AF654261

Perspectives on Political Order

Perspectives on Political Order

East and West

RAMASHRAY ROY

RAWAT PUBLICATIONS
Jaipur • New Delhi • Bangalore • Hyderabad • Guwahati

ISBN 978-81-316-0596-7

© Author, 2013

No part of this book may be reproduced or transmitted in any form or by any means, electronic or mechanical, including photocopying, recording or by any information storage and retrieval system, without permission in writing from the publishers.

Published by
Prem Rawat for **Rawat Publications**
Satyam Apts, Sector 3, Jawahar Nagar, Jaipur 302 004 (India)
Phone: 0141 265 1748/7006 Fax: 0141 265 1748
E-mail: info@rawatbooks.com
Website: www.rawatbooks.com

New Delhi Office
4858/24, Ansari Road, Daryaganj, New Delhi 110 002
Phone: 011 2326 3290

Also at *Bangalore, Hyderabad* and *Guwahati*

Typeset by Rawat Computers, Jaipur
Printed at Chaman Enterprises, New Delhi

Contents

Preface

Perspectives on Political Order: East and West is an enlarged version of *Political Order: The Vedic Perspective* published by the Indian Institute of Advanced Study, Shimla. Due to certain compelling reasons *Political Order: The Vedic Perspective* had to be radically revised. In the course of revision it was considered very desirable to add some more material dealing with the concept of 'order' in China to make the study more useful. *Perspectives on Political Order: East and West* is the result of the effort to enlarge the scope of the study with a view to providing a larger perspective so that comparison across countries and across different conceptions of political order and the evaluation of their relative merit can become possible.

The relevance of this study lies in the fact that students of political science seldom concern themselves with abstract but highly significant subjects and focus more on the externalities of the political system. As a result of this neglect, it proves very difficult to fathom the depth of a large body of information employed to make the external aspect of political order apprehensible. Also, it becomes very difficult to relate the information about the external aspect of the political system with the underlying idea that gives it unity and coherence. *Perspectives on Political Order* aims at overcoming this lacuna.

In writing *Perspectives on Political Order: East and West* I have received help from many sources but they are too many to record here. I do, however, mention Kamlesh who helped me in getting a neatly typed manuscript. I am also grateful to the publisher – Rawat Publications – especially Shri Pranit Rawat, who has shown exemplary courage against the main current of the market and has published it with great care. I leave it to the readers to judge whether this study stands the test of their critical appraisal.

1

Introduction

It does not need any demonstration to suggest that the role of political order in fashioning, shaping and regulating progressively larger areas of human existence today has become central. As this role expands, questions about what impact it makes on the quality of life and the content and direction of human development surge up for satisfactory answers. It needs to be emphasized that the use of certain symbols, such as freedom, equality and the like, to judge the merit of a political order, is not helpful because these symbols constitute labels that take their essence from something other than themselves. This "something" is constituted by a philosophical or ideological perspective that determines what these symbols should concretely mean in different temporal and spatial contexts. It also represents a set of abstract ideas that offer a consistent and interconnected account of man and his world. It is these ideas that get embodied in a particular arrangement of institutions equipped with normative, legal or pragmatic rules, regulations and procedures. It is the combination of abstract ideas and principles, on the one hand, and their concrete manifestation in the institutional arrangement, on the other, that constitutes the notion of order. Thus, the notion of order is immanent in the concreteness of a particular institutional structure; it is this notion that animates the functioning of the institutional order and fills it with content and gives it a particular direction.

What also needs to be added is that in its abstract form, the notion of order is ethereal and eternal, beyond the flux of change produced by the ongoing process of change in the phenomenal world, the world of here and now. But then it enters the stream of history by getting embodied in an institutional arrangement and is buffeted by the winds of change passing through the stages of growth and decay. It must, however, be made clear that it is not the notion of order in its abstract form that is subject to growth, decay and recovery. It is rather its institutional garment or manifestation that undergoes the process of change. Thus, the notion of order is both immanent in relation to a particular institutional arrangement as well as external to and beyond it. It is external in the sense that it can be abstracted from its institutional setting and cast into a set of principles defining the place, status, and role of different elements both in their separation and connectivity.

This is by no means a unique feature of the notion of order; all such abstract notions that are capable of being given an institutional body exhibit this feature. However, it must be emphasized that the notion of order has no relevance apart from the pragmatic situation in which it is supposed to play its proper role. It is the pragmatic situation that forces a sensitive soul to take stock of the obtaining reality that has become oppressive and intolerable and develop a paradigmatic example of order that can put society on the right track. Such a sensitive soul can either be a sage or mystic or a philosopher. In creating a paradigmatic example of right order, the sensitive soul opposes his insight into or knowledge of "the healthy order of society, to the surrounding order, which he diagnoses as affected by disease, a *nosos*".[1] He becomes a visionary in the real sense of the term insofar as he can see and penetrate into the dense fog of reality that has become somewhat opaque and oppressive and gain an insight into or a vision of the true structure of order. It is this vision that he projects for wider acceptance in opposition to the prevailing order of things.

The need for the sage or the mystic or the philosopher to engage in an exercise of creating the example of paradigmatic order arises with a view to getting over an emergent crisis. The crisis occurs because the statesman has failed in his responsibility of creating a state reflecting the notion of right order or has allowed it to gradually slide into a deplorable condition when he was in complete charge of things. When the statesman fails in discharging his responsibility of creating or preserving political order and keeping it on a proper course, the sage or the philosopher has to intervene and project himself as a political authority. As a consequence, the affairs of political order no longer remain the exclusive domain of the statesman and the constitutional organs of government. The field extends to incorporate even private citizens who undertake to enquire into the nature and articulate the result of their enquiry concerning right order.

It is quite likely that the outcome of such an enquiry leading to the articulation of right order may or may not be acted upon or may not prove durable and degenerate, if acted upon. And yet the fact remains that it is not the paradigm, but the institutional carrier of the paradigmatic idea that, under the sway of certain adverse environmental factors impinging on it, gets derailed. This is symptomatic of the intractability of the disease that does not respond to the treatment of the statesman functioning as a political healer.[2] The private person, whether a mystic, sage or a philosopher, is not discouraged even when he is confronted with a manifold of such derailments because his sensitivity ever remains sharp and is distressed by the growing disorder in man's psyche and its reflection in the external world. After all, the disease of a society remains even if it proves intractable. And, it is this persistence of the disease of society that evokes his sympathy and prompts him to suggest a way out of the prevailing *nosos.*

When a mystic, sage or a philosopher is moved to intervene, he makes his diagnosis and suggests remedial action; his prognosis is inspired either by meditation or by the revealed word of God or the philosopher's love of wisdom. Whatever may be the case, each of them gives expression to the truth of being as he visualizes it. It is entirely a different matter that his prescription of right order fails to penetrate the society. This is not due to some defect immanent in the vision but it is due to internal resistance. This failure does not in any way invalidate the vision of the right order yielded either through contemplation or the revealed word of God or the philosopher's love of wisdom. It ever retains its pristine grandeur and is ever available for study and execution.

What happens is that the intractability of deformed society to the healing vision articulated by someone may lead to the conclusion that the society will, perhaps, never be truly formed by the order of meditation, revelation or philosophy. That this has happened in history can be seen by the failure of Israel and Hellas. As Voegelin points out, both Israel and Hellas were conscious of being set off by their leap in being toward attunement with transcendent order, from the empires which had not broken the cosmological form, and even more so from societies on the tribal level. Both had expressed the consciousness of their higher order by referring to the surrounding mankind as goyim and barbarians.[3] What is also interesting is that in both societies men appeared – Moses in Israel and Plato in Hellas – to articulate the truth of existence as a paradigm for ordering society.

While Moses did this on the basis of the revealed word of God, Plato gave expression to the philosopher's love of wisdom. However, both these attempts came to naught.

The failure of repeated attempts at ordering society in light of the vision of right order forces on the consciousness the realization that society can never be truly formed by the vision yielded by meditation, the revealed word of God, or the love of wisdom. As a consequence, the field splits up in two, one represented by those who claim to be the carriers of the vision of right order and those who live in and manage the affairs of the world affected by the degeneration of order. This split, then, becomes visible in many areas of life. Referring to the many splits that appear in society, Voegelin notes:

> The men who had experienced the universality of transcendent order were in search of social carriers of order other than the finite societies of their origin, because membership in the finite society seemed no longer to exhaust the meaning of human existence. The prophetic existence of the servant of God was separated from the collective existence of the Chosen people under the Torah; the philosopher's *bios theoretikos* from political life; the universal humanity from parochial humanity. There began to differentiate a spectrum of order, which required membership in a plurality of societies as its adequate form. In faint outlines there began to appear the fundamental division of spiritual and temporal order, of state and church.[4]

The split between those who articulate the vision of right order and those who manage political affairs did not stop here. A further split occurred as the maturation of the possibility that the science of order could be abandoned eventually in favour of the science of the pathological states of society. With science of order disappears the tension between health and disease, and the diseased state acquires a neutral character of normality. In the theory of politics the pathological case becomes the "nature of man". This is fully exemplified by Hobbes. It is true that he was shocked by the evils of the surrounding society. But, as a theorist, he did not admit its pathological character and indulged in institutional devices as remedial action and evoked the idea of Leviathan as the power structure that would keep the nature of man in check.[5]

The various splits that we referred to above point to three essential components of a social order. They can be identified as the mystic, sage or the philosopher, the statesman or the politician, and the common man, whose nature has to be kept in check by the existent power structure. These components represent respectively the spiritual realm or religious sphere, the domain of politics and the world of the common man whose needs, expectations and aspirations lend content and direction to politics. It can be argued that after the science of order has been eclipsed completely by the pre-eminence of the science of the pathological states of society, the utility of the mystic, sage or the philosopher has come to an end. However, it must be emphasized that, as Voegelin points out, "... The disease of a society remains a disease even if nothing can be done about it; and the understanding of right order is not invalidated by the impossibility of putting it to use.[6] And, the mystic, sage or the philosopher must be moved by the intractability of the pathological state of the society. This also impels the *politikos* as the physician to suggest the proper remedy for the persistent malady of sick society. This is indicative of the fact that even when the diseased nature becomes the nature of man, therapeutic desire of the *politikos* as the physician does not disappear.

It is true that science of order has become, in recent times, a subject that is treated as an untouchable; it does not mean either that society has no underlying pattern of order, however flawed it might be or that it does not need the intervention of the sage or the philosopher for prescribing a new order. Even a state that has fallen into a pathological state does not necessarily lack order; no matter what the nature of order or no matter how theoretically and philosophically deficient and deformed that order may be. It is also possible that the nature and the constituent elements of order may not have been explicitly articulated. However, it does not, for that matter, negate the structure of order on which the society rests and reflects in its functioning. It is quite likely that the social order may not be able to satisfy different groups of people who may, then, be led to criticize the prevailing order. This presupposes the prior existence of some standard that may be used to examine and evaluate the prevailing order and identify its deficiencies. As such, even when the science of order has been ignored and neglected, it still exists, albeit in a fragmented state lacking a coherent and systematic rational account, and functions as a standard for examining and evaluating the prevalent order.

The second element of the political order is comprised of the managers of the political order who are responsible for organizing, managing and regulating political affairs and giving it a particular direction. The mystic, sage or the philosopher confines his task to constructing a paradigm of order and is seldom inclined or willing to undertake the responsibility of giving an institutional expression to his own paradigm. The task of giving a practical shape to the articulated paradigm of order falls on the shoulder of the statesman politician. It is he who works out the structure and defines the various aspects of political order, lays down the institutional basis, and formulates its procedural dimension. There might be what is known as the original lawgiver who might have laid the foundation of the political order and elaborated its structural and procedural bases. However, after he is gone, its care passes on to other hands that might or might not prove capable in preserving the legacy that they received from their predecessors.

This might be due either to personal inadequacies or the complexity of the circumstances in which a particular politician statesman finds himself. If the affairs of the state are not handled correctly, the political order may undergo a period of ups and downs till it is put on the right keel by some capable leader who succeed in overcoming the difficulties that may have accumulated over the years to interrupt the smooth working of the political order. His successful leadership may also be reflected in his ability to cut through the external manifestations of the creeping disorder and come to a correct diagnosis of the basic cause and be able to mend the deteriorating health of the political order and prove a capable statesman as a physician. However, he cannot ensure that the political order will always remain functioning smoothly without any trouble. This is so because the health of the political order depends, to a very large extent, on certain contextual factors that go on changing over time throwing challenges to the manager(s) of the system.

One of the contextual factors of great significance is, of course, the character of politics that constitutes the crux of political order. Politics has its grounding in the nature of what has been designated, in recent times, as civil society. Needless to say that civil society is marked by heterogeneity of interests engendered by diversity of human nature. It represents an aggregation of a multiplicity of interests and points to a highly differentiated membership of civil society in terms of socio-economic location, resource endowment, level of political consciousness, etc. It is this differentiation that gives a particular but definite shape to the interests that different groups of people hold and articulate. Since it is not possible for these groups of people to fully depend on their own resources to either safeguard or promote their interests, they have no alternative but to channel their demands into the political process. However, there exist other interest groups whose concerns may not be compatible with other interests. And, since the resources available for satisfying all the demands that are challenged into the political process, there ensures a stiff competition among different, not necessarily compatible, interests, for privileged access to and control over scarce societal resources.

It is against this background that we can appreciate the importance of civil society as the prime source of politics. It is in the civil society that different kinds of needs of the people arise. When these needs are channelled into the arena of politics, they have to be recognized and classified into several categories for quick, delayed or deferred disposal. It is quite likely that certain group demands are by nature such that the managers of the political system may not recognize either as legitimate or as politically justifiable or feasible. As a result, such demands even when vociferously pressed may remain unfulfilled and gradually lead to a situation in which conflict between those who voice such demands and the government that denies satisfaction of these demands may flare up. Alternatively, when interest becomes the primary defining element in differentiating different groups of people competition among different groups for access to scarce societal resources seems to be natural. It is this assumption of naturalness that is the only significant characteristic of societies.

Competition does not pose any problem as long as it remains peaceful. However, given the important fact of the scarcity of societal resources, not all demands that are channelled into the political process can be satisfied. In such an eventuality, certain factors intervene to transform the situation of peaceful competition into a conflictual one. These factors pertain, to mention only a few of them, to the intensity with which demands are pressed, political ordering of these demands in terms of priority, the nature of counter-pressures for recognition and fulfilment, the quantum of resources available, etc. And if certain demands remain unfulfilled despite mounting pressures, the possibility of alienation and political radicalization opens up. In addition, the possibility of conflict erupting in the political arena is also created. Once this happens, it affects not only the political system but also a wider spectrum of socio-economic interests.

When multiplicity of interests rooted in the variety of human nature characterizes a society, it lends a special flavour to politics. And, what makes politics a continuous process of contestation is due to the fact that not all interests are compatible with each other. As a matter of fact, interests prove antagonistic in a situation where self-interest provides the woof and warp of politics. It can be promoted and pursued only at the expense of others in a situation of scarcity. This being the case, it is not unexpected that conflicts among antagonistic interests would at times be generated in the political system. As conflicts or conflict-like situations come to mark the functioning of the political order, the even tenor of the life of the people is disturbed. As disturbance persists, economic life and relations, too, come to be affected and their efficiency tends to decline and wilt. This produces a chain reaction adversely affecting the capacity of the system to perform its basic responsibilities.

Needless to say that such a situation is an anathema to the political managers of the system. They must intervene to bring the system back to its normal pattern of functioning and prevent the system from sliding further in the mire of the threateningly accelerating disorder. The intervention of the political functionaries of the state points to the fact that orderly conduct of politics is necessary for the health of the system. It further means that the ability and efficiency of the political system in maintaining a peaceful public order and the capability of fulfilling the needs, hopes and aspirations of the people comes to depend, to a large extent, on the disorderly conduct of politics on the part of the citizens who constitute the political system.

The orderly conduct of politics by citizens is possible only when they are imbued with a living consciousness of some larger interest apart from the interest of each and every citizen. Such a consciousness presupposes a live awareness of and attunement with certain higher, trans-individual values. It is the attunement with and commitment to these trans-individual values that make it possible to transcend the narrow concerns of his separate existence. This transcendence, in turn, becomes the basis of a harmonious community living.

This is not to suggest that the sustenance of a good, cohesive and harmonious community living is a responsibility that only citizens have to bear and discharge. Equally, if not more, important is the role of the political leaders who are responsible for maintaining and safeguarding public order. It is incumbent on them to discharge their responsibility dispassionately and without any motivation of personal gain from the office they hold. The need for them to be above their personal interest is much more pressing for them since they are supposed to be the exemplars of behaviour and the keepers of public morality. If they deviate sharply from the behaviour expected of them, it lays the foundation of personal corruption. Personal corruption then translates itself, in due course, into the corruption of a large segment of the population. As a result, the whole society is corrupted. It must be kept in mind that corruption does not begin from below; it always begins from the top and, then, gradually seeps down below affecting a large section of society.

It is against this background that political leaders at the top must present before those they rule an exemplary behaviour. It is necessary not only for protecting the system from the corroding touch of corruption. It is also necessary for putting before the citizen a standard of morally correct conduct. It is this standard that functions as a beacon for others to guide them in the dark, stormy and turbulent sea of uncertainties that are faced by the common man. One of the reliable guides in directing the traveller in the sea of life is *mahajan* (the great soul) or *spudaios*, the wise man of Aristotle. Even when the wise man is not physically present to guide men in proper conduct, his example is ever present before the public eyes to inspire the common man to emulate his example.

The need to keep political life and relations free of the turbulence likely to be caused by citizens who might become excessively unruly in pressing their demands, on the one side, and the politician who may turn arbitrary and despotic, on the other, cannot be denied. However, this eventuality can be avoided only when both the citizen and the politician rise above their own self-interests and give their allegiance to certain trans-individual values that become instrumental in facilitating and promoting the good of one individual compatibly with the good of all. Additionally, it is also necessary to buttress these "invisible observers" of human conduct with visible watchdogs of laws of good conduct and law enforcers. This becomes necessary because the there is ever-present the danger of the tendency to ignore the counsel of the "invisible observers" when pressed hard by the urge to fulfil a particular insistent need.

It is to obviate such an eventuality that a political order needs to be supported in its struggle for escaping the hazards of the movement of time by both "invisible observers" and visible body of laws and the institution of law enforcement. These two together constitute the internal and external bulwark of the city, that is, the political order, that protect it from decay and degeneration consequent upon the corruption of the citizen and the politician. And, since it is necessary that both these elements must not work at cross-purposes, their compatibility and harmonious enmeshing becomes a *sine qua non* of a good and salubrious political order. But it must be added here that the relationship between the internal and the external control mechanism needs to be more than compatible. What is also required is that in their enmeshing they should also be instrumental in preserving the necessary balance between the three universals.

These three universals – universal divinity, universal humanity and universal world – constitute the three most important parameters of human existence. The world represents the phenomenal world that provides man with his abode; it also constitutes the nexus of relationships in which the individual finds himself. This relationship is forged with a view to satisfying certain needs that every individual *qua* individual has and must seek to fulfil if he wants to ensure his well-being. These needs include certain emotional social, economic and spiritual needs in addition to biological needs. It is the fulfilment of these needs that bring men together and necessitate the formation and the continuity of such groups as family, different kinds of peer groups, associations, communities, societies, etc. All these groupings define the parameters of the location of the individual in the phenomenal world and signify certain rights and obligations that individuals bear to each other. It is this network of rights and obligations that assumes a particular character of man-man relationship.

One very important aspect of man-man relationship is the character of economic needs and the structure of economic life and relations that develop in the process of the fulfilment of man's economic needs. It is these economic needs that constitute the basis of individual interest. It is the promotion of self-interest that brings the individual to interact with other members of society in his immediate environment and in the society at large. It also establishes a pattern of interaction between man and nature. It is man's interaction with nature that enables him to fulfil his myriad needs involved with provisioning not only for the individual alone but also for all those who are either dependent on his economic activities or tied up with him in a process of exchange. The significance of the fulfilment of economic needs of man is beyond doubt in as much as it is one of the crucial elements that contributes immensely to individual well-being.

That the fulfilment of economic needs constitutes just one vital aspect of human well-being is indicated by two crucially important factors. If one of these factors is the nature of economic needs themselves, the other factor pertains to the relationship these needs have with other aspects of human existence. Obviously, this relationship has certain implication for other dimensions of human existence. We can conceive, broadly speaking, of two different ways of defining the nature of these needs as well as two different modes of their fulfilment. The way human needs are defined and the mode of their fulfilment as well as the nature of their relationship with other dimensions of human existence have an important bearing on the type of political order that comes into being and functions. It must be emphasized that the proper understanding of the nature of needs and the mode of their fulfilment is crucial in as much as man is more than a bundle of passions and the aggregation of his material needs.

This realization makes us aware of the fact that, whether we recognize it or not, man is a resident of two orders of existence, i.e., his mundane life constituted by his pragmatic affairs and the life of spirit. Every society, as Voegelin reminds us, is "organized for survival in the world and, at the same time, for partnership in the order of being that has its origin in world-transcendent divine being. It has to cope with the problem of its pragmatic existence and, at the same time, it is concerned with the truth of its order."[7] Man's residency in two orders of existence makes it incumbent upon him to reconcile the demands of his pragmatic existence with the demands that his concern with the truth of its order makes on him. To reconcile them is to be aware of the quaternarian community comprising of man and society and world and God. Alternatively, this quaternarian community can be thought of as being constituted, as the Vedic world view underlines, by *martyas* (mortals) and *amartyas* (immortals) and *prithiwi,* the world and *dyau,* the heaven.

The question of how this quaternarian community can successfully overcome the stresses and strains of man caught inexorably in the movement of time depends on whether or not we recognize the existence of the quaternarian community and the need of its preservation. It in quite likely that the existence and the relevance of the world unseen, as symbolized by the terms immortals and *dyau*, can be either completely lost in forgetfulness or totally ignored treating it as irrelevant for man's well-being. In such an eventuality, man's well-being tends to be defined in terms of the fulfilment of ordinary life needs of man alone without any reference to other dimensions of human existence. It is assumed that the fulfilment of ordinary life needs constitutes the basis for the development of other capacities including moral sensitivity. It is not surprising, therefore, to find Lord

Keynes asserting forcefully that "economic development is the possibility of development".

The significance of this assertion lies in the widely prevalent belief that it is only through the ever-rising standard of living that the development of man's capacities – technical, intellectual as well as moral – is possible. To put it differently, the way to moral and spiritual development of the individual can be paved only through the creation of equitable distribution of ever-rising material prosperity. It is the sharing by all in material prosperity that can ensure the individual his felicity, become instrumental in the actualization of his hidden potentialities, push up the level of collective well-being, and impel the chariot of civilization on the path of progress.[8] Needless to say that what this perspective on man and his world does is to make the development of man and society highly dependent on the level of material affluence. The non-material aspects of man's existence can, this perspective insists, be meaningful and fruitful only if the material aspect of man's existence is treated as of central importance in realizing total well-being of the individual.

When material aspect of human existence is put on the highest pedestal, quest for material security and affluence becomes the prime concern of man. The primacy of this quest is justified on the ground that desires are natural, that is, they are endowed to man by nature. As such, it is incumbent on him to fulfil the demands of his nature in order to be happy. And, since the tendency of seeking felicity is engrained in human nature, it is also rational for the individual to ensure his happiness; he must therefore satisfy his desires as and when they become pressing. It is rational in yet another sense. The world-view that gives preference to the search for felicity as the basis of development of humanity also treats individuals as self-defining; as such, each individual becomes an autonomous centre of energy and power. Separated from other individuals, the individual himself must look for his own well-being. Self-help is the central theme of this approach to the understanding of the nature of man and his world. This understanding underlines the fact that each individual must look for himself. As such, it is rational for him to seek the satisfaction of his desires unconcerned with and without expecting any help from others.[9]

When the pursuit of self-interest is considered to be both natural and rational, it leads to some very undesirable consequences for man himself and his relationship with other men as well as with nature.

This is due to the fact that, given the primacy of material improvement as the basis of improvement in all spheres of man's existence, it becomes necessary for all to compete in a situation of scarcity for getting access to and control over scarce societal resources. Thus, the scarcity of resources and the intense competition that ensue for getting access to scarce societal resources combine to lead to ever escalating demands for goods and services. It is natural, then, that a crowd-like situation would emerge.[10] A person standing at the back of the crowd must make an attempt to move closer to the front of the crowd to have a better view of whatever happens there. There are only two ways of succeeding in this: he would either push his way though by trampling over other's toes or wait for the whole crowd for making an advance in which he too gets the opportunity to have a share in the resources. Hirsch puts it:

> Taking part in the scramble is fully rational for any individual in his own actions, since in these actions he never confronts the distinction between what is available as a result of getting ahead of others and what is available from a general advance shared by all. Thc individual who wants to see better has to stand on tiptoe. In the game of beggar thy neighbour, that is what each individual must try to do, even though not all can.[11]

However, in many cases, the crowd remains stationary and the desire of the individual to move ahead becomes impelling or, alternatively, even if it moves, the relative position of persons located at lower echelons of income hierarchy remains unchanged. The individual is, then, impelled by the propelling force of his desires to trample on the toes of others since to stand on tiptoe does not make the view any better. The competition for occupying advantageous positions and ensuring privileged access to and control over scarce societal resources becomes very acute. This competition may and normally does encourage the production of more and more goods and services. However, as more material goods are added to the existing ones, it further intensifies competition.

It is this adverse consequence of the installation of the material aspect of human existence on the highest pedestal that is responsible for the unbridled competition for privileged access to scarce societal resources. It is this competition, again, that introduces a mismatch and a break between individual well-being and collective good leading eventually to the collapse of the structures of cooperation in society. As these structures collapse, interdependence and harmony also evaporate. With the worsening of harmonious social relations, the policy of "beggar thy neighbour" takes a stronghold of the individual.[12] Apart from the adverse social consequences of the predominance of the value of material advancement, it also cripples humane orientation of man because he ignores the development of other physical, psychological, intellectual and spiritual capacities, on the one side, and it leads to the depletion and devastation of natural resources, paving the way for eco-disaster, on the other.[13]

It is against this backdrop of the mismatch between the private and the public aggravated by the predominance of the material aspect of life that the need for rulers and legal system for regulating individual conduct and social relations could be appreciated. It is quite obvious that in a society where it is effectiveness in winning a contest, in the sense McIntyre uses it,[14] the erosion of internal checks – checks that reflect the internalization of certain moral values – become ineffective and gradually get dissipated, certain external controls over human motivation and behaviour become necessary. The externally imposed controls take the form of rules, regulations and laws for regulating individual conduct and social relations. But certain factors integral to the society, where goods of effectiveness are valued and coveted, if not by all, then, at least, a large number of its members rob these rules, regulations and laws of their educative and transformative significance; they are interpreted simply in terms of punitive measures and can be willingly accepted if the benefits outweigh losses when the law is violated. Thus, its exemplifies a wilful violation of law under the sway of rational commensuration.

These factors, as already pointed out, are ingrained in the underlying order that lends meaning and relevance to the socio-political system committed to giving utmost importance to the goods of effectiveness. Needless to say that the underlying order leads to the creation of the state out of private passions and is responsible not for educating, disciplining and regulating human motivation but only to take care of the consequences of self-interested actions. If the state undertakes the responsibility of forming human motivation by trying to change human nature, it amounts to the infringement of individual freedom. It therefore invites criticism and condemnation. If, on the other hand, individual freedom is given a free rein, it tends to lead to a situation where what Aristotle calls *pleonexia* may prevail[15] to pervert social life and relations. But the state in the modern times cannot either allow this situation to prevail or to root out the factor that allows this situation to arise. One of the reasons for the inability of the state to deal effectively with this dilemma is the fact that the worldview that instals the satisfaction of one desire after another ceaselessly, also celebrates the enjoyment and exercise of freedom by self-defining subjects. The dilemma can be resolved only when certain curbs on the exercise of individual freedom is imposed by the state in a situation whether neither the conscience of the individual nor the society at large is in a position to check and restrict the exercise of freedom by individuals and groups. In addition, to restrict freedom is to render ineffective the dynamic quality of the society that values and promotes goods of effectiveness. It is true that the unrestrained exercise of freedom creates discord. However, as Kant points out, discord is necessary for commitment of the exercise of freedom and freedom is necessary for realizing human capabilities. Man does prefer to have order, but nature will have discord.[16]

Social discord can be minimized, if not totally eliminated, if certain conditions of social living and interaction are fulfilled. In the absence of a social order that educates, forms and regulates human motivation and conduct, one can think of a system where an elaborate structure of rules, regulations and laws is created to promote the value of reciprocity and support cooperative interactions among individuals and groups. For cooperation to flourish, Pareto optimality principle must operate. This signifies a situation, in which each of the competitors for privileged access to and control over scarce resources is able to maximize his satisfaction or felicity, to the degree that that the preferences of others allow.[17] The efficient operation of the Pareto principle presupposes two essential conditions. Without the satisfaction of these conditions, Pareto optimality principle will remain ineffective.

One of these conditions pertains to the stability of expectations. This means that a person is quite capable of knowing or interpreting in what ways other persons are going to or actually act. This also means that individuals are able to grasp the "meaning" of actions of others or anticipate future events, in particular, the manner in which others are going to react to their own behaviour. It is with a view to safeguarding the condition of reciprocity that an elaborate structure of rules, regulations and laws is created. The rules, regulations and laws are meant to enforce reciprocity so that mutual obligations are recognized and acted upon. In this perspective, justice is simply the outcome of a situation in which reciprocity is maintained with the help of external control, particularly the law. What gives concrete content to the idea of justice is primarily the relative power position of competitors in the race of life. And, what makes justice possible is that rules and laws are minimally acceptable to all.

What is important to note in this regard is that a perfectly just person is no more or no less a person who obeys the rules of justice. On this view justice lacks content until an enforceable set of rules or laws defining the relationship of each person to every other in respect of the pursuit of their respective goals have been formulated. As such, the virtue of justice is only secondary to and definable only in terms of the rules of justice.[18] Similarly, the idea of order is, in this perspective, only secondary to the idea of individual felicity. Given the primacy of individual felicity, coupled with that of the exercise of freedom for realizing self-defined purposes, order is supposed to evolve only as an outcome of a condition in which reciprocity becomes a value to be jealously guarded. What is distinctive about this perspective is that it treats the satisfaction of desires of the individual as a first order goal. But this goal must be realized in a way that the attainment of happiness must not come in the way of another person's search for happiness.

This means that every person must attempt to attain his happiness together and compatibly with each other. This becomes or should become every individual's second order goal. As Taylor puts it: "Now if intelligent calculation can show how to shape man and circumstances so that men achieve happiness, and all of them achieve it together and compatibly with each other, then is this not the highest goal, and that is according to reason (intelligent calculation) and nature (universal desire for happiness)."[19] Building society on this "rational" and "natural" principle, a perfect order can emerge. On this view, instead of seeing nature as expressing a meaningful order, one which is to be accounted for in terms of ideas, we see it as a set of interlocking elements whose relations can be explained in terms of efficient causation. The order (as against disorder) in things does not consist in their embodying ideas, but rather in their meshing without conflict and distortion.[20]

It is this concept of order that is projected on the human realm and is posited as a goal to which every person should not only aspire but also reflect in his own behaviour. To quote Taylor again, this "means that man comes to realize natural order when the company of desiring subjects comes to achieve full satisfaction (happiness) each compatible with all others. The perfect harmony of desires is the goal, which nature and reason prescribe to man."[21] Needless to say that order in the human realm is modelled upon the prevailing conception of order in the natural domain. It is, therefore, not surprising to find, Frances Edgeworth voicing the hope that:

> Mecanique Sociale may one day take her place along with Mecanique Celeste, throned each upon the double-sided height of one maximum principle: the supreme pinnacle of moral as well as of physical science. As the movements of each particle, constrained or loose, in a material cosmos are continually subordinated to one maximum sum-total of accumulated energy, so the movements of each soul, whether selfishly isolated or linked sympathetically, may continually be realizing the maximum energy of pleasure, the Divine love of the universe.[22]

The hope of a harmonious social order emerging out of the clash of aggressively pursued self-interest by individuals and groups never gets realized. Devoid of any *a priori* idea of order shaping and being reflected in the socio-political institutional arrangement and practices the idea of order emerges out of the continuous interaction between different socio-economic interests. Whatever order we can discern at any particular time underneath the ever-restless and flowing current of politics is the outcome of the interplay of socio-economic forces. It is this interplay that lends a particular content as well as direction to political affairs. We can, therefore, see that, since order is itself the product of the dynamic interaction among powerful socio-economic interests, it cannot be expected to exercise a benign influence on human motivation. In the absence of order capable of educating, disciplining and regulating human motivation and conduct, different emergent socio-economic interests usually tend to be aggressive in the pursuit of their objectives without any due regard to the consequences of their actions for the good of others.

It is thus apparent that in a society dedicated to the acquisition of "goods of effectiveness," the problem of reconciling the good of one individual with the good of all individuals is a recurrent one. It cannot be solved by the state since this involves curbing and controlling the exercise of freedom by individuals and groups. To do so is to undercut the dynamic element that lends vigour and vitality to the society that celebrates goods of effectiveness. Nor can the institution of law succeed in curbing the tendency towards self-aggrandizement because of the operation of the factor of what Darrell Dobbs calls "rational commensuration".[23] It refers to a situation in which calculation about the costs and benefits of acting in a particular way that is likely to infringe a moral or legal norm becomes an integral part of human conduct. In such a situation, law loses its educative function and becomes merely one of alternative factors in the calculations of costs and benefits in making a choice of action.

It is not, therefore, surprising to find law proving increasingly ineffective in disciplining human motivation. Rational commensuration points to the fact that rationality does not recognize any authority beyond itself and can ignore even the command of what we understand to be divine commandment. Devoid of any connection with something superior to it capable of exercising a restraint on its excesses, rationality degenerates, in a situation where passion dominates human motivation, into rational commensuration. It then tends to erode rather reinforce morality. It could be argued that even a society that has erected the edifice of public order on the foundation of private passions still retains a measure of culture that can exercise some sobering influence on the wayward movement of desires. But here, again, we encounter a difficulty. In modern times, it has, for all practical purposes, lost its intellectual, chiefly educational, vaguely prescriptive and, above all, evaluative significance.[24]

The dominance of rational commensuration has certain adverse consequences for man himself as well as the world in which he lives and acts. In the first place, the predominance of rational commensuration signifies that there does not exist anything else more valuable than the life of passion. And, since the life of passion is the only reality that the individual recognizes, socio-political institutions must be so fashioned that they defend and sustain the life of passion. It does not need to be argued that such a perspective on human existence reduces the totality of what man stands for to only a part of his nature. This reduction throws up a utilitarian perspective on man and his world. It further means that there are no higher values that man should aspire and act to realize. In the second place, it also paves the way for what Voegelin characterizes as "an attempt to create an absolute cosmos out of the finite forces of human desire and will."[25] Such an attempt is symptomatic of the denigration as well as displacement of ideas, values and practices not germane to the value of utility. In such a situation, the public order is constantly buffeted by the contrary winds of freedom and order.

It is expected that the ill-effects of the contrary pulls of freedom and order could be checked by the mediation of politics. This mediation can not only diminish the rigours and volatility of the contention of antagonistic interests, but also, it would protect the public against disorder by persuading the contestants to terminate their conflict on the basis of partial satisfaction of their demands through a process of negotiation, bargaining and compromises.[26] But, since this process can yield only partial satisfaction, compromises prove tenuous and *ad hoc* and temporary. Moreover, such compromises encourage other socio-economic interests to forcefully state their claims for greater access to and control over strategic societal resources. Thus, the political system assumes more and more a character of an entity performing its function of deciding, "who gets what, when and how".[27] Power becomes the determinant of who gets what, when, and how; scarcity engendered by escalating demands for more and more goods and services intensifies conflicts. Also, it makes it difficult for underprivileged socio-economic interests to get their demands fulfilled.

As a result, the simmering discontent frequently erupts into violence reflecting the growing fragility of order and that it is not only unable to satisfy rising demands for goods and services but also incapable of maintaining order when its gets disturbed. Ironically, the need for order becomes more pressing when forces of disorder raise their head. With a view to escaping or, at least, minimizing the depredations of the rising disorder, it is necessary to render politics compatible with the requirement of order. And, since politics associated with a social order that instals goods of effectiveness on the highest pedestal does not and cannot prove compatible with the requirements of order, it is desirable to treat politics as something other than the mechanical process of ensuring partial satisfaction through a process of negotiation, bargaining and compromise. It needs to be hitched to some higher values so that it can be freed from its bondage to private interests and be deployed for individual well-being compatible with the requirements of collective good.

In view of this, it is necessary to view politics as something that rises above the givens of nature and society and becomes attuned with certain trans-individual, transcendental values. Accordingly, when the political is rescued from its purely intermediary role and conceived of as an activity that teaches men in civic virtues, it becomes the apt instrument of serving the public weal. As such, political life, as Schaar puts it,

> occupies a middle terrain between the sheer givens of nature and society, on the one side, and the transcendental ends towards which men aspire, on the other. Political action is that type of action through

> which men publicly attempt to order and to transform the givens of nature and society by the light of the values which are above or outside the order of the givens.[28]

In transcending the givens of nature and society, the political order transforms a mere aggregate or multitude of isolated separated individuals into a political community equipped with a vision of order, an institutional arrangement reflecting and safeguarding that vision, and practices associated with public institutions and grounded in certain values that promote and protect civility. Given the crucial role of civility, interpreted in the sense of the attunement of the individual with the need to preserve the public order and safeguard its sanctity, we can ask: What are the transcendental values that can preserve the sanctity of the political community over time? In answering this question, what must be kept in mind is the composite nature of man. While man is mortal, he seeks immortality; he lives, it is true, in a finite world and is, therefore, himself finite, but he is surrounded by an infinite world and aspires for infiniteness.[29]

Looked at from this perspective as such, man is the resident of two inter-penetrating worlds, one finite and the other infinite. As such, man must, therefore, be governed by those values that articulate and express the realization of his membership in a larger order. This realization becomes translucent when he becomes alert to the fact that "God and man, world and society constitute a primordial community of beings."[30] It must, however, be emphasized that this primordial community is merely a possibility; the partnership envisaged in the quaternarian community has not yet become a reality. For it to become real, it is necessary to create an institutional structure grounded in a vision of order that can link the finite with the absolute as the basis of realizing the primordial community. And, since the political sphere constitutes the pre-eminent, effective and indubitably the most visible domain, it must be the means of linking the finite with the absolute.

Thus, the problem pertaining to the political sphere is the conflict between the finiteness and absoluteness, the givens of nature and society and transcendental values associated with the realm of the absolute. The solution to the problem can be found only when the political gets grounded in ontology. When it is so grounded, it performs as what Voegelin calls a "shelter" function. It is with the help of this shelter function that man attempts to give to his life a semblance of meaning.[31] A political order grounded and inspired by this vision is capable of reaching the emotional and spiritual centre of man's existence making it possible for individuals to outlive their fragmentary personal lives by a projection into the life of a larger community. As such, the political order

> provides a structure of meaning into which the singe human being can fit the results of the biologically and spiritually (productive, procreative) energies of his personal life, thereby (relieving) the life from the (disordering) aspects of existence that always spring up when the possibility of life ending in annihilation is envisaged.[32]

It is, then, apparent that there are different versions of political order. We have so far indicated two different notions of political order stipulating different conceptions of man and institutional patterns of managing interpersonal and inter-group interactions. But, the matter does not stop here. In the West itself, throughout the history of political philosophy, there have been varying notions about the nature of order and these have ranged from the Greek idea of individual self-fulfilment, through the Christian conception of the political order as kind of *preparatio evangelica*, to the modern liberal view that the political order has little to do with psyches or souls. Similarly, in India, the main concern has been with restraining the self-aggrandizing tendency of power. It is in this connection that the traditional Indian perspective gives so such attention to the harmonious relationship between *secerdotium* and *regnum* or making power the proper tool of promoting public weal. In Chinese civilization, Confucian thinking has been principally concerned with the proper relationship been *jen* (goodness, humanity) and *li* (propriety).

The variety of the notions of political order, it can be argued, have had their heyday and have no relevance in modern times. But to argue this is to ignore the dysfunctionalities that the regnant liberal version of political order and its expression in political institutional arrangement make it incumbent upon us to look for a proper notion of order that is salubrious for individual well-being and collective good. But, then, most of these paradigms of political order are things of the past and cannot be revived and restored in a changed situation However, their study can surely yield an insight into the true structure of political order. Thus, the significance of the study of these various notions of political order is not to bring the past back, but open the horizon of the future.

With this objective in mind, we discuss in what follows certain relevant issues related with the question of political order and examine different paradigms taken both from the West and the East. The emphasis in this study is on the Vedic perspective on political order. This emphasis on the Vedic perspective is due to the fact that the Veda has been treated as simply a collection of hymns detailing certain rituals as integral parts of the process of *yajna* (sacrifice).[33] This tendency is still operative despite Jan Gonda's warning that we should avoid the Scylla of considering the Rigveda as a collection of magico-ritualistic texts produced by self-interested priests as well as the Charibdis of secularizing that ancient corpus.[34] When these antithetical views are avoided, the Veda appears in its true light as legacy of a whole civilization, a mirror into man's psyche and its vision of life in all its intricacies.[35]

The Vedic hymns, as Miller puts it,

> are imbued with the poetry and feeling of nature and this constitutes part of their charm. But behind the mythological vision of the cosmos emerges a remarkable insight into the working of the universe, the underlying oneness of all life behind the multiplicity of forms and forces that hide it, the one law of transformation, of growth and decay, of evolution, of order and adjustment whereby all things are kept more or less in equilibrium, all disorders being restored back to order, this causing friction, conflict, and in man's case, suffering.

But, the nature Miller talks about is, as *Isopanishad*, puts it, the abode of the absolute. And, the Veda as the articulation of the inner experience of the beyond, concerns itself not only with the question of what does the awareness of reality signify, but also with the structure of that reality, the process through which this structure comes into being, and the existential and spiritual ramifications of this inner experience for man and his world. In view of all this, it is necessary to bring out the original insight, an insight that in comparison with other notions of political order emerges as quite formidable. The Vedic insight into the structure of the cosmic order and its institutionalization in political order in the phenomenal world is quite important but ill understood. Its contribution to the philosophy of political order cannot simply be ignored.

Notes

1. Eric Voegelin, "What is Political Order," in *Drama of Humanity and Other Miscellaneous Papers 1939–1985*), vol. 33 of the *Collected Works of Eric*

Voegelin, eds. William Petropoulos and Gilbert Weiss (Columbia: University of Missouri Press, 2004), p. 56 (to be cited hereinafter as CWEV).

2. One of the functions that Aristotle assigns to the *Politikos* is that of the physician. As he notes:

   And by human *Arête* we mean not that of the body but of the soul; and happiness we also call an activity of the soul. Now if this is so, the *politikos* clearly must know something about the psyche, just as the man who is to heal the eyes or the body as a whole must know something about the eyes or the body .... The *politikos* must study the psyche; and to the extent that is sufficient for the purposes of his inquiry. *Nichomachean Ethics*, 1102a 8–25.

3. Eric Voegelin, *Order and History: The Eucmenic Age,* IV, (Baton Rouge: Louisiana State University Press, 1974).
4. Ibid., p. 116.
5. See CWEV, Vol. 33, p. 59.
6. Ibid., p. 57.
7. Eric Voegelin, *Order and History: Plato and Aristotle,* III, (Baton Rouge: Louisiana State University Press, 1974) III, p. 2.
8. Immanuel Kant, *Political Writings,* Ed. Hans Reiss (Cambridge: Cambridge University Press, 1977).
9. This is precisely what Thomas Hobbes argues in his *Leviathan*.
10. See Fred Hirsch, *Social Limits to Growth* (London: Routledge and Kegan Paul, 1977), p. 10.
11. Ibid.
12. Loc cit.
13. Loc cit., p. 4.
14. Alasdair McIntyre, *Whose Justice? Which Rationality*? (London: Gerald Duckworth Co. Ltd., 1988). McIntyre defines the goods of "effectiveness" as the capacity to acquire something that is valued in a situation of scarcity leading to competition among individuals and groups for privileged access to and control over scarce societal resources.
15. Aristotle uses the term *pleonexia,* in two important interrelated senses. One of these senses refers to self-aggrandizement signifying a tendency to seek to have more than one deserves. *Pleonexia* also means the toleration of exploitation and oppression willingly.
16. Immanuel Kant argues that discord awakens in man all his latent powers and the first real steps are taken from the rudeness of barbarianism to the culture of civilizations. The Arcadian shepherd life evinces complete harmony, contentment and mutual love. However, without discord, all their talents would have, forever, remained hidden and embryonic. To quote him:

As gentle as the sheep they tended, such men would hardly have given to their existence a higher worth than belonged to their domesticated cattle. Thanks be then to Nature for this unsociableness, for this envious jealousy and vanity, for this unsuitable desire for possession, or even of power. Without then all the excellent capacities implanted in mankind would slumber eternally undeveloped. Man wishes concord, but Nature knows better what is good for his species and she will have discord.

Quoted in Lucio Colletti, *From Rousseau to Lenin: Studies in Ideology and Society* trans. John Merringlon and Judith White (New York: Myth Review Press, 1922), pp. 159–60.

17. Fred Hirsch, op. cit., p. 4.
18. Alasdair MacIntyre, op. cit., p. 36.
19. Charles Taylor, *Hegel and Modern Society* (Cambridge: Cambridge University Press, 1979), p. 75.
20. Loc. cit.
21. Loc. cit.
22. Francis Edgeworth, *Mathematical Physics*, p. 12. Quoted in George J. Stigler, "Economics or Ethics, in Sterling Mcmurrin, ed., *The Tanner Lectures in Human Values*, II (Salt Lake City: The University of Utah Press, 1981), p. 168.
23. Darell Dobbs, "Reckless Rationalism and Heroic Reverence in Homer's Odyssey", *The American Political Science Review*, 81, 2 (June 1987), pp. 491–508.
24. See A. Marquior, *The Veil and the Mask: Essays on Culture and Ideology* (London: Routledge and Kegan Paul, 1979), p. 39.
25. Eric Voegelin, *History of Political Ideas: Helenism: Rome and Early Christianity*, Athanasios Moulakis (Columbia: University of Missouri Press, 1997), I, General Introduction, p. 28.
26. As a matter of fact, Sheldon Wolin defines politics in these terms. According to him, politics include basically three types of activities including (a) a form of activity centering around the quest for competitive advantage between groups; individuals, or societies, and (b) a form of activity conditioned by the fact that it occurs within a situation of change and relative scarcity; and (c) a form of activity in which the pursuit of advantage produces consequences of such a magnitude that they affect in a significant way the whole society or a substantial portion of it. *Politics and Vision: Continuity and Innovation in Western Political Thought* (Boston: Little, Brown and Company, 1960), pp. 10–11. Given these aspects of politics, negotiation, bargaining and compromises constitute the defining characteristics of politics.
27. Ibid.

28. John H. Schaar, *Escape from Authority The Perspectives on Eric Fromm* (New York: Basic Books, 1961), p. 296.
29. Eric Voegelin, *Order and History: Israel and Revelation I* (Baton Rouge: Louisiana State University Press, 1957), p. 1. This primordial truth about the quaternarian community is supposed to exit, as the Veda sees it, in the intimate relationship between mortals and immortals, and Prithivi and Dyau.
30. Eric Voegelin, *History of Political Ideas*, I, p. 225.
31. Ibid., p. 226.
32. See Herman Oldenberg, *The Religion of the Veda*, trans. Shridhar B. Shrori (Delhi: Motilal Banarsidass, 1988); and Maurice Bloomfield, *The Ancient Religion of India: From Rigveda to Upanisada* (Delhi: Ideological Book House, 1972).
33. Jan Gonda, *The Vision of the Vedic Poets* (Delhi: Munshiram Manohar Lal, 1984), p. 13.
34. Jeanine Miller, *The Vision of Cosmic Order in the Vedas* (London: Routledge and Kegan Paul, 1985), p. 1.
35. Ibid.

2

Varieties of Order

History has witnessed a variety of political order in time and space. But common to all of them, whether empirically encountered or imaginatively crafted, is the prime objective of blending and coalescing of a diversity of individual perspectives into a cohesive collective purpose. The realization of such an objective depends on the extent to which individuals are able to see above their own self-interest, rise above the narrow concerns of their own existence and attune their thinking and action with the need of the preservation of a good, healthy social order of which they form a part. Or, at least individual actions, even if motivated by pure self-interest, are such that they do not militate against and collide with such actions by other individuals. In such a case the least that can be expected is compatibility between the actions of one individual with actions by others. Whether it is the conscious awareness of the desirability of rising above one's own exclusive good for desisting from jeopardizing the good of others or whether it is the compatibility as the product of myriads of self-interested action of individuals, an element of self-transcendence is necessary.

The need for self-transcendence arises from the fact that the human world exhibits an enormous measure of diversity in respect of preferences, expectations, capacities and achievements. All these characteristics pertain to the individual *qua* individual: to the individual's idea about himself as to what he is and what he wants to become. Both these facets of the individual's idea have a very important bearing on the determination of life purposes of the individual as well as the selection of means by him for realizing these purposes. These are the two major forces in the individual's life that have an intimate relationship with his ideas of what he is and what he wants to be. But, since there is a diversity of human nature, it is not surprising to encounter a plethora of individual needs embedded in these two aspects of the individual life; all these needs clamour for fulfilment. And, what must be emphasized is that whatever the individual thinks of himself or about giving a particular shape and direction to his existence, it involves access to certain resources, both internal and external, for realizing his purposes. Insofar as external resources are concerned, they are available only in the external world – both society and nature. It is in this context that we can appreciate the fact that the question of self-transcendence cannot be settled by a reference to the individual's existence alone.

The reason for this lies in the fact that man is not self-sufficient. The individual person alone in his separateness from others cannot hope to exist since he has to rely heavily on his fellowmen for help and support in seeking to mobilize the resources necessary both for his subsistence and also for his psychological and spiritual development. These two aspects of the individual's existence – physical subsistence and intellectual and moral development – have associated with them certain needs that must be fulfilled for his proper sustenance and growth. Thus, both his subsistence needs and needs created by the necessity in terms of traditional or moral sensitivity, are such that they can be fulfilled in a situation where it is possible for the individual to get the help and cooperation of others in his immediate as well as remote environment.

It is this compulsion emanating from the existential condition of man that makes him dependent on the help and collaboration of others in meeting the demands of his existence. The need to collaborate with others imposes on the individual to forge a relationship with others of mutuality or reciprocity. The need to establish relationships with others on the basis of reciprocity and interdependence creates a network of relationships between individuals. Every individual thus finds himself enmeshed in this network of relationships and must discharge the responsibilities that it imposes on them. It is also this nexus of relationships that defines what an individual socially and economically is, what status he occupies in the social order and what role he is expected to perform.

Man is thus essentially a social being; his existence as a solitary man living outside the periscope of society is certainly to turn out to be a process of continuous battle against malign forces of nature even for a troubled survival. This perilous existence impels man to depend on others for a danger-free existence as well as for life-long support and succour. The compulsions of living, let alone that of a good living, are such that the individual cannot ignore, erode or avoid the relationships he is led to establish with others. If he does not need others' help and collaboration, he is either a beast or a god.[1] The entire network of relationships that envelops an individual's life and protects him from regressing into animal existence can be summarily denoted as society. The membership of society links the individual's existence to a larger order. This larger order in a way represents the aggregation of all the individual members who compose it.

It is true that a contemporaneously regnant world view treats society as nothing more than the sum total of all individual members. However, such a view holds no water in view of the fact that despite its denigration to a subordinate place as compared to the individual, society retains its primacy not only because it protects the individual from the hazards of isolated solitary living but also because it furnishes the individual with resources with which he can enrich his life materially, intellectually, morally and spiritually. The importance of society in providing and maintaining the necessary condition for sustaining and making human existence better than animal existence elevates society to something more than a mechanical aggregate of separate and isolated individuals.

Given the status of society as the protector of the individual from the hazards of living and as that of making a natural man into a social being, underscores the shelter function of society. It is in this sense that primary function of society is to provide shelter to individuals. This shelter function comes into play when society links the finite existence of the individual with the infinite; it is this linkage that constitutes the source of truth, meaning and value. And, it is with the help of these essential elements of human existence that society protects the individual from the hazards of mortality and existential problems. What should be underscored here is the fact that the shelter function of society is limited not only to mere protection of individuals from the hazards faced even in sheer survival, it also includes that of inculcating in man certain physical and intellectual capacities that enable him to solve problems he faces in the process of living and chart out a path for reaching safely the destination of his life's journey.

In no way information is likely to help the individual in acquiring or training and disciplining his orientation in a way that helps him in refraining from upsetting the delicate balance that the social order seeks to maintain with the help of a particular institutional arrangement and a pattern of everyday practices. For this, training of mind through what we know as formal education is not of any help either because its usefulness is restricted to preparing man for using his brawn and/or brain power skilfully and effectively for participating in the creation or sharing in the good life of modern conception. Formal education or education in formally organized institutions of learning does not in any sense help individuals in training the mind for self-transcendence. As stated earlier, shelter function is limited not only to mere protection of the individual from the hazards that sheer survival faces mankind, it also includes that of inculcating in him certain physical and intellectual capabilities that enable the individual to solve problems he faces in the process of living and chart out a path for reaching safely the destination of his life's journey.

Even more important aspect of the shelter function of society is the shaping of cultural and moral life of the individual and of giving it a definite content and an appropriate direction. It is against this backdrop that the more important shelter function of society comes to light. This shelter function pertains to the cultural and moral life as a necessary prop of orientation supportive of self-transcendence. Insofar as the cultural and moral life of an individual is concerned, what is important is that the enrichment of individual life and its role in the preservation of the social order depends on the extent to which he has grasped the truth of his existence and its relationship with the larger order. His live consciousness of the awareness of this truth of his existence is instrumental in injecting in his life certain values without which his life may not prove to be anything more than sailing blindly in the sea of uncertainties and unforeseen dangers. The perilous voyage of life receives, as the result of the awareness of being a part of a longer order, a strong intimation of the direction and purpose of the life's journey in the world of here and now. The fundamental role of the apprehension of truth, meaning and value is both individually ennobling and socially salubrious.

It is through the apprehension of truth, meaning and value that the individual becomes aware of the need to rise above the merely material aspect of his life and cultivate certain values in his life not only for rising above the level of the animal and for living a cultured life but also for making himself a more useful member of the society he is a part of. The individual *qua* individual is born as a natural being with certain appetites associated primarily with the physical needs of survival. But he is more than the sum total of his physical needs; he has also a non-physical aspect of his existence. If he gets completely immersed in the everyday concerns of fulfilling just his physical needs, he exposes himself to the dangers of blunting the growth of his individuality to its fullest limit. He is likely to emerge as an incomplete human being, a "broken totality" as Iris Murdock calls it, for which nothing counts but only his own material needs and his egotistic self. Such an incomplete person is likely to turn out to be a parasite who only seeks to take but not to return in exchange for what he gets from others.

Whatever needs a person may harbour in his breast, they are to be fulfilled in a social setting. On one view, the meaning of "social setting" may just refer to society, as a potential means for the realization of individually defined purposes. In this sense, its role is limited to just providing the resources necessary for meeting individual demands for them. However, what needs to be noted here is that the conception of society, either as a providential instrument for realizing individual purposes or merely as an arena where individuals endeavour to fulfil their needs, is inadequate in the sense that it does not bring forth the real import of society. It is an undisputed fact that, due to the operation of several factors, resources do not ever prove sufficient for satisfying all demands. And, when scarcity is a perpetual characteristic of society, the distribution of scarce resources in a situation where demands for resources exceed their availability, call for a basis or a criterion with reference to which resources could justifiably be distributed.

That there must be a criterion for deciding how scarce resources are to be distributed among claimants for access to and control over scarce societal resources does not need any demonstration. But, the formulation of such a basis or criterion for distributing scarce resources is not enough in itself. There are certain other conditions that must be met before a preferred basis for distributing scarce resources can become workable. In the first place, whatever basis or criterion may be preferable, it also must seem to be just and acceptable widely. What this implies is that it must not seem to favour some and put some other's interest and good in jeopardy; it must meet the fundamental criterion of transcending individual interest for protecting collective interest and fulfil the condition of universality by answering to some objective, dispassionate and trans-individual principle. In the second place, more than the selection of such a trans-individual basis for the distribution of scarce societal resources, its operation must be such that it does not exceedingly favour one class of persons at the expense of others. It is not at all surprising to find a particular governmental set-up working in a partisan spirit and favouring its own supporters and potential supporters with a view to strengthening its support base. This is most likely to raise serious doubts in public mind about the legitimacy of the preferred principle of distribution. And, lastly, in case there are distortions in the working of the principle of distribution, there must be some institutional mechanism to correct these distortions and remove or, at least, control the factors that cause distortions.

In view of this, the conception of society that reduces it to the status of a mere potential instrument for the realization of individual purposes proves to be awfully inadequate. This is so for the reason that the need fulfilment of different individuals and groups involves not simply the question of the desirability of each individual or socio-economic group having its own unrestricted access to societal resources. It also involves the difficult questions of the justifiability and propriety of the claim for access to societal resources by individuals and socio-economic interests. These claims cannot be expected to be compatible to each other. They are usually antagonistic and conflicting in many situations. In such situations individual choice cannot be expected to be a reliable basis either for formulating a principle of distribution of scarce societal resources or for providing a reliable basis for formulating a principle resolving the conflicts that may arise because of the antagonistic nature of interests. It becomes the responsibility of a larger entity to formulate principles, rules and procedures not only for installing a principle of distribution but also for setting in motion a procedure for resolving conflicts arising out of antagonistic claims for entitlement.

It is true that the choice of the individual, both in terms of choosing ends and means considered to be appropriate for realizing a particular individual purpose, cannot be given a complete free play. The reason for this lies in the fact that the individual is liable to err by selecting improper ends as well as undesirable means. Both are liable to infringe moral codes of a society as well as the laws it has framed for safeguarding decency and social peace and concord. It is often argued that even if the moral code a society has inherited from tradition or has evolved in the process of its own evolution, has, for some reason, become moribund or ineffective, law can successfully replace the watchman located in the interior of the individual. This watchman usually performs the role of a counsellor and advises him about what to do and what not to do. In most cases, then, the law, even though it is imposed on the individual from a source external to him, is considered to be as efficacious as the benign rule of morality.

A little consideration is enough to prove that this claim is untenable. The claim that law is effective in controlling the wayward movement of man's desire and his action rests on the belief that the command of law is universally respected and honoured, and that it is self-sufficient in itself in the sense that it does not need any helping hand from any source beyond itself. It is universally accepted because, it is claimed, the commands of law are backed by penal action on the part of the state. This argument is grounded in the belief that, first, every infringement of law automatically brings its own penalty, and second, law stands above conflicting interpretations and punishes only the guilty one. Both these grounds are suspect because not all infringements are brought to the notice of the agencies responsible for law enforcement. The reason for this lies in the fact that, in many situations, cases of infringement are never brought to the judicial agency either because of the fear of reprisal from powerful interests or the incapacity to bear the burden of litigation. It is also suspect because in many cases even those are penalized who have not committed the offense they are charged with; as a result, the culprit goes scotch-free in many instances. It is in this sense that we can appropriate Plato's indictment of the law as a tyrant[2] because its command fails to discriminate between the really guilty and those who are only seemingly guilty. It is also a tyrant because it does not make any discrimination between different situational contexts in which human beings act.

In addition, there are also profound difficulties in the argument that law is something that stands above the will of contending socio-economic interests and finds its grounding in some trans-individual source that is recognized as universal and, therefore, independent and impartial. It must be recognized that law-making and law-adjudication both take place in a situation where the goods of effectiveness, in the sense MacIntyre uses it, that is, goods involving riches, power, prestige, status, etc., do not recognize any value as higher than themselves; for them, goods, not value, are sacrosanct.

And, since the conception of any good standing above the good of all individuals taken separately becomes a dominant orientation, conflict for privileged access to societal resources will rage unabated unless certain limits must be imposed on individual motive and action. In the absence of invisible watchman residing within man's interior, such limits have to be defined and imposed from an external source. The creation of such limits is the domain of law-making and law-adjudication. And, the principle of law-making in a situation devised to protect and promote the well-being of all through the quest for goods of effectiveness must inevitably make some combination of interests as the ground for legislation and law-adjudication.

The principle of such a combination is supposed to be derived either from an aggregation of interests (Bentham) or from a procedure of law-making to which everyone subscribes in self-interest (Locke and Rousseau), or from an ideal procedure of law-making which everyone can agree upon in self-interest and which can be shown to lead to a particular desired distribution of wealth and power (Rawls). All these formulations encounter a formidable difficulty, that of finding a neutral way of combining individual subjective values. Without reliable standard located outside the individual, subjective preferences to determine which interests to combine in what measures, and in what ways, law-making will amount to *ad hocism* and be determined by the relative power positions of individuals and groups.

In addition, the possibility of finding a procedure to which everyone can subscribe to it in self-interest gets embroiled in the dilemma of generality *versus* concreteness. If the standard lacks specificity, it will be less adequate for evaluating and yielding guidelines for coping with the concrete; it will, then, tend to give preference to individual subjective ends. Insofar as the question of making shared values the ground for law-making is concerned, it should be noted that if shared values are treated as neither individual nor subjective, the basic tenets of modern world view will be violated. It is tantamount to hoping that the replacement of one premise by another in the world of ideas will alter the course of history. If, on the other hand, shared values are nothing more than the coincidence of individual values, the search for the ground for law-making in shared values encounters the same difficulties faced by other approaches.

Apart from the difficulties encountered in law-making and law-adjudication, it must also be borne in mind that the law is the product of human will. As such, it can also be changed by will. Moreover, in a situation in which there operates a continuous process of competition and conflict in regard to the pattern of distribution of available societal resources is made more acute by persistent efforts of different socio-economic interests to have privileged access and control over these resources. What also adds to this competition is the phenomenon of unequal distribution of societal resources – a distribution that is favourable to some and unfavourable to many others. It is this inequality that not only leads to conflicts, but also stimulates effort to change the law to remove inequality as far as possible. And, since none of the patterns of distribution of societal resources is expected to remove inequality totally and completely, the search for distributive justice becomes a permanent feature of a society that is always on the move.

In addition, it is also unrealistic to suppose that law can somehow rise above the interests and errors of human beings who formulate them. As Aristotle notes, the law itself must be either democratic or oligarchic, for example, and so will share in the defects inherent in these regimes.[3] Thus, the law as the means of regulating and controlling human motivation and conduct proves very ineffective, social control itself loses its salience inasmuch as society is produced to a mechanical aggregate of self-defining subjects,[4] and, as a result, drained of this significance as a source of values and control. Moreover, society, as Colletti argues, is not an end, that is, an indispensable condition for man to be truly man; its task is merely to "create an external formal order, i.e., a politico-juridical order which, through the law, consolidates and reinforces the absolute prerogatives of the 'natural man' in his isolation from others."[5]

External sources of control prove ineffective precisely because in a system that has been built to promote the acquisition of the goods of effectiveness there occurs a large-scale erosion of what Alfred Lowi calls "auto-control".[6] As pointed out earlier, the fulfilment of ordinary life needs constitutes the pivot around which human existence revolves. In one version of life according to nature, man could, by exercising rationality the excesses of what Aristotle calls *pleonexia*,[7] that is, the tendency towards self-aggrandizement, could be curbed by exercising rationality with which every man is equipped. It is nature that endows man with rationality. However, rationality signifies principally calculative, prudential and instrumental reasoning. Moreover, it serves as a handmaiden of desires.[8] But another version, credited to Rousseau, endows ordinary life purposes with higher significance; their realization is considered *sine qua non* for the flowering of man's potentialities, including moral ones.[9] As Taylor points out:

> To fulfil the true impulse of nature in us is not just to meet biological needs but also to satisfy a higher aspiration. It is, at the same time, a moral fulfilment. From Rousseau on, the true 'voice of nature' is at one and the same time both the impulse of biological need and an aspiration to what is experienced as moral self-realization.[10]

Needless to say that both these versions of preventing the slow but certain erosion of auto-control do not work because both of them promote man's immersion into materiality. Immersion in materiality does not allow self-transcendence so necessary for ensuring compatibility between the good of one individual and the good of all individuals. Also, the other effect that it produces is the manipulation/exploitation and, as a result, the transformation of nature. This becomes necessary to appease the growing hunger of man for goods and services as a passport to the alluring land of terrestrial heaven promised by the regnant worldview. Manipulation/exploitation of nature for satisfying human greed for ever larger doses of goods and services has cumulated, over the years, into what is known as pollution of nature leading gradually to eco-disaster. The possibility of eco-disaster has reached such a stage where it now poses the threat of the extinction of the human race.

The failure to resist the temptation to get immersed in materiality is instrumental in downgrading of society as a disciplining and controlling association. It also robs it of its crucial role of acting as a socializing agent responsible for instilling in men values that elevate their consciousness of the need to reconcile the good of one with the good of all. In a situation where society has been deprived of performing its proper role has become an established fact, respect for law too falters and gradually fails in checking depredations of *pleonexia*. It is against this background that we can appreciate why Plato underlines the fact that the youth in his own days had no respect for law and raises the question how respect for law can be cultivated. As he notes, the main reason for this is the youth's turning away from the gods.[11] This can be corrected only when the true significance of divinity is demonstrated to them. And, for Plato, the importance of cosmogony lies precisely in this.

Given the strongly operating tendency to become indifferent to the true role of law in keeping man on the path of virtue, the question that assumes central important is: What it is that supports law to retain its respectability and, therefore, remains acceptable to all? In other words, the law alone in its solitary majesty needs to be clothed with dignity to be respected and remain acceptable. The kingly garb must be woven with golden warp and woof for its majesty to remain resplendent and radiate awe and obedience. What needs to be emphasized here is that both law as king's command and as the voice of the people in its collective wisdom are liable to falter on the slippery ground of the powerlessness of the people caught in the snare of treacherous reality. Such people tend to be swayed by fear or interests. When the sense of fear of the king/law gets weakened or when the individual is swept away by the storm of desires, the majesty of law loses its shine and it is then seen in its true colour as what in reality it is.

In general, what the law is in its true colour is simply an expression of coercion, a "dictatorial prescription". It lacks what Plato calls a *prooimia logon*, a prelude or a preamble.[12] It is *prooimia logon* that explains to the person punished by law the reason for it and why he should avoid infringing the law. But why should the legislator add a prelude or a preamble to the legislation dealing with unlawful behaviour? Plato makes it clear that the legislator is like a physician who has been given the responsibility of treating the sickness of the soul so that a person afflicted with this disease that is, *nosos* (sickness of the soul), recovers and regains his true persona and his proper social station. The legislator or *politikos* as Aristotle calls him, combines, according to Aristotle, three different roles in one, that of the law-giver, the physician and the statesman. The true *politikos* is, Aristotle makes it clear, supposed to be a man who has concerned himself with particular care with the nature of *Arete*, for he wishes to make the citizens good and law-abiding men. As he says:

> And by human *Arete* we mean not that of the body but of the soul, we also call an activity of the soul. Now if this is so, the *politikos* must clearly know something about the psyche, just as the man who is to heal the eyes or the body as a whole must know something about the eye or the body. All the more so, since political science is more honourable and better than medicine. And even among physicians, the better ones labour hard at acquiring knowledge of the body. The *politikos*, therefore, must study the psyche, and he must study it with these objects in view, and to the extent that is sufficient for the purposes of his inquiry.[13]

Needless to say that Aristotle borrowed this formulation of the functions of the *politikos* from his predecessors, especially from Plato. When Plato speaks of the legislator as a physician, Plato refers to a particular stream, perhaps the only respectable stream, of thinking about the proper role of the *politikos*. In his view, the *politikos* is nothing less than a physician who is an expert in the art of healing the diseased order of society. As an expert, he is well versed with the nature or essence of true order. This means that he knows fully well the *eidos* or idea that undergirds a particular polis. The *eidos* or idea is the aggregate of symptoms that enables the physician to diagnose the disease; it is, as it was called by Greek physicians of the late Roman imperial period, a syndrome.[14] This use of the term "syndrome" was to come later. However, Plato used the term *eidos* or the idea not to point to the aggregate of symptoms that characterizes a diseased state of society, but the characteristics of a healthy order.

But what is a healthy order? The answer to this question has taken a variety of forms both in the East as well as in the West. The various formulations of what is a healthy order have taken their inspiration from the vantage point from which a thinker views the phenomenon of order and fixes its salient characteristics. If one changes the vantage point from which to perceive the character of a healthy order, that is to say, if one holds a particular *eidos* or idea that must animate a particular social order, the formulation of order and the identification of its characteristics both undergo a sea change. Given the fact of a variety of conceptions of a healthy order, it is not at all possible to give a straightforward answer to the question of what is a healthy order.[15] What is also interesting to point out is that the conception of order takes, broadly speaking, two main forms. One of these forms refers to the *a priori* nature of order that precedes any actual society; this *a priori* conception of order acts as a font of inspiration as well as the source of guidelines for both the formation of an empirical healthy social order and as a reference point for evaluating its institutional props and their actual functioning. The source of inspiration of an *a priori* idea of a healthy order can be found in a particular conception of reality the thinker holds. It is this idea of reality as cognized by the thinker that yields the conception of a healthy order. Obviously, the idea of reality will change over time and space and will, as a consequence, yield entirely different conceptions of order. It is, therefore, necessary to make explicit at the very outset the different ways in which reality we are located in, confronts us, and shapes our consciousness of ourselves as well as our relationship with different elements of reality.

We can, to begin with, symbolize this reality as a line with two poles. While one of these is occupied by the divine entity no matter how it is conceived, defined or articulated, the other pole is occupied by the entity we know as man. In between these polar points, one defined by the divine or God and the other symbolized by man, there exist a number of other points that we can call the 'world in the aggregate'. Man shares this world with other fellowmen and this sharing shapes his life experience and lends a particular character to his consciousness. Looked at from this perspective, the structured reality can be seen to comprise three 'universals'. They are: the universal humanity, universal divinity, and universal world.[16] Voegelin speaks of humanity not because the category 'man' is vacuous, but because the term 'man' in its generic sense remains undifferentiated since we do not have any idea about his mode of existence or vital differences between men located in different factual orders. In view of this, it is preferable to use the term 'humanity' inasmuch as it refers to man in a mode of understanding himself in his relationship to god, world and society.[17]

Obviously, these modes change. Nonetheless they indicate the way the self-understanding of man is structured and changes in the course of the inexorable movement of time. What also needs to be added here is that these three universals constitute a unity; however, for analytical purposes they need to be distinguished from one another. The reason for this lies in the fact that when the universal world assumes predominance in the minds of men, the relationship between all these three universals undergoes a change. As Voegelin remarks, "as soon as you isolate the one or the other, the other two become senseless."[18] As he notes further, "only the three together are adequate description of reality that formerly was experienced in the primary form of cosmic experience, and now, on the level of consciousness, splits into these three universals, which cover all of reality. It is necessary to maintain a proper balance among these three universals in order for reality to retain its wholeness and its true import."[19]

However, this balance can and does get lost. "When it does happen, the other two universals, that is, the universal of divinity and that of humanity, lose their proper meaning and true role in man's existence. Take, for example, the case of the universal man. When the universal world is hypostatized and made into an absolute reality as it has been the case in modern times, the balance is lost."[20] The first consequence of the loss of balance with the universal world made into an absolute reality is that the very conception of God or divinity changes. If earlier God was considered to be world immanent in the sense the *Isopanishad* underlines it, God is considered to be something apart from and beyond it, a world transcendent God. But, the matter does not stop here. In course of time, when we come to the nineteenth century, Feuerbach's psychology of projection reduced God from an independent transcendental entity to simply the function of man. For Feuerbach, all religious ideas, especially the idea of God, came to be conceived as a projection of the contents of human mind into a beyond.

Today, the psychology of projection is practically an accepted part of the science of psychology. However, if the God underwent a diminution, it was completely eliminated by Marx. Feuerbach still left the matter at the level of the psychology of projection while Marx more consistently said, "Why should we project? Let us pull these projections back into ourselves where they started."[21] That simply meant the pulling back into our humanity and thereby we ourselves claim becoming gods, or if not gods, at least supermen. With the total eclipse of gods, man himself emerges as the symbol of divinity and assumes all the power that previously used to be the preserve of gods. Once man assumes the powers of divinity, he claims to refashion the conditions of his own existence. But what stands out is the fact that his existence is now defined primarily, even exclusively, in terms of his existence in the phenomenal world confined in and preoccupied with the concerns of living at the minimum and living well at the maximum.

But this is not the only consequence that follows from the expulsion of gods from the God's creation. It does allow man a complete freedom in shaping his destiny by assuming the power of transforming and or manipulating nature with a view to satisfying his myriad desires, to be sure. However, exercising this power indiscriminately, man changes nature in many vital ways and alters the socio-economic conditions of his existence. In making continuous modifications in the essential conditions of his existence, man himself is turned into something that is subjected to the agency of history. With his subjection to history, he emerges only as a possibility.[22] This means that the traditional Aristotelian idea of *entelecheia*, that is, the inborn tendency implanted by nature in man which governs the course of the growth and development of man, is discarded in favour of the shaping of man by external forces. These external forces, relating especially to socio-economic conditions of man's existence, as we have already indicated, go on changing.[23]

These changes come about mainly as a result of man's effort to fulfil his needs, needs particularly pertaining to the acquisition of wealth, power and prestige. With a view to fulfilling his needs, man takes the help of technology. The use of technology escalates and proliferates needs; proliferation of needs calls for the continuous upgrading of technology for transforming/manipulating nature to force it to yield more and more of its hidden treasure. As technology continues to be upgraded, there is further fillip to the escalation and proliferation of needs. As a result, a dynamic relationship comes to be established between need fulfilment and technological changes. It is as the result of this dynamic interaction between need fulfilment and technological innovations and upgradations that certain changes, sometimes very radical changes, take place in man's environment, both social and physical. These changes, however, occur in the course of the movement of history. It is as a consequence of these changes occurring in history that affects the growth and development of man as well as in the environment in which he lives and works with nature and the myriad changes that occur because of this interaction. It is this process of change that Giambatista Vico identifies as the main factor in the self-making of man. This signifies the fact that it is in this process that man creates institutions, fashions culture and makes history. And, in making history, man makes himself.

It is also in this process that man himself changes. By this is meant certain changes in the nature of man himself. He does not simply, as Kant underlines, actualize his potentialities that lie deeper in his breast, but he also develops moral sensitivities. As Spinoza puts it, "interacting with other men, the individual becomes aware of the fact that they all belong to the same kind. This awareness also becomes instrumental in instilling in him the essential component of sympathy. There are several stages of the development of morality in man's existence. This movement is gradual: it moves from the awareness of belonging to the same kind to the development of a sense of sympathy or 'kindness'." This perspective on man, needless to say, is quite different from the one that is grounded in the constant awareness and crucial importance of God in man's existence.

What is clear from the above is that when the universal world is picked up and made into an absolute, the two other universals lose their significance. Humanity is interpreted in terms of man's ability to acquire as much of the material resources as possible as a means of the development of his personality and moral character. As such, man turns out to be the function of the world. This is indicative of the fact that when one of the universals is hypostatized and created as an absolute, exclusive reality, fateful changes occur in the status and significance of the other two universals. In this process, the universal that is created into an absolute exclusive reality also gets deformed. The deformation of meaning and significance of the universals is symptomatic of the loss of balance between these universals and affects the phenomenon of order not only in terms of its conception but also in its effectiveness in keeping human existence on an even keel.

Given the fact that both the conception of order as well as its role in securing human happiness, concord and harmony in the social universe, the very conception of order can be influenced by the crucial fact that there are two varieties of order. One variety has its reference to reality that has divinity in it as an integral part, while the other reality will be no-God reality – a reality from which the essential role of divinity or God has been squeezed out or which relegates God to insignificance. Obviously, these two varieties of reality will have important consequences both for man and his world as well as the order man erects to regulate his life and to protect himself from the dangers of living in an uncertain world. Insofar as the conception of order is concerned, reality with God will underlines *a priorily* existent order that is reflected in nature since the order observed in it has been imposed on it by the divine entity. The order observed in nature then becomes the source of order in the human world. As such, God also becomes the source of order that regulates the human world also. Such an order is not something that man's imagination forges with a view to catering to his needs. It is already there installed by the Creator and must be embraced by man to ensure his personal fulfilment and social concord, peace and harmony.

In contradistinction to this, the conception of order in a reality with no divinity or God rejects any notion of order either emanating from God or the one that is immanent in nature. But since a social order cannot remain for long safe from the advancing flood of disorder, a statesman or a law-giver must undertake the task of constructing order. This is tantamount to the art of a craftsman who looks around to identify the materials that are available in his environment and are appropriate for crafting whatever image of order he has in mind. Similarly, a statesman or a law-giver has as his material the human stuff which provides him with ideas about what the character of the order he designs must be and what function it must perform. Such an order has a primary reference to some conception of man for whom order is designed. This means that the image of man underlying the conception of order appropriate for a reality with God must be qualitatively different from the one meant for a reality without God.

The basic difference between the images of man held by two different orders of reality has to do with the question whether man is completely a conditioned being or he has in him to transcend his conditioned existence. This difference refers to the fact that while the conception of order with God does recognize that man is a conditioned being, his ultimate destiny is unconditioned, the order of reality with no God treats man as fully conditioned biologically, psychologically, sociologically and intellectually. The first kind of order treats man, as T.S. Elliot underlines:

> For man is joined spirit
> and body, and therefore must serve as spirit and body.
> visible and invisible must meet in his Temple;
> You must not deny the body.
>
> — Choruses from the Rock

In this perspective, man is thus a conjoint entity incorporating both spirit and body; consequently, man is a conjunction of the finite and the absolute. By virtue of this, his prominent concern in the words of Saint Augustine is *amor Dei*, the love of God. And it is *amor Dei* that keeps order in the individual's soul and, through it, in the society at large. This order is preordained and reflects a balance not only in different psychic forces but also in society and nature. It is not therefore surprising to find Elliot giving expression to this as under:

> Talking of right relations of man, but not of relations of men to God.
> 'Our citizenship is in heaven'; yes, but that is the
> Model and type of your citizenship upon earth.
>
> — Choruses from the Rock

In contradistinction to this, the order germane to reality without God has passed through, as Voegelin demonstrates, several stages of construction, underlining different approaches to the formulation of the idea of order such as economic, psychological, ethical, etc. However, what stands out in such constructions is the image of man as a *homo economicus* (economic man engaged in the necessary functions of production and reproduction aimed at the fulfilment of ordinary life needs). These needs are basically concerned with the acquisition of wealth, power and prestige. And, since every individual is engaged in this enterprise, it leads to competition and conflict underlining the fact that the idea of *libido dominandi* (desire to dominate) as the ordering principle in one's life assumes prominence. This desire cannot be eliminated nor can it be given a free hand in society lest it unleashes a rule of exploitation and oppression leading to *matsya myaya* (the rule of the shark). As such, any idea of order must be based on mechanical balance among autonomously given entities. It is true that this balance tends to get disturbed but, then, counter-balancing forces, it is claimed, intervene to restore the balance or establish a fresh balance. In other words, the conception of order in this perspective is not *a priorily* given or pre-ordained. Order ever evolves. Thus, the process of order finding a new level as a result of the dynamic interaction of autonomously given entities is supposed to be open-ended.[24]

Based on the varieties of reality, one with God and the other without it, there have evolved several paradigms of order. Speaking of order of the first variety, Voegelin identifies three such paradigms. These paradigms he calls cosmological, anthropological and sotereological. As has already been pointed out, all these paradigms are concerned with the truth of reality and each of them seeks to penetrate to this truth but in its own different way. In seeking to penetrate to the truth of reality each paradigm makes a definite statement about this truth. By doing this, each articulates, through the use of certain symbols, a society's interpretation of its existence in the presence of God. In Voegelin's words: "The symbols in which a society interprets the meaning of its existence are meant to be true; if the theorist arrives at a different interpretation, he arrives at a different truth concerning the meaning of human existence in society."[25]

Needless to say that the truth of existence by which a society lives is simply the result of a particular way of viewing reality; it cannot claim to be the only or even the whole truth. Otherwise, there would not be another such interpretation about reality.[26] Whatever the case, all of these different ways of perceiving reality have one common feature. All of them emphasize the need to engage in the quest for *homonoia*, that is, spiritual agreement between men in reflecting happiness as a consequence of the attuning of the soul with the divine entity. But this is possible only when men live in agreement with the divine part of themselves. All men participate in their divine part, though in varying degrees of intensity; and, hence, the love of men for their own divine self makes it the common bond between men.[27] As Voegelin notes, "Only in so far as men are equal through the love of their noetic self is friendship possible. It is the friendship with the divine part of the self that, as Heraclitus underlines, provides the ground of *xynon* or shareable commonality."[28]

The three different formulations of the truth of reality by which a society organizes its experience of existence put forth three different perspectives, from which one can perceive truth. It is this particular way of perceiving truth of reality and the organization of social order based on the insight gained from a particular way of perceiving reality that enables a society to claim that it represents something beyond itself, that is, the transcendent reality. It is this claim, made especially by the ruler of a political system to present himself as the representative of the transcendent reality on this earth, enables him to project himself as the sustainer of the transcendental order on this earth. This is what makes that political order a model of cosmological order. It refers to a society that understands itself as the chosen representative of the transcendent order, that is, the order of the cosmos. A political order claiming to be cosmological considers itself as representing: "a cosmic order in the medium of human society."[29] In this perspective, ruler-ship signifies "the task of securing the order of society in harmony with cosmic order; the territorial empire is an analogical representation of the rhythm of the cosmos. It is in this sense that the society claiming to be the representative of the transcendent reality becomes a cosmological type of order."[30]

Another paradigm of order, what Voegelin calls the anthropological principle, is associated with Plato who posits a homology between the individual person and the state; this is well reflected in his oft-quoted phrase that polis is man writ large. What is distinctive about this interpretation of order is that it treats the politically organized society as a cosmion – a replica of the cosmos pregnant with meaning. It underlines the fact that "a political society in existence will have to be an ordered cosmion, but not at the price of man; it should be not only a micro-cosmos but also a macro-anthropos."[31] This signifies that in its order every society reflects the type of men of whom it is composed. This suggests that differences of social order are due mainly to the difference of human types. If a social order degenerates, it is because the order in man's interior has degenerated. The way out of the disorder of society is possible only if a philosopher whose soul is attuned with the divine ground of being and who can have a deeper insight in the true order of things can suggest and fashion a well-ordered political order. Such a political order will reflect a type of man whose psyche is well-ordered because his soul is open to the experience of the transcendent.

What Plato does, through his anthropological principle, is to elaborate the basic elements of a noetic order, that is, order based on the attunement of the soul to the substratum of reality. However, he completely ignores the fact that men are also vulnerable to the counter-pull of passion. And a less noetically minded person is likely to go under in the struggle of reason and passion. To be true to the demands of the noetic order, what is also necessary is an element of faith that can keep a person steadfast on the difficult path of virtue. Christianity, through its soteriological principle, as Voegelin argues, supplies this element. On this interpretation the phenomenal world is profane because it is afflicted with disorder. And, the soteriological principle reveals reality as moving towards a state undisturbed by forces of disorder. A perfectly ordered society will emerge as the final state of this movement. For this, what is necessary is a strong faith in the word of God conveyed to the world by his son – Jesus Christ.

Two things are at once apparent. In the first place, Voegelin has completely ignored the Vedic perspective that combines in it the anthropological principle as well as a stress on what is known as *shraddha* (literally, firmly situated in truth or faith). In the second place, he has not made any reference to the character of order in a reality without God; such an order is exemplified by the conception of order as articulated in liberal philosophy. Also, there is the Chinese conception of order articulated principally by Confucius through the use of two central concepts *jen* (goodness, humanity) and *li* (propriety). In the following pages we discuss the liberal, the Platonic Aristotelian, the Confucian and the Vedic formulations of order. This will help not only in appreciating the characteristics of different conceptions of order that we meet in the world of ideas and in pragmatic existence in the course of history, but also in reaching to a definitive understanding about the comparative merit of each of these conceptions of order.

Notes

1. Aristotle, *Politics*, 1253 25–30.
2. Plato discusses this in *The Laws.*
3. Aristotle, *Politics*, 1288a 34–39.
4. See Ramashray Roy, "Freedom and Order: A Fresh Look," *Gandhi: Soundings in Political Philosophy* (Delhi: Chanakya Publications, 1984), p. 51.
5. Lucio Colletti, *From Rousseau to Lenin: Studies in Ideologies and Society,* Trans John Marrington and Judith White (New York: Monthly Review Press, 1972), p. 150.
6. Afred Lowi, *Beyond Liberalism* (New York: W.W. Norton, 1969), pp. 20–21.
7. Aristotle, *Nichomachean Ethics*, 1129–69.
8. See Robert M. Unger, *Knowledge and Politics* (New York: The Free Press, 1975).
9. See particularly, Immanuel Kant, *Political Writings*, ed. Hans Reiss (Cambridge: Cambridge University Press, 1980), pp. 44–45.
10. Charles Taylor, "Growth, Legitimacy and the Modern Identity," *Praxis International*, July 1991, p. 43.
11. *The Laws.*
12. Ibid., 722a.
13. Aristotle, *Nichomachean Ethics*, 1102a 8–25.
14. Thucydides applied the term in the *History of the Peloponnesian War* to a state of social disease for the first time when he explored the *kinesis* of the 5th century that culminated is the disaster of the Great War in the 4th century.
15. Eric Voegelin, *The Collected Works of Eric Voegelin* (34 vols.)*: The Drama of Humanity and Other Miscellaneous Papers 1939–1985* (Columbia: University of Missouri Press, 2004), Vol. 33, pp. 267–68.
16. Ibid., p. 186.
17. Ibid., p. 220.
18. Loc. cit.
19. *The Drama of Humanity* ... op. cit., pp. 225–26.
20. Ibid.
21. Loc. cit.
22. Stanley Rosen, "Man's Hope," *Social Research*, 48, 3 (Autumn, 1981), p. 20.
23. E.M. Wood, *Mind and Politics: An Approach to the Meaning of Liberal and Socialist Individualism* (Berkeley: University of California, 1972), p. 100.

24. Sheldon Wolin, *Politics and Vision: Continuity and Innovation in Western Political Thought* (Boston: Little, Brown and Co., 1960), pp. 10–11.
25. Eric Voegelin, *The New Science of Politics: An Introduction* (Chicago: The University of Chicago Press, 1987), p. 53.
26. This is evident from the fact that a variety of order has been articulated from different points of views.
27. Aristotle, *Nichomachean Ethics,* 1166a 22 ff; 1177a 12–18, 1177b 27–117898.
28. Eric Voegelin, *The New Science of Politics*, op. cit., p. 77.
29. Ibid., p. 54.
30. Ibid., p. 4.
31. Eric Voegelin, *Order and History: The Economic Age,* V (Baton Rouge: University of Louisiana Press, 1974.

Passion, Ethics and Order

Two different ways of looking at the phenomenon of order in society and world are related to the relationship between the two universals, that is, the universal 'divinity' and the universal 'world'. Differences in the ways of conceiving this relationship between these two universals lead to other differences relating to the nature of man, the status of society, the pattern of interaction of man with nature, and so on. One way of formulating this relationship is to posit the idea of the world with God. The conception of order for the world without God employs a particular conception of man and the phenomenal world. Another version of this type of order recognizes God, to be sure; however, the sustenance of order, no matter how it has been conceived, depends on man's commitment to a system of ethics that precisely defines man's relationship with others in society depending on the age and rank of each of the members. The main difference between the two varieties of the conception of order centres on law versus ethics.

In contrast, the conception of order based on the recognition of the world with God may have different understandings of the status of the God in the world. In one version, God is not recognized as inhering in the world; he is apart from it as a transcendent being; he is the creator of the world, to be sure; however, he has no further role in keeping order in the world. The transcendental entity does not create the world, because it does not descend into any being nor does it allow any being to enter into it. In contradiction to this, another version posits the God as the one who becomes the world through his procession from the non-material into material and inheres in the world as an integral part of it. Given this difference, however, the divine entity is the source of order both in nature and the human world. In both the versions, nature is not an accidental concourse of a lifeless object; it is something that has come to be by the providence of the God and, as Plato sees it, it is "truly a living creature with soul and reason."[1]

The cosmos, as a truly ordered cosmos with soul and reason, is the abode of man who forms an integral part of it. This cosmos, in Jonas' words, constitutes the exemplar of order; it is, at the same time, the cause of all order in particular beings. Thus, while all particular beings display the cosmic order in themselves, they reflect it only in degrees approximating the whole.[2] In this view of order, the relationship between the particular beings and the divine entity is defined by reciprocity between them. That is to say, the divine being has no presence except through its recognition and conscious acceptance by particular beings. Similarly, particular beings have no significance except with reference to the absolute being and with other particular beings. This relationship has been characterized as the Great Chain of Being in which each particular being is linked with all other beings and all linked with the totality.[3] What is distinctive about this perspective is the "fitting together of different components with each other and of these components with the whole; it is this fitting together that results in order and yields harmony. Harmony is thus symptomatic of the manifestation of the One through its manifold beings; the manifested world is subsumed under the idea of *sarvam* (all that is spread all around before one's eyes).[4] Thus, the phenomenal world, besides being the consequence of the procession of the One into materiality, is also the abode of its creator and is, therefore, ordered in the same way as nature; however, order in the human world is nothing more than a possibility.

The reason for this lies in the frailty of human beings in completely moulding their life according to the principle of conduct derived from the intuitive understanding of the structure of order proper for society. Insofar as the intuitive insight into the structure of order is concerned, we should note two things about intuitive understanding of order: one, the source of order in the world is not directly perceptible and, two, how the world came into being nobody knows. Both the nature of the creator God and the manner in which he created the world can be apprehended only through what Plato calls "a likely story". It is only through the medium of the likely story that we can know something about the creator and the way this world came into being. And, this likely story and its telling is based on the intuitive insight one has into the structure of order though it is not accessible to everybody; a rare mystic, sage or philosopher can gain it, although their ways differ sharply from each other. The mystic or the sage relies on the experience he gains, as a result of the unwavering attunement of his soul with the divine ground of reality that results in a flash of eternity on his consciousness and illumines, even though only vaguely, the shape of the structure of order. It is this flash of eternity that yields a paradigm of order suitable for the human world. This paradigm is then elaborated into a complete profile of order with its ritual, cultural, institutional and procedural aspects and then rationally justified through myths and symbols.

In contradistinction to this, the philosopher's relies on his reasoning capacity without perhaps the help of any experience of the transcendent. Consciousness of disorder pervading a society prompts him to find its way out based on his own understanding of the source of the sickness that has afflicted it. In doing so, he performs the role of a physician who possesses a deeper understanding of the sickness of the soul of the individual, that is, *nosos*. For him, it is this sickness that spreads out from the diseased individual soul and gradually pervades the entire society. Once he identifies the cause of the disease, he can then prescribe what needs to be done to curb disorder. Although reason plays an important role but his reasoning power is incapable by itself to penetrate the mystery of the transcendent. In order to be able to penetrate to the depth of this mystery, he has to take recourse to myths and symbols.

The use of symbols and myths is also evident in the case of the sage and the mystic in fashioning a likely story of creation, that is, cosmogony. The primary function of cosmogony is to lay bare the structure of reality as it has come to be as the result of the process of creation; in laying bare the process, it also identifies the creator of the cosmos and his relationship with the cosmos. In addition, cosmogony also places man in a larger context that includes the visible part of the cosmos and the invisible world beyond it. Awareness of the larger order makes man conscious of the limitations of his existence. This consciousness acts as a stimulus for him to the fact that he can attain fullness by acknowledging the need of keeping alive his connection with the larger world. Also, it helps man to shape his life experience in accordance with the demands of the preservation of this larger order without which his own existence will be threatened with perils and loss of value and meaning.

The expectation is that if order has to prevail in society, individual persons must not only imbibe the principles inherent in order, they must also actively pursue these principles in their personal lives and social relations. This means a perfect match between the ways people think and work and the principles of correct living. It is only this perfect match that sustains order and prevents it from degenerating into disorder. But, this match ever remains elusive mainly because of two reasons. First, different likely stories of creation present different images of the transcendent entity, the manner of creation and the projection of different ways of living. What is also important is that each of these stories claims to be the only true story.

This truth claim can be sustained as long as different civilizations grounded in different cosmologies remain isolated from each other. But once they come into contact with each other, different truth claims are put to closer scrutiny and when questions about their truth value are asked, commitment to the way of life comes to be shaken. Secondly, individuals sharply differ in their mental make-up, skill and capability and, consequently, their understanding of the principles of correct living and their commitment to these principles vary sharply. As a result, many individuals fail to live up to the principles of correct living. This affects adversely the prospect of order. Given the fact that there are different ways of conceiving the phenomenon of order, it is necessary to subject at least a few of them to closer scrutiny. What follows is an account of the liberal world view and the Confucian perspective on order.

It must be emphasized that the problem of order arises because there exists a strained relationship between freedom and order. Freedom, needless to say, is necessary since without it, man's development gets stunted and his creative power gets blocked or remains undeveloped or underdeveloped. This is most likely to happen when order restricts freedom of choice to the extent that it loses its significance. If, however, freedom is not restrained, the aggressive pursuit of self-interests promotes *pleonexia*. That is why, the relationship between freedom and order constitutes a key element in the conception of order. Two polar perspectives on the relationship between freedom and order can be easily identified. One perspective treats freedom as primary and order as a secondary principle necessary to insure the pursuit of individual advantage compatibly with others. Even on this view, order necessarily means constraint and, therefore, some constraints on the exercise of freedom. However, constraints may not be based on some *a priori* idea of order. They are usually governed by duly established procedures, or the 'rules of the game' that are legitimate because, supposedly, commonly agreed to and the substantive issues involved in the conflict. Politics is concerned primarily, even exclusively, with this process.[5] Another perspective considers the social world to be characterized by disorder caused mainly by the aggressive pursuit of self-interest. This brings inevitably into operation the "law of the shark"[6] and engulfs social existence in the war of one against all making life a constant struggle. A viable order, capable of containing this struggle, cannot be sustained on the basis of principles derived from the givens of society and nature. Order has to be grounded in something else, in the ends that are beyond the subjection of shifting interests and opinions, that is, in some trans-individual principle. Only then can order be stamped on society and the chaotic impulse of self-aggrandizement of individuals and groups can be successfully checked.

These are, no doubt, antithetical perspectives. The former perspective, an anthropocentric humanism as Dante Germino calls it,[7] constitutes the dominant paradigm that came into prominence when a shift in worldview occurred in Europe in the seventeenth century. This shift epitomizes the rejection of worldviews that considered man as forming an integral part of a larger, conceptual order and made a distinction between a life completely devoted to satisfying ordinary needs, to production and reproduction, on the one hand, and a life given to actualizing certain higher purpose – search for truth, reality and meaning, good citizenship, grace of God, etc., on the other.[8] True, man must satisfy his ordinary needs through production and reproduction. However, such a life is incomplete, barren and imperfect. A wholesome complete and perfect good life is that in which activities are grounded in and informed by the pursuit of some higher purpose. This is possible only when man relates himself to a larger order. On this view, man is not a self-complete and self-sufficient subject who defines for himself his ends and selects means to realize them. It is the larger order that is the locus of norms and values that shape man's ideas, customs and institutions.

True, the larger order is separated from the real world. However, man is endowed with reason, faith or both to apprehend the true structure of the conceptual world. Since rationality is a natural endowment equally shared by all men, the apprehension of the true nature of things produces a shareable commonality of ends and means. Morality and freedom consist in conforming to and moulding one's behaviour on the pattern of the model extant in the conceptual world. Norms and values exist *a priori* and are independent of the vagaries, whims and arbitrariness of individuals, institutions and societies. On this view, the real world in itself does not have any inherent moral order. Norms and values are, in this perspective, transcendent, not immanent.

However, with the shift in the worldview in the seventeenth century, man stood alone in the vast but indifferent world. Cut adrift from the larger order, man emerged as a "broken totality".[9] The eclipse of the larger conceptual order meant the denial of higher purpose in life. The significance of life was seen to consist in the satisfaction of ordinary life needs. The pursuit of happiness was, subsequently, identified with the augmentation of fortune,[10] and the appeasement of desires became the defining and organizing principle of man's life activities. As desires vary from person to person in space and time, no external agency can prescribe and legislate what desires to satisfy and what to postpone and suppress. Consequently, it devolves on man himself to define his purpose. This means that man must enjoy autonomy to discover his purpose in himself. Also, for man to become a true subject, he must follow an internal purpose and, in doing so, he should not owe allegiance to any pre-existing order except the structures that come into being as a consequence of his consenting to their creation.

The freedom to define one's own purpose implies the freedom to execute. To execute a contemplated project requires representing things clearly and contemplating comparative costs and benefits of various alternative means of attaining a given end.[11] The power to plan and execute is thus the hallmark of modern man. This presupposes an attitude of disengagement towards the external world. To look for significance in the external world is to circumscribe one's ability and willingness to use and manipulate the external world for realizing one's purpose. To be disengaged is a necessary condition not only for implementing projects but also for safeguarding freedom. As Taylor points out, "To be able to look on everything, world and society in this perspective would be to neutralize its significance and this would be kind of freedom – the freedom of the self-defining subject who determines his own purpose, or finds them in his natural desires."[12]

The denial of the larger order saw man emerging as a self-complete, self-defining and self-sufficient subject who defines his own purpose,[13] his projects and treats the external world – both society and nature – as potential means. In this transformation, man must have freedom to plan and implement his projects. Reason is essential in both planning and execution. But rationality does not mean apprehension of true nature of things; it is now understood as instrumental reason, nothing more than prudential, calculating reason subservient to desires that constitute the dominant element in man. The necessity of satisfying desires for seeking happiness transforms the external world into potential means and drains its significance. The value of utility comes to pervade man's relationship with the external world. Society becomes nothing more than a mechanical aggregate of self-defining subjects who enter society as the carriers of "natural liberty" that they are supposed to have enjoyed in the state of nature.

The modern conception of nature, along with the predominance of the idea of man as a natural man, has replaced the traditional idea of nature as saturated or permeated by mind which, as Plato sees it, constitutes the source of regularity and orderliness in the natural world. "Similarly, mind or intelligence, in all its manifestations, is the ruler," a dominating or regulating element, imposing order first upon itself and then upon everything belonging to it, primarily its own body and secondarily that body's environment.[14] Analogically, then, Plato conceives order to be established when intelligence rules over desires in the case of man and the philosopher-king governs all others in a *polis*.

But, the worldview based on this idea of nature was replaced by the ascendance of what Collingwood calls 'Renaissance cosmology'. This cosmology rests on the denial that the world of nature is an organism and the assertion that it is devoid both of intelligence and life.[15] As such, nature cannot order its own movement in a rational manner; as a matter of fact, it is quite incapable of moving at all. It is true that nature does display regularity of movement and manifests orderliness. But both regularity of movement and orderliness we identify with nature are not due to its own intelligence; this intelligence is external to nature itself. The regularity it exhibits and the orderliness it displays have their genesis in "laws of nature" imposed from outside by a *deus ex machina*. The Renaissance cosmology, thus, projects a mechanistic view of nature. Instead of being seen as an organism, as in the Greek view of nature, the natural world is supposed, in the Renaissance cosmological perspective, to be a machine, an arrangement of bodily parts designed and put together and set going for a definite purpose by the intermeshing of different part of the machine that the world is. Order, in this perspective, is equated with mechanical intermeshing of various parts of the machine without distortion or conflict. As Taylor points out:

> ... instead of seeing nature as expressing a meaningful order one which has to be accounted for in terms of ideas, we see it as a set of interlocking elements whose relations can be explained in terms of efficient causation. The order (as against disorder) in things does not consist in their embodying ideas, but rather in their meshing without conflict and distortion.[16]

This model of order finds its fullest expression in the Newtonian view of natural order expressed through the concept of equilibrium. In Newton's view, nature comprises a myriad of autonomous and unconditionally viable forces in constant interaction with each other. Equilibrium signifies stability within a system composed of autonomous forces. But, this equilibrium is, despite this relative durability, tenuous; it is frequently disturbed "either by an outside force or by a change in one or other elements comprising the system ... ."[17] However, inherent in nature is the property that is capable of restoring the old equilibrium or creating a new one. Thus, the natural system is self-regulating even though subject to occasional disturbances.

When this conception of order is projected on to the human world, individuals are treated as autonomously given entities, self-complete and self-defining subjects who interact with others for the purposes of fulfilling their needs. The primary impulse for individuals is the search for felicity, which generates energy impelling individuals to satisfy their desires as and when these make their irresistible appearance. Impelled by this energy, individuals interact with each other and the external world, both society and nature, for ensuring their felicity. For Hobbes, who identifies felicity as the central, if not exclusive, concern of individuals, which consists of satisfying one desire after another. For this, generation and exercise of power not only for retaining what one has but also for acquiring/possessing what one thinks is necessary for his felicity becomes *sine qua non*.[18]

The search for felicity came to occupy the centre stage in man's existence only after the banishment of God from his own creation and the rejection of higher life purposes along with it. The void thus created was filled by the dominant concern of fulfilling ordinary life needs involved with the process of production and reproduction. These needs relate to the acquisition and enjoyment of wealth, prestige and power. It is expected that if everyone is driven by the energy of his own desires to seek what he needs, personal as well as collective good will well be served. On this view, the only dynamic entity is the individual who, as the centre of energy and enterprise, serves the collective good by securing his own happiness inasmuch as collective good is nothing but the sum total of individual goods.

In this perspective, vitality, vigour and dynamism of the system depends on the extent to which the individual performs. The performance of this role, efficiently and effectively, raises the level of collective welfare. But it is necessary that that he does not encroach upon or become a hindrance to the performance of a similar role by others. On this view, then, as Taylor observes, "... man comes to realize natural order when the company of desiring subjects comes to achieve full satisfaction (happiness) each compatibly with all others. This perfect harmony of desires is the goal which nature and reason prescribe to man."[19]

Edgeworth posits a homology between what he calls "mechanique social" and "mechanique celeste". If the law of self-interest (engendering a psychological motion) rules the moral universe, the law of physical motion rules the physical universe.[20]

The maximum energy of pleasure can be generated only when the movement of each soul reflects the absence of conflict and distortion and thereby sustains order. This perspective, then, presupposes a particular understanding of human nature which underlines the hope that actions are the expression or are caused by desires and according to which chains of practical reasoning always terminate in some 'I want' or 'it pleases me'.[21] The translation of desire into action, although the key to individual felicity, is not possible unless one creates, acquires, or mobilizes the resource of power. And, power, in this perspective, signifies nothing more than bending others' will to one's own in order to realize one's self-defined purposes.[22]

Central to this perspective is the strategic importance of the exercise of individual freedom both for determining one's purposes and for realizing them. To realize self-determined purposes requires the conversion of freedom into power in the sense referred to above. And, since everyone is engaged in the same enterprise, social life becomes intensely competitive; individuals and diverse social-economic interests vie for articulation, ascendance and control. In such a situation, the important thing is to ensure privileged access to and control over strategic societal resources by the use of superior power, if necessary; winning in a situation of scarcity when everyone is engaged in the same enterprise assumes central importance. It is no wonder, then, that efficacy in performing entrepreneurial tasks of transforming society and nature for provisioning and, beyond that, laying the firm foundation of the good life of modern conception constitutes a basic factor forming and sustaining the modern identity of man.[23]

Efficacy, in this perspective, means to ensure privileged access to and control over societal resources in relation to others or, as Mahatma Gandhi puts it, to establish maximum inequality in one's own favour.[24] The use of efficacy in creating, acquiring certain goods – riches, power, status and prestige – is necessary to ensure, as this perspective claims, individual felicity. It is what MacIntyre calls "goods of effectiveness" which can be had by winning in the race of life. Winning may, perhaps, ensure felicity in the Hobbesian sense, but can it guarantee justice? It can very well do so, if elaborate rules that have to be developed in order to regulate interpersonal interactions, especially the process of exchanging goods and services, are, on the one hand, quite precise, unambiguous, and extensive and, on the other, universally acceptable. This is necessary in view of the fact that, as Unger points out, "a society of individuals who seek to achieve their particular objectives and to satisfy their needs of comfort and honour must be characterized by mutual hostility and mutual dependence. Both hostility and dependence are based on the nature of human ends and on the scarcity of means to satisfy them."[25] Impelled by the intense competition in which individuals are engaged for the search of wealth, power and prestige, they must forge alliances. But such alliances ever remain precarious, tenuous, fragile and temporary.[26] And yet, the mobilization of power resources is absolutely necessary for protecting and promoting individual and group concerns. This creates a situation in which the tension between freedom and order aggravates.

This is the natural consequence of the conditions of mutual antagonism and of the drives that underlie these conditions.[27] Groups form and re-form because of the perception of the similarity of interest and conflict among them poses a threat to order; to safeguard order, limits must be placed on their exercise of freedom; however, this amounts to the infringement of freedom and enfeebles those dynamic factors that lend strength and vitality to the system. This is a dilemma which cannot go unresolved if the disastrous consequences of the opposition between freedom and order are to be avoided.

The solution to the problem of freedom and order is sought in the rule of law, that is, the making and application of elaborate impersonal rules or laws.[28] The main objective of these rules or laws is to minimize, if not completely eliminate, the occasions of open conflict as the direct consequence of natural antagonism, on one hand, and promote cooperative interactions among individuals and groups, on the other. But for cooperation to flourish in a condition of mutual antagonism, two conditions must be fulfilled. In the first place, competition for access to and control over societal resources must be not only fair but also such that it allows unrestrained operation of what is known as Pareto optimality principle, that is, the existence of a situation in which each competitor can maximize his satisfaction (or felicity) to the degree that the preferences of others allow.[29] In the second place, there must exist stability of expectations signifying the strand of cognition or interpretation by which individuals and groups grasp the "meaning" of the actions of others or anticipate future events – in particular, the manner in which others will react to their own behaviour.

In order to create and safeguard these two conditions necessary for cooperative interactions, elaborate rules or laws have to be framed and enforced. These rules or laws have to prescribe reciprocity; that is, they have to define a bargaining situation specifying what is to be exchanged for what.[30] Justice, in this perspective, is, then simply the outcome of a contract, an episode of explicit negotiation.[31] What gives concrete content to the idea of justice is primarily the relative power position of contestants. And, what makes justice possible is that rules or laws are minimally acceptable to all. What is interesting to note in this context is that a perfectly just person is no more or no less a person who always obeys the rules of justice which lacks content until an enforceable set of rules or laws defining the relations of each person to every other in respect of the pursuit of their respective goals has been formulated. As such, the virtue of justice is only secondary to and definable only in terms of the rules of justice.[32]

This introduces a break between individual well-being and collective good. The key to personal welfare now depends on one's ability to stay ahead of others. Even if the level of generalized economic growth rises, the competition for occupying advantageous positions and ensuring privileged access to and control over societal resources becomes very acute.

For addition to the material goods that can be expanded for all will, in itself, increase the scramble for those goods and facilities that cannot be so expanded. Taking part in the scramble is fully rational for any individual in his own actions, since in these actions, he never confronts the distinction between what is available as result of getting ahead to others and what is available from a general advance shared by all. The individual who wants to see better has to stand on tiptoe.[33] He has necessarily to engage in the game of "beggar they neighbour". It is against the backdrop of the mismatch between the private and public, aggravated by the process of economic growth itself, that rules and laws for regulating individual conduct and social relations are needed. It is quite obvious that the goods of effectiveness, such as wealth, power, prestige, status, etc., do not recognize any other goods as higher than themselves or in any way sacrosanct. And, since there is no conception of good that stands above the conflict for privileged access to societal resources, the winning in a situation of scarcity by the employment of power becomes inevitable. However, this is an enterprise in which everyone is engaged. It is no wonder, then, that efficacy in performing entrepreneurial tasks of transforming society and nature for provisioning and, beyond that, laying the firm foundation of the good life of modern conception, constitutes a basic factor forming and sustaining the modern identity of man.[34]

It is interesting to note that there does not exist any principle of good that can impose certain artificial limits on conflicts in want of natural limits derived from a principle of trans-individual principle. Consequently, artificial limits must be created and imposed on conflicts with a view to promoting harmonious cooperative social relations. The creation of these artificial limits is the domain of law-making and law-adjudication. And, the principle of law-making in a situation devised to protect and promote the goods of effectiveness must inevitably make some combination of interests as the ground for legislation and adjudication. The principle of such a combination is supposed to be derived either from an aggregation of interests (Bentham) or from a procedure of law-making to which everyone subscribes in self-interest (Locke and Rousseau), or from an ideal system of procedure of law-making which everyone can agree upon in self-interest and which can be shown to led to a particular desired distribution of wealth and power (Rawls). All these formulations encounter a formidable difficulty, that of finding a neutral way of combining individual, subjective values. Without a reliable standard located outside the individual, subjective preferences to determine which interests to combine in what measures, and in what ways, law-making will amount to *ad hocism* and be determined by the relative power positions of individuals and groups.

In addition, the possibility of finding a procedure to which everyone can subscribe in self-interest gets embroiled in the dilemma of generality *versus* concreteness. If the standard lacks specificity, it will be less adequate for evaluating and yielding guidelines for coping with the concrete; it will, then, to give preferences to individual, subjective ends. Insofar as the question of making shared values the ground for law-making is concerned, it should be noted that if shared values are treated as neither individual nor subjective, the basic tenets of the modern world view is assuredly violated. It is tantamount to hoping that the replacement of one premise by another will alter the course of history. If, on the other hand, shared values are nothing more than the coincidence of individual values, the search for the ground for law-making in shared values encounters the same difficulties faced by other approaches.

Apart from the difficulties encountered in legislation and adjudication, it is also to be kept in mind that the law is the product of will. As such, it can also be changed at will. Moreover, in a situation where none of the patterns of distribution of material benefits satisfies all, efforts to change the law as the legitimizing source of distributive justice are continuous'y made. In addition, it is also unrealistic to suppose that the law can somehow rise above the interests and errors of human beings who formulate them. As Aristotle notes, the law itself must be either democratic or oligarchic, for example, and so will share the defects inherent in these regimes.[35] Thus, the law as a means of regulating and controlling human motivation and conduct proves very ineffective. Social control itself loses its salience inasmuch as society is reduced to a mechanical aggregate of self-defining subjects[36] and is drained of its significance as a source of values and control. Moreover, society, as Colletti argues, is not an end, that is, an indispensable condition for man to be man; its task is merely to "create an external, formal order, i.e., a politico-juridical order which, through the law, consolidates and reinforces the absolute prerogatives of the "natural man" in his isolation from others.[37]

External sources of control prove ineffective precisely because in a system built to promote goods of effectiveness there occurs a large-scale erosion of what Alfred Lowi calls "auto-control".[38] As has already been pointed out, the fulfilment of ordinary life needs constitutes the pivot around which human existence revolves. In one version of life according to nature the excesses of what Aristotle calls *pleonexis*,[39] that is, the act of self-aggrandizement, could be curbed by a resource to rationality; however, rationality signifies only calculative, prudential and instrumental reasoning. Moreover, it is simply a hand-maiden to desires.[40] But another version, associated with Rousseau, endows ordinary life purposes with higher significance; their realization is considered *sine qua non* for full flowering of man's potentialities.[41] As Taylor points out:

> To fulfil the true impulse of nature in us is not just to met biological needs but also to satisfy in higher aspiration. It is, at the same time, a moral fulfilment. From Rousseau on, the true 'voice of nature' is at one and the same time both the impulse of biological need and an aspiration to what is experienced as moral self-realization.[42]

Since the fulfilment of ordinary life needs holds the key not only to personal felicity and the development of individuality, but also to civilizational progress through what Giambatista Vico calls "self-making of man", the struggle for privileged access to and control over scarce societal resources gets accentuated. As a direct consequence of this, the political order becomes primarily an arena of rival interests with each interest vying for articulation, ascendance and control. It is as a result of the continuous process of competition and conflict among different socio-economic interests for ascendance and control that politics is characterized as a process of "who gets what, when, and how". What underlies this perspective is the fact that politics is supposed to derive its nature from the consequences arising out of the competition between individuals, groups and societies for comparative advantage in a situation of scarcity that affects significantly the whole society or substantial part of it.

Competition for comparative advantage often leads to active conflict. This constitutes an invitation to political intervention to bring the contestants to a settled compromise through negotiation and bargaining. But all such compromises yield only partial satisfaction leaving the way open for further conflicts. It is the contestation for comparative advantage that is supposed to produce change that disturbs the relative power positions of diverse socio-economic interests and modifies the objectives for which individuals and groups contest. The impetus for and response to changes provoke conflict and produce destabilization which calls for a new equilibrium. This continuous process, that is, the disturbance of the prevailing equilibrium and the need to establish a new one, characterizes the political system, based on the goods of effectiveness. And, the role of politics in it is to ensure civil stability without blocking change. As such, politics constitutes "an activity expressive of society's needs for constant readjustment."[43]

It is, thus, obvious that order, in this perspective, is not a set pattern; it lacks any *a priorily* defined purpose or goal and, as such, is without any final cause; it is something that is open-ended; it ever evolves. And, in its evolvement, it is not influenced by any set principle of justice, but by the current fashion of opinion and power. As a result, it guarantees neither justice nor civic stability; changing power equations making might into right constantly sways it. This amply underlines the fact that society lacks substantive vision of collectively agreed upon collective purpose except to maintain the system for individual gains. This means that there must be certain common ends that the political community must seek to realize in collective life and relations. In the lack of this vision, the political order must depend for its effectiveness on the appropriateness and legality of procedures of public decision-making.

However, no matter how legal the procedures may be, law-making favours some more than others. In such a situation, cries go up for equalizing life conditions for overcoming inequalities tolerated, condoned, or created by the political order itself. If the political order responds to these cries forcefully and effectively, the way is paved for it to assume more and more power threatening the very existence of the political order as an association of free and equal citizens; this tends to drown individual liberty in the sea of repression and oppression. If it settles for a path of least interference, its legitimacy is gradually eroded and the political order is faced with the prospects of uncertainty and instability.

A political order committed to securing and safeguarding the goods of effectiveness must necessarily become a rule-bound system if for no other reason than to provide a neutral ground for making public decisions in a world marked by subjectivity. The effectiveness of a rule-bound system depends largely on not only the obedience of the law but also on the respect of the law, that is, the internalization of the value of the need to submit to the rules framed to govern people's conduct in a particular situation. The rules confirm not only the fact of having something in someone's use and control, they also define the right to so use and control it. This means that in order for everyone to have his own, even in the material sense, the system must create a condition in which each is ensured the unimpaired possession and enjoyment of his rights. This further means that everybody must develop the disposition to govern one's conduct. It requires at the least the respect of the right of those whom that conduct affects. But, for various reasons, this disposition fails to develop in a large number of cases, or does not take strong roots, if it develops. That is why, the system continues to be buffeted by strong cross-currents of the pursuit of antagonistic interests without finding a resting place.[44]

The preceding discussion highlights a perspective on order for a world without God. These attributes illustrate the raising of one of the universals – the universal world – to the status of an absolute. The result is the downgrading of God and the determination of what man essentially is with what the world signifies. The result is the constant tug-of-war between freedom and order. This makes the sustenance of order difficult. But can an ethical system grounded in role playing by different persons and sections of society maintain order in the world without an abiding faith in God become effective? To answer this question, a reference must be made to the Homeric and Confucian worldviews.

If "having one's own" in the material sense as the basis of a system concerned with the goods of effectiveness proves a fragile foundation for a political order, what about its other sense, that is, the performance by everyone of his socially ascribed role-specific responsibilities without let and hindrance and efficiently and excellently? For example, the Homeric world view of order is based on this conception of "having one's own". For Homer, the universe has a single fundamental order, which structures both nature and society. To be virtuous or just *(dikaios)* is to conduct one's actions and affairs in accordance with this order. In this perspective, society is hierarchically constituted in which different roles associated with specific social stations are graded. *Dike* (justice) consists in faithfully and efficiently carrying out the roles one's social station demands. This means that everyone should know where does he stand in the network of social relationships, what he is expected to do and how best he can do so that he does not usurp or encroach upon the role of others. To usurp the role of others amounts, in this perspective, to violating *dike* and infringing the honour (*time*) of others. A person, who performs his role well and pays back what he owes to others, is *agathos* (good, excellent).[45]

Dike incorporates the idea of everyone doing whatever his role requires. As such, the order based upon it has both personal and social ramifications. At the personal level, it means thinking well or soundly about what one should do not only in respect of one's own role performance but also in respect of the manner, in which he should perform his role so that it does not harm, encroach upon, or prevent others from performing their role. Thus, what is distinctive about the Homeric world view is that the role performance by a particular person necessarily involves and has ramifications for other role occupants. In this sense, what is required of a person in his role is to give what is due to others who perform such roles that stand in determinate relation to his own. As such, two features of Homeric *weltenschauung,* that is, the concept of *dike* and practical reasoning (*phronsesis*) associated with it, deserve special mention. As MacIntyre points out, both are embedded in and draw part of their distinctive character from the larger conceptual scheme in which they are at home.

Both *dike* and *phronesis* are interrelated.[46] And, to learn to make a connection between the two, on the one hand, and to attain even a higher level of excellence in performing one's role, on the other, are factors that cannot be reduced to rules. One learns these things in a social environment – from its values, institutional arrangements, etc., through socialization developing the disposition to apply a particular standard of action in varying contexts. *Phronesis* thus means not simply that a person is well conversant with the rules governing or associated with his role. Additionally, it also means that he knows how a particular norm of behaviour can be applied in particular contexts of action in accordance with the particular structure and specific demands of particular contexts. To act on the *phronesis* is to safeguard *dike.*

The emphasis on performing one's role with excellence as well as fairly and justly means that "each person and each performance have to be accorded what is due to him or her and to it is respect of merit."[47] Thus, justice is defined in terms of merit and desert. But, there usually exists a multiple of standards of desert and ways of ordering them.

This requires a unified standard if the community of role occupants is to function well on the basis of an overall shared standard of just apportionment, just recognition and just rewards and punishments. This is possible in a form of community which provides itself with a well-defined and easily recognized standard so that its members could structure their common life in terms of a form of activity whose specific goal (is) to integrate within itself so far as possible all those other forms of activity practised by these members and so to create and sustain as its specific goal that form with which, to the greatest possible degree, the goods of each practice could be enjoyed as well as these goods which are the external rewards of excellence.[48]

Obviously, this form of activity is politics (*politiei)* and it is the *polis*, which concerns itself with this form of activity; its concern is not with any particular desert or achievement, but with desert and achievement per se. Thus, we can understand the construction of a *polis* as the expression of a set of principles about how goods are to be ordered into a way of life. In such a *polis*, then, human beings will enjoy whatever is best for them; this will be *eudaimonia* (happiness)[49] and would be indicative of how best to flourish.

Two things, however, upset the order of things in the Homeric worldview. First, it is necessary for a person wishing to display justice in his conduct that he must always carry on a dialogue with his *thumos*, that is, the energy that carries him forward in translating his purpose into action, but what usually happens is that passions swell *thumos* and frequently lead to actions that are destructive.[50] Thus, passions are causes that swelling the *thumos* and thereby divert one from doing what will he otherwise do. And, when this happens, *dike* is violated. Second, it is also incontestable that there are many *aretais* (virtues) as there are specific functions and roles to any society. And, there may be as many incompatible as well as conflicting opinions about how these different *aretais* are to be ordered and integrated in a particular way of life.

Thus, *thumos*-directed action raises the question of what controls and disciplines *thumos*? Additionally, there is also the question not simply of giving allegiance to a particular scheme of ordering but also of accepting as valid and, therefore, legitimate the conceptual framework in which a particular scheme of ordering is embedded. Apart from the question of consensus about the way of life, it also raises the question of what virtue must be considered to be the "super" virtue that can subsume and define all other virtues and integrate them in an ordered whole. It is clear from the Homeric emphasis on *thumos* as the main guiding principle that these questions will ever remain unanswered. This is so for the reason that Homer cannot see beyond *thumos* and also offer anything else than a heroic ideal that common men cannot make the beacon of their shuddering ship. What about the Confucian world view? Does it offer a better alternative?

The Chinese idea of political order can be best expressed by the Chinese character signifying man (the base line), the heaven (the top line) and the king (the middle line) who joins and safeguards virtue in personal and public life by acting as the surrogate of the cosmic order, symbolized by the term "heaven," and joining both the heaven and earth (the diagonal line dissecting all the three lines).[51] The role of the king in maintaining order can be compared with a lynch pin that holds diverse elements together in a bond of unity. This is forcefully expressed in *Shih-Ching* 249 and 205: the former underlines the fact that the king orders both the people (in the collective sense) and men (in the individual sense) by receiving the blessings of the heaven when he receives its mandate to rule. The latter expresses the idea that the king below the heaven is the overlord of all land and men inhabiting this land. It is the responsibility, then, of the king to preserve the social order.[52]

Behind this surface meaning of the symbol lies a long-drawn out process in which all the three terms defining the symbol have undergone changes. Take, for example, the term "heaven". Chinese thought at the dawn of the Chinese civilization, especially during the Shang dynasty (1751–1152 B.C.), was dominated by the fear of the spiritual beings. This fear led the Chinese to make use of divination in order to find out the pleasure of the spirits. When the Chou overthrew the Shang in 1112 B.C., they turned to man and his ability to perform things that earlier depended solely on the pleasure of spirits. Since human skill in doing things was seen to be more effective, man was in ascendancy. As a result, the tribal anthropomorphic Lord *(ti),* who controlled human destiny at his whim, was replaced by the impartial and universal heaven (*t'ien*).[53]

With the coming of Confucianism, the abstract category "heaven" was given a definite content. As we shall see later, the key concept in Confucianism is the superior man who is wise, humane, and courageous; who is motivated by righteousness instead of profit; and who studies the way (*tao*) and loves men. In the course of becoming a superior man, a person develops his humanity and contributes significantly to the establishment of harmonious development of the individual and society together. When the individual behaves correctly and society operates in the right manner, the Way is said to prevail. The Way is the moral law, or moral order. It is the Way of heaven. Thus, heaven was no longer conceived in Confucianism as the anthropomorphic Lord (*ti*) but the greatest of all spiritual beings. To Confucius, heaven was the origin of all things, the Supreme Reality, whose purpose manifested in the Way.[54]

Similarly, the term "king" went through several transformations in the course of history. What is remarkably distinctive about the Chinese experience is the idea that an empire of some sort existed from the beginning. This empire was perfectly virtuous and was ruled by mythical figures (three such figures are already mentioned). What must be emphasized is that China had, from the very beginning, tribal clans, each with its own overlord. The division of the Chinese society into tribal political organizations headed by an overlord created several territorial units known as *kuo*. These *kuos* were all rival to each other for predominance. However, alliance among some of them was instrumental in paving the way for the establishment of an empire; the empire was consolidated further by expansion or sinification of the tribal groups at the periphery of the empire as well as the organizational structure given to the hierarchization of power.[55]

As the Po-hu-t'ung reports, the king, who was the son of heaven, *t'ien-tzu,* because Heaven was his father and the earth was his mother, exemplified the meaning of the pre-imperial kingship. The king, in turn, is the father and mother of the people; and in that capacity he rules over "all under Heaven".[56] The dynasty the king founded was displaced either by superior power or treachery of a minister. It is the working out of this process that saw the rise of three dynasties – Hsia, Yin and Chou. Insofar as the organizational structure of dynasties is concerned, it was defined by the pre-imperial conditions indicating a group of territorial states under different chieftains forming separate ritual units. If one of the chieftains became strong enough, he could subject neighbouring territories to his rule under the title of *wang.* Once such a kingdom was established, it could be conquered by one of the member-states, perhaps only recently drawn into the orbit of civilization. This is what seems to have happened in the case of the conquest of the Shang kingdom by the Chou and their barbarian allies on the western border.[57]

The earlier tribal societies represented not only a *t'ien-hsia* ("all under heaven", a religio-cultural entity) but also a ritual community. A chieftain who became king was the ritual head of the community that understood itself as the ecumene. And, though, for reasons of state, the conquered were liberally massacred, the survivors of the former regime had their respected, if insignificant, status among the lords of the newly established Chou kingdom. Thus, the newly established kingdom included the lords of the new kingdom as well as that of the old ones. In the newly established Chou kingdom, the society displayed three levels of political and social hierarchy: the king, the ruling society, and the common people. The supreme rank – *wang* – was occupied by the leader and his descendants who formed the dynasty. The ruling nobility, whose distinguished members were established as lords of territories, of the *kuo,* with lesser families as sub-vassals, formed the next rank. They were collectively called the "Hundred Clans," though probably they never exceeded thirty. Among the commoners, there were *jen* (the members of the clan society) and *min* (non-clan commoners).[58]

The kingdom, as already pointed out, consisted of several territorial states headed by chieftains. In this multi-clan kingdom, the king was, besides being the ruler of the ecumene, also the ruler of a territorial state, of a *kuo*, like other lords. He was also a member of numerous clans whose other members also might hold lordships. The union of three positions – a ruler of ecumene, a lord of a *kuo,* and a clan member – was the distinctive mark of Chinese society under the Chou. Thus, a kingdom represented both a power structure as well as a cultural entity. Keeping of peaceful relationship between *kuo* as a power structure and *t'ien-hsia* stressing the ritual and cultural aspects of ecumenical rule constituted the principal responsibility of the king.[59]

The *t'ien-hsia*, the ecumene in the cultural sense, is associated with *wen* meaning the art of peace. *Wen* is, however, opposed by *wu*, that is, war. *Wen* and *wu*, furthermore, have operational powers: *wen* operates through the attraction of its prestige (*te*), whereas *wu* operates through the force (*li*). The necessity of holding the kingdom together becomes tangible in the institution of the *po*, as a regional protector of the realm at times when the king's own force proves insufficient to maintain peace. Thus, a corresponding series of symbols emerged: To the series *t'ien-hsia*, *wen*, *te, wang* there corresponds the series *kuo*, *wu, li, po.* But finally *kuo* was replaced by *chung-kuo* with the coming of empire. The *kuo* as power organization of Chinese society is thus distinguished from the cultural substance, which it is supposed to shelter.[60]

It is interesting to note that the scholars conceived the idea that well-being in the *ti'en-hsia* came first and the ruler second. However, pragmatically, the order can be reversed and then only *kuo* as a power organization remains with its entire self-aggrandizing tendency towards power and pelf. Ku Yen-wu points in his work (published in 1670) to the distinction between good and bad regimes. As he says: "when the superior man attains station, he desires to work out the *tao*, the Way; when the small man attains station, he desires to serve his own interests."[61] Ku Yen-wu further writes: "The desire to work out the Way (*tao*) manifests itself in making *t'ien-hsia* of *kuo-chia*; the desire to serve one's own interests manifests itself in wounding men and destroying things." To *t'ien-hsia* the *kuo-chia* means to transform the empire, which is nothing but a power organization, into a carrier of ecumenic civilization in the Confucian sense."[62]

The possibility of the making *t'ien-hsia* of *kuo-chia* depends on the *t'e* (virtue) of the king. As Mencius (*The Books of Mencius,* VII, B, 132) says: "There have been men without goodness (*t'e*) who have attained a *kuo;* but no man without goodness has ever attained the *t'ien-hsia*."[63] But before Confucius introduced the idea of *jen,* the concept of *t'e* was in vogue. *T'e* connotes a substance which, when possessed by a person, makes him a king. The *t'e* of the emperor harmoniously combines "heaven and earth," that is, the cosmos; the *te* of the king also harmoniously combines goodness (*jen*) and righteousness (*i*) (*Po Hu Tung*).[64] The personal *t'e* must be distinguished from the collective *t'e*. The personal *t'e* is proper to individual who, in the role of an "ancestor", contributes to the *t'e*-charge of the family, or in the role of a "virtuous ruler," recovers the fortunes of the dynasty for a while. The collective *t'e* is proper to a family, which by virtue of the accumulated *t'e*-charge, can aspire to royal rank. The family which has acquired the necessary *t'e*-charge, then, may ascent to the rule of the ecumene, if it receives the decree or appointment, *ming*, of Heaven. For the time of its heavenly appointment, though not before or after, finally, the dynasty of the family is conceived as a unit of ecumenic order with regard to time, space and substance.[65]

What emerges from this account of the increase and decrease in the charge of *t'e* is the moral perspective that Confucian scholars project on *regnum.* The distinctive mark of this perspective is the important distinction between the state as a power structure and the state as the protector and sustainer of the cultural life of the individual and the community he is part of as well as the maintenance of the ecumene as a cultural entity. The power of every dynasty springs from a virtue (*t'e*) or a prestige (*ti* or *to'-yin*), which passes through a time of fullness (*chang* or *sheng*), then declines *(ngai)* after an ephemeral resurrection (*hing*), becomes exhausted and is finally extinguished (*mie*). The dynasty then ought to be extinguished, suppressed (*tsuch* or *mie-tsuch*); exterminated, for it no longer has heaven on its side (*pu-tien*). Heaven (*tien*) ceases to treat its kings like sons (*tsu*).[66]

A family can only provide China with kings, sons of heaven *(t'ien tsu)* during the period in which heaven grants its investiture (*ming*). This investiture, this heavenly mandate is always temporary. Heaven is changeable, and inexorable. Its favour is lost and wears away not because the heaven is fickle but because king transforms the kingdom from a cultural ecumene to a power structure and uses it for the advancement of his own selfish ends. When the king turns autocratic ignoring the way of the heaven he becomes a tyrant, his *t'e* is exhausted and the dynasty comes to an end sooner or later.[67]

As such, every dynasty that retains its power when the time has passed away only possesses it *de facto, de jure*, it is a usurper. The heavenly mandate, that authorizes a dynasty to rule, is the fruit of merit (*kong*) of a greater ancestor. But, due to the complete erosion of *te* of the king, the family forfeits its right to rule. The founders of the dynasties whose hour has come fulfil a heavenly mission by suppressing the dynasty that has become out-of-date and maleficent. They are the ministers of a divine chastisement and their victory is the proof that heaven has entrusted to them its mandate. The last sovereigns of a dynasty are essentially tyrants and rebels against the way of the heaven, blinded with pride. The royal virtue is obtained by obedience to the heavenly commands.[68]

What we must note is that this perspective on statecraft offers a theory about how a kingdom is gained and lost and why. It is a theory which is, at the same time, a condemnation of statecraft that promotes indulgence in and expression of the need to satisfy the king's passions to the complete neglect of public weal. Confucius understood human relations in moral terms – affection between father and son, righteousness between ruler and the people, attention to their separate functions between husband and wife, proper order between old and young, and faithfulness between friends. But, in all these relationships, the relation between the king and his people was given the central importance because on it depended the stability of society.[69] Thus, the Confucian ideal of *regnum* is a moral order that tends to degenerate over time and reduce the *t'ien-hsia* to *kuo-chia*. And, when this happens, the sovereign turns into a tyrant and his reign needs to be brought to an end. As such, a person who succeeds in extinguishing a dynastic rule that has turned into misrule is performing a moral act sanctioned by the command of the heaven. The peaceful performance of this moral duty is possible only when a particular person has acquired *t'e*. His *t'e* makes even the improper means in extinguishing a tyrannous dynasty a moral act.[70]

The king as the keeper of the heavenly order is also the lord of men who inhabit a particular territory. The king constitutes an exemplar of virtue and inspires men he rules over to become virtuous. And, when men become and remain virtuous, the territorial unit becomes a cultural entity. It is against this background we can appreciate why the self-designation of the Chinese people equates Chinese society as comprised of civilized mankind of which it is the sole carrier. The equation of the civilized mankind with Chinese society has derived from its geographical location. At the time of An Yang, China was never one society among others; from its beginning the history of Chinese society was for its members, to the best of their knowledge, the history of mankind. In the absence of cultural contacts with other societies, the process of organizing different peoples in an imperial order was inspired by endogenous forces operating within the geographical bounds of Chinese society. Chinese ecumenism received its peculiar colouration from the unbroken consciousness of the identity of China with mankind."

What these endogenous forces were can be gleaned from numerous designations that refer to the structure of political order. In 8th century B.C., China appeared as an unstable confederation of over-lordships. At the beginning of the Chun-Chien epoch, Chinese unity was already sketched out on a federal plan. The expression, which was to mean simply China, had then the meaning of Chinese Confederation (*Chong Kuo)* formed of over-lordships of varied importance. These over-lordships felt themselves connected less by the force of political relationship than by a certain community of civilization. A shade of difference can also be discerned between the expression *Chong Kuo* and *Shang Kuo,* the latter designating the over-lordships (*kuo*), which were formerly in confederation and possessed superiority. *Wu,* the superior over-lord qualified as *hsai* – the name of the first dynasty, also signifying "civilized". And equivalent of *hsia* is *hua* (flower); the expression *Chong hua,* the central flower, is in the end applied to the whole of China.[71] Thus, *hsia* and *hua* come to mean the superiority of the *Chong hua* over all others. The currency of *Chong hua* can still be seen in the designation of the Chinese Republic (Taiwan) as *Chung hua Min-Kuo* (Central Flower Republic); even communist China has expanded the style to *Chung-hua-jeng-Min Kung-Ho Kua* (Central Flower People's Republic). The term *chang-kuo* thus acquired geopolitical and civilizational connotation in addition to its cosmological meaning.[72]

Thus, the substantive meaning of the territory occupied by the Chinese people refers to the superior civilization, not because the political order is defined in terms of the free display of naked power by the sovereign, but because the *regnum* follows the way of the Heaven and exemplifies the virtue reflected in *wu*. However, as we have already seen, virtue (*te*) goes through a process of decline till another replaces one dynasty. Confucian thinking posits the idea of a 500-year cycle in which a dynasty rises, continues to rule but finally it gets extinguished. Needless to say that such a periodization has a philosophical rather than a historical character. Its philosophical character is derived from the attempt to justify the role of the sage in putting a stop to declining order and define afresh the moral and pragmatic content of order and, if need be, he can also play an active role as an administrator to stem the tide of disorder and instal order again. The sage estimates the historical situation by relating it to the cycle and finds his own role by placing himself in the position to check the lapse of order. Confucius was the prominent sage to intervene by his writings and suggest a framework of order that could check the slide of order into disorder.[73] As he said, if there was no virtue in the kingdom the sage had no choice but to intervene. "If right principles prevailed through the empire, there would be no use for me to change its state."[74] This was again repeated by Mencius when one of his disciples found him discontented on leaving the state of Chi; his disciple, Chung yu reminded Mencius that he had formerly said that the gentlemen neither murmurs against heaven nor is he angry with men, Mencius sets him right by saying:

> That was then, today is different. Every five hundred years there must be a king (*wang*); and in between there must be men who create order within their generation. Since the Chou, more than seven hundred years have passed. Hence, the number has been exceeded already. If we

> examine the situation of the time, the possibility is there. But Heaven does not yet want the ecumene pacified and ordered. If it wanted the ecumene pacified and ordered in the present generation, who is there but myself? How should I be not discontented?[75]

It is clear, thus, that in case heaven does not act, it becomes incumbent on the sage to take on the role of the heaven and not only suggest ways and means of pacifying and ordering the ecumene, but also of taking on this responsibility himself. Even his son, Ssu-ma Chien, claims in his autobiography that he, too, could not avoid the responsibility of setting things right. This claim on the part of the sage indicates the susceptibility of the *regnum* to forsake the path of virtue and be gripped by the allurement of power. This slide from virtue to power, then, invites disorder. This is symptomatic of the vulnerability of a paradigmatic perfect state of virtuous life and relations to human frailty from which even the monarch is not immune. It is to bolster the life of virtue that the sage has to intervene. But what exact path this intervention must take? We have three different answers to this question. If in China, the sage restricts himself mainly to reconstructing and/or reorienting the edifice of a virtuous state, in Greece, the philosopher actually becomes king and directs and manages human affairs. In contradistinction to these two historical models, ancient Indian thinking suggests a complementary role of *sacerdotium* and *regnum*, a syzygy between the two in which king acts according to the counsel of the priest. However, there is a vital difference in the Chinese and the Indian perspectives. If the sage in China can both advise and actively intervene in the administration, the Purohit in India strictly restricts himself to rendering advice.

But what framework of order is discernible in Chinese, especially Confucian, thinking? How does his thinking, especially its fundamental tenets, relate to the question of order in general and political order in particular? It should be kept in mind that the Chinese political order was conceived to be the earthly, this worldly copy of the heavenly order. But, the two are always in tension. Confucian thinking stems from this tension. The tension is precisely this. In confrontation with the world, Confucianism (and Taosim) keep harking back to the ideal qualities of the *tao,* the governing principles of the cosmic and social order and the "golden past" when the *tao* was thought to be in perfect operation (during the days of legendry figures of Yao and Shun).[76] This meant that the given world was at ethical variance with the *tao* and the "golden past". Public indictment and personal criticism against the socio-political order that abounded in the Chinese literature of every age expressed no acceptance against the socio-political order "as given".

What became accepted in the Confucian thinking was the world as interpreted by the Confucian orthodoxy. Meanwhile, the concrete forms and qualities of the *tao* and the "golden past" were subject to interpretation by authoritative men of knowledge just as God's will was interpreted by the Hebrew prophets. The knowledge of the sage was to advance propositions for controlling or remoulding the world as he found it in conformity with the various interpretations of *ideal* ethical demands by the *tao*. In Confucian and in general Chinese moral tradition, there was pressure for transforming the given world in conformity with ideas that were often disguised under the label *tao* or the "golden past". The *tao* was the abstract concept, not the concrete form, of cosmic and social order;[77] it received its content from the sage who juxtaposed reality against what he thought virtue to be.

For Confucius, however, this abstract concept could be given a concrete form if the two central concepts of Confucian thinking – *jen* (goodness, humanity) and *li* (propriety) – were embraced by the individual in giving a proper shape to his life in society. *Jen* referred earlier to different kinds of particular virtues; however, at the hand of Confucius it emerged as an umbrella concept that gave meaning to all ethical norms. *Jen* thus performs an integrative function. *Jen* refers to personal morality, while *li* points to propriety, particularly in the context of social interactions, underlining the phenomena of society as the basis not only of community but also of cultural community living. *Jen* as personal morality describes the highest human achievement reached through moral self-cultivation. In contrast, *li* refers to the "boundaries of right," the boundaries that have to be respected in concrete social situations where what matters is reciprocity informed by the motivation of respecting the integrity of the other.

Li can be considered as externalization of *jen* in a specific social context. To cultivate equilibrium in one's inner being, without, however, eliminating all worldly ties and without withdrawing from the service of society, is the essence of *li*. *Li* means standards of this world, whereas *jen* means the summon of choice and answerability. *Li* signifies the fact that a man lives in society, *jen* points to the equally important fact that man is more than the intersection of social forces. *Jen* gives meaning to *li*; without the manifestation of *li*, *jen* is also inconceivable in Confucianism. It is interesting to note that *jen* in its etymological meaning is "man in society" and consists, according to some schools, of the sign of one and the sign of two, the primordial form of human relatedness. This is expressed in Peter Boodberg's suggestive translation as "co-humanity".[78]

Li as a process of humanization is manifested in four developmental stages: (1) cultivating personal life (*hsiu-shen*); (2) regulating familial relationship *(ch'i-chia);* (3) ordering the affairs of the state *(chi-kuo*); and (4) bringing peace to the world *(ping t'ien-hsia).*[79] There is evident a series of concentric circles and the centre of which stands the individual himself. It is expected that the individual will graduate from ennobling his own life to making the world a better place through intervening stages. What is emphasized here is a process of gradual inclusion, not developing humanity in the abstract. It is, therefore, not surprising that Mencius attacks universalism of Motzu. From the Mencian perspective, the central issue is not so much the desirability of universalizing one's basic value commitment as much as how, by concrete path, it can be universally manifested. Setting up an abstract standard of indiscriminate love without coming to terms with concrete human situations is to ignore the very context in which the ideal is to be actualized. Hence, the Confucians believe that the realization of universal love must begin with a concrete process of gradual inclusion.

It is on the basis of the application of the principal Confucian tenets that the making of *kuo-chia* into a *tien-hsia* means the transformation of the empire, which is nothing but a power organization, into a carrier of ecumenic civilization in the Confucian sense. What is projected in the Confucian perspective is a social philosophy that, even while it attempts to move from the temporal to some form of pure form of transcendental metaphysics, always returns to the social, this worldly affairs,[80] especially in later interpretations. And, the social life comes to be predominantly characterized by family relations. Dominated by ideas of respect, domestic morality seems in the end to become mixed up with a ceremonial of family life. On the other hand, the relations of society, animated first by the spirit of contest, or the passion for prestige, it seems, end by being governed by an exclusive taste for decorum. Civic morality having gravitated towards an ideal of strained politeness seems to tend solely to organizing among men, a regulated system of relations, in which the actions befitting each age are fixed by edict, as are also those for each sex, each social conduct and each actual situation.[81]

Finally, in political life, where the stage is reached of advocating the principle of government by history, it appears that it is claimed as sufficient for everything to follow solely the virtues of traditionalist conformity. As Max Weber remarks, "the Messianic hope for a this-worldly savior-Emperors is found in China, as in almost all patrimonial associations. But this hope is not hope for an absolute utopia, as was the case in Israel."[82] This hope was the hope of adjusting to the world, to its orders and conventions. This was unavoidable because even though a reference was made to heaven, it lacked substantive content, which was given to it by thinkers and sages as each of them conceived of it.

The idea of order and derivatively that of political order took it inspiration from a super-divine, impersonal, power identical with eternal existence. The heaven revealed itself to the regime on earth, in the firm order of nature and tradition, which were part of the cosmic order and, as elsewhere else, it revealed itself in what occurred to man. Thus, what was desired was the preservation of this cosmic order in the social universe through the mechanism of *regnum*. The success of the *regnum* depended on the extent to which it conformed to the ways of heaven and did not allow the *t'e* to erode. In this, the fusion of the laws of nature and of rites into the unity of *tao* was to serve as an unfailing instrument of keeping order.[83]

The preceding discussion has highlighted some of the essential features of liberal, Homeric and Chinese worldviews. It has also underscored the limitations and deficiencies each of them suffers from. It is, therefore, necessary to discuss the Hellenic perspectives before we move on to discussing the traditional Indian perspectives focusing, in the main, on the Vedic perspective.

Notes

1. Plato, *Timaeus* in F.M. Cornford, tr. *Plato's Cosmology* (London: Routledge and Kegan Paul, 1971), pp. 33–34.
2. Hans Jonas, *The Gnostic Religion: The Message of the Alien God and the Beginning of Christianity* (Boston: Beacon Press, 1963), p. 242.
3. V.C.C. Collum, *Manifold Unity: The Ancient World's Perception of the Divine Patterns of Harmony* (Calcutta: Rupa and Co., 1995), pp. 59–60.
4. It needs to be emphasized that the cosmos Plato talks about is not, in any sense of the term, the manifestation of the One. The Platonic form does not enter anything not does it allow anything else to enter itself. As such,

there exists a duality in the world and its supposed creator. This has profound consequences for man and his world. Needless also to say that this duality does not exist, as will be clear later, in Vedic cosmogony.

5. Sheldon Wolin, *Politics and Vision: Continuity and Innovation in Western Political Thought* (Boston: Little Brown and Co., 1960), p. 43.
6. The law of the shark or *Matsya Nyaya* points to the phenomenon of the big fish eating the small ones.
7. Dante Germino, *Machiavelli to Marx: Modern Western Political Thought* (Chicago: Chicago University Press, 1972), pp. 7, 16.
8. For a brief but succinct discussion on this subject, see Charles Taylor, "Growth, Legitimacy and the Modern Identity of Man," *Praxis International*, 1, 2 (July 1981), pp. 112–14. See also his *Hegel and Modern Society* (Cambridge: Cambridge University Press, 1979).
9. This phrase is Iris Murdoch's and can be found in her *Sartre* (Collins, the Fontana Library, 1968), p. 85.
10. For a useful discussion on this subject, see Albert, O. Hirschman, *The Passions and the Interests: Political Arguments for Capitalism Before its Triumph* (Princeton: Princeton University Press, 1977).
11. On this point, see Charles Taylor, The Concept of a Person, B.N. Ganguly Memorial Lectures, Centre for the Study of Developing Societies, Delhi, March 1981, 3rd Lecture Typescript, published as *Social Science as Praxis* (Delhi: Oxford University Press, 1985).
12. Ibid.
13. Cf. Then, the Supreme Maker ... cast man in his own image, and having placed him in the center of the world, spoke to him thus: "... The nature allotted to all other creatures, within laws appointed by ourselves, restrains them. Thou, restrained by no narrow bonds, according to thy own free will, the where power I have placed thee, shall define they nature thyself." Pico, *Oration on the Dignity of Man;* Quoted in J.H. Randall, Jr., *The Making of the Modern Mind* (New York: Houghton, Mifflin, Co., 1968), p. 123.
14. R.C. Collingwood, *The Idea of Nature* (Oxford: Oxford University Press, 1976), p. 3.
15. Ibid., p. 5.
16. Charles Taylor, *Hegel and Modern Society*, op. cit., p. 75. Cf. David Hume in *Dialogues Concerning Natural Religion: Look Around the World*: Contemplate the whole and every part of it. You will find it to be nothing but one great machine, sub-divided in an infinite number of lesser machines which again admit of subdivisions to a degree beyond human senses and faculties can trace and explain. All these various machines and even their most minute parts are adjusted to each other with an accuracy which ravishes into administration all men who have even contemplated them.

The curious adopting of means to end throughout all nature, resembles exactly though it much exceeds the production of human ... intelligence.

17. Hans Morgenthau, *Politics among Nations: The Struggle for Poser and Peace* (New York: Alfred A. Knopf, 1964), 3rd edn., p. 168.
18. Thomas Hobbes, *Leviathan* (New York: Dutton, 1956), p. 79.
19. Op. cit. Cf. Elie Halevy, *The Growth of Philosophic Radicalism* (London: Faber and Faber, 1972), p. 15. Cf. also Mandeville when he underlines the relationship between private vice and public benefit.
20. Francis Edgeworth, *Mathematical Physics* (1981), quoted in George J. Stigler, "Economics or Ethics".
21. Alasdair McIntyre, *Whose Justice? Which Rationality*? (London: Gerald Duckworth Co. Ltd., 1988).
22. Max Weber, "Power (Macht) is a probability that one actor within a social relationship will be in a position to carry out his own will despite resistance, regardless of the basis on which this probability rests." *The Theory of Social and Economic Organization,* ed., Talcott Parsons (New York: The Free Press, 1966), p. 152.
23. On this point, see Charles Taylor, "Growth, Legitimacy and the Modern Identity," *Paraxis International,* 1, 2 (July 1981), pp. 112–14.
24. M.K. Gandhi, "Unto the Last," *Selected Works of Mahatma Gandhi*, ed., Shriman Narayan (Ahmedabad: Navajivan Publishing House, 1969), 6 vols., Vol. 4, pp. 8–9.
25. Roberto M. Unger, *Knowledge and Politics* (New York: The Free Press, 1975), p. 65.
26. On this point, see Dov Ronen, *The Quest for Self-determination* (New Haven: Yale University Press, 1979).
27. Ibid., p. 67.
28. On this point, see Adolph Lowe, *On Economic Knowledge: Toward a Science of Political Economy* (New York: Harper and Row, 1965), Part 2, Section 2: see also his "Toward a Science of Political Economy" in Robert L. Heilbroner, ed., *Economic Means and Social Ends: Essays in Political Economy* (Englewood Cliffs, N.J.: Prentice-Hall, Inc., 1969), p. 11.
29. MacIntyre, op. cit., p. 36.
30. Loc. cit.
31. Loc. cit.
32. Loc. cit.
33. Ibid., p. 10.
34. Taylor, op. cit.
35. Aristotle, *Politics*, op. cit., p. 1281a 34–39.
36. See my "Freedom and Order: A Fresh Look", in *Gandhi: Soundings in Political Philosophy* (Delhi: Chanakya Publications, 1984), p. 51.

37. Lucio Colletti, *From Rousseau to Lenin: Studies in Ideologies and Society,* trans. John Marrington and Judith White (New York: Monthly Review Press, 1972), p. 150.
38. Alfred Lowi, *Beyond Liberalism* (New York: W.W. Norton, 1969), pp. 20–21.
39. Aristotle, *Nichomachean Ethics,* 1129b 9.
40. See Unger, op. cit., pp. 39–55.
41. On this, see Immanuel Kant, *Political Writings,* ed. Hans Reiss (Cambridge: Cambridge University Press, 1980), pp. 44–45.
42. Taylor, "Growth, Legitimacy, and the Modern Identity", op. cit., p. 113.
43. Sheldon Wolin, *Politics and Vision: Continuity and Innovation in Western Political Thought* (Boston: Little Brown and Co., 1960), p. 11.
44. It is for this reason that Michael Oakeshott's restatement of what Noel O'Sullivan calls the civil model of political order must prove ineffective. See Oakeshott, *On Human Conduct* (Cambridge: Cambridge University Press, 1975) and O'Sullivan, "The Political and the Concept of the Public", *Studies in Humanities and Social Sciences,* IV, 2 (1997), pp. 1–22.
45. MacIntyre, op. cit., pp. 14–15.
46. Ibid., p. 23.
47. Ibid., p. 33.
48. Ibid., pp. 33–34.
49. According to John M. Cooper, the traditional English translation of *eudaimonia* as happiness is not a good choïce. As Aristotle points out, only gods and human begins are capable of being *Eudaimon* and among humans only adults, since it is only acceptable to a call a child *eudaimon* in the expectation that his adult life will be such as to make him later on *eudaimon. Nichomachean Ethics* (NE) 1099b 32–34, 1178 b 23–31, and 1100a a-L). Again *eudaimon* is not the possession of single days (NE 1098a 18–20) or short periods of time but only of the whole adult life of a certain sort of person. Cooper therefore prefers human flourishing rather than happiness as the proper rendering of *eudaimonia. Reason and Human Good in Aristotle* (Cambridge, Mass: Harvard University Press, 1975), p. 89, fn. 1.
50. Homer himself offers a very good example of this. See, Illiad.
51. Ax Xinzhang Yao put it: "According to Confucian understanding, the world is sustained by and structured around, three ultimates *(sanji),* which are also termed the three powers of the universe (*sancai*): *Tain (heaven), di (Earth)* and *ren (humans).* These three powers work together in an organic cosmos so that "heaven, Earth and humans are the region of all things. Heaven generates them, Earth nourishes them and humans perfect them." *An Introduction to Confucianism* (Cambridge: Cambridge

University Press, 2000), p. 139, the quotation is from *Chunqiu Fanblu Yiz heng* (Beijing: Zhunghva Shuju, 1985).

52. It needs to be emphasized that the universal way, the central concern of Confucianism, is understood to originate from heaven and therefore to be the source of the meaning and value of human. However, the universal way was manifest most perfectly in the wisdom of the ancient sage kings (*Xianuakg zhi dao*) *Lunye Yizhu*, 1–12 (Beijing: Zhonghua shuja, 1960) and in the way of life of good people. (*shanren Zhi dao),* ibid., 12. 20. And, as Confucius sees it, the order embedded in the way of heaven has to be maintained primarily by the king and if he fails in it, by the sage. Yao, op. cit., p. 140. See also Marcel Granet, *Chinese Civilization* (Cleveland: Meridian Books, The World Publishing Co. 1964), p. 9.
53. See "Chinese Mythology," *Encyclopaedia Britannica,* p. 410.
54. *Encyclopaedia Britannica.*
55. Eric Voegelin, *Order and History: The Ecumenic Age*, V, (Baton Rouge: Louisiana State University, 1974), p. 284.
56. Ibid., p. 289. As Shih-ching 205 underlines: All below heaven, None but the kings, land; All on the land, None but the king's men. It should be noted that the king, besides being ruler of the ecumene, furthermore was the leader of a territorial state, of a *Kuo*, like the other lords. He was, finally the master of a numerous clan whose other members also might hold lordships.
57. Voegelin, op. cit., p. 288.
58. Ibid.
59. Ibid.
60. Ibid., p. 289.
61. Ibid., pp. 292–93.
62. Yen-wu, Ku, quoted in Voegelin, ibid., p. 293.
63. Voegelin, op. cit., p. 293.
64. Tjan Tjoe Som, *Po. Hu Tung: The Comprehensive Discussion in the White Tiger Hau (*Leiden: E.J. Brills, 1949), Vols. I. and II, Leiden 1952).
65. Voegelin, op. cit., p. 294.
66. Granet, op. cit., p. 14.
67. Ibid.
68. Ibid.
69. Yao, op. cit., pp. 165–69; see also R.P. Krame, trans *King Tzu Chia You: The School Sayings of Confucius* (London: E.J. Brill, 1950), p. 212.
70. Mencius elaborates, in *The Book of Mencius,* VI, B, on the traitorous usurpation at four occasions: "the Five Hegemons (*po*) were traitors to the Three Royal Dynasties (*san-wang*); the lords (*chu-hou*) of the present

time are traitors to the Five Hegemons; the nobles (*ta-fu*) of the present time are traitors to the lords of the present time." This traitorous usurpation is, a Mencius sees it, the sure sign of the erosion of *te'* and its replacement by personal greed. Mencius attributes this to the decay of royal substance which course in three phases. To quote him (VII, A, 30): The mythical emperors Yan and Shun possessed the substance (perhaps the Confucian *(jen)* by nature; the founders of the dynasty acquired it, and the Hegemons of the Chich-Chin period borrowed it." Mencius concludes that "when some body borrowed something and does not return it for a long time, who will still be aware that it is not his property". It signifies the exercise of power without morality.

71. Voegelin, op. cit., p. 282.
72. Ibid., pp. 282–83; Granet, op. cit., p. 76.
73. Voegelin, op. cit., pp. 116–17.
74. Confucius, *Analect*, 18.16.
75. Mencius II B15; quoted in Voegelin, op. cit., p. 281.
76. G.K. Yang, Introduction, Max Weber, *The Religion of China,* trans. and ed. Hans H. Gerth (New York: Free Press, 1951), p. XXXVII.
77. Ibid.
78. Tu Wei-Ming, *Humanity and Self-Cultivation: Essays in Confucian Thought* (Berkeley: Asian Humanities Press, 1979), p. 27.
79. Ibid.
80. Cf. Etienne Balazs, "Even when it attempts to detach itself from the temporal world and arrive at some form of pure, transcendental metaphysics those can be no hope of understanding it without recognizing its point of departure to which sooner or later it returns." "la crise sociale et la philosophic politique a la fin dies Han, " *Toung Pao*, 39 (1949), pp. 83–131. For an English version see, "Political Philosophy and Social Crisis in the end of Han," in Etienne Balazs, *Chinese Civilization and Bureaucracy: Variations on a Themes* Trans. H.M. Wright, ed., Arthur F. Wright (New Haven: Yale University Press, 1964), p. 195.
81. Granet, op. cit.
82. Max Weber, *The Religion of China* (New York: Free Press, 1968), p. 145.
83. Ibid.

4

The State Within Us

For Aristotle, the best regime is the one that is capable of dispensing two kinds of particular justice, distributive justice and corrective justice.[1] By shifting his focus from general justice, that is *dikaiosyne* in the sense of goodness or righteousness yielding what Plato calls *sophia,* Aristotle relates justice to the relationship between the state and its members, on the one hand, and that among its members, on the other. For example, distributive justice refers to the pattern of distribution of offices and honours among its members. This pattern to enjoy legitimacy must conform to a conception of a particular relationship between desert and reward. To make desert the basis of distributing offices and rewards is to ensure that a particular hierarchy of goods, men and different constituents or parts of society must be maintained for avoiding the possibility of morally worst men occupying higher positions. This means that the pattern of distributive justice must be backed up by a just and proper disposition pertaining to the correct location of goods, persons and parts of a whole on a scale of values or degree of perfection.

It is evident that any hierarchical ordering of society and individual lives and relations must be based on a particular gradation of various goods on the basis of certain values or virtues. And, the knowledge that yields a standard for ordering various goods is what Plato calls "synoptic vision". It is the "synoptic vision" that engenders "the ability to see the connection of things,"[2] or, *politeia* (i.e., the ability to establish a principled relationship or authoritative order among various goods). This is precisely *sophia* which Aristotle leaves alone and prefers, as we have seen, *phronesis* based on deliberation. This means that Aristotle prefers the *polis* to be founded upon and reflect in its functioning justice between citizen and citizen *sub specie civitatis* rather than justice as between man and man *sub specie humanitatis.*[3] And, when dirempted from *sophia* the basis of absolute justice, particular justice comes to be based on the sanction of the law. In this sense, distributive justice consists in obedience to that principle of distribution that defines the order created by the law.

The order based on desert and merit and sanctified by the law can, thus, be safeguarded against disruption only on the basis of total commitment to the rule of law. As such, a good citizen *qua* citizen is required not only to obey but also to respect the law. In this sense, *dikaiosyne* means doing every thing which the law requires, that is, "... the exercise of all the virtues by each citizen in his relationship to other citizens".[4] But the citizen's *arete* (virtue) is an uncertain commodity; fluctuations in it may disrupt order. When this happens, it becomes necessary to restore order. Restoration of order is what Aristotle calls "rectificatory justice" which has the important function of restoring, as far as possible, that just order which was partially destroyed by some unjust action or actions.

Three essential conditions must exist in order for this double-barreled conception of justice to become effectively operative. First, there must exit a widespread and deep-rooted consensus about the appropriateness of the existent pattern of distributive justice. Without such a consensus, the *polis* will be constantly harassed by the contest of alternative versions of distributive justice, each of which will be pressed with passion and power for recognition as the sole basis of state policy. But this consensus does not prove durable if it is based on agreement among powerful socio-economic interests. A slight shift in their perspectives causes enormous change in consensus pitting one interest against another in a battle for political dominance. And, since the diremption of *phronesis* from *sophia* signifies the forceful separation of the concept of a good citizen from that of a good man, *phronesis* degenerates into deliberation.

It must be emphasized that deliberation does not aim at some end beyond the action to be done. Deliberation is concerned with the efficacy of different means for realizing a particular end beyond its own determination; it calculates costs and benefits of a particular course of action. It does not, and cannot, calculate the good and bad consequences of a particular course of action. And moral reasoning is concerned precisely with the consequences of particular action for others. And moral reasoning requires a life that is impregnated and regulated by a moral outlook. This means opting for a way of life, *bios*[5] in the true sense of the term, in which some ultimate end determines the adoption of appropriate action in a particular situation. On this view, ethics is linked with *bios* as a clear and comprehensive unity, a deliberately shaped life pattern. It is the consensus about the way of life that constitutes the sub-stratum of the consensus about the appropriate pattern of distributive justice. Thus, to be a good citizen, it is necessary to be a good man, which, in turn, requires the cultivation of *sophia*. Without it, distributive justice lacks an anchor to firmly hold it against the contrary winds of interests and fashions of opinion.

Second, if for any reason, the pre-existent pattern of distributive justice comes to be challenged and violated, Aristotle expects that the imbalance caused by the disruption of order can very well be redressed by rectificatory justice. Aristotle gives us to understand that rectificatory justice aims at restoring *status quo ante* rather than establishing a new equilibrium based on consensus about a new, widely acceptable pattern of distributive justice. But the very need to take recourse to rectificatory justice is symptomatic of the fact that the pre-existing pattern of distributive justice has become unacceptable because it is felt to be unfair by many. Any attempt to go back to the old pattern of distributive justice will mean the continued discontent and, perhaps, active resistance by those socio-economic interests adversely affected by the pre-existent pattern of distributive justice. In such a situation, restoration of the *status quo ante* involves legality, that is, excessive use of the existing laws by the emergent dominant powers to extract resentful submission to and unwilling obedience of the prevalent mode of distributive justice. This further paves the way for the erosion of legitimacy of the state.

If, on the other hand, the felt injustice is sought to be rectified on the basis of legitimacy, that is, a new consensus on basic values, it not only signifies the abrogation of the antecedent distributive justice but also the inauguration of an open-ended process of the raising of new demands and their satisfaction moving, in this process, from one mode of distributive justice to another *ad infinitum* till the political system breaks down under the burden of its own anxiety to continue in existence. Thus, there are problems in relying on rectificatory justice to safeguard a particular pattern of distributive justice. The source of these problems lies in the attempt to restore the pattern of distributive justice without ensuring that the values underlying justice remain universally acceptable and continue to animate, influence and regulate political life and relations.

And, lastly, as suggested earlier, the stability of the social system in terms of its value system and institutional arrangement has a very significant bearing on the capacity of the political system to defend and maintain a particular mode of distributive justice. But every social system is prone to change and the process of change affects not only the structural properties but also their constitutive principles. In this process, it is quite likely that every thing of value may change beyond recognition. This also applies to distributive justice. In time, the substantive idea of what constitutes distributive justice may undergo drastic changes with each new conception of justice being justified on one ground or another.

This has two very profound consequences. In the first place, in want of an absolute standard beyond the grasp of king Whirl, it is very difficult to determine whether a particular pattern of distributive justice is, in fact, justice. In the second place, this puts state-society relationship under a very heavy strain. Aristotle criticizes Plato for ignoring diversity and advocating complete unity. "Is it not obvious", Aristotle asks, "that a state may at length attain such a degree of unity as to be no longer a state? – since the nature of a state is to be a plurality ..."[6] But Aristotle loses sight of the fact that diversity or plurality proves disastrous for political life and relations if it is not woven into a unity of purpose and perspective.

What should be the basis of this unity, of integrating the diversity into unity without destroying or emasculating diversity? Interest cannot provide such a basis because it is itself a surrogate for diversity; the state, too, cannot be the basis of such a unity insofar as it represents something higher than itself, something which, when fully reflected in political life and relations, creates and sustains a political community. And, as Aristotle himself makes it clear, the *polis* exists for justice; it is not only founded on the idea of justice, it also exists to defend and enforce justice. But, as we have already seen, for justice to retain its salience for guiding and regulating political life and relations, something more than the rule of law becomes necessary. The very commitment to respect and obey law that Aristotle prescribes as the firm foundation of civic virtue has to be engendered by a moral outlook which is cultivated not by *phronesis* but by *sophia*.

Without it, commitment to respecting and obeying the law itself suffers erosion.

The erosion of the legitimacy of the law or its ineffectiveness in correcting violations of justice increases the importance of social order in educating men in the virtues of a good man without which a man cannot become a good citizen. To the extent that society performs this role well, the state will receive support from society when it is confronted with growing disaffection and dissatisfaction. If, however, society lacks those principles that forge, strengthen and reinforce bonds of unity, the state is increasingly faced with challenges to its legitimacy and authority but finds itself severely handicapped in coping with them successfully. It can hope to cope with them only when it aligns itself with powerful socio-economic interests. But, then, it has to pay not only a heavy price for it; it also reneges in discharging its responsibility of dispensing and safeguarding distributive justice. The fact, however, remains that while Aristotle assigns central importance to character building in a community, he does not consider society to be an apt medium of the training of character; it is the *polis* which he considers appropriate for this.[7] But when the *polis* is starved of the sustenance of *sophia*, it engenders only cankers of self-love, dissension and conflict; it does not educate men in the virtue of citizenship.

Aristotle does seek to embed justice and, therefore, political order in practical reasoning which, according to him, is the surrogate of rationality and morality. Practising *phronesis*, a person can, Aristotle argues, develop the capacity of avoiding two vicious features of character, that is, *pleonexia,* acting so as to aggrandize oneself, whether one's desert entitles one to it or not (*Nicomachean Ethics*, to be referred hereafter to as NE 1129b9) and suffering injustice voluntarily. Thus, to act virtuously is to act in accordance with a mean, a middle state between two extremes; it is what is known as moderation or temperance. It must be pointed out that moderation is, in fact, the distinctive feature of a person who is blessed with two character traits. First, such a person is capable of controlling his passions. In a moderate man passions are expected to be in harmony with other parts of his being especially his reason. Second, he must develop the capacity, in Gandhi's words, of resisting tyranny, that is, the adverse consequences of someone's action for others, on the one hand, and wilful violations of justice, on the other.

Needless to say that if we put emphasis on moderation as the basis of political order, the locus of order is shifted from the exterior to the interior of man. However, the implications of moderation are such that they demand more than *phronesis*. It must be stressed that harmony in man's interior is not automatic; it has to be nurtured and nourished by each individual by his own self-effort. that allows and supports healthy individual growth. The effort at self-transformation demands, on the one hand, acting on oneself and, on the other, a social order that allows and supports healthy individual growth. But, as Aristotle himself recognizes, most people prefer to have more and more of good things in life. The cause of this is zeal for life, but not for the good life (NE 1257b41). And, insofar as the environing social order is concerned, society itself becomes incapable of controlling and shaping individual conduct. Thus, Aristotelian perspective on political order must get its sustenance and succour not from man's interior but from his exterior, that is, the laws, the constitution, etc. But, then, political order becomes anaemic and infirm. It is against this background that the question of the relationship between man's interior and political order assumes importance. This leads us to examine Plato's thinking which articulates one mode of this relationship.

The central problem for Plato is the question of civic wholeness. This question has three different dimensions: the *pratimana* (model) of civic wholeness, ramification of this *pratimana* for man, and the nature of political institutional arrangement appropriate for safeguarding civic wholeness. In elaborating these dimensions and determining their relationships, Plato establishes a homology between man and the *polis* (*Republic* [Rep.], BK. II, 368). Since the *polis* is man writ large, there exists a structural similarity between justice at the level of the individual and justice as it applies to the *polis*.[8] The homology between man and *polis* has its roots in certain common features shared by both. As Plato makes it clear, the state comes into being in order to facilitate the fulfilment of man's various needs. The fulfilment of these needs gives birth to many occupations based on division of labour and specialization. As a simple society makes transition to a complex society, man's needs proliferate and, along with it, occupations become more and more diverse and specialization, too, becomes very elaborate. Corresponding to man's needs, occupational groups emerge to fulfil these needs. All these occupational groups can, broadly speaking, be categorized in three classes: those who produce or facilitate exchanges of goods necessary for fulfilling diverse needs, that is, artisans; those who are responsible for protecting the *polis* from internal disturbances and external aggression, and those who are responsible for guiding the *polis* and ruling. They constitute the three vitally important parts of the *polis*.

Corresponding to these three classes in the *polis*, there are appetites, spirit and intelligence as three parts of the soul. Taking these three classes in the *polis* and the three parts of the soul, Plato distinguishes, as Jaeger puts it,[9] three types of desire and pleasure, and corresponding governing principles. Each part of the soul has a different desire, set on a different object. The part that desires loves profit in the broadest sense of the term. The spirited part loves honour. The reasoning part loves knowledge: it is *philosophos*.

The homology between man and the *polis* goes farther than this. Each of the parts of the soul can and, in fact, does become the ruling principle. Depending on which part of the soul happens to be the ruling principle in a man's life, there will be different types of men. This is also true of the *polis*; its type will, as in the case of man, be determined by the type of persons whose life pattern reflects a particular ruling principle. Thus the homology between man and the state that Plato establishes conveys the idea that, for Plato, there is an intimate relationship between the order of man, and the order of the *polis*.[10] In Voegelin's words:

> Man is equipped with a pattern of life, the paradigm of his choice in Hades, and associated with it is a daemon of a more or less virtuous complexion. The same structure of paradigm and daemon is to be found in the *polis*. It has a pattern of institutional order, its politeia; and it has a daemon, represented by its ruling part.[11]

Every individual chooses for himself a way of life, his *bios*; it is this life pattern, which the individual embraces of his own free choice, that shapes and moulds his character. It is this character that becomes the individual's life-long companion and determines his conduct. Plato equates, following Heraclitus, character with daemon; on this view, daemon means God not in his absolute being but in his active relation to man.[12] And, in its active relation to man, daemon as character has an important bearing on the individual's *arete*; if the individual finds himself in a position to regret his self-chosen life pattern, he cannot blame anyone else but himself. Thus, the individual has his pattern of life; it shapes his character which, in turn, is supposed to bring him happiness. Similarly, a state has its own distinctive pattern of institutional arrangement which shapes and regulates political life and relations, and, above all, it has its ruler whether an individual or a dominant social class. Thus, as there are various types of men, so are there various types of states distinguished by their respective pattern of life and ruling principle.

Given the diversity of the type of men as well as that of states,[13] Plato must answer four questions before his idea of political order could be fully grasped. First, are all life patterns or, by the same token, all states equally good or preferable? Second, if they are not all good and preferable, what life pattern should be considered good and preferable? Third, what must be the basis for determining the best pattern of life that should be preferred? And, lastly, if the best pattern of life in case either of the individual or the *polis* can be determined, how does this life pattern become a reality both in the case of the individual and the *polis*? Two issues are concretely involved in answering the first question. In the first place, if something is already written in large letters, why should one take the trouble of reading the same thing written in small letters? And, since the *polis* is man writ large, the kind of life pattern that is good and preferable can very well be discerned from the consideration of what is the best form of government.[14] In the second place, there is, of course, a homology between man and the state. It is also true that both man and the state are associated with certain paradigms of life patterns. But, these paradigms are innumerable and different kinds of *arete*, too, live in different states. These paradigms by themselves are unable to yield the knowledge of what constitutes a good life. One has, therefore, to go beyond these paradigms in order to apprehend what good life is.[15]

In explicating what good life is, Socrates, when convinced of the futility of dialectical reasoning in demonstrating what justice is, adopts the strategy of showing justice (Rep. II, 368–371) in the "whole city" (Rep., 368 E 2–3). In showing this, he first creates a simple city, a city that can cater to nothing more than the subsistence needs or plain necessities of its small population. Glaucon characterizes this city as only fit for pigs (Rep., 372 d 4–5) and argues that it is not a true city since it does not provide for relish for a person like Glaucon; nor does it accommodate those who are blessed with spiritedness. Socrates accedes to Glaucon's demand to create a city that should provide for "relish" (Rep., 372 C 2), Glaucon's demand means substantively that the city must provide for "the supplement to the indispensable staples of human life". In effect, it means "... The inclusion of the full array of goods and services commonly accepted as pertaining to an elegant life style".[16] What does the city become when it gears itself up to provide for an elegant lifestyle?

It is quite clear that if the city is organized to serve the demands of an elegant lifestyle, it must admit a multiplicity of goods and services requiring a very large number of specialists who must be trained and recruited to service limitless appetites. In other words, the simple city populated by a small number of people will inevitably grow in size; it will have a greatly enlarged community; it will be swollen up with a whole multitude of callings not ministering to any bare necessity.[17] With the increase in the size of the community, the territory which was large enough to support a small population proves too small to support a large population. As a result, "we shall have to cut off a slice of our neighbour's territory" and if they too are not content with bare necessaries, "they will want a slice of ours". This will inevitably end in war.[18] War will necessitate a big standing army. With all this, the *polis* will become too large to allow, for example, a shoemaker to try to become a farmer. Specialization holds the key, then, to the smooth functioning of the *polis*. It means that men engaged in different occupations necessary for providing goods and services for endlessly proliferating needs of the people need to be well trained in their respective fields and must be equipped with the greatest amount of skill and practice.[19] This must also be true of those who are to guide and rule over the destiny of the *polis*.

But what kind of skill and education is necessary for the guardians? To determine this, it is necessary to take note of the problem inherent in installing order in a state committed to satisfying a multitude of appetites. In such a case, the polis is in no condition to exclude any good or service as long as it is technologically possible to provide them. This simply means that the *polis* lacks a basis to discriminate between appetites; in want of such a discriminatory standard, all desires will carry equal weight. It also means that there will consequently be no order or hierarchy among the myriad of goods and services that the city permits. "Like the inflamed appetite it is obliged to admit, the city is itself limitless. It possesses as yet no principle according to which its order or even its completion may be determined."[20] It is in this context that the question whether a state which seeks to respond to all appetites has become complete or, to put it alternatively, where in such a *polis* does justice reside?[21] If the state lacks justice, the attempt to supply Glaucon's demand for relish produces nothing more than a "promiscuous heap; stuffed and multitudinous"(Rep., 373 b 3–4).

What Plato drives at by asking where justice lies in a city grown large in trying to meet the demands for ever more goods and services emanating from inflamed appetites is to draw attention to a very significant character of the *polis*. He intends to underline the fact that a city may grow big as a consequence of incorporating a multitude of demands and a diversity of occupations displaying a host of technical expertise. But, the growth of the city in this manner is no assurance either that it has grown into a well integrated political community or it has become whole in the sense of reflecting civic wholeness. As a matter of fact, in want of civic wholeness, diversity or, to put it in its contemporary usage, pluralism, poses a problem to the viability and vitality of the *polis* inasmuch as it promotes particularism and self-aggrandizement rooted in self-love. Given the preponderance of self-love, what is there to keep the watch dogs of the *polis* from turning into wolfs and devouring their fellow citizens? Moreover, in the absence of civic wholeness, the *polis*, when facing a crisis, finds very few citizens to defend it against the ruler's abuse of power.[22] Thus, the *polis* does not become whole or complete by allowing unrestricted increase of goods and services. The wholeness evidently depends instead upon the establishment of a principled relationship among the *polis*' diverse parts. This principled relationship or authoritative order is what Plato calls *politeia*.

But how is the pattern of principled relationship among various parts of the city to be apprehended? Plato considers all those who are immersed in appearance to be unable to develop a synoptic vision which is necessary to apprehend what *politeia* is; to apprehend *politeia* sharpsightedness is an essential condition (Rep., 368d 3–4). In speaking of the synoptic vision as the product of sharpsightedness, one must, Plato insists, make a distinction between "all knowing" and "deep knowing" or, as Plato himself puts it, between the exhaustive technical wisdom of the poet and the real wisdom of the philosopher (Rep., 398 a1). The poet knows – and knows passionately – too many things. His wisdom touches upon all things and is, therefore, very comprehensive. However, while

> mimetic expertise is exhaustive in its reach, it remains piecemeal in its comprehension. Despite its dazzling capacity for representing anything and everything, the one thing merely mimetic expertise cannot imagine

> is the governing principle that prescribes the proper place of (all beings) and so provides definition to their community as a whole.[23]

Compared to the poets who exemplify "all knowing", the statesman ranks higher because, despite the fact that the statesman's knowledge is much less exhaustive than that of the poet, the knowledge he possesses pertains to something whole, even if it is by no means finished or complete.[24] But it is quite likely that the statesman, too, may be suffering from what Plato calls "cognitive bewitchment" induced by the needs and appetites of the body.[25] To quote Plato:

> For the body is a source of endless trouble to us by reason of the mere requirement of food; ... and by filling us as full of loves, and lusts, and fears, and fancies, and idols, and every sort of folly, prevents our ever having, as people say, so much as a thought. For whence come wars, and fightings, and factions? Whence but from the body and the lusts of the body?[26]

When a person comes under the irresistible allurement of the body, he attaches equal value to all his desires; he is simply unable to distinguish between which desire he should honour, which to reject and which to satisfy only to a particular extent. And, when he lets in every desire that appears without being invited, it is tantamount to handing the rule over himself to each of his desires as it comes along and harasses him till it is appeased. As Plato notes, the person under the rule of his desires

> ... will set all his pleasures on a footing of equality, denying to none its equal rights and maintenance, and allowing each in turn, as it presents itself, to succeed, as if by the change of the lot, to the government of his soul until it is satisfied. When he is told that some pleasures should be sought and valued as arising from desires of a higher order, others chastised and enslaved because the desires are base, he will shut the gates of his citadel against the messengers of truth, shaking his head and declaring that one appetite is as good as another and all must have their equal rights.[27]

Welcoming and embracing all the desires as he does, his life exhibits "no order or restraint, and he has no wish to change an existence which he calls pleasant, free, and happy".[28] This state of affairs leads to what Plato describes as *polypragmosyne*, that is, the readiness to engage in multifarious activities which are not a man's proper business and *allotriopragmosyne* (meddlesome-ness, officious interference) (Rep., 434b-c; 444b).[29] Apart from meddlesome-ness, unthinking submission to appetites also signifies, as Nussbaum puts it, changeability of the soul. "A soul kept in such a way is at the mercy of any ruler." Such a soul can too quickly change its course in obedience to a new mastering desire. "And because its desire leads it, so frequently, to attend to vulnerable things it, can all too rapidly be stripped of what it really values."[30]

In order for the soul to escape being stripped of what it values, it is necessary for it to "escape from the servitude of many mad masters" (Rep., 329c). But how does one escape from the servitude of many mad masters? As long as a person lives an appetitive life, he is like a vessel full of holes; no matter how much and how long one fills it with water, it always remains empty. Similarly, no matter how long and how many desires a person satisfies, satisfaction ever eludes him. Such a person is like a loathsome bird that execrates as rapidly as it eats, and is constantly doing both.[31] A soul bewitched by the body becomes accustomed "to hate and fear and shun(s) that which is hidden from the eyes, to be grasped only by the intelligence and with the help of philosophy ...".[32]

A necessary consequence of the bewitchment of the body is immersion into materiality that, in turn, leads to the distortion of perspective. When the soul is totally turned towards appearance, reason becomes cramped and deformed; it, then, ceases its search for the true and the good; it is, as Plato points out, wholly consumed in *logizomenos*, that is, calculation (Rep., 366a 6–7). And *logizomenos* is the prime source of synoptic incapacity. What is also interesting is the fact that no rational argument can help a person in the grip of appearance; he can only become a *philodoxos* (lover of opinion), not *philosophos* (lover of wisdom). Moreover, even if a *logos* accounting for the superiority of justice is needed, no amount of argument can benefit a person who does not recognize any truth higher than what his opinion leads him to believe. If anything, the operation of dialectical argument or, for that matter, any well-reasoned argument, will inevitably deteriorate into eristics if the distinction one makes fails to correspond to the proper articulation of the whole (Rep., 454 a 1–9).

A *philodoxos*, even when he is highly dissatisfied with the prevailing state of affairs, will only mouth another opinion bereft of or far more removed from real knowledge. This is nothing more than "spinning of shard" (Rep., 521c 5), that is, when alienated from the perverting reality, however pernicious it may be, a person immersed in appearance is like an isolated piece of a shattered whole. As such, he cannot adequately contemplate the human good. In order, therefore, to accurately discern the nature of human excellence, he must heal his own soul and thus develop a capacity for synopsis.

Two things are very clear. First, as long as man is engrossed in an appetitive life, it is difficult for him to apprehend truth. Second, the true and the good cannot be apprehended through dialectic, that is, through an intellectual definition. To see the true and the good is possible only through the soul's eye. As Plato points out, "... every soul possesses an organ better worth saving than a thousand eyes, because it is our only means of seeing the truth ..." (Rep., 527 D-E). However, the soul is buried deep down in "some barbaric slime" (Rep. 533D) and cannot see clearly. It is, therefore, necessary to train the mind to develop the capacity of putting many particulars together to realize the single idea behind them. It is what Plato calls "synoptic vision". It is possible only when the soul turns round (*periagoge*) from the world of appearance towards the source of light that makes the eye of the soul to see, distinguish between what is only apparently good and what is really good. As the sun is the source of light in the physical universe, so is the "Idea of Good" the source of truth and meaning in the social world. And, the "Idea of Good" can be grasped only when the soul is rescued through *periagoge* from its bondage to appetites and is attuned to the divine ground of being which is the source of the true and the good.[33] When the "eye of the soul" is fixed on the Good, it yields the knowledge or the synoptic vision with the help of which one can perceive the pattern of right ordering. This is true in case both of the individual and the *polis* (Rep. 540a-b).

Insofar as the question of right ordering is concerned, Socrates had already suggested a hierarchy of values reflecting a clearly graduated theory of goods, which places spiritual goods highest, physical goods below them, and external goods like property and power in the lowest place.[34] Following Socrates, Plato too, imposes a hierarchy on goods which treats the soul as the divine in man and is the locus of intelligence through which the divine ground of being can be apprehended. And since it constitutes the divine part of man, the soul must rule over spiritedness and appetites. It is, therefore, man's primary responsibility to care for his soul; it is only on this basis that man's quest for the knowledge of values and of truth, *phronesis* and *aletheia,* in short, the vision of *agathon*, can be successfully completed. It is the *vision* of the *agathon* that forms the soul through the experience of the transcendence and makes it possible to put one's interior in order by installing the soul as the sensorium of divine as the ruler over other faculties.[35]

Installation of the soul as the ruler in man's interior signifies the adoption of a way of life, *bios* in the true sense of the term. The soul, when properly, trained, becomes the locus of *sophia* which, in turn, represents a particular ethical code by which man can organize his life activities. Living by such a code man develops the capacity to resist nature and attains *eudaimonia,* perfect happiness. This underlines the fact that "... man cannot reach ... harmony with being through the cultivation and satisfaction of his own senses and his bodily nature ... but only through complete mastery over himself in accordance with the law he finds by searching his own soul."[36]

This harmony represents, both in the case of the individual and the *polis,* cooperation of different parts which becomes evident when, on the one hand, these parts reflect a hierarchy in which the apex is occupied by the best and, on the other, each of these parts performs its naturally endowed or socially sanctioned roles in the great chain of being. Following this principle, it is the soul in the individual being that should be the ruling power and it is the philosopher-king who must be the ruler in the *polis.*

It is true that when the soul's eye is turned towards the divine source of values and truth, man attains *sophia* and thereby puts his interior in order so that he remains either unaffected by the swelling of appetites or becomes capable of preventing them from raising their head. In order to seek the vision of the *agathon*, what is needed is *periagoge*. But how does *periagoge* become possible? To put it differently, what kind of knowledge can turn the soul around from the life of passion to the life of wisdom? Plato does not believe, to quote Jaeger, that

> it can be done through a single experience, a sudden movement of the soul, an instantaneous flash of light which burst upon a man without any trouble on his part. Nor can it be achieved by the ordinary education of the guards: for athletics deal with the world of coming-to-be and passing away, with growth and diminution, while 'music' only creates rhythm and harmony in the soul, without giving knowledge.[37]

There is one kind of knowledge that can rekindle and sharpen the soul's eye; it is mathematical studies which "forces the soul to turn towards the region of that beatific reality which it must by all means behold".[38]

In working out the homology between man and the *polis*, Plato, as is evident from the preceding discussion, locates the source of a benign political order in the order in man's interior. In other words, the state within each of us is the model as well as the ground of the state outside us. It is the order or disorder of the soul that becomes the source of order or disorder in society.[39] Thus, when the entire soul is "turned away from the changing world" and contemplates reality and "that supreme splendour ... called Good,"[40] the state within becomes well-ordered. A man thus formed, "a wise man" (Rep. 591 s), will keep his eye fixed on that *politeia* within himself (79 e), and do whatever he can to preserve its order intact by steering a middle course between extremes of wealth and poverty, public honours and insignificance (Rep., 591 e-592a).

But, is the Platonic prescription of ordering man's interior, we must ask, workable? For various reasons, the Platonic paradigm of a well-ordered *polis* seems to flounder on the rock of several ambiguities and uncertainties. First, Plato seems to be in two minds when it comes to the question of ruling. It is true that Plato correctly insists that the best element in both man's interior and the *polis* should rule. However, it is not quite clear whether the act of ruling should be based on *praxis* (doing) or *techne* (making).[41] Plato does think it necessary to have a synoptic vision in order to identify the *politeia* for putting diverse elements of the *polis* in order. But once the *polis* based on *politeia* has come into being, does it really need a philosopher king or well educated guardians? It is here that Plato seems in two minds. He makes a distinction between what is ideal and what is only possible and acknowledges that "it is in the nature of things that action should come close to truth than thought" (Rep., 473b-c). Given this, it may not be possible to embrace and realize the idea of the philosopher king or of the king to become *philosophos.* In this eventuality, there is no other alternative but to rely on *techne* or making to cast the *polis* in the ideal mould.

Second, even if the apprehension of the Good is *sine qua non* of founding the best *polis,* it is not clear either how contemplation of the Good is possible or effective in sustaining what Cochrane calls *platonopolis*[42] As Plato himself admits, rational discourse is quite incapable of apprehending the Good.[43] It is, therefore, not surprising that Plato talks of the soul turning round to the source of light. This turning round *(periagoge),* Plato argues, is possible with the help of mathematical studies. It must, however, be pointed out that it is true that the world exhibits, as Pythagoras argues, harmony and this can very well be demonstrated by numbers representing harmonic scale. But so are dissonances in this world. Moreover, as Gadamer argues, numbers constitute a sequence which "remains primarily a mere model of systematic deduction in general ..."[44] It is true that a sum of numbers does symbolize unity of many. But this unity cannot be attributed to particular numbers constituting the sum. Also, numbers can be combined and divided in many ways. However, the results of combinations and divisions of numbers are anticipated in the very steps of mathematical operations. Also, numbers represent properties of something else; they are not themselves that something. And God, what is also interesting, does not indulge in mathematics; only men do.

Third, it is true that Plato seeks to lift man up from the realm of appearance (that is, the realm of becoming) to the realm of being and form man's ethos in a way that justice is safeguarded. This does not, however, seem to be within the range of possibility for different reasons. As Plato himself admits, *logos* proves very tender and fragile under the fury of the storm of self-interest engendered by appetites. It is quite evident that Plato categorizes people into three main types, each type reflecting not only a particular natural endowment of inclination but also immutability of tendency to resist becoming something else than what a person is. However, Plato insists that when the philosopher-king takes society and human character as his canvass, he must begin by scraping it clean so that "he is given a clean surface to work on or has cleansed it himself".[45] That is why, Plato does not put reliance on *logos* alone; he has to prescribe certain institutional devices, like censor, communal sharing of certain objects, strict educational pattern, etc., to keep man on a proper path.

It is evident, then, that *logos* is neither accessible to or is capable of controlling and regulating the conduct of all. It has, therefore, to be helped by the law which can force men to conform to the idea of justice. Thus, the *polis* grounded in the idea of justice has the law as its guardian; the law, as Pindar says, becomes the king.[46] It is true that the law has a great educational potential in making man a citizen; it represents a new *aretę* which becomes effective only when wisdom and power join hands in safeguarding and promoting justice. But the law, as Plato recognizes, is a tyrant who tends, on the one hand, to ignore distinctions which ought to be made in certain situations, and, on the other hand, to freeze a particular social situation as well as a particular behaviour pattern foreclosing the possibility of growth and innovation. The replacement of ethos by the law symbolizes the denigration of the social aspect of communal life. This is so for the reason that the law attains primacy as an instrument of controlling man's behaviour only when social life and relations get denuded of their significance and authority. But, then, the law itself comes to be treated as a means by those who become competitors for controlling the power apparatus of society.

And, lastly, Plato posits a basic opposition between form and matter. Plato treats matter as chaotic and resistant to order. The *polis* is no exception to these. Given the duality inherent in Platonic thinking, matter cannot change its nature. It therefore works as a limiting factor and makes intelligence struggle, perhaps in vain, against the challenges that obstreperous matter poses. It is, therefore, not surprising that Plato has to make both the law and power the ally of *logos*. But, as the helplessness of *logos* increases, the role of the law and power in maintaining order also increases eclipsing *logos* still further. As *logos* finds its hold slipping, power dictates the kind of the law necessary for keeping in leash autonomous individuals intoxicated by the ambition of controlling the power apparatus of the *polis*. The law then emerges as the product of will which can be changed by will.

It is enough to suggest that Platonopolis is encumbered with several problems which it cannot solve or avoid. It is true that Plato's notion of justice is undoubtedly evocative. However, it fails to generate transformative power. One important reason responsible for this is, of course, the exclusion of a large number of persons from the charmed circle of the rare few capable of breaking through the barrier of *doxa* (opinion) and reaching the promised land of *episteme* (knowledge). Devoid of knowledge, they must be condemned to live a life of appetite and sink not only their own soul in the mire of ignorance and unhappiness but also making the *polis* extremely vulnerable to injustice. The political system that is created to safeguard justice is not able to accomplish anything more than forcing people to perform their self-chosen or socially sanctioned roles efficiently and effectively. It induces only conformity; it does not shape the people's consciousness to strive to move towards the best. And the devices the political system relies on for making individuals to conform to certain standards of public life do not induce or train men to transform their own lives. If the law and political institutional arrangement lack the power to make men truly men, so is the social system quite incapable of doing anything else than becoming the means of realizing individual purposes or constituting the arena where different interests contend for ascendance and control. Thus, a large number of people are unable to escape the snare of appetites. If dialectic fails to kindle the sparks of divine nature of man, then, Plato believes, *thanatos* (the fear of death) can engender *periagoge.* Eros (love) can then take over and facilitate the soul's attunement to the divine ground of being. Needless to say that even Thanatos proves, as Yaksha-Yudhishthir *samvad (*dialogue) in *Mahabharat* demonstrates, ineffective.

All this suggests that the ground for a durably just political order must be sought in a perspective that satisfies three vital conditions. First, it must forge a link between the finite cosmos of meaning and the absolute to be sure; however, it must not take human nature to be immutably frozen. It must, of course, consider human beings to be conditioned beings, to be sure; but it should also take into account the real possibility that the ultimate destiny of man as a conditioned being is unconditioned. Plato notes, it is true, that "no two people are born exactly alike. There are innate differences that fit them for different occupations."[47] It is also true that these innate difference are, for most individuals, definitive of their ethos. However, ethos itself can be changed through self-effort aimed at self-development. As such, the perspective linking the *asya loka* with *asau loka*[48] must grant man the possibility of self-transformation in the deeper spiritual sense.

Second, it is true that not all men are capable of self-transformation even if they earnestly wished for it. But this does not mean that if they lack the capacity of self-transformation, they also necessarily lack the capacity or the motivation to adopt a mode of conduct that makes them good men as a vital precondition of becoming good citizens. It does not help to put, as Plato does, the "Tree of Knowledge" in opposition to the "Tree of Life". This is evident from Plato's reduction of truth in reality to truth in language. In this reduction two things happen. In the first place, the soul gets divorced from the senses and creates its own world that stands over against the world of senses and seeks to count it out of reckoning for the purposes of living. In the Platonic scheme is reflected a picture of what Cochrane calls "a multiple soul, a composite ... of discrete elements confronting one another in a struggle to be concluded only by the final release of mind from its prison house in matter and by its return to the source of its being, the 'life' of pure form".[49] It is paradoxical that the soul that is supposed to redeem man-in-the-flesh must first redeem itself only by repressing the flesh.

In Plato's view, the soul, even when it is a part of the body, is opposed to it; unless the body is vanquished and crushed, the soul cannot redeem man. Thus man in flesh is decidedly a stumbling block to the soul's flight to the ethereal realm of idea. In this sense, Plato considers "individuality, the existence of man in the flesh, not as the vehicle for the expression of personality but as an obstacle to its realization, an obstacle to be surmounted only by an utter repudiation of the life of sense".[50] To see opposition between the soul and the body is to preclude, *ab definitio*, the formation of a well-integrated personality. As such, it is necessary to project a perspective that allows for the development of a well-integrated and well-balanced personality which cares not only for the soul but also its locus, the body.

And, lastly, the institutional structure most appropriate and effective for supporting, controlling and regulating human behaviour in a situation marked continuously by the interplay between the forces of unity and diversity must be devised. Given the multiplicity of interests and opinions, it is but natural that the unitarian perspective will tend to take on different hues in different localities and regions. Variations in the control principles derived from the primordial insight into the structure of reality may develop. It is also possible that these variations may in time erode the substance of these principles even if their outer form is somehow maintained. The corrosion of the primordial insight, the principles derived from it and the institutional arrangement based on and reflecting these principles, is not unnatural in a situation characterized by the process of becoming. However, it creates problems for the well-being of the individual and the collectivity he is a part of.

It is in this context that the question of an appropriate institutional arrangement assumes importance. This question refers particularly to the comparative merit of what in modern times is called "civil society" and the political order. It is to be stressed here that the political order concerns itself with only a narrow range of human activities which can be, strictly speaking, justifiably termed as "political". A wide range of activities that have a great bearing on the development of correct ethos are beyond the pale of what is usually known as "political". These activities have to do mainly with what Aristotle calls "the realm of necessity" which he erroneously characterizes as the sphere of instrumental reason. The very distinction between the realm of necessity and the realm of freedom is odious because it introduces opposition where there is no opposition. If a man does not learn to be a good man in the realm of necessity, it is very doubtful whether he would become a good citizen in the realm of freedom, that is, the political realm. It is also very clear that political order does not succeed either in transforming a man totally engrossed in everydayness into a good citizen or in keeping him on the path of right conduct. It is against these considerations that the civil society must be considered to be the proper place where man learns how to become a good man and, consequently, a good citizen. Given this, it is necessary to restore to the civil society its original significance as a proper agency for educating men in proper values and developing appropriate ethos.

It is against these considerations that the Vedic perspective seems to be eminently appropriate for providing a suitable basis for creating a durable political order. It is a perspective that offers a distinctive and very profound insight into the structure of reality that, in turn, yields a very interesting way of looking at the political and its governing principles. It is also a perspective that takes into account different considerations articulated earlier. As such, it is necessary to properly delineate what this perspective is and how it is relevant for exploring the nature, role and function of political order. But before we do so it is necessary, first, to remove some of the misconceptions that have prevented a proper appreciation of the Vedic perspective for understanding and evaluating the nature and function of the political order. Three of these misconceptions – the supposedly acosmic nature of the Vedic perspective, the failure of the Vedic perspective to make a transition from faith to reason, and the inappropriateness of mythopoesis as a vehicle of thought about the unknown – are examined here.

The basic thrust of Indian thinking, as Zimmer notes, is not information but transformation. This has a reference to the need of becoming aware of the hidden truth within every being and then realizing it. This need arises because of the fact that immersion into phenomenal world, the everydayness organized around the fulfilment of ordinary life needs, is the source of *klesha,* unhappiness. Unhappiness cannot be overcome by changing the external world with a view to making it compatible with one's perspective and concern. That is why it is necessary to turn around from information to transformation. The question of transformation does not arise as long as the self, the centre of experience, is understood only in the *bhoktri* sense. This understanding of the self is not only partial but also the source of a distortive perspective on life. To quote Zimmer, "the naive awareness of the hidden truth of the self ... is the primary cause of all misplaced emphasis, inappropriate attitudes, and consequent self-torments of this auto-intoxicated world."[51]

If the totality of human existence includes *sakshi suparna* as a part of individual being, then, turning inward and attuning one's soul to the divine ground of being becomes necessary not only to apprehend the hidden truth of one's being but also for totally reorienting one's attitude not only about one's own self but also about its relationship with the external world. This becomes possible only when the distortive perspective is totally given up by a conscious endeavour aimed at self-transformation as the catalyst of self-knowledge. In this perspective, self-knowledge represents "a radical changing of man's nature and therewith a renovation of his understanding both of the outer world and of his own existence; a transformation as complete as possible such as will amount when successful to a total conversion or rebirth".[52] Thus, Indian thinking is inspired and informed by the realization that "the truth of life and experience is necessarily transcendent" and calls for "the continuous and consistent effort to transcend the empirical level ... ".[53] But this does not mean that, except for a rare particular school of philosophy, the tradition of Indian thinking advocates the world as totally unreal and, therefore, to be completely shunned. As a matter of fact, the dominant tendency is to attain freedom by self-transformation and then to organize pragmatic affairs in the light of this freedom. As such, there is no substance in the charge that Indian thinking, particularly the Vedic thinking, is acosmic.

Insofar as the question of the inability of the Indian tradition of thinking, especially the Vedic perspective, to make a transition from faith to reason is concerned, it must be pointed out that to consider this tradition as nothing more than an expression of faith is mistaken for two vital reasons. One, the dichotomy between faith and reason itself is erroneous since faith is not possible without the solid input of reason. Two, to insist that a discourse must move away from faith to reason is tantamount to arguing that reason has somehow a better claim to articulating the experience of the unknown. Insofar as rational discourse is concerned, Plato argues that it is well nigh difficult to say which opinions about the God are "altogether and in every respect exact and consistent"; as a consequence, "we ought to accept the tale which is probable and enquire no further".[54] Again Plato argues in the *Seventh Letter* that logical cogency may compel us to recognize the truth, for example, of Euclid's theory. But this is not possible in the realm of ideas. This is so for the simple reason that none of the four available means, *onoma* (name or word), *logos* (explanation or conceptual determination), *eidolon* (appearance, illustrative image, example, figure), and the knowledge or insight itself produced by the first three either singly or in combination with others, can provide certainty that in them the thing itself will come to be known as it truly is.[55]

In view of the inadequacy of rational discourse in apprehending the unknown what can be said of mythopoesis as the vehicle of the experience of the beyond? Voegelin argues that philosophy is better suited than mythopoesis in bridging the gap between insight and its demonstrability. However, what is important from the traditional Indian point of view is not demonstration but evocation through communication of the experience of reality beyond the scope of rational discourse. Myths and symbols prove very effective in this. Moreover, the strictures passed by Plato against poet's inability to have a synoptic vision does not apply to Vedic seer-poets.[56] The Vedic seer-poets possess divine vision which enables them to know the hidden truth knowing which a person becomes all-knowing capable of apprehending the structure of truth and reality.

It is also important to note that the Indian tradition of thinking makes a distinction between *buddhi* (thinking in concepts) and *bodhi* (direct experience, enlightenment). This distinction underlines the fact that the knowledge acquired through conceptual thinking is inferior to the knowledge acquired through mind's eye, through the direct knowledge of the unknown. It does not mean that the knowledge gained through the senses (*Vijnana*, knowledge of a multitude of things) is non-essential. It only means that *vijnana* must be subordinated to *jnana*. And since the seer-poet has the vision of the Beyond, the articulation by him of the experience of the Beyond is *darshan*, that is, philosophy. It is the central concern of *darshan* to communicate this experience evocatively first and intelligently only afterwards. In evocating this experience mythopoesis and symbols are as effective as any other mode. And if this evocation aims at arousing and sharpening consciousness, then, hymns are as good a medium as any other. Hymns are a form of poetry that does not enrage, dissimulate or lull. It is a kind of poetry that celebrates the *Atman* and the *Brahman*, the soul's bursting forth into hymns when suddenly and irrepressibly touched by an exalted reality. It is interesting to note that Plato himself considers hymns to.the God (as well as songs in praise of good individuals) as a form of poetic representation which is free of criticism. In the hymns to God, there is no danger of self-estrangement that may be, and usually is, induced by the potent magical play of poetry. As Gadamer puts it, "He who praises address both himself and the one before whom he praises (and in a certain sense one who is being praised), for he speaks of that which binds them all to one another and gives them all a common obligation."[57]

The Vedic hymns sing of this common obligation, of the existence of a primordial community between man and God and society and world or, still better between *martyas* and *amartyas* and *Prithiwi* and *Dyau*. And it is this common obligation that is celebrated in the Veda as the firm, reliable and benign basis of political order. In the following chapters we articulate the nature of this common obligation, its reflection in political order and its ramifications for collective life and relations.

Notes

1. It must be pointed out that the Greek term for justice, that is, *dikaiosyne*, has a much wider sweep than the term "justice" indicates; it is something more than legal and includes ethical notions belonging to the word "righteousness". It is against this background that we can appreciate the first distinction that Aristotle makes between "general" and "particular" justice. For Aristotle, general justice is the same as goodness or righteousness or that which "answers to the whole of goodness ... being the exercise of goodness as a whole" (NE 1129b 25–30 and 1130a 5–10). Particular justice is a part of general justice, to be sure; however, it is concerned with the specific form of goodness which consists in behaving fairly or equally to other men. Again, Aristotle makes a distinction between two kinds of particular justice, distributive justice and rectificatory justice. Distributive justice pertains to the state in distributing offices, honours, and other benefits among its members, while rectificatory justice is that which the state seeks to maintain between one member and another (NE 1131a1).
2. Plato, *Republic* (Rep.) 537b8–539d7.

3. On this point see, Ernest Barker, *The Politics of Aristotle* (New York: Oxford University Press, 1958), p. 364.
4. Alasdair MacIntyre, *Whose Justice? Which Rationality?* (Notre Dame: University of Notre Dame Press, 1988), p. 103.
5. On this point, see Werner Jaeger, *Paideia: The Ideals of Greek Culture,* II (Oxford: Oxford University Press, 1939), p. 46.
6. *Aristotle, Politics,* 1261a15.
7. Aristotle treats both family and village as the realm of necessity and, therefore, concerned only with instrumental reasoning. In contradistinction to this, the *polis* represents the realm of freedom and it is participation in public affairs that makes man a true citizen (*Politics*, Book I).
8. *Republic*, in *Works of Plato*, tr. B. Jowett (New York: Tudor Publishing Co., n.d.), 4 volumes in one, vol. 2, p. 59.
9. Jaeger, op. cit., p. 249.
10. The homology between man and the state gets a clear enunciation in Book VIII of *Republic* where Socrates puts it as follows:

    Do you know, I said, that governments vary as the dispositions of men vary, and that there must be as many of the one as there are of the other? For we cannot suppose that States are made of "oak and rock" and not out of human natures which are in them, and which in a figure turn the scale and draw other things after them?

    Yes, he said, the States are as the men are; they grow out of human characters. Jowett translation, p. 307.
11. Eric Voegelin, *Order and History: Plato and Aristotle*, III (Baton Rouge: Louisiana State University), p. 85.
12. See Jaeger, op. cit., p. 248 and Voegelin, op. cit., p. 55; *Plato* (Baton Rouge: Louisiana State University Press, 1966), pp. 52–59.
13. In consideration of this, it is quite clear that Aristotle is obviously mistaken when he accuses Plato of doing away with pluralism.
14. It does not need to be pointed out that in answering the first question, Plato also answers the second question and *vice versa.*
15. It is quite clear that Plato is raising not just the substantive question of "what good life is" but also the epistemological question of how one arrives at "the idea of what good life actually is".
16. Darrell Dobbs, "Choosing Justice: Socrates' Model City and the Practice of Dialectic," *American Political Science Review*, 88, 2 (June 1994), p. 266.
17. *The Republic of Plato*, tr. F.M. Cornford (New York: Oxford University Press, 1965), p. 61.
18. Loc. cit.
19. Ibid., p. 62.

20. Dobbs, op. cit., p. 267.
21. *The Republic of Plato*, tr. F.M. Cornford, op. cit., p. 58.
22. For a similar argument, see Fred Hirsch, *Social Limits to Growth* (London: Routledge and Kegan Paul, 1995).
23. Dobbs, op. cit., p. 267.
24. It is in this context that Plato's reference to Hesiod's saying that "Half is more somehow than all" (*Works and Days*, 40) can be appreciated (Rep. 466v 2–3). For a useful discussion on this, see Dobbs, op. cit., p. 268.
25. Plato, *Phaedo*, 81B.
26. Ibid., Jowett edition, III, p. 197.
27. *The Republic of Plato*, tr. F.M. Cornford, op. cit., p. 268.
28. Loc. cit. See also Martha C. Nussbaum, *The Fragility of Goodness: Luck and Ethics in Greek Tragedy and Philosophy* (Cambridge: Cambridge University Press, 1986), chapter 5.
29. See also Voegelin, *Plato*, op. cit., p. 64 and *Order and History*, III, p. 66.
30. Nussbaum, op. cit., p. 137.
31. Plato, *Gorgias*, 493A.
32. *Plato's Phaedo* 81B, tr. R.S. Bluck (London: Routledge and Kegan Paul Ltd., 1966), p. 80.
33. On this point, see Jaeger, op. cit., II, pp. 283–85.
34. Jaeger, op. cit., p. 39.
35. On this point, see Voegelin, *Plato*, pp. 112–16.
36. Jaeger, op. cit., p. 45.
37. Ibid., p. 301.
38. *The Republic of Plato*, tr. F.M. Cornford, p. 244.
39. Cf. Voegelin, *Order and History*, III, p. 69.
40. *The Republic of Plato*, tr. F.M. Cornford, op. cit., p. 232.
41. For a fruitful discussion on this point, see Peter J. Steinberger, "Ruling: Guardians and Philosopher-Kings," *American Political Science Review*, 83, 4 (December 1989), pp. 1207–25.
42. Charles N. Cochrane, *Christianity and Classical Culture: A Study of Thought and Action from Augustus to Augustine* (Oxford: The Clarendon Press, 1940), p. 80.
43. See *The Seventh Letter.* See also, David Grene, *Greek Political Theory: The Images of Man in Thucydides and Plato* (Chicago: University of Chicago Press, 1965), Phoenix Books, pp. 111–13; and Hans Georg Gadamer, *Dialogue and Dialectic: Eight Hermeneutical Studies on Plato*, trans. P. Christopher Smith (New Haven: Yale University Press, 1980), chapter 5 and Ramashray Roy, *Beyond Ego's Domain: Being and Order in the Veda* (New Delhi: Shipra Publications, 1999), chapters 2–3.

44. Gadamer, op. cit., p. 202.
45. *The Republic of Plato*, tr. F.M. Cornford, op. cit., p. 209.
46. Pindar, *Fragments*, 112.
47. *The Republic of Plato*, tr. F.M. Cornford, op. cit., p. 56.
48. See *Chhandogya Upanishad*, 1.8.9.
49. Cochrane, op. cit., pp. 425–26.
50. Ibid., p. 426.
51. Heinrich Zimmer, *Philosophies of India*, ed. Joseph Campbell (London: Routledge and Kegan Paul, 1952), p. 12.
52. Ibid., p. 4.
53. Jan Gonda, *The Vision of the Vedic Poets* (Delhi: Motilal Banarsidass, 1984), p. 18.
54. Plato, *Timeaus*, *The Collected Works*, trans. Jowett (Oxford: Oxford University Press, 1952), III, p. 717.
55. For a fruitful discussion on this point, see Gadamer, op. cit., pp. 93–123.
56. For a discussion on this point, see Ramashray Roy, *Beyond Ego's Domain: Being and Order in the Veda*, op. cit., chapter 2.
57. Gadamer, op. cit., p. 66.

5

Reconstructing the Vedic Vision

Referring to the tradition of thinking about statecraft, A.L. Basham observes as follows:

> From the days of Plato and Aristotle European thought has turned its attention to such questions as the origin of the state, the ideal form of government, and the basis of law, and politics has long been looked on as a branch of philosophy. India also thought on such questions, but she had no schools of political philosophy in the western sense. The problems which form the stock-in-trade of the European political philosopher are answered in Indian texts, but in a take-it-or-leave-it manner with little discussion; often indeed the only argument in favour of a proposition is the citation of an old legend used much as Plato's adaptations of older myths to reinforce his theories.

Continuing further, Basham underlines the fact that even while India did not have formal philosophy, the science of statecraft

> ... was much cultivated, and a number of important text-books on this topic have survived. *Dandaniti,* the administration of force or *rajaniti,* the conduct of kings, was a severely practical science, and the texts cursorily dismiss the more philosophical aspect of politics but give comparatively detailed advise on the organization of the state and the conduct of governmental affairs.[1]

Several things are worth noting here. First, Basham does not think that the Vedic literature, especially the four principle Vedic texts, yield any significant clue to the understanding of the character of political thinking in ancient times. He does acknowledge that significant contributions to the discussion about state, law and political administration were made under the rubric of *dandaniti* or *rajaniti.* But these discussions took place much later. We should also note that Basham is not alone in thinking so. Note, for example, that V.P. Varma argues that by rendering the term "*rashtra*" as nation, "we assume an amount of mature political development that perhaps was not present in the Vedic India of 1500 B.C."[2] He further notes that

> In the realm of political thought the Hindu thinkers did not produce any magnificent work. The Hindu thinkers did not concern themselves with the analysis of the significant problems of political philosophy at an advanced theoretical level. Their analysis of the fundamental concepts of political theory and public law is also not very penetrating and profound. Their main aim was to categorize the duties of the king and to prescribe to him pragmatic rules for political and imperialistic success.[3]

Second, it is also evident that whatever writings the Indian scholars produced on the statecraft are bereft of any philosophical value; they focus mostly on the pragmatic aspect of the statecraft. This suggests several things. In the first place, lacking the integrating framework of philosophical analysis, these writings are not much better than "do-it-yourself" variety of instructions to the kings or those aspiring to be kings. It is true that Basham does refer to the lack of philosophical tradition in the western sense. However, this distinction loses its meaning when he characterizes the tradition of political thinking in ancient India as lacking rigorous logical investigation in which arguments, pro and con, are weighed, evaluated and accepted or rejected. In the second place, Basham's remark suggests by implication that the realm of politics has never been treated as significant in itself; as a result, it did not enjoy autonomy requiring systematic and coherent analysis in its own rights. As such, Indian tradition failed to stimulate the evolution of competing schools of political philosophy.

These undercurrents swirling around Basham's observations raise several questions both about substantive and methodological aspects of political discourse in ancient India. First, are the meaning and significance of philosophy, in general, and political philosophy, in particular, exhausted by: "rational" discourse? If not, what is the real significance of philosophy, or, to put it differently, political philosophy? And, is not there any other way to express philosophical truth except in discursive, logical language? Second, is it necessary to treat the arena of politics or statecraft as autonomous and significant in itself? It must be emphasized that the realm of politics emerged as an autonomous discipline only after the phenomenal world and its concerns assumed primacy after the existence of any transcendental entity was denied. Such a denial makes interest the central concept of politics and the fulcrum of political order. As such, the important question that needs to be answered is whether interest-centred politics can make people's life better or make the political order durable and benign.

Needless to say that to treat the domain of politics as sufficient unto itself has serious ramifications for human existence. In the first place, it truncates human existence and makes it incomplete. It reduces the totality of man's existence to a part of his being, that is, his passions. With passions occupying the centre stage of man's life, his rationality assumes only an instrumental role responsible for calculating costs and benefits of alternative but competing ways and means of realizing a given end. What is also to be noted in this regard is that when rationality is reduced to calculative reasoning, it loses its authority to judge, regulate or control passions. The consequence is that man becomes an externalized creature whose expectations from the external world skyrocket without being ever pacified. As a result, man never remains at peace either with himself or his environing world. In addition, the tension between what is individual and what is communal, that is, collective, gets aggravated posing a severe threat to public order.

The cumulative result of this is that the realm of interest is forcefully separated from the realm of values without itself being capable of filling the void caused by the defection from the source of values. Needless to say, this source is that entity which is said to constitute the substratum of reality. The realm of interest partakes of meaning and cultivates and sustains meaningful human relationship only when it is linked with the absolute as the source of meaning. To link the realm of interest with the source of values is to attune the soul to the divine ground of being and to restore to it its true role of keeping the unruly mob of passions under leash so that they do not introduce incompatibility between what is private and what is public.

It is this linkage between the finite world of human existence and the absolute as the source of meaning that restores to human existence its totality, fullness and meaningfulness. It is also this linkage that enables the political realm to lift man up from the defiling depth of the givens of society and nature and enables him to relate himself to something larger than his private narrow and fragmented existence. Again, it is this linkage that constitutes the ground of political thinking in ancient India. As Varma puts it:

> ... there is a fundamental spiritual and moral note in Hindu thought which is surpassing in its proclamation of the sacred character of the individual human personality ... (T)he fundamental theme of Hindu philosophical speculation is the spiritual nature of man. Man is not the materialistic-ritualistic agglomeration of physical and chemical elements or the temporary embodiment of a blind force ...[4]

It is the spiritual nature of man, or at least the possibility of man becoming spiritual that is at the back of political thinking in India. As such, political thinking in India does not take human existence as divided in different and separated compartments; it deals human existence as a totality of which the political realm is one significant but organically linked aspect. As such, it is not politics, as an autonomous domain that carves out, independent of other cognate areas of human existence, the domain it must operate in, the goals it must seek, and the way these goals must be realized. In short, in the Indian tradition of political thinking, politics is a field that is neither self-defining nor self-legitimating; it is a field, which is subservient to the worldview that prescribes and sanctifies the desirable pattern of life. It is this pattern of life that delimits the boundaries of the domain of politics and defines the way it must operate.

What is important, then, is the linkage function of politics or statecraft; it "links practical political conduct of life (*Vyavahar*) with the pursuit of ideal ends (*Purushartha*) ..."[5] Thus, the central thrust of Indian thinking is what Sri Aurobindo characterizes as the raising and enlarging of the internal man, the mind, the soul, the spirit. But it aims, at the same time, at shaping his external existence and making of it a rhythm of advance towards high and great ideals.[6] It is these ideals that constitute the animating source of statecraft. And since the realm of politics is joined with the transcendental realm of values that constitutes for it both the animating as well as controlling factor, discursive logic, which Basham thinks indispensable for philosophical discourse, does not prove to be a robust, or even reliable, medium of expressing what is ineffable. As Pande notes:

> All religions contain within themselves basic and seminal political conceptions none of which allows our understanding of political reality to be reducible to a merely technical comprehension ... (T)hese basic political conceptions reach us as elements embedded in systems of faiths and carrying with them a force and authority which goes beyond the mere recognition of factual constraints or the persuasiveness of mere reason.[7]

It is against this background that the term "philosophy" in the Western sense appears too inadequate.[8] And it is this inadequacy that impels Indian scholars as well as Plato to take the help of myths and symbols in order to make articulate what in rational discourse is incapable of being articulated. As such, the real worth of Indian thinking about statecraft cannot be ascertained on the basis of its conformity with the Western tradition of political thinking. Nor can this be done on the basis of whether or not the Indian textbooks provide only practical advice to kings.[9] It does not need to be demonstrated that practical suggestions without the foundation of theoretical/philosophical thinking are like rudderless boats whose movement is inordinately influenced by the fast flowing cross-currents of changing opinions.

The fact that there exists a remarkable degree of consensus on the objectives and *modus operandi* of the state and political institutions is an unfailing testimony to the fact that a single, uniform and self-consistent worldview underlay political thinking in ancient India. Whether this worldview and its components formed an integral and explicit part of discussions on statecraft or not does not really affect in any way[10] the embeddedness of political thinking in the worldview that sought to improve the quality of man's existence in the phenomenal world with the help of certain spiritual insights and experiences. That the political discourse in ancient India does not consciously and deliberately incorporate this spiritual dimension must not be construed to mean either that such a dimension does not exist or that it has no connection with whatever political discourse we associate with the tradition of thinking in ancient India.

Once we recognize this spiritual dimension which provides the basic framework for the discussion on statecraft in India, certain things follow. First, it is not enough to admit, *en passant*, that Indian perspective on statecraft is grounded in a spiritual insight or experience. What is necessary is to show how this insight or experience influences and is related to the structure of political thinking in India. Thus any evaluation or critique of political discourse in ancient India must, in order to be fair, make it explicit what this spiritual insight or experience is and how it embeds political discourse. Second, if we admit the embeddedness of political discourse in the spiritual ground, then we must also admit that, for various reasons, the spiritual insight or experience that underlies political discourse is special to India. It is rooted in special features of the lived world in India. As such, it cannot be properly viewed and reviewed from the perspectives that have been forged elsewhere outside India; nor can it be fruitfully compared in the light of experiences outside India.[11] Indian experience of political reality must be explored and apprehended in its own terms.

Third, coupling of the transcendental realm of values and the immanent domain of pragmatic concerns through the political[12] is symptomatic of the attempt to make the real what is still unreal or non-existent reality. It is the conscious participation in this non-existent reality that endows the political with the capacity to transform the givens of society and nature in the light of certain preferred values. This participation engenders certain experiences that cannot be fully articulated with the help of discursive logic; myths and symbols have, therefore, to be used for articulating the experience of the transcendent reality. It is in this sense that symbols are not concepts that refer to objects existing in time and space; they are carriers of a truth about non-existent reality.[13] Thus symbols, or the language used to convey the experience of the transcendent, convey no other truth than that of the engendering experience. It is in this sense that language of political ideas is evocative rather than descriptive. As such, to treat the language in which political ideas are couched as descriptive of certain existent facts in real life is to misrepresent reality.

And, lastly, political ideas and institutions are expressions of a particular cultural ethos. They are the external aspect or secondary derivations of the original insight into the structure of order and cannot be well understood without exploring their linkage with the engendering primordial insight. What is also important in this regard is the way this primordial insight is developed into an institutional arrangement and its governing ideas. While the primordial insight remains unchanged, beyond the corrupting influence of time and space, its manifestations in ideas and institutions are susceptible to change in time and space. But however much they change, they remain bound up with their engendering experience rooted in the primordial insight into the structure of order. The process of change and variation, even when they assume different forms in different times and space, is guided and governed by the central tenets of culture. It is, therefore, essential to treat the primordial insight and its institutional expression as an organic system. As such, the appraisal of the different elements of a political system must not view political ideas and institutions in isolation or separation from the cultural ethos that impinges on their genesis, growth and change. They can be viewed as the foreground and the background of a picture in which the foreground is defined and etched out against the background which, in turn, becomes articulate and meaningful only by a reference to the foreground. "The true nature of the Indian polity," notes Sri Aurobindo, "can only be realized if we look at it not as a separate thing, a machinery independent of the rest of the mind and life of the people, but as a part of and in its relation to the organic totality of the social existence."[14]

How far does the contemporary reconstruction of the Vedic vision of political order conform to the considerations outlined above? To answer this question, it is necessary to identify and articulate the cultural and intellectual influences that have gone into the shaping of the contemporary reconstruction of the Vedic vision of political order. This is what we now turn to discuss. One of the major influences working on Indian scholars has, of course, been a strong sense of nationalism that impelled them to react with vigour against disparaging comments by Western scholars on the lack of tradition of political philosophy (or science) in India. National fervour, when aroused by negative evaluation by Western scholars of political thinking in India, led Indian scholars to look back to their own cultural and intellectual heritage whose sources lay in the distant past. It did stimulate a series of serious explorations of ancient texts including the Veda in order to draw conclusions that may serve in modern times. It was quite natural that in drawing these conclusions most of them would take benefit of their modern intellectual training. It is not that they were not aware of the problems involved in expressing ideas originating millennia ago in English words and idioms current today. However, many of them were unable to escape the over-powering influence of modern Western thought-ways in interpreting ancient texts. This can be illustrated in several ways.

To return to the nationalistic fervour as a springboard of contemporary reconstruction of the Vedic vision, K.P. Jayaswal is credited with fathering Indology in India. As K.B. Krishna observes:

> Since the discovery of *Arthashastra* (1906) there has been a regular crop of books. A national historical school arose, much to the detriment of scholarship. Jayaswal set the ball rolling. He made a special study to find out what constitutional progress, if any, ancient Indians had

achieved. In 1911 and 1912 some results of the study were published in the legal journal, the *Calcutta Weekly Notes* and the Calcutta monthly, *Modern Review*. A connected paper was read to the Hindi Literary Conference in 1912 and its translation published in the *Modern Review*, 1913 under the title, *An Introduction to Hindu Polity*.[15]

As Jayaswal himself notes:

> Before the publication of the Introduction there had been no work in any modern language on the subject. The Introduction fulfilled its purpose. Today the subject finds place in University teaching. And the author has had the satisfaction of seeing his results quoted and reiterated, with or without acknowledgment almost every year; the subject has become popular ...[16]

There is no doubt that the *Hindu Polity* by Jayaswal was the first ever systematic exploration of, to use Bhandarkar's words, whether or not Indians "ever showed activity in the political field and made any contribution to the political science".[17] However, the beginning of the nationalistic tide beating against the hard rock of Western prejudices goes, as R.S. Sharma observes, much earlier.[18] As he notes, during the last three decades of the 19th century, several nationalist leaders engaged themselves in demonstrating the hollowness of the imperialist ideology. Many scholars, associated with the freedom movement, conducted research on different aspects of the past history of India and made a strong case about socio-political progress India made in the past. Since then the study of India's past was influenced mainly by nationalistic feelings.[19]

These feelings were aroused by the comments of Western scholars such as Hegel, Max Muller, Bloomfield, Dunning and others that India did not have any tradition of political thinking. Indian scholars took umbrage to the charge that "the Hindus made no contribution to the science of politics and India has therefore no place in the political history of the world".[20] It is not possible to undertake here an exhaustive survey of what Western scholars have to say about the lack of systematic political thinking. However, it is necessary to present here a few specimens of their observations. Hegel, for example, argued that since there was the absence of freedom both as an abstract will and as subjective freedom, Hindu political existence presents only a people but no state. But Hegel does not remain content with the finding that there is no state in India. He goes on to discover in India unmitigated despotism. As he notes:

> If Asia generally has been the scene of despotism and tyranny, the worst part of Asia in this respect has been India because, whereas in other Asian countries ... there had been protests and struggles against despotism, in India there has not even been any expression of resentment against it.[21]

Thus, for Hegel, India has nothing either intellectually or practically to contribute. This is so for the simple reason that there was no concern in ancient India with matters practical; her sole concern was abstract thought unrelated to seeking solutions to practical problems either analytically or practically. As Max Muller puts it:

> The Hindus were a nation of philosophers. Their struggles were the struggles of thought; their past, the problem of creation ... It might therefore be justly said that India has no place in the political history of the world.[22]

For the last 300 years, what Descartes calls "practical philosophy" dedicated to the observation and measurement of the movement of stars and other heavenly bodies with a view to tapping their energies to serve man's purposes in this world, has been regnant. As a result, it is very difficult for a Vedist like Max Muller, who has been deeply influenced by and firmly entrenched in the worldview celebrated by scientists and philosophers since Descartes, to really appreciate the true import of the struggles of thought aiming at disconcealing the mystery of creation. However, what is astonishing is that even hardnosed political theorists like Willoughby and Dunning find no merit in Indian political thinking. Whether they are Vedists or philosophers or social scientists, they all regret the lack of the spirit of much vaunted and celebrated liberty in the early political writings of India. Willoughby, for example, considers these writings nothing more than confused heaps of religious and ethical dicta unrelated to any general principle and hence useless to the political theorist.[23] But Willoughby is not alone. Note, for example, that even Hobhouse considers the ruler of the Vedas, Manu, as the autocratic monarch.[24]

Confronted with such pronouncements – pronouncements that are mostly based on insufficient knowledge or appreciation of the Indian perspective on man and his world – condemning what is considered to be the glorious chapter of Indian history as worthless, Indian scholars were bound to react. They felt it was incumbent upon them to resurrect their glorious past and paint it in beautiful colours. However, all these colours do not fit very well. As we shall see shortly, they blend poorly and represent different pigments and dissolving agents. At least five different colours, which have been used to paint the tradition of political thinking in ancient India, can be identified for our purposes. These colours represent different vantage points from which different Indian scholars view, examine, evaluate and form their conclusions about the intrinsic merit of the tradition of political thinking in ancient India.

One of the sore points for most Indian scholars is the much-vaunted superiority of the tradition of Western political thinking especially Greek political thought. Greece is not only supposed to be the birthplace of political thought. It is also claimed to be the first country in the world to be blessed with city-state. This is something that some Indian scholars cannot stomach. They find in this claim nothing but Western arrogance bred of ignorance of the Indian experience and therefore hardly justifiable. Thus, the claim of Western superiority in the sphere of political philosophy is one-sided and distortive of reality. They therefore seek to redress the balance by demonstrating to the world the merit of the tradition of political thinking in ancient India which, for some of them, still remains unmatched. Note, for example, that explaining the purpose of his study, Mukerjee refers to the fact that Western and Westernized scholars always seek to prove the superiority of Western culture. He therefore proposes to place side by side a critical account of political ideas and institutions of India and Greece to make an appraisal of their achievements. By doing so, he would like "to correct the lopsidedness perpetrated by Western scholars who always overestimate Greek values and achievements".[25]

Given the recognition of the tradition of political thinking in ancient India, evaluation of its merit differs from scholar to scholar. Note, for example, that while Beni Prasad admits that political institutions in India are as old as those of the Greeks, he finds it difficult to trace their development or to visualize their working with any clarity and fullness.[26] India did have political ideas and institutions. However, some of them find it unjustifiable to compare them with those that developed in the West. As Bandopadhyaya argues:

> ... Our ideas may not be confused by the analogy of developments elsewhere in which we find some elements of similarity but which owing to diverseness of time, environment, or political instinct, never tally with one another. It is more so in India where social and political development has been on the lines quite different form those of the West and a careful enquiry brings home to us the nature of this divergence ...[27]

Bandopadhyaya thus underlines the fact that political ideas and institutions take on different characteristics because of their rootedness in a different socio-cultural milieu. In view of this Bandopadhyaya underlines the need to evaluate political ideas and institutions in terms of the socio-cultural system in which they are embedded. As such, comparison of such ideas and institutions across socio-cultural systems is misleading and therefore futile. Given the fact of the intimate relationship between political ideas and institutions and their environing and embedding socio-cultural environment it is necessary to take the former in their own term. But it is not very easy to do so since these ideas and institutions have developed and assumed their form over centuries. In this process of development, the one prominent milestone is Kautalya's *Arthashatra,* the first ever-systematic treatise, which proved beyond doubt that the observation of Western scholars that India lacked the tradition of political thinking was baseless. Bhandarkar, however, admits that there is some truth in the estimate of Western scholars that India did not have any place in the political history of the world. But he points out that this appeared to be the correct view only uptil very recently when Kautalya's *Arthashastra* was brought to light.[28]

Arthashastra thus constitutes, for many Indian scholars, the cut off line dividing scattered, unorganized political ideas and systematic formulation and ordering of these ideas into a coherent whole. In Altekar's words:

> Though there was no systematic literature in the political science composed in the early period, usually called the Age of the Vedas and the Brahmanas there are scattered passages in the Vedic literature, which throw considerable light sometimes dim, sometimes clear on the theory and practice of government in the contemporary times.[29]

For Altekar and others, the real, systematic discussion of political ideas and institution begins in about 8th century B.C., an age of specialization when grammar, etymology, prosody, astronomy, etc., began to form separate schools. The beginning of school of politics, properly so called, has to be ascribed to this age of specialization … .[30] This is indicative of the fact that the scholarly discussion of political ideas and institutions took a systematic form only after a long period of gestation whose beginning is uncertain, dim and tentative. It may perhaps be quite true. However, the fact remains that, for several Indian scholars, ancient India's contribution to political thought has not been less valuable than that in the West. But some scholars feel that it has been rather quite significant and unique. In Ghoshal's words, "The Indians belong to the category of people who have left their impress upon the pages of history as the founders of original systems of political thought. ... There is no reasonable room for doubt regarding either the native source of their inspiration, or else their national stamps."[31]

It is enough to indicate that Indian scholars are very emphatic in their assertion that Western scholars are quite wrong in their belief that India lacked the tradition of political thinking and that it has no place in the history of political ideas. Countering this, what they consider Western prejudice, they firmly assert that, contrary to the Western denial of any tradition of political thinking, India did, in fact, have a rich tradition of thinking about political ideas and institutions. It is this tradition that these scholars seek to reconstruct and elucidate its distinctive features with a view to establishing its importance and relevance. They are quite aware of the fact that in reconstructing the ancient Indian thinking on political ideas and institutions, the Indian experience of political reality should not be looked at from a non-Indian perspective. The reason for this is not far to seek. Approaches to political reality are governed by highly differentiated socio-cultural experiences. As a result of this, it is not unusual that even similar concepts and words through which the experience of political reality is expressed refer to entirely different substantive entities. Thus concepts and words as the vehicle of expressing certain experienced reality acquire differential contents because experiences of reality organize themselves according to changing configurations of various components of reality in time and space. As such, the experienced reality and its various elements cannot be properly and legitimately expressed in concepts and words that are over laden with senses that acquired significance in another time and space.

In reconstructing the experience of political reality in ancient India, Indian scholars remind themselves of the impropriety of the effort to translate this experience in the idioms and language of today. As already pointed out, Bandopadhyaya underlines the sharp difference in socio-political situations prevalent then in ancient India and that prevailing today in the Western world and argues that this difference prevents proper comparison between political ideas and institutions in the two cases. He also underlines the fact that "it is often difficult to render the ideas expressed by words of Indian vocabulary by using similar ones from the terminology of the West". To illustrate this, he refers to such words as polity and *Rajya* and argues that "the word Polity, for instance, never connotes the ideas contained in the word *Rashtra* and it is doubtful whether the word *Rajya* can be safely rendered into English by the word State."[32] Thus, to see equivalences and similarities between the ancient Indian and the modern Western experiences is hazardous. Pointing to the difficulties confronting the effort to find equivalences, Drekemieir observes:

> In some cases it may be instructive to turn to the West for examples to suggest a parallel or to paint a moral. The images and constructions we use will fit only imperfectly. For even the concept of the State (as we know it) has no exact counterpart in Indian political function if not always readily distinguished from other social fanctions.[33]

And yet the fact remains that there is discernible a strong tendency among Indian scholars to project modern ideas back on the ancient political texts and interpret them in the light of modern experience of political reality. To quote Drekemieir again:

> An unfortunate feature of a good deal of the interpretation of Hindu political thought has been the willingness of Indian scholars, trained in Western history, to force an equation of Hindu and Western theoretical concepts. Often a certain similarity does exist, but then the Western concept is allowed to shape the Indian situation.[34]

Thus, even while Indian scholars are against seeking equivalences between the ancient Indian and modern Western political experiences or using Western concepts for elucidating Indian situation, they tend to ignore their own warning. As a result, the corpus of writings by Indian scholars dedicated to reconstructing the ancient Indian perspective on political life and relation represents more an effort to bring it closer to the modern perspective on politics than to really apprehend, appraise and appreciate its real worth. As Pande puts it:

> Indian scholars learnt from their Western teachers the scientific analysis of facts from their own past and their evaluation according to the modern Western standards. But their patriotism added one more thing to their history writing, this was the kind of interpretation of their ancient tradition which could bring it closer to the modern perspective current in the West. It was reflected largely in the interpretation of ancient politics because it was in this sphere that the lack of a past

> tradition was experienced most. These interpreters did not cast doubt on the old presuppositions, they cast doubt on the Western interpretations of old goals and sought to show that in reality facts were entirely different.[35]

Despite their insistence of the incompatibility between the experiences of political reality in ancient India and in the modern West and despite their admonition to use Western concepts and terms, most of the Indian scholars find it difficult to escape the long shadow on their thinking of the Western perspective on man and his world. The Western way of looking at things has undeniably made its impact on the way most Indian scholars view their own past. This influences their perspective, may be unconsciously, but nonetheless its impact is very deep. It not only seeps through the concepts and terms these scholars use, but also through the modern values that they have come to owe their allegiance to and the way ancient civilization is viewed by the modern man. The projecting back of the modern way of looking at the world and doing things on the political experience of ancient India is evidenced in two interrelated ways. Apart from the fact that the ancient history of India and its political ideas and institutions are studied and analysed in terms of the modern conception of history as the movement of universal history, the Vedic and certain institutional aspects of political experience in ancient India, too, are viewed in the light of modern sensitivity and outlook.

Insofar as the modern notion of history is concerned, it is influenced by the idea of progress that underlines the fact that the golden age of human civilization lies not in the past but in the future. Its past describes only the childhood of man's existence. This childhood is characterized by undifferentiated social existence, very low level of material well-being, predominance of myths, superstitions and ritualistic religion. Mankind has gradually been advancing towards affluence and cultural and intellectual excellence. It is this image of universal history moving from one level of material and cultural achievement to other higher levels that moves scholars reconstructing ancient Indian political experience. When this notion of history is brought to bear upon the Vedic experience, the society as it was then is identified with a tribal society[36] in which religion and politics mingled without any differentiation and the intermeshing of religion and ritualism reinforced irrationality. As Bandopadhyaya observes:

> As the primitive mind is always swayed by fear, it invokes the blessings of the gods and tries to appease their anger. Gradually, formalities and practices are introduced to safeguard divine sanction for all acts and with it is evolved a code of ritual, which not only confines itself to the acts of the individual but embraces the actions of the community as a whole.[37]

Thus, for Bandopadhyaya, the origin of religion in India as elsewhere lies not in the spiritual quest to "know thyself" but fear, fear of natural elements and human marauders. What is also important is the association found by Bandopadhyaya between primitivism and non-rational explanation of political phenomena. As he notes, the commixture of politics and religion "marks the transition from primitive ideas of cosmology to a rational explanation of the relation of the forces and factors regulating the phenomenal world".[38] That this is not an isolated instance of misconceived interpretation of the Vedic world is confirmed by what Altekar argues. Referring to the contract theory of Locke and Rousseau, Altekar admires them for formulating a rational and secular theory which thrashes threadbare, and exposes the fundamental principles of political association, define the limits of political authority, etc. In contrast, the Indian writers, Altekar argues,

> did not live in an age of rationalism; they looked at the question from a semi-religious and semi-sociological point of view. They have, therefore, neither gone deep into the fundamentals of the problem, nor defined precisely the limits of the powers of the state and the people.[39]

It is obvious that Altekar considers only constitutional government and the rational mode of explanation as legitimate. When compared against them, the ancient mode of governance as well as the mode of explication proves quite unsatisfactory. This is quite apparent when he argues that it is true that Indian writers prescribe regicide if the king fails in his duty. However,

> ... what precisely will constitute a breach of contract ... and *what is the secular constitutional machinery* by which people can enforce the performance of the terms of the original contract is nowhere clearly described. The permission to remove a tyrant or to kill him no doubt assumes the ultimate sovereignty of the people and invests them with supreme authority. This remedy, however, is drastic and difficult; it would have been more useful if our authorities had recommended a less extreme but more practicable remedy *in the form of an everyday constitutional check.*[40]

This tendency to look back and project, either in admiration or in criticism, on ancient Indian political ideas and institutions modern concepts is quite prominent among Indian scholars. If Altekar finds the Hindu notion of "contract theory" lacking in comparison with that of Locke and Rousseau, Jayaswal nevertheless sees the full flowering of democratic institutions in the Vedic age. As he points out, "Going back to the oldest literature of the race, we find from the Vedas that national life and activities in the earliest time on record were expressed through popular assemblies and institutions."[41] Similarly, he refers to Hindu republics as another illustration of the communal self-governing habits.[42] Referring to this tendency, Sri Aurobindo comments:

> Indian scholars have attempted to read the modern ideas and types of democracy and even a parliamentary system into the past of India, but this seems to me an ill-judged endeavour. There was a strong democratic element, if we must use the Western terms, in Indian polity and even institutions present a certain analogy to the parliamentary form, but in reality these features were of India's own kind and not at all the same thing as modern parliaments and modern democracy.[43]

In reconstructing the Vedic vision of political ideas and institutions, the only source available is the Veda. It was Jayaswal who quoted copiously from the Vedic texts in support of his arguments. Since then Indian scholars have invariably resorted to this practice. In using Vedic texts for reconstructing the Vedic vision of political order, Indian scholars have not only treated the Veda as a prime source that contains significant clues to the history, manners and institutions of the primitive people who came from outside and made India their homeland. Also, their eager hunt for clues leads them to force their own sense on the Vedic texts and fabricate their own interpretation from hymns that are more of allusions to the unknown than to real manners, institutions and history. In this process, what is there in the Vedic texts is completely ignored and what is not there assumes enormous size and shape. As a result, the *arche* text that pierces the veil fully obscuring the secret of the unknown and provides its glimpses is reduced to the status of a historical document throwing even, if only a very dim light, on the patterns of living in the dark primitive age in India. The result is that a text that is highly evocative of certain not easily communicable spiritual experiences has been treated as descriptive document and has undergone several hieroglyphic transformations.

In this process of transformation, the Vedic text has not only been cut off from its perennial spiritual fountain-head. It has also generated a lot of controversy among Indian scholars about the true import of certain Vedic notions seemingly applicable to political ideas and institutions. Deferring the discussion of textual manipulations, it is necessary here to make explicit the view they have of the Vedic world and how they treat some of the elements – for example, the relationship between *sacerdotium* and *regnum* and divinity of the king – of the Vedic vision of political order which Indian scholars consider as kingpin of the Vedic vision. Insofar as the understanding of the Vedic world is concerned, most Indian scholars show a similar perspective as do Western scholars. For Drekemieir, for example, the Vedic and post-Vedic account of life and ancient India is "the story of the ancient heroic ideals, and of the norms of conduct that replaced it"; it is symptomatic of the non-rational and symbolic experience of a civilization emerging from a tribal culture.[44]

Drekemieir is not simply content with identifying the Vedic civilization as basically tribal. He goes on to aver that "Vedic texts reveal on the whole a sensitivity to native, a belief in the magical and the occult, an optimistic outlook, and a sense of man's significance."[45] Vedic society showed a marked tendency towards warfare that, in turn, made it necessary to seek the help of the gods. This, in its own turn, increased the power of the priesthood. This gave a distinct materialist cast to the Vedic sacrifice and led to the development of complex, highly specialized and complicated rites in which technique became all too important. The Rigveda, Drekemieir points out, "confronts us with a Homeric world of warrior-gods ... ancient heroes and tribal chieftains who took on supernatural powers as the stories of their battles expanded in the telling."[46] Moreover, these gods are representations of natural phenomena rather than guardians of morality. It is natural because the Veda does not contain an explicit ethic. The ethical was replaced, in Vedic society, by the ritual which served as the means to comprehend the supernatural and manipulate it through certain formalized actions. In the Vedic society, as Drekemieir argues, the ritual provided "a means of acting out and thus reducing strains and frustrations produced by the uncertainties and rationally inexplicable occurrences of life."[47]

That this characterization of the Vedic world is not confined to Western scholars alone has been indicated earlier. To take another example, let us turn to discussing how the relationship between

Sacerdotium and *regnum*, one of the pillars of the Vedic vision on political order, has been handled by both the Western and Indian scholars. As is well known, the key to the understanding of the Vedic vision and political ideas and institutions based on it underlines the need of syzygy between two conjoint principles, intelligence (*Brahma*)[48] and *Kshatra* or wisdom and power respectively. Two important questions need to be answered in this regard. First, does this coupling of *Brahma* and *Kshatra* describe a relation between unequal partners so that the relationship between *sacerdotium* and *regnum* deteriorates in a relationship of super-ordination-subordination? Second, if divinity is claimed for the king, how can the *regnum* be supposed to be inferior to or lower in rank than *sacerdotium*?

Needless to say that these two questions are interrelated in the sense that the question of the divinity of the king and that of his position *vis-à-vis* the Purohit can be resolved not in isolation from each other. But contemporary literature reconstructing the Vedic vision of political order makes this question a tangled web. To begin with, after an extensive review of the Vedic literature Gonda comes to the conclusion that "the ancient Indian-European kingship was, in important aspects, a sacred institution".[49] He refers to Rigveda (RV) (IV. 42.4) in which Indra claims to be the lawful king as against Varuna.[50] It is true that Brahmans, who constituted the first in rank[51] and were "convinced of their own divinity, by their mighty spiritual and intellectual influence supported and strengthened the position of the ruler with a variety of rites and theories and who proclaimed its superhuman character".[52]

As against Gonda's emphatic assertion of the divinity of the king, Drekemieir views the relationship between *sacerdotium* and *regnum* in a slightly different manner. In so doing he seeks to combine two desparate streams of apprehending truth in reality, that is cosmological identified with the ancient Middle Eastern kingdom of Babylon, Mesopotania and Persia and the Vedic one. In combining these two streams, Drekemieir adds an historical dimension. The main objective of the political system in ancient India was to keep people on the path of righteousness in a *varna*-divided society or, in other words, the furtherance of the material and spiritual well-being of the people. As the guardian of the political order, the king, on the one hand, acts on this earth as the representative of the Supreme Being and, on the other, must look to the Brahman for defining what is righteousness and how it must be safeguarded. In respect of the former, the political order comes to be "interpreted as analogous to the cosmos, its creation a repetition of the divine creation of the cosmic system".[53] The king's kingdom is the analogue of the cosmos and he must, as the earthly agent of the divine ruler, care for his kingdom, for its purity and its sanctity.

But, the question of what constitutes right conduct in conformity with *dharma* is the domain of the Brahman. As such, the king must seek the advice and guidance of the Brahman in the discharge of his kingly duties. In the beginning the Brahman enjoyed dominance. "For centuries the Brahman was successful in securing his power by his magical control of the ritual."[54] But, then, the era of great heterodoxy and/or the drive of the king to acquire autonomy challenged the dominance of the Brahman who was compelled to enter into a closer alliance with the political authority and the state became, in effect, the guarantor of religion. "For with the possibility of new bases of legitimation the Brahmans were confronted with the alternatives of making concessions to the king or losing their status."[55]

The Brahmans did make concessions to the king but at the same time two things helped them consolidate their position. In the first place, increase in the incidents of war made it necessary to seek the assistance of gods through sacrifice and offerings. In the second place, *dharma* as the sovereign principle ruling the conduct of the king, Drekemieir argues, was ultimately removed from popular interpretation and appeal.[56] Brahmans, being the sole custodian of *dharma* with access to sacred learning, were able to consolidate their position by developing complex, highly specialized and complicated rites. This no doubt preserved the political importance, if not dominance, of the Brahman who remained indispensable for the legitimacy of the king's rule. However, it created a dilemma that, it is argued, ancient political thought could never resolve. *Danda* was indispensable for ensuring compliance with *dharma* that is the higher power and must regulate the exercise of *danda*. However, it is dependent on *danda*. This dilemma, as Drekemeier observes, is real and Hindu political thought could never escape from this dilemma of royal power and priestly authority.[57]

This dilemma has been much played upon by Western scholars, two scholars, Louis Dumont[58] and J.C. Heesterman[59] must occupy our attention before we return to Indian authorities. Dumont recognizes that Brahman and Kshatriya go together, they are often designated as two prime forces, and must be united in order to make

Kingship a successful and effective institution. However, "as soon as this necessary union has been stated, the hierarchical distinction between the two forces' manifests itself". This distinction, as Dumont argues, is based on a series of oppositions, the principle of which is religious. For example, the twice-born (the upper three *varnas*) is opposed to the *Shudra*, the first two of the twice-born are opposed to the third; and the first two are opposed to each other. It is this ingrained opposition that, Dumont argues, is at the root of the dilemma of priestly authority and kingly power".[60]

At the root of this dilemma is, of course, the fact that "the *Brahman* does not fall under the jurisdiction of the *Kshatra,* the *Brahman* being the source or rather the womb, from which the *Kshatra* springs, is superior; the *Brahman* could exist without the *Kshatra*, but not conversely."[61] However, the Brahmans, even while they proclaim their spiritual pre-eminence, are temporarily dependent on the royal power.[62] It is thus the combination of the temporal mastery of the king and the spiritual superiority of the Brahman coupled with his temporal dependence on the royal power that, Dumont argues, has led to an unsymmetrical relationship between the Brahman and the king. This has subordinated the Brahman to the Kshatriya.

In substantiating his conclusion, Dumont argues that the subordination of the Brahman is symptomatic of the gaining of autonomy by the politico-economic domain from the Brahaminical absolute values.[63] In support of his conclusion he offers his theory of what he calls renouncer's individualism and that of *artha* which counter poses itself against *dharma*. Insofar as the former is concerned, Dumont creates two ideal-typical categories: man-in-the-world, that is, the Brahman who does not invent ideas but adopts them, and the renouncer, that is, the individual-outside-the-world who is the real creator of values.[64] The renouncer, in leaving the world, seeks to consecrate himself to his own liberation as well as to invest himself with an individuality "which he apparently finds himself uncomfortable with since all his efforts tend to its extinction or it transcendence".[65] But what is important in this regard is that "he thinks as an individual and this is the distinctive trait which opposes him to the man-in-the-world and brings him closer to the western thinkers".[66] And, as against the Brahman, who is mainly the preserver, the renouncer is in a position to put everything in question.

Now, Buddhism, for all practical purposes, is the religion of the renouncer. It is these renouncers who explain the story of genesis in a secular way. This story starts from the primeval chaos and presents a kind of gradual genesis of mankind through its differentiation and degeneration. Men came finally, in order to preserve property, to elect one of themselves as Mahasammat, "Great Elect", charged with the maintenance of social order. This story of genesis achieves, at one and the same time, two purposes. By opening up choices of individualized religion, it successfully challenged the religious monopoly of Brahmans which was further reinforced by the rise of the Kshatriyas to political ascendance and dominance. In short, it was instrumental in strengthening secular forces in society as against the Brahmanical religious ideas.

The process of secularization was further helped by the gaining of autonomy by *artha* as against *dharma* freeing pragmatic affairs of man from the stranglehold of *dharmic* injunctions. *Artha*, as Dumont points out, refers to rational action directed to well considered acquisition of worldly goods. What is interesting is that Dumont finds an opposition between *dharma* and *artha* because "*dharma* is (action in conformity with) the universal norm, and hence disinterested, while *artha* is (action in conformity with) interest, without regard to the universal norm".[67] But, then, how is it possible to recognize *artha* as a life-purpose if it negates the supremacy of *dharma*? The answer to this question lies in the hierarchy of life-purposes: "*artha* is recognized only in the second place, we may say in matters indifferent to *dharma*, *artha* remains finally contained within the all-embracing *dharma*, confined within *dharma* prescribed limits."[68]

This is, as Dumont argues, a situation parallel to that of *Kshatra* in relation to *Brahma* in the sense that the same process of secularization is also in operation here. This entails the gaining of autonomy by that which traditionally is supposed to be only subordinate. As a result, "*artha*, like *kshatra*, is severed from the whole of being, made in some way autonomous, special, or, as we would say in our modern language, 'rational'.[69] What is also interesting to note is that Dumont sees an equation between Brahman and *dharma*, on the one hand, and that between Kshatriya or the king and *artha*, on the other. Given this, the upshot is that

> the political sphere is severed from the realm of values. It is not in the political sphere that the society finds its unity, but in the social regime of castes. The system of government has no universal value, it is not the state in the modern sense of the term ... Force and interest work only for strife and instability, but these conditions may thrive without anything

> essential being part in question; much to the contrary, social unity implies and entertains division.[70]

Dumont's analysis is not necessarily limited to explaining the changed relationship between *Brahma* and *Kshatra*; it is meant to take in its ambit the character of politics in India, in general. But, whatever may be its claim, Dumont's analysis is, for all that, full of holes and, therefore, without any use. First of all, it is the degeneration of what refers, in *Brahadaranyaka Upanishad* (I. 411), to abstract, cosmogonic forces, that is *Brahma* as consciousness (*manas*) or intelligence and *Kshatra* as energy (*prana*) or will into sociological categories. In this process the true import of what *Brahadaranyaka Upanishad* says has not only been distorted but also it has become the source of a false dilemma. In the second place, Dumont's use of the term in connection with renouncer is sloppy and misleading insofar as the individual in Western sense symbolizes a man completely dedicated to appeasing his passion and, therefore, completely immersed in materiality. As a result, his individuality is marked by egocentrism and *pleonexia.*

In contract, the renouncer turns his back on the world and its concerns, and seeks to submerge his individuality into the universal self so that he gets rid of his individuality in the Western sense. Moreover, the renouncer himself is bound to the norms enunciated by the man-in-the-world, i.e., the Brahman. And, in the third place, Dumont's imposition of modern sociological, particularly, Weberian, categories on the relationship between *dharma* and *artha* not only confuses the real import of this relationship but also introduces opposition where there is no opposition. As is well known, the theory of Purushartha not only identifies the four ends of life as worthy of pursuit but also underlines the need to subjugate the pursuit of *kama* and *artha* to *dharma* so that none of the former two becomes autotelic and endangers social harmony and peace. It is not the opposition between *dharma* and *artha* that is the cause of the drive of *artha* towards autonomy but the emergence of man as a self-defining subject as a result of the banishment of the God from his creation.

It is evident that the application of modern sociological reasoning to experience in ancient times does not prove rewarding. Yet mental habits die hard and the relationship between *sacerdotium* and *regnum* continues to be analysed in terms of modern sociological theories. The case in point here is Heesterman who, like Dumont, finds the source of dilemma between spiritual authority and temporal power in *Brahadaranyaka Upanishad* (I. 4.11) but he is not satisfied with Dumont's explanation and offers a new one. Heesterman argues that the relationship between the Brahman and the king cannot be explained in terms of the distinction between a spiritual and the temporal being carried out in an absolute form. This distinction, as a matter of fact, he argues, is absolute and involves a contradiction which cannot be resolved, much less erased.[71] Space does not allow a fuller discussion of Heesterman's arguments except to point out that, in his view, the two orders – that of spiritual authority and temporal power – are, it is true, represented as opposed ideal patterns. However, in actual fact, the difference is rather a matter of degree since each of the two is ambiguous. The egalitarian order necessarily leads to differences of rank. However, the king's position remains embedded in the constituent relation of the community, whose unity he must represent. "Power and authority are therefore not exclusively the king's; they are diffused throughout the community."[72]

Add to it the fact that kingship is constituted by a network of personal relations evidenced, according to Heesterman, not only by Ratnins' relationship with the king as reflected in Rajasuya Yajna but also by other factors. It means that "power and authority are situated at cross-roads, that is to say, of the personal relations which make up the polity. Power and authority are dispersed".[73] In such a situation, the king can be nothing else but a living expression of the balance of these relationships and their opposing pulls and pushes, which tie him down and prevent him from acting on his own. He does not transcend the community by his right or otherwise; at best he is a *primus inter pares.*[74] The upshot is that the Indian system "makes the king supreme only to deprive him again of his supremacy".[75] In order to buttress his case Heesterman refers to what he calls the fight between Prajapati and Death through sacrifice[76] and puts a highly dubious interpretation to it. As he says, "the exclusion of the primordial rival, Death, and the assertion of the unopposed lord of life, Prajapati, who is at the same time the prototype of the sacrificer, amounted to a revolution of the socio-religious system". But a heavy price had to be paid; it was "complete divorce from social reality"; that is, "the sacrifice was cut loose from community".[77]

For Heesterman, the place of sacrifice in the classical view is the ideally ordered world, in any case, a non-existent reality, the ideal, completely sealed off from the world of social relations, a pressing, unrelenting existent reality, the real. But both are opposed to each other as Prajapati and Death or the Brahman and the king. The problem, then, is to reconcile them and make their coming together easy and benign. However, as Heesterman views it, in the individualized sacrifice the single sacrificer turns his back on society and strikes out in a world exclusively his own. As such, "the ideal sacrificer, like the ideal Brahman, stands outside society; he is a renouncer".[78] Thus, the problem of transcendence was sought to be solved by introducing a dichotomy in the universe; that is the worldly sphere of social relation and the outer-worldly sphere of the individual, cut off from society and thereby transcending it. This also applies to the separation between the Brahman's spiritual authority and the king's temporal power. "Authority could only be made transcendent on condition that it be free from involvement in the social world and its attendant struggle for the distribution of power."[79] By the same token, society stands condemned, because it lacks authority that is borne by the Brahman alone. But he can exercise his authority as long as he keeps himself free from involvement in the social world. "In particular he should shun the holder of power."[80] As such, "the dichotomy excludes, in principle, any relation between power and authority".[81]

It is quite obvious that Heesterman, just like Dumont, misreads his sources and offers explanations that cannot be substantiated unless one injects modern sociological point of view. But, the projection back of modern perspective on the ancient world is quite endemic. Note, for example, that Bandhopadhyaya accepts without any critical examination, the Western scholars' interpretation of the relationship between *sacerdotium* and *regnum.*[82] He also accepts the cosmological interpretation of the king's position in the world.[83] Similarly, the question of the divinity of the king evokes a response from Indian scholars which is not dissimilar to the Western approach. Also, it has divided them in two opposing camps, one camp arguing in favour and the other denying the divinity of the king.[84]

The preceding analysis sharply underlines the way how what is basically evocative has been treated as descriptive setting in motion a process of hieroglyphic transformations. As a result, not only the totality of the Vedic perspective on political order has been violated, but also this perspective and its institutional manifestations have been dirempted from their socio-cultural environment. With the violation of the wholesomeness of the Vedic perspective, it becomes difficult to comprehend its real import and appreciate its deeper significance. What is, therefore, attempted in the following chapters concerns the setting down of a framework that puts the Vedic vision of political order in a proper perspective.

Notes

1. A.L. Basham, *The Wonder That Was India* (London: Sidgwick and Jackson, 1961), p. 79.
2. V.P. Varma, *Studies in Hindu Political Thought and its Metaphysical Foundations* (Delhi: Motilal Banarasidass, 1959), p. 12.
3. Ibid., p. 254.
4. Ibid., p. 255.
5. G.C. Pande, *Jain Political Thought* (Jaipur: Prakrit Bharati Sansthan, Centre for Jain Studies, University of Rajasthan, 1984), p. 5.
6. Sri Aurobindo, *The Spirit and Form of Indian Polity* (Calcutta: Aryan Publishing House, 1947), p. 2.
7. G.C. Pande, op. cit., p. 1
8. For a discussion on this, see Ramashray Roy, *Beyond Ego's Domain: Being and Order in the Veda* (Delhi: Shipra Publications, 1999), Ch. 2.
9. It is interesting to note here that Indian scholars who have sought to reconstruct the ancient Indian perspective on statecraft are not at all certain whether this perspective could be identified as purely metaphysical or purely practical. This can be illustrated by the diametrically opposed observations of Beni Prasad and V.P. Varma. Note, for example that Beni Prasad avers that it is true that works on law or polity are certainly numerous but, for the most part, they are theoretical. See *The State in Ancient India* (Allahabad: The Indian Press Ltd., 1928), p. 1. In contrast, Varma notes that the Hindus thought that political matter required not so much of utopian and idealistic theoretical construction as a pragmatic and practical handling. See Varma, op. cit., p. 52.
10. It is to be noted that even in modern times writings on politics or economics, for instance, do not articulate the conception of man, which provides the basic framework for its own discipline-bound discussions. Each of these disciplines takes the concept of man for granted or as already given elsewhere.
11. For difficulties involved in comparing perspectives on life across culture, See Voegelin, "Equivalences of Experience and Symbolization in History," in *Eternita e Storia; I Valori permanenti nel Divinite Storico* (Florence: Valecchi, 1970), pp. 215–34.

12. The term "political" signifies, as is evident from Plato's *Republic*, the constitutive principle which installs order on a multitude of goods. It is in this sense, that the term "political" is used here.
13. For a useful discussion on this, see Voegelin, "Immortality, Experience and Symbol," *Harvard Theological Review*, 60, 3 (July 1967), p. 1.
14. Sri Aurobindo, op. cit., p. 19.
15. K.B. Krishna, *Theories of Kingship in India* (Vijaywada: Vishalandhra Publishing House, 1932), p. 19. Dr R. Bhandarkar expresses the same opinion but, of course, without implying what Krishna explicitly says about the detrimental effect of Jayaswal's work. Bhandarkar observes, "The importance of the subject (Hindu polity) was first perceived with prophetic vision by K.P. Jayaswal ... who began by contributing thought provoking articles to the *Modern Review* in 1913." See *Some Aspects of Ancient Hindu Polity*. The Manindra Chandra Nandy Lectures, February 1925 (Varanasi: Benaras Hindu University), Preface.
16. K.P. Jayaswal, *Hindu Polity: Constitutional History of India in Hindu Times* (Calcutta: Butterworth & Co. (India) Ltd., 1924), Part I, Preface. See also R. Bhandarkar, op. cit.
17. R. Bhandarkar, op. cit., p. 1.
18. R.S. Sharma, 1990 and ibid., p. 16.
19. Ibid., p. 16.
20. G.W.F. Hegel, *The Philosophy of History* (New York: Dover Publication, 1956), p. 161.
21. Ibid.
22. *History of Ancient Sanskrit Literature,* p. 31. It goes to the credit of Max Muller that at least he recognizes the unique contribution of the Hindus to the realm of religion and philosophy. As he notes, "the only sphere where the Indian mind found itself at liberty to act, to create, and to worship, was the sphere of religion and philosophy." But insofar as the sense of nationality is concerned, he is emphatic in his verdict that "the Indian never knew the feeling of nationality, and his heart never trembled in the expectation of national applause." Ibid., pp. 30–31. It is really heartening to note that a scholar like Max Muller, who claimed to know all the secrets of the Veda, could also decipher the heartthrobs of Indians long dead.
23. A. Willoughby, *Political Theories of the Ancient World,* 1903 (reprinted in 1973).
24. L.T. Hobhouse, *Social Evolution and Political Theory,* 1911 (reprinted in 1977).
25. K.P. Mukerjee, *Ancient Political Experience* (Colombo: M.D. Gunasena & Co. Ltd., 1961), Preface.

26. Beni Prasad, *The State in Ancient India* (Allahabad: The Indian Press, 1928), p. 1.
27. N.C. Bandopadhyaya, *Development of Hindu Polity and Political Theories* (Calcutta: R. Camberay & Co. 1927), 2 vols., Preface, p. VII.
28. R. Bhandarkar, op. cit., p. 3. cf. K.M. Panikkar, "The discovery and publication of Kautalya's *Arthashastra* gave the first shock to this complacent ignorance in which both Western and Eastern scholarship had busied itself." Panikkar further comments that the publication of *Arthashastra* made the orientalists busy in untangling the problem of its authorship, probable date of its composition, etc. But the bewildering variety of literature produced to settle these questions one way or the other does not, Panikkar points out, conceal the significance of the book. Whoever wrote the treatise, it was clear that the science of politics as such has been a matter of enquiry and study in ancient India; that thinkers had long busied themselves with explanations of the nature and character of sovereignty of the organization and functions of the state and its relations to individuals and all the other problems of corporate social life. See *The Ideas of Sovereignty and State in Indian Political Thought* (Bombay: Bharatiya Vidya Bhawan, 1963), pp. 2–3.
29. A.S. Altekar, *State and Government in Ancient India* (Delhi: Motilal Banarsidass, 1992), p. 5; cf. H.N. Sinha, "the picture of the Indo-Aryans presented to us by the Rig Veda is only in the form of silhouette. The outlines are buried in the haze and silence of the past". See *The Development of Indian Polity* (Bombay: Asia Publishing House, 1963), pp. 15–16.
30. A.S. Altekar, op. cit.
31. U.K. Ghoshal, *A History of Hindu Political Theories* (London: Oxford University Press, 1927), p. 41.
32. U.K. Ghoshal, op. cit., p. 1.
33. Charles Drekemieir, *Kingship and Community in Early India* (Bombay: Oxford University Press, 1962), p. 4.
34. Ibid.
35. G.C. Pande, *Bharatiya Parampara Ke Mool Swara* (New Delhi: National Publishing House, 1981), p. 18. Author's translation from Hindi.
36. cf. K.P. Mukerjee, op. cit., p.12; Drekemieir, op. cit., p. VIII.
37. Bandopadhyaya, op. cit., p. 143. For another angle on ritualism, cf. H.N. Sinha, "But frequent warfare enhanced the importance of sacrifice also, since the assistance of gods helped them in winning of wars, they had to be invoked by sacrifices as frequently also ..." op. cit., p. 4. See also Charles Drekemieir, op. cit., pp. 23–27.
38. N.C. Bandopadhyaya, op. cit.
39. A.S. Altekar, op. cit., p. 33.

40. Ibid.
41. Jayaswal, op. cit., p. 12.
42. Ibid., p. 23.
43. Sri Aurobindo, op. cit., cf. Nanda K. Acharya, "There is a school of scholars headed by K.P. Jayaswal that defines Hindu democracy in modern terminology. This is nothing but misunderstanding the true character of republican elements in ancient India", *The Cultural Politics of the Hindus* (Delhi: Surya Prakashan Mandir, p. 1973), p. 67.
44. Charles Drekemieir, op. cit., Preface, p. VIII.
45. Ibid., p. 12.
46. Ibid., p. 13. It must be said that Drekemieir is explicit in his Western bias when he imposes the Homeric world with a list of occult added on the Vedic world.
47. Ibid., p. 27.
48. For a detailed and penetrating discussion, see Ananda K. Coomaraswamy, *Spiritual Authority and Temporal Power in the Indian Theory of Government* (New York: Kraus Reprint Corporation, 1967) and "Kshatrasya Kshatram", Ch. 10 of Ramashray Roy, *Beyond Ego's Domain: Being and Order in the Veda* (Delhi: Shipra Publications, 1999).
49. Jan Gonda, *Ancient Indian Kingship From the Religious Point of View* (Lieden: E.J. Brill, 1969), p. 141.
50. Ibid., p. 103.
51. The primacy of Brahman as a sociological category is usually inferred from the Purusha Sukta (Rv. X. 90) and *Brihadaranyaka Upanishad*, I.4.11 ff.
52. Jan Gonda, op. cit., p. 139.
53. Charles Drekemieir, op. cit., p. 15.
54. Ibid., p. 6.
55. Ibid.
56. Ibid., p. 10.
57. Ibid.
58. Louis Dumont, "The Conception of Kingship in Ancient India", *Contributions to Indian Sociology*, VI (December 1962), pp. 48–77.
59. J.C. Heesterman, "Power and Authority in Indian Tradition" in R.J. Moore, ed., *Tradition and Politics in South Asia* (New Delhi: Vikas Publishing House, 1970), pp. 60–85.
60. Louis Dumont, op. cit., pp. 49–50.
61. The source of this argument goes back to Brihadaranyaka Upanishad, I. 4 II which says:

    In the beginning this was called Brahman, one only. Being one he did not flourish. He specially projected an excellent form, the Kshatra, those who are Kshatra among gods Indra, Varuna, Soma, Rudra, Parjanya, Yama, Mrityu (Death), and Ishana. Therefore, there is none higher than the Kshatra. Hence, the Brahman worships the Kshatriya from a lower position in the Rajasuya sacrifice. He imparts that glory to the Kshatriya. The Brahman is the source of the Kshatriya. Therefore, although the king attains supremacy (in the sacrifice) at the end he resorts to the Brahman, his source.

62. In arguing the temporal dependence of the Brahman on the royal power, Dumont takes support mainly from two sources. In the first place, he quotes Hunter who argues that "from the very ancient times, the leaders of the Brahmans recognized that if they were to exercise spiritual supremacy they must renounce earthly pomp. In arrogating the princely function, they gave up all claim to royal office." *Indian Empire*, p. 136, quoted in N.N. Law, *Aspects of Ancient Indian Polity* (Oxford: Clarendon Press, 1921), pp. 44–45. In the second place, Dumont supports his argument with the observation that in Indian villages a relationship of dependency between Brahmans and dominant caste can be observed even today. Needless to say that both these evidences are misleading. The first argument reduces the relationship between *Brahma* and *Kshatra* to expediency in addition to committing a fallacy which confuses the office of the Purohit with the whole Brahman class. The second argument is misleading because it judges the character of the dim and distant past in the light of the present.
63. Louis Dumont, op. cit., p. 75.
64. Louis Dumont, "World Renunciation in Indian Religions," *Contributions to Indian Sociology*, IV (April, 1960), p. 49.
65. Ibid., p. 46.
66. Loc. cit.
67. Louis Dumont, *Kingship in Ancient India*, op. cit., p. 66.
68. Loc. cit.
69. Loc. cit.
70. Loc. cit.
71. J.C. Heesterman, op. cit., p. 65.
72. Ibid., p. 73.
73. Ibid., p. 67.
74. Loc. cit.
75. Ibid., p. 66.
76. *Jaiminiya Brahmna*, 2.69–70.
77. J.C. Heesterman, op. cit., p. 80.
78. Loc. cit.
79. Loc. cit.

80. Ibid., p. 81.
81. Loc. cit.
82. N.C. Bandopadhyaya, op. cit., p. 100.
83. Ibid., p. 144.
84. Bhandarkar is a prominent member of this camp while Jayaswal opposes it with Altekar standing in-between.

6

Political Order

Non-Vedic Perspectives

One of the adverse consequences of absolutizing the universal world and making it a basis for the construction of a framework of order relates to the inherent tension between the two dimensions of the individual's existence. These two dimensions refer to the fateful divide between the private world of the individual and his public face. This problem defies solution as long as man, unaware of the ennobling potentialities immanent in his spiritual personality, remains a captive of his materially dominated individuality. However, as the classical world view, especially, the Vedic world view recognizes, even while man is immersed in materiality, he is quite capable of transcending his conditioned existence and seeking the divine essence buried deep in his psyche.[1] It is in this context that we can appreciate that man's psyche is thought to be bivalent. The psyche of man is, no doubt, enveloped in materiality; however, it also contains a divine spark which, when fully kindled, may bring enlightenment to him. As Tucci puts it:

> While it (the psyche) may disperse more and more into negation of that light until it entirely obscures it, it may also, as though impelled by the glimmer that is not entirely extinguished in it, disengages itself from the night, discover once more our essential divinity, and induce us to find our way back along the path that leads beyond the plane of *maya.*[2]

Needless to say that it is getting across the plane of *maya* that, in the Vedic perspective, gives men a sense of fullness or wholeness (*sarvata)* that, in turn, induces the feeling of *ahati* (i.e., the feeling of remaining uninjured).[3] To acquire *sarvata* is to become *Arya* (i.e., to be hospitable to the guest from beyond), to be open to transcendence, in the true sense of the term. And to be a true *Arya* is to engage in the pursuit of light, *jyotish abhayam* (the light that makes one fearless).[4] What is important in the classical Indian thinking is not the struggle between good and evil, a contest between virtue and sin that is said to derive from the opposition between the body and the soul.[5] What is important is the opposition between the luminous Consciousness and its opposite, the psyche and the subconscious generally called as *maya.* This opposition is not permanent and it can be overcome by the process of integration consequent upon the realization that, as Tucci puts it, there is an essential unity "between God and the world, between the Absolute and life, and the conscious Being and the psyche".[6] This realization is a precondition of integration that must occur at different levels – between man and God, and between man and the world.[7]

Integration is possible principally by realizing the truth of one's own being by conquering the base nature. Conquest of the base nature is possible by realizing that being human involves being sensitive to the sacred. But this realization and the conquest of the base nature of man are attainable through a mystery. As Heschel reminds us,

> ... the acceptance of the sacred is an existential paradox: it is saying "yes" to a "no"; it is the antithesis to the will of power; it may contradict interests and stand in the way of satisfying inner drives.
>
> To our sense of power the world is at our disposal, to be exploited to our advantage. To accept the sacred is an acknowledgement that certain things are not available to us, are not at our disposal.[8]

On the possibility of this conquest rests a benign political order that the classical Indian thinking aims at forming and institutionalizing. In such a political order, power is not banished; it is rather wedded to righteousness. To wed power to righteousness and to create political institutional arrangement so that it becomes the embodiment of the "political" in Plato's term. By insisting that the political has the function of linking the finite with the absolute, Plato liberates political from its submission to the givens of nature and society. The "political", as Schaar puts it, occupies,

> a middle terrain between the sheer givens of nature and society, on the one side, and the transcendental ends toward which man aspires on the other. Political action is that type of action through which men publicly attempt to order and to transform the givens of nature and society by the light of values that are above and beyond the order of nature.[9]

On this view, the "political" performs the function of linking the finite and the absolute, forges a primordial relationship between world and God, and man and the world. It is this perspective that makes it necessary to treat political philosophy as an integral part of *philosophia perennis*, a philosophy that embodies "wisdom (*vidya)* which links practical conduct of life (*vyavahar*) with the pursuit of ideal ends of life (*purusharthas*), on the one hand, it is a strategy or *niti,* on the other a moral wisdom *(dharma, vidya*). Grounded in *agama* or tradition, it is at once Reason or Prudence, Theory and Art."[10] It is this perspective that illustrates the Vedic vision of order as well as that of both Jainism and Buddhism even though these two streams of thinking are considered to be quite opposed to the Vedic worldview, especially its Brahmanical conception of *dharma* and the practices associated with it. This and other vital differences[11] make the Jaina political thinking somewhat different both from the Buddhist and the Vedic thinking. First, according to Jaina thinking, man by nature is a spiritual being to whom righteousness comes naturally. Righteousness is *dharma* that consists in detachment. This is very forcefully suggested in the dialogue between King Nami and Indra.[12] As Pande points out:

> *Dharma* is basically virtue which is grounded ultimately in the spiritual nature of man. Moral conduct thus becomes conduct in accordance with and conducive to spiritual life. Spiritual life itself is life of detachment, purity, peace and, above all, non-violence. To be good or to follow *dharma* is to be spiritual.[13]

Second, complete detachment is the basis of righteousness that, in turn, makes a society a *dharmasangha* or *aryasangha* in which every man follows *dharma*. Keeping in mind the fact that every man, in the Jaina perspective, is of equal worth (*atmatula*),[14] the living of a virtuous life makes society an association of moral men. And it is society as an association of moral men that the Jaina thinking postulates as the first pristine beginning of human society in history. By doing so, it underlines the fact that the essential principle of human conduct as well as of social organization cannot be force or naked power; instead, it must be righteousness. And to make righteousness the basis of social order is also to treat the self "as a value lying beyond the instinctive processes of nature and (to underscore) the similarity between oneself and others .... The basis of society as a moral association (*dharmasangha* or *aryasangha*) is, thus, not instinct or force, but spiritual recognition deriving from rational reflection as well as a tradition of faith."[15]

The first society may have begun as a *dharmasangha* or *aryasangha,* but, then, two factors intervened to push it on the path of decline progressively eroding the rule of righteousness. In the first place, man, despite his spiritual nature, still has in him a touch of materiality that inclines him towards egoism forcing him to make the distinction of "I" and "They". As a result of this distinction, possessiveness took hold of men and competition for privileged access to material resources raised its ugly head. The undue influence of egoism on men's mind inclined them to overlook the well-being of others and create a situation in which social cooperation broke down disrupting, in the process, harmonious relationship. Thus, it is the egoistic impulses that prove to be the prime factor responsible for the erosion of the foundation of society as a moral association.

In the second place, everything in this phenomenal world is governed by time, *Kala*, which, as Jinasena points out in *Adipurana*, is not only without beginning and end (*anadinidhanam*); it is also the cause of all changes in the world.[16] Time is only a concomitant cause which becomes active only when *vikara* (that is, changes as the result of the action of certain internal or external factor or cause) becomes operative (I.iii 4); time moves in a circle and its movement symbolizes the rise and fall in social order as a moral association. The ascent of the cycle of Time signifies *utsarpini* when good times, as a result of progressive improvement in the righteous behaviour of the people, come. In contrast, its downward movement, called *avasarpini*, denotes decline in the righteous behaviour of the people (I.iii.14). Both of them have six different stages each representing a particular level of righteousness existing at a particular time and its concomitant social order.

Both *utsarpini* and *avasarpini* follow one after the other like the two successive lunar fortnights (I.iii.21). In their rotation, they underline two factors of great importance for Jaina thinking as it impinges on the installation, maintenance, and the rise and fall of the state. One of these factors relates to the progressive decline of the good time due to a parallel decline in virtuous living. Note, for example, that in the first-time division, men and women had fabulously long lives and perfect bodies; they enjoyed chaste life and perfect happiness and lived upon the products of wish-fulfilling trees (*kalpavriksha*).[17] However, the subsequent ages saw the progressive decline leading to changes in nature, in the behaviour of the animal world and the means of subsistence and physiological conditions. With the good life taking a downward plunge, successive Patriarchs, blessed with superhuman attributes, intervened to make people adjust to changing conditions. But failure in arresting the progressive decline created a situation where people began quarrelling. With the increased tempo in the fall of man, the successive Patriarchs progressively increased the penalties for offences; penalties began with "ha" (alas) which graduated to "ma" (don't) leading up to "dhik" (condemnation) (III.iii.214–16). But as men became very prone to crimes, imprisonment, death, and corporeal punishments were prescribed.

Thus, the account of the evolution of society in a cyclical fashion presented in the *Adipurana* underlines three basic components of Jaina thinking about political order. These are: the notion of cyclical time, human decline, and the original founding of civilized human and universal sovereignty. As Pande points out, "... these ideas constitute a philosophy rather than a history." The seemingly historical account is, as a matter of fact, symbolic of the hazards that living according to certain spiritual principles implies. What it points to is the inexorable decline in moral values and the growing ineffectiveness of spiritual law in regulating human conduct when men get attached to their own ego and seek to improve their worldly life. It is this situation that makes *danda* (punishment) and the state necessary for safeguarding and upholding *dharma* in society.

And, lastly, if a society remains a moral association and people do not deviate from the path of righteousness, there is no need either for *danda* or for a king ... it is only after the spiritual fall of man has taken place that the need for maintaining law and order as a precondition of securing a good life based on righteousness arises. It also follows that when conditions for life according to and reflecting dharmic tenets are present, there is no need at all of political order, king or laws to sustain and preserve order and safeguard the public from the hazards of the tendency towards self-aggrandizement engenders. Society as a moral association is, by definition, a society of good men who have realized to the fullest their spiritual nature; they have available to them the knowledge that can yield the principles of good governance. Thus, the source of good governance is not the king or the law, but good men who possess the requisite insight and knowledge to apprehend and articulate the virtues of the king and the properties of good laws.

But since the movement of time induces the decline of righteousness in society and the erosion of the respect for *dharma* disrupts order, it is necessary to shore up the tottering edifice of law and order so that the virus of chaos can be prevented from wasting the texture of society as a moral association. This requires the installation of the political order headed by a king who can safeguard and regulate public life and relations by appropriate laws, and employ *danda* in the case of those who infringe laws. However, they are not unmixed blessings insofar as the state is the surrogate of coercion and, therefore, violative of the fundamental principle of *ahimsa*. As Pande puts it:

> ... within the imperfect conditions of human life as actually given, the state functions as a habitual condition of moral life and although in this sense it is indirectly good, it is at the same time necessarily evil on account of its coercive nature. Nor is this morally mixed institution an essential or ultimate condition of the highest type of human life, which is that of spiritual realization. Morally, thus the state has value as well as disvalue.[18]

It is against this background that the need for making *dharma* the real sovereign who rules through the agency of the king can be appreciated. Thus, the king must subordinate himself to the suzerainty of *dharma* and mould his conduct according to *dharma*, more particularly to Jaina *dharma*.

Like Jainism, Buddhism, too, rejects the Vedic world view as well as the idea of political order grounded in it. However, just as Jainism, Buddhism also insists on grounding political life and relations in *dharma*. Also, Buddhism, just as Jainism, sees the appearance or the installation of political order as a necessary consequence of moral decline to the point of no return. This is quite evident from the Buddhist account of genesis.[19] When, after the dissolution of the universe, a new universe appeared, self-luminous beings, made of mind and very light, made their appearance before anything else in order to achieve the extinction of existence and *karma*. They fed upon the essence of the earth. Then the earth appeared; it was a lake of butter. Some beings, prompted by greed, ate this essence. As a consequence, they became heavier, rough and hard and lost their proper attributes. Then, the sun, the moon and other things appeared. Gradually, vanity, conceit, too, appeared and the distinction between ugly and beautiful persons raised its ugly head.

Gradually, rice without husk and powder appeared to provide sustenance to the beings. However, greed increased which, in turn, led to acquisitiveness and possessiveness. People began taking more of rice than they required. This further led to stealing. Even after several reminders, the promise not to steal anymore remained unfulfilled. Then people hurriedly gathered together and selected one of the most kind-hearted, authoritative persons to dispense reproof or approval for which he was to receive one-sixth of the rice produced in everyone's fields.

So originated the idea that Maha-sammata means "elected by the great body of the people". So originated the idea that *rajan* means he who is worthy of the rice portions from the rice fields. So originated the idea that an anointed (noble) means he who achieves security for his country (and) is as a parent to towns and provinces. That is how a king can say, "I am king, an anointed noble, and one who has achieved security for my people."[20]

As is evident from the Buddhist account of genesis, it is the decline of morality consequent upon greed, acquisitiveness and possessiveness that disrupts the state located in the interior of everybody. This, in turn, makes it necessary to create a political order headed by a king in the external world, an order that is distinct and separate from society. But the installation of the king to rule over men, look to their welfare, protect them from others as well as from their own cupidity is symptomatic of the decline of society as the agent that instils virtue in the hearts of men. As a result, the king, as an external authority, must discharge all these responsibilities. To be able to do so, the king must safeguard the well-being of the people he rules over. This means that, as the Mahakapi in the *Jataka* story[21] 407 told the king:

> The happiness of kingdom and of army and steel
> And city must be dear to thee, if thou would'st rule indeed.

Also, the king must subdue his passions (*Jataka* 490); he should never injure a right lest it recoil on the king himself (*Jataka* 422). He should not covet what belongs to others and should never betray a friend (*Jataka* 527). What is interesting to note in different *Jataka* stories is the emphatic underlining of the dictum, *raja kalasya karanam*, that is, it is the king who causes good or bad times. This is clearly indicted in *Jataka* 334 which explains why the fig offered by Bodhisatta to King Brahmadatta tasted sweet one time and bitter another time. The key to this is whether the king rules righteously or not. If the king rules unrighteously:

> The bull through floods a devious course will take,
> The herd of kine all struggling in his wake.

So if a leader tortuous paths pursue,
To base ends will he guide the vulgar crew,
And the whole realm an age of license rue.

But if the bull a course direct should steer,
The herd of kine straight follows in his rear.

So should their chief to righteous ways be true,
The common folk injustice will eschew,
And the realm shall holy peace ensue.

Thus, if the king does not follow the right course of action, then, as *Jataka* 422 recounts, drought comes when a wet spell is needed. As such, the king must rule righteously if he is to be true to his calling. But we must ask with King Brahmadatta (*Jataka* 521) as to what course of life is the best for a king? And as is evident from the answers his three bird-sons and daughter gave to his question, the king should rule righteously abiding in the three truths. That is, he should put away all falsehood, he must do what he has to do according to the oath he takes at the time of his coronation, and he should not allow his passions to sway him and should remain alert. In addition, he should always stick to the two maxims that nicely summarize the king's duty: first, he should keep whatever is his own and second, take good counsellors. And, above all, the supreme powers of limbs, of wealth, of counsel, of caste, are learning. It is by the strength of learning that a man becomes wise and succeeds in life.

Thus, wisdom, as the supreme power, is the key to good government. And wisdom can be acquired if one knew what is good and true. As *Jataka* 515 notes, the good and the true implies:

A king all wicked ways should carefully eschew,
Nor, like bewildered fool, an evil course pursue.

To loss of his own soul he never should transgress,
Nor e'er be guilty of deeds of unrighteousness,
Himself ne'er be engaged in any evil way,
Nor e'er in wrong path a brother lead astray.

Thus, what is emphasized in Buddhistic doctrines is the need for a king to be righteous; if, as *Anguttara Nikaya* (II: 74–76) points out, he becomes unrighteous, his officers and others, too, will become unrighteous. With it the whole society becomes corrupt. Thus, the key to the society as a moral association lies in the extent to which the king rules righteously. This is possible only when the king becomes *swarat,* that is, when he achieves self-rule (autarchy). And, as *Jataka* 544, underlines, one treats the body as a chariot and controls its charioteer – the mind – by the soul.

> The body is called a chariot, swift and provided with the mind as a charioteer; having the abstinence from all injury as its axle, liberality as its covering, a careful walk with the feet as the circumference of the wheel, a careful handling with the hands as the side of the carriage, watchfulness over the tongue is the prevention of the wheel's rattling. Its parts are all complete through truthful speech, it is well fastened together by the absence of slander, its frame is all smooth with friendly words and joined well with measured speech, well-constructed with the respectful salutation of humility as the carriage pole, with the shaft of gentleness and meekness, with the rope of self-restraint, according to the five moral precepts, and the key of absence of anger, and the white umbrella of righteousness, driven with a thorough knowledge of the proper seasons having the three sticks prepared in his assured confidence, having humble speech as the thong, and with the absence of vain-glory as the yoke, with the cushion of unattached thoughts, following wisdom and free from dust, let memory be thy goad, and the ready application of firmness thy reins, mind pursues the path of self-control with its steeds all equally trained, desire and lust are an evil path, but self-control is the straight road. As the steed rushes along after forms and sounds and smells, intellect uses the scourge and the soul is the charioteer. If one goes with his chariot, if this calmness and firmness be steadfast, he will attain all desires, O King, he will never go to hell.[22]

If the king attains self-control, he becomes like a father to his subject. According to *Jataka* 432, "just as an aged father ought to be cared for by an able-bodied son, so too ought all the people to be protected by the king … ." It is in this sense that *dharma* becomes *kshatrasya kshatram.*

It is clear from the above that both Jainism and Buddhism lay emphasis on a morally well-informed political society. Both of them put equal emphasis on self-control as a basis of good governance. But does either Jainism or Buddhism provide the true basis of self-control necessary for the king to discharge his responsibilities well? Needless to say that without such a basis, the proposal of self-control for making the king the real sovereign under the over-lordship of *dharma*, will remain simply a slogan and will, consequently, fail to become *praxis* in the real sense of the term. Both Jainism and Buddhism insist on the needs of cleansing the "soul" of its impurities, that is, the incrustations of materiality, so that it regains its primordial, pristine purity that it loses in the process of living itself. Its purity is lost when the individual, obeying the dictates of his passions, engages in action motivated by his well-being without any consideration for the well-being of others. As a result, the moral sense gets beclouded; this, in turn, creates a situation in which conflict of interests leads to social discord paving the way for violence. With the breakdown of social concord, society as a moral association, too, breaks down.

The loss of purity by the soul indicates that righteousness, the seedbed of morality, cannot cohere with prudence whose real significance lies in making the most advantageous combinations of ends and means with a view to optimalizing utility. If it is the only significance that prudence has, then, it rests on *phronesis,* not *sophia or prajnan.* In such a case, self-interest takes on the responsibility of directing the management of man's pragmatic affairs. When this happens, order in man's interior is disrupted and his soul gets afflicted with *nosos,* that is, sickness of the soul. When the sickness of the soul spreads wide and achieves a critical size in the mass of men, social order, too, becomes fragile and disorder in many spheres of life becomes visible. It is claimed that the threat of the widespread disorder should not prove to be a cause of worry or frustration. There are certain key elements in society that can curb disorder and prevent it from striking deep roots. It is, for example, suggested that there is the invisible watchman located right in the depth of the individual's psyche; this watchman is quite capable of guiding successfully the individual in making decisions regarding the right course of action that he should take. If the invisible watchman fails to perform this role, there are great souls, that is, *mahajanas* (wise men, *spudaios*) who, because they are virtuous and good, can become a model of proper conduct for others. They can also become the source of control for others as well as constitute a standard against which the conduct of others can be judged, approved or condemned.

Even if the influence of the great souls fails to induce individuals to walk straight on the path of virtue, there is law that incorporates two very important factors that are capable of keeping men moving straight on the path of virtue. In the first place, law prescribes the boundaries determining what is good and what is bad. If a person is himself not capable of determining what right conduct is, law can effectively guide him in this. In the second place, law is also a command whose violation invites punishment. The fear of punishment is most likely to incline men to respect law and obey its command. Also, noteworthy in this connection is that there is the state to enforce the command of law and maintain order. What must be kept in mind is that it is the growing disruption of order both in the interior of the individual's psyche and in society that paves the way for the creation of the state and the installation of a king. The state becomes necessary to protect and preserve the crumbling ramparts of social order under the rising fury of the flood of *pleonexia.*

But as has already been indicated, none of these factors is capable of warding off the waves of this flood. This flood, it must be emphasized, is caused by the rising tide of self-interested action. The ravages of self-interested action inspired by self-aggrandizement by individuals and groups cannot easily be shored up by any of these factors. This is all the more true of the state. The state, as Unger notes, is like the gods in Olympia, "who were banished from the earth and endowed with superhuman powers but condemned to undergo the passions of the mortals".[23] It is, therefore, very difficult to maintain that the state can rise above the conflict occurring incessantly among private values seeking articulation, ascendance, and control. It is this characteristic that renders the command of the state less than right insofar as it is inexorably enmeshed with power positions of different socio-economic interests. Given the fact that only one set of views, interests and preferences prevail over others, "the morality of requiring all to abide by the decisions of some as a matter of duty or, less ambitiously, as a matter of inclining before the threat of force, has always seemed problematical".[24]

Needless to say that when the natural tendencies of the average man, who is moved to act by the impulse of aggressiveness, self-interest, and acquisitiveness, all ideals, whose pursuit is supposed to elevate man morally, lose their salience. But it is also a fact that without the re-education of natural impulses, political order will ever be buffeted by the crosscurrents of conflicting interests. To protect the political order from these crosscurrents so that it remains benign, it is necessary to inculcate in men a coherent order of values – values that are embedded in and derive their sustenance from their spiritual nature of man. Is this inculcation possible within the framework of Jainism or Buddhism? Both for Jainism and Buddhism, the truth of existence is one, a single whole. As such, the principles grounded in this truth apply equally to all spheres of life even though technical and practical details of each of these spheres may differ from one another.

It is, therefore, necessary to ask whether the political order based on the Jaina and Buddhist perspectives and inspired and influenced by their world views can create and maintain benign political order.

The birth of the state is in itself indicative of a widespread decline in morality. The loss of morality implies *dukkha* (unhappiness, misery) for individuals and growing difficulties for the social order. In view of this, the existence of *dukkha* and the continuity of the state go hand in hand. By the same token, the state will have to continue to take care of the adverse consequences for other individuals and the society at large of *dukkha*-influenced actions of the individual as long as the causes of *dukkha* are not obliterated. And the continuity of the state either as a guardian of virtue in public life or as a coercive arm of the people in their collectivity is indicative of the fact that *dukkha* is the natural condition of man. In addition, it also leads to the conclusion that it is very hard to overcome or totally obliterate *dukkha* or its causes. This is, no doubt, a pessimistic conclusion leading to the inference that all efforts to eradicate *dukkha* or its causes are futile. This inference is reinforced by the cyclical theory of the movement of time, which points to the secular tendency of moral decline over time in every society.

But this is not the conclusion Jainism and Buddhism reach. For one thing, their adherence to the theory of cyclical movement of Time is testimony to their optimism insofar as they deny the permanence of *dukkha*. If the wheel of Time moves downward, it is also bound to take an upward swing sooner or later. This upward swing of Time is certain to bring back good times. The upward swing of the wheel of Time is symptomatic of not only the arrest of moral decline but also of moral recovery by a large number of people in the society. And moral recovery is, by the same token, indicative of the possibility of the eradication or, at least, attenuation of *dukkha*. The turning of the wheel of Time is not an automatic process, although it appears to be so. It needs help both of gods and mortals to make its upward swing. If the gods help this process by descending down to the earth as *avataaras*,[25] the mortals do so by attaining self-transformation through self-development. Self-transformation involves the quest for freedom from the bondage to base human passions. The possibility of self-transformation denies the immutability of human nature. Thus, the belief in the mutability of human nature reinforces optimism about the possibility of overcoming or eliminating the causes of *dukkha*.

Thus, if the decline of *dharma* is inexorable, so is its upsurge. This is the basis of optimism in Jainism.

The overcoming of *dukkha* calls for self-transformation, the true source of liberation. It is this liberation that becomes the basis of improving the quality of personal lives and collective existence. As Pande puts it:

> The quest for liberation requires the transformation of the whole of life. Without right behaviour there can be no inner tranquility, illumination and liberation. Whether the area of behaviour is political or economic or personal, the same basic principles need to be applied. Business ethics can only be the behavioural norms of an ethical person engaged in business just as political morality can be the mode of action of a moral person in politics.[26]

It is this holistic and unitary principle of moral regeneration of man that both Jainism and Buddhism espouse. Both believe in the idea that once man regains his higher nature through self-transformation and, as a result, attains freedom from bondage to his base passions, he can engender principles of right living from the freedom he acquires. These principles apply not only to personal but also to public dimensions of his existence. Believing as they do in this central principle and its efficacy in ordering, disciplining and regulating all life activities, both Jainism and Buddhism see the possibility of reordering or, at least, maintaining the dignity of political life and relations in the moral regeneration of man. It is not surprising that both Jainism and Buddhism, therefore, locate the question of the improvement of political life and relations and the possibility of the attainment by public order of higher moral caliber and moralizing influence in the context of the cleansing of the soul[27] of its impure and polluting incrustations of materiality so that it regains its primordial spiritual purity.

Once the soul becomes pure, it attains knowledge that yields a profound insight into the structure of reality and enables man to rise above the contingent experiences of finite existence and act judiciously and morally not only in personal but also in public affairs. It is true that Jainism and Buddhism differ sharply in some important details of religious experience. However, they share a common perspective on man and his world. Note, for example, that Jaina thinking considers the soul as pure spirituality transcending all possible sensible experiences.[28] In its essential nature, the soul possesses *kevalajnana* (prefect knowledge) which mirrors the entire universe, enjoys omniscience and infinite happiness. But it gets gradually incrusted with materiality as a result of man's involvement in *samsara* (the phenomenal world). This involvement is caused by *kamma* (*karma,* action) aimed at satisfying desires for worldly pleasures. Jainism makes a basic distinction between *karma* that harms and that which does not harm. The harming *karma* is designated as 'delusory', that is, *mohaniya.* It is *mohaniya karma* that constitutes the principal source of *jiva* (life form) getting immersed in everydayness.[29] It brings about attachment to incorrect views and incapacitates the individual to lead the religiously correct life. "At one level, it interferes with the normal functioning of the intellect and senses; at another, it prevents the functioning of the developed mental capabilities of the *jiva* including the omniscience which is otherwise natural to it."[30]

Central to Jaina philosophy is thus the concept of *kamma* or *kriyavada* which underlines the crucial significance of *kamma* both in dragging the *jiva* down in the heap of harming *kamma* and in wiping the soul clean of its impure, polluting incrustations of materiality. *Mohaniya* (harming) *kamma* obscures perception and distorts knowledge. As a result, the innate energy of the soul to resist *mohaniya kamma* by keeping passions in leash is gradually lost. When the individual falls a prey to his unruly worldly desires, to the lure of possessiveness, he comes under the sway of his passions (*kashaya).* This engenders the influx of *karmic* matter that sticks to the soul and makes it impure so much so that its proper functions are totally obscured. As a consequence of this, the soul wanders in the *samsara* and is forced to undergo varied experiences of misery and unhappiness. "Those who are led by their desire, who seized by Time dwell in the heap (of *kamma*) are born again and again."[31]

The immersion of *jiva* in the heap of *kamma*, that is, actions that bind it to the world, has certain adverse consequences both for the individual and the social order he is an integral part of. At the individual level, the progressive influx of karmic matter robs the soul of its primordial qualities and drags the individual into the mire of self-forgetfulness and makes for what Coomaraswamy calls "self-is-ness". The result is that the individual becomes highly selfish and comes to "believe in the world, believe in reward, believe in action: 'I did it'; ' I shall cause another to do it'; ' I shall allow another to do it'. In the worlds these are all the causes of sin ... ".[32] It is *kamma*, actions influenced and inspired by the attachment to the notion of "self-isness" that becomes the cause of misery and brings forth evil consequences.[33] Buried in the heap of *kamma,* the individual cannot rise above the trap of the phenomenal world. "As in a lake a greedy leaf-covered tortoise cannot rise up; as the trees do not leave their place, thus men, born in various families, cry bitterly because they do not reach liberation."[34]

Insofar as social order is concerned, actions originating in the ignorance of the true self do not only signify suffering for the individual. It also bodes disruption of social order as a consequence of the shattering of social concord and harmony insofar as it demolishes the foundation of sociality. Bondage to desires leads to self-regarding action; excessive concern with the satisfaction of one's own desires produces negative characteristics – false belief, lack of discipline, carelessness, passions and mental, physical and verbal activities that reflect harming *kamma*. Under the influence of these characteristics, the individual is prompted to perform all sorts of violent actions and comes to be in thrall to the whirlpool of the senses.[35] The essence of self-regarding action lies in the fact that it tends to disregard the fundamental integrity of persons by treating them as not significant in themselves, for their own intrinsic worth. They are treated as merely instruments for the realization of individual purposes. Obviously, such an attitude is grounded in *pramada*, that is, wrong attitude towards life. Thus, as Pande puts it:

> *Himsa* (violence), the root evil, has two parts, viz., the presence of *pramada*, or wrong attitude, and the infliction of injury to life. Egoistic passions are inherently other-disregarding and constitute *bhava-himsa.* The infliction of injury positively as *aghata* or negatively as *pratibandha* on any aspect of vital activity physical, vocal or mental or breathing, etc., constitutes *dravya-himsa.*[36]

Needless to say that *dravya-himsa*, that is, violence done to objects in the external world, is directly linked with *bhava-himsa* or violence that breeds in the interior of man. As has already been pointed out, the source of *bhava-himsa* is, of course, *pramada.*[37] It is under the influence of *pramada* that the individual becomes dead to the well-being of others. He is completely drained of the awareness, natural to the soul in its pure condition that all living creatures experience, to a greater or lesser extent, the same sort of feelings. As a result, he becomes immune to the desire for friendship with all creatures. This *pramada* is, as discussed earlier, the consequence of ignorance of what one really is, that is, the forgetfulness of the fact that his soul is pure intelligence and is above the fluctuations of the phenomenal world. All actions that originate in self-forgetfulness are injurious to others because they are self-regarding and other-disregarding. They are symptomatic of the self-aggrandizing tendency of the individual and spring from *bhava-himsa* leading to *dravya-himsa*. And since *himsa* is the basic cause of moral decline, widespread recourse to it atrophies and degenerates social order as a moral association.

But, then, is the human condition characterized by suffering and misery indispensable? Is the lure of *mohaniya kamma* so compulsive and, therefore, inexorable, that it cannot be evaded or avoided? It is true that, as Shrivarya underlines, "there is nothing mightier in the world than *karma*; *karma* tramples down all powers, as an elephant a clump of lotuses.[38] It is also true that it is *kamma* which is responsible for the manifest differences in the status, attainments and happiness of *jivas* (life forms). But the reference here to the almighty *kamma* is metaphysical; it is the accrual of *kamma*, both good and bad, that determines what one becomes and how this *samsara* works. But there is another aspect of *kamma* that pertains to individual action, which can be both harming and non-harming. If the individual can engage in *mohaniya kamma*, he can also exercise his freedom to engage in action that liberates or accumulates merit necessary for his liberation. It is on the basis of actions that one can liberate one's soul; as a result, the individual regains its primordial purity. It can, however, be argued that if the individual is already deeply immersed in the heap of *kamma*, how can he exercise his freedom to extricate himself from this heap and thus redeem his soul? It must, however, be pointed out that Jainism believes that, even in the state of bondage, the power of the soul, that is, its omniscience, is not completely lost.[39]

As such, the individual can certainly redeem his soul if he so wishes. Redemption of the soul lies, on the one hand, in shunning bad *karma*, and on the other, in engaging in good action aimed primarily at one's own well-being and then the well-being of the world around. But this requires self-effort by the individual himself. The beginning of this effort is the recognition that the individual himself is responsible for his troubles and he alone can do something to get out of them. Recognizing this, he should also recognize that he does not have to look anywhere else but within himself, to the dweller in his own interior. As *Acharangasutra* puts it:

> Man! Thou art thy own friend; why wishest thou for a friend beyond thyself? Whom he knows as a dweller on high, him he should know as a

> dweller far (from sin), him he should know as a dweller on high. Man! Restraining thyself (from the outward world) 'thou will get free from pain'. Man! Understand well the truth! Exerting himself in the rule of truth a wise man overcomes Mara.[40]

Thus, the first step towards liberation is the realization that the individual is his own enemy since he ignores the demands of his soul and indulges in worldly pleasures. This realization must persuade the individual to desist from serving his desires, to turn his back on the world, and seek actively to purify his soul. The soul can be purified when the individual, committed to crossing the miseries of *samsara,* engages in stopping the further influx of karmic matter and expelling its past accumulation. The process of stopping the further accumulation of karmic matter is called *samvara.* This means not only self-discipline in the two-fold sense of turning one's back on the world and a firm resolve and appropriate action matching this resolve not to seek again the pleasures of this world. But this is not enough for crossing the miseries of the world. What is also needed is the process of *nijjara*, that is, self-mortification. This means that "one should mortify (one's flesh) in a low, high and highest degree, quitting one's former connections, and entering tranquility".[41] Thus, as Pande notes, "the three planks of the early Jaina view ... are the conception of an immaculate spiritual substance, of a material principle of defilement and of an ascetic process of purification. All three are interwoven in the close synthesis of a theory of *samsara.*"[42]

Needless to say that Jainism posits the ideal of the hero who conquers himself and, through it, the world. "He who conquers many conquers one. Knowing the misery of the world, the heroes go on the great journey; they rise gradually; they do not desire life."[43] Or, again, "carefully abstaining form pleasures and ceasing from bad works he is a hero, guarding himself, who is grounded in knowledge."[44] To become a hero is to be dead not only to one's lower nature but also to the world. But this death does not come all at once; it is supposed to occur gradually. Jainism identifies 14 *gunasthanas* (stages of quality) delineating how the individual can proceed gradually through a series of levels to final deliverance.[45] The point of departure for this deliverance is, of course, the state of ignorance and superstition of the initiate. But the individual progresses towards liberation through a harsh regime of austerity, meditation and suppression of passions. Given the perseverance, the initiate transforms himself into a complete ascetic. He becomes a sage,

> who correctly possesses these (sensual) perceptions, viz., sounds and colours, and smells and tastes, and touches, who self-possessed, wise, just and chaste with right comprehension understands the world ... one who knows the law, and (is) righteous. He knows the connection of whirl (of births) and the current (of sensations with love and hate). Not minding heat and cold, equanimous against pleasure and pain, the Nirgrantha does not feel the austerity of penance. Waking and free from hostility, a wise man, thou liberatest (thyself and others) from the miseries.[46]

Such a sage is really a hero who, "examining karman and the root of karman, viz., killing, examining (it) and adopting its contrary, he is not seen by both ends. Knowing this, a wise man who knows the world, and has cast off the idea of the world, should prudently conquer the obstructions to righteousness."[47]

When a man achieves liberation, he becomes enlightened signifying that he has now the true understanding of the world, the self and others. This understanding manifests itself in non-violence because it engenders the awareness that all living creatures, like oneself, do not wish to suffer in any way.[48] In other words, this understanding, since it is based on the recognition of the spiritual nature of the self, leads one to the search for freedom. This, in turn, prompts the individual to discipline himself by exercising full control over his passions. This discipline yields the further recognition of spiritual equality of all beings (*atma-tula*) and it, therefore, leads to the practice of *ahimsa*. *Ahimsa,* for the Jainas, constitutes the ideal that every man should adopt and practice; it is, thus, the source of the principle that must guide the conduct of every man and which, when acted upon, makes it possible for the society to become a moral association in the true sense of the term. It is, again, this understanding that installs *dharma* as the true ruler of man and society. *Dharma,* in the Jaina view, is different from the Vedic conception that treats *dharma* as the command of the Veda; instead, it is virtue "grounded in the spiritual nature of man".[49] But since the spiritual nature of man tends to get befogged, it is the purpose of *dharma* to clear the fog of ignorance. *Dharma,* in the sense of "that which carries", provides the support and creates conditions for the soul to retain its natural state.

At the root of the Jaina world view are, thus, three basic conceptions that distinguish Jainism from other world views. These are: *Atmavada, Lokavada* and *Kriyavada.* What these concepts refer to is that man is pure spirituality. He is surrounded by a world of material bodies inhabited by souls of different grades of perfection and imperfection. He, however, gets enmeshed in materiality when he acts under the sway of his worldly desires. As a result, his soul gets engulfed in the influx of *kamma* and loses its omniscience. Bereft of the right perspective on life, the individual engages in actions that harm him as well as the world surrounding him insofar as he exploits the world for his own benefit. This further degrades his soul, causes injury to the *loka*, and further enmeshes him in the mire of materiality. He is, however, endowed with freedom of action and he can, if he so chooses, utilize his freedom and extricate himself from this mire and can, with the help of right *kriya* (action), regain the primordial purity of his soul. Once he does do so, he treats everything as *atma-tula* and ceases to do violence and injure others. The practice of non-violence installs *dharma* as the real ruler who then supports and sustains good governance.

For Jainism, then, it is the spiritual reawakening of man that holds society together, preserves social order and makes the political order just and benign and capable of sustaining a moral order. Buddhism, too, calls for such a reawakening, although it takes a somewhat different metaphysical path and differs in certain essential details from Jainism. The point of departure for such a spiritual reawakening, for Buddhism, is the world of becoming as a source of *dukkha*. To say that there is the world of becoming is also to say that there is something that becomes. And if there is nothing apart from that which is pure becoming, there is, then, no question of crossing the sea of becoming. By the same token, it is futile to seek to become something that does not become, does not change, and is not transient. The King of Whirl does not tolerate any other king who can replace him. As such, there is no escape from the world of becoming and, therefore, from suffering.

But this is not what Buddhism signifies. Buddhism associates the phenomenon of becoming with the self (*atta, sambhava*), that is, the sense of "I", the psycho-physical individuality. But what is this psycho-physical individuality called the self, the Ego-consciousness? It is true that, for all practical purposes, people, engaged in managing their pragmatic affairs, do identify themselves as the doer of things or have to bear the consequences of their actions. In all this, they are conscious of their agency and the sense of "I-ness". Endowed with this sense, they are also concerned with the movement of Time insofar as it affects their worldly condition. But do they know what they mean by the notion of the "I"?[50] What men call their psycho-physical body is only short-lived; it is mortal. "Brief is man's life, a trifle, fleeting, with many an ill … . (It is) like a cow about to be slaughtered, whose every step brings her nearer to death … ."[51] The body, which receives so much attention from its owner, is impermanent and what is impermanent is "painful, liable to change". As such, "… whatever is body that is past, future, present, subjective or objective, gross or subtle, low or excellent, far or near – all body should be viewed, with right wisdom, as it has come to be thus: This is not mine, this am I not, this is not my Self".[52]

In short, whatever takes a "material shape is impermanent, that is suffering. What is suffering is not the Self. What is not Self, that is not mine, that am I not, that is not my Self".[53] Attachment to the impermanent self is the source of *dukkha*. "Evil is done by the self, by the self one comes to grief."[54] It is this attachment that is, according to Buddhism, the source of becoming and, therefore, *dukkha*. The source of *dukkha* is the corruptibility of all things born, composite and mutable, their liability to suffering, disease, decay and death. They corrupt by drawing men into the vortex of becoming (*bhava-cakka, samsara)* and arousing in them desires for worldly pleasures. These desires are not only endless and insatiable but also irrepressible and rebellious. The turmoil of desires sets all sensations, all sensibilia (for example, the tongue and its tastes, the mind and its thoughts) on fire – the fire of appetite, resentment, and delusion (*rago, doso, moho)*, birth, ageing, death and sorrow.[55]

When the senses catch fire, the process of becoming (*bhava*) takes hold of empirical individuality (*atta-sambhava),* the self. And, the self encircled by the fire of the senses is always harassed by the presence of the phenomenon of wanting (*tanha,* thirst). But it is not possible to quench this thirst, because it produces indetermination (*anicca)*, *dukkha,* and *anatta* (self-forgetfulness, un-self-isness). Self-forgetfulness is indicative of the fact that man, caught in the vortex of becoming, chooses mortality instead of immortality. And, as long as he prefers mortality, frustration, misery and unhappiness continue to haunt him all through his life. That is why he is called upon to awaken to the perils of the senses on fire and seek immortality by self-consciously impugning the life of appetites. For this, it is necessary to recognize that man has to set out in earnest to overcome his worst enemy, that is, his own self, and make it a servant and ally than his master. The first step towards this is to recognize and acknowledge the predicament that confronts every man. This means that one has to know the appetitive congeries for what they are and learn to distinguish one's Self and its interests from the Ego, that is, his self and its interests.[56]

In order to put an end to his suffering, the individual needs to understand and eradicate the causes of becoming. This understanding brings home the realization that the fires of ego-consciousness are those of *raga, dosa* and *moha* and they can be quenched only by practicing their opposites.[57] This calls for the practice of opposite virtues and the acquisition of right knowledge (*vijja*). It is, as a consequence of the knowledge and the practice of the opposite virtues that the fires of ego-consciousness are quenched and the individual attains liberation (*nibbana*). To attain *nibbana* is to tame the self; to tame the self is to stir up unsluggish energy that calls up un-muddled mindfulness, becalms the body and guards the pure Self.[58] But this becalming of the body is possible only when it is admitted that "the Self is the lord of the self, for what other lord could there be?"[59] As such, the self must be restrained by the Self.[60]

The individual who cultivates his Self for conquering his self is a person who swims against the current. And swimming against the current, his mind is "fired by the desire of the Untold (*anakkhata*)" and is, consequently, freed from love and hate.[61] But the knowledge which stimulates the individual to seek the Untold cannot be communicated.[62] Every one has to carve out the path of this own liberation. It is true that the Buddha does point the way and enunciate the *dhamma* that should guide the seeker in his search for liberation. However, "the Buddhas do but tell the way, it is for you to swelter at the task".[63] In this sweltering, it is faith in the *magga* (the way) shown by the Buddha that sustains the seeker and finally conduces to knowledge[64] insofar as it implies authority, that is, Buddha's authority resting upon his own spiritual experience and the words spoken by him.

Liberation in the Buddhist perspective is thus a moral discipline requiring the taming of the self by cultivating the Self. This means blocking the process of becoming (*bhava*) that has its origin in wanting (*tanha*) and its location in the psycho-physical individuality, the self. To block and reverse this process requires the individual to cast the anchor of his self, floating in the sea of suffering, in the Self.

As is evident from the above account, both Jainism and Buddhism underline the corruptibility of man in a corrupt world caused by self-forgetfulness that unleashes man's appetites from the discipline of morality. As a consequence, man comes under the sway of his lower nature, associated with the psycho-physical individuality and has, therefore, to undergo suffering and misery. This has certain ramifications for the public order too. Thus, the standard of the good differs from person to person indicating not only that there is a lack of consensus about the good that is common for all; it is rather each person who decides. It is this human condition that makes the creation of the state inevitable in the first place. It is also the continuation of this condition over time that makes it necessary to keep the political order above the conflicts of particular interests and protect and defend its integrity against interested attacks. Again, it is this that makes it necessary that the state should function in a way that reflects its groundedness in certain moral principles. It is against this background that both Jainism and Buddhism articulate their thinking on political order. It is, again, against this background that their search for the common good transcending various conceptions of individual goods can be appreciated. And, the common good that they identify is the good of the soul. It is this good that liberates the individual from the depredations of his passions and upholds the public order and keeps it attuned to moral imperatives.

It is true that the good of the soul, when pursued actively, liberates the individual from the bondage of his passions and restores order in the soul and, through it, in the individual as a psycho-physical entity. The order of the soul, then, ensures order in society. This, in its own turn, restrains temporal power and its drive towards auto-telism and self-aggrandizement. The rule of *dharma* disciplines the rule by the king in his ruling and keeps him disciplined, virtuous, and just. But just as the pleasure of the body, the good of the soul, too, is something that cannot be shared by others. Nor is it a good that can be acquired by all; only a few can ever hope to acquire it and hope to cross the sea of suffering, and attune their soul to the divine ground of being. But the trouble is that those who have succeeded in obtaining the good of the soul prefer to live in the pure realm of the spirit and decline to have anything to do with the affairs of the mortals.[65] Thus, a spiritually arrived person, that is, the Enlightened One, tends to dichotomize the world between sacred and profane; the former he prefers because of his exclusive concern with immortality and the latter he abhors and condemns because it tends to overlook, even ignore, the question of the purity of ends and means. He, therefore, prefers to replace prudence by morality. Or, alternatively, if this replacement proves difficult to attain, he insists on fully informing prudence by morality.

The need to harmonize prudence and virtue is a pointer to the fact that, since man is a combination of both spirituality and materiality, both of these must also be harmonized so that man's well-being can be ensured. As Dobbs puts it, since human condition is twofold in nature,

> a pair of requisites must be satisfied for a human being to know himself: each of us must acknowledge the gulf separating himself from the divine and, at the same time, honour his own capacity for divine intelligence by developing it to the highest peak of excellence. Such self-knowledge would expose the mortification of ascetics and the pride of intellectuals as inadequate and merely piece-meal responses to the human condition. For what the human condition calls for is both reverential and intellectual endeavour, not merely severally or alternatively but at the same time.[66]

How do Jainism and Buddhism reconcile the diverse demands of the two worlds, the world of the soul and that of the body? Can the dilemmas arising out of the claims of these worlds be satisfactorily resolved? Can the political order be able to function righteously, or, at least, effectively, if it relied totally on the otherworldly teachings of Jainism and Buddhism? What answers can we expect from them to these questions? Jainism, for instance, claims to be a body of knowledge that is grounded in the authoritative insights of Ford-makers, insights they acquired through the experience of transcendence. This knowledge, it is claimed, facilitates reorientation of a person's attitude towards oneself and the world. However, the path Jainism envisages cannot be followed by householders as they must engage in violent actions and are in thrall to the whirlpool of the senses.[67] Freedom from action is only for the homeless mendicant and the ascetic. Only they can acquire the right mental stance towards the world. But to become a homeless monk requires fortitude in the face of great difficulties,[68] which householders lack. That is why the householder's life is stigmatized as worthless and dangerous.[69] The ideal is, therefore, the difficult but noble life of the ascetic; it is this life that alone can lead to liberation.[70]

Jainism would like every householder to become an ascetic. But, then, no body will be left to cater to the needs of the ascetic. Apart from this, certain metaphysical assumptions integral to Jainism preclude the possibility of everyone becoming a monk. Although *jivas* (life forms) are fully and equally endowed with the qualities of bliss, energy and omniscience, two factors make the embodied *jivas* unequal in qualities and highly differentiated in status. First, owing to the operation of *karma*, *jivas* become variously embodied. Second, not only the *jivas* form two classes; *sthavara* (stationary) and *trasa* (moving), they are also graded in a hierarchy depending on the number of senses they possess. As a result, receptivity to spiritual experience or the capacity of grasping the significance of the received Word greatly varies. As such, only a few can become spiritually reawakened. This blocks the emergence of society as a moral association and makes the state inevitable for maintaining the integrity of the social order.

It is true that Jainism and Buddhism require the ruler to follow *dharma* in performing his kingly duties. But since enlightened persons keep themselves away from the affairs of the mortals, only a spiritually imperfect person will become a king. But, then, he will be as prone to the allurements of the world as any ordinary person. What is there, then, to keep him steadfast on the path of virtue and prevent him from being moved in the performance of his duties by anything else than his conviction of the spiritual values of Jainism?[71] Perhaps the Word of the Ford-makers is expected to retain its originality! However, it is very difficult to see that, while the words of the Vedic seers get distorted in the stream of history, as Jainism claims, how the words of Ford-makers can remain immune to the ebb and flow of time! Moreover, given the unequal endowment of receptive as well as retentive capacity and differences in layman's attitude and approaches to life, the Word does not carry equal weight for all.

Two other factors should also be noted here. First, while the lay community is necessary for the consolidation and expansion of Jainism, and for the sustenance of the Jaina monks, laymen are exhorted to conquer their passions by withdrawing from the world of the senses and abstain from violence and possessions. In the hope that the layman would finally leave the world and become an ascetic, Jainism formulates an idealized course of the layman's life into 11 stages called *pratima*. It stipulates that the layman will progressively abandon worldly needs and, finally, after leaving his household, devote himself completely and whole-heartedly to the search for his liberation. However, this ideal became completely otiose over time. This is reflected in the downgrading of the ideal of *upasaka* to *shravaka*.[72] Moreover, as Dundas points out:

> What is important in Jain lay behaviour is not precise conformity to a canonical pattern of religiosity ... but the manifestation of pious

> intentions and correct ethical dispositions through public participation in religious ceremonies, worship and community affairs, the enhancement of oneself and one's fellow Jains through religious gifting and the correctness of one's business affairs and family alliances.[73]

But even this proves difficult to attain in a society that, in the Jaina perspective, is corrupt and corrupting. And since it is not possible for the Jainas to live in isolation from the non-Jainas, it is most likely that they too would not remain untouched by the corruption pervading the surrounding society.

More or less all this applies also to Buddhism and its ideas pertaining to temporal power. Buddhism underlines the fact that all existence, both individual and collective, is imperfect. Thus, any society or group, including the Sangha itself, is subject to change (*anicca, anitya*), and conditioned (*dukkha*) by many interdependent factors (*samudaya*).[74] Thus, corruption is inevitable. However, Buddhism believes that corruption can be arrested if the king is guided by *Dhamma* as taught by the Sangha. Thus, as Grimm points out, " the status and the welfare of the king, of society and of the Buddha *sasana* are correlated and interdependent; they need each other for stability."[75] This means that the weakness of any of the links in this chain of interdependence caused by a fall in the high standard of conduct is sure to drag the political order in the mire of corruption and degeneration. This degeneration is bound to be very fast in the absence of a well-ordered social universe.

Thus, both Jainism and Buddhism do stress the need of a good and just king. They, however, insist that a king to be good must mould his conduct according to the tenets peculiar to each of them. But, apart from positing the ideal of good king and a good social order, they do not suggest the ways and means of reconciling the claims of the body and the soul nor of prudence and morality. In view of this, it is necessary to examine the Vedic perspective on political order.

Notes

1. See J.L. Mehta, *Philosophy and Religion: Essays in Interpretation* (New Delhi: ICPR, 1990), pp. 278–79.
2. G. Tucci, *The Theory and Practice of Mandala* (London: Rider and Co., 1974), p. 12.
3. J.L. Mehta, op. cit.
4. Ibid., p. 279.

5. It must be emphasized that an irreconcilable opposition between body and soul has been posited in Western thought since Pythagoras. The body is supposed to be the prison-house of the soul and the soul can attain its purity and divinity only by escaping from the body. See Werner Jaeger, *Paideia,* op. cit.
6. G. Tucci, op. cit., p. 9.
7. This is symbolized in the Vedic perspective by three terms, "*aham*", "*ayam*" and "*om*". *Aham* symbolizes the ego principle, equivalent to Maritain's concept of individual. *Aham* has to be transformed into *ayam*, that is, a person's identification with the cosmos, which becomes possible only through the attunement of the soul to the divine ground of being (*om*).
8. A.J. Heschel, *Who is Man?* (Stanford: Stanford University Press, 1965), p. 48.
9. John H. Schaar, *Escape from Authority: Perspectives on Eric Fromm* (New York: Basic Books, 1961), p. 296.
10. G.C. Pande, *Jain Political Thought* (Jaipur: Prakrit Bharati Sansthan, Centre for Jain Studies, University of Rajasthan, 1984), p. 5.
11. For other vital differences between the Vedic and the Jaina thinking, see, Pande, op. cit., pp. 1–20.
12. Max Muller, ed., *Sacred Books of the East, Jain Sutras,* tr. Herman Jacobi (Oxford: Clarendon Press, 1895), Vol. XLV, Part II, pp. 35–46.
13. G.C. Pande, op. cit., pp. 23–24.
14. It is the equality of spiritual person that constitutes the basis of *ahimsa* (non-violence).
15. G.C. Pande, op. cit., p. 31.
16. Acharya Jinasena, *Adipurana,* tr. and edited by Pt. Pannalal Jain (Varanasi: Bharatiya Jnanapitha, 1944), vol. I, ch. 3, *shloka* 2 (I.III.2).
17. Ibid., I.III.14.
18. G.C. Pande, op. cit., p. 33.
19. This account is available in *Mahavastu*, tr. J.J. Jones (London: Luzac & Co., 1949) vol.1, pp. 285–301.
20. Ibid., p. 292. It is interesting to note that U.N. Ghoshal and others including Drekemeier superimpose on this myth a modern view on the origin of the state by arguing that the Buddhist story of genesis refers to a state of nature out of which emerged the state through a contract between the people and the king. See Ghoshal, *A History of Indian Political Ideas* (London: Oxford University Press, 1966), p. 64; Charles Drekemeier, *Kingship and Community in Early India* (Bombay: Oxford University Press, 1962), pp. 104, 109. That this superimposition is unwarranted is indicated by the fact that the state of nature that Hobbes, Locke

and Rousseau describe is, for one reason or the other, not a fully ordered and, therefore, completed state. It is incomplete because in this state life is "short, nasty and brutish" or property is not safe or reason is lacking. But none of these features applies to the pure and pristine, fully moral society. Moreover, what the story of genesis describes is not the actual state of affairs but a paradigmatic one. As such, Mahasammata is no contract in the sense in which Hobbes, Locke and Rousseau mean it

21. *The Jataka or Stories of the Buddha's Former Births*, ed. E.B. Cowell (London: Luzac & Co., 1957) have been used here.
22. Ibid., p. 125.
23. Roberto M. Unger, *Knowledge and Politics* (New York: The Free Press, 1975), p. 73.
24. Jassay, op. cit.
25. *Avatar* can be both *purna avatar* (full incarnation) in which the whole of the God incarnates according to the need of the time, or it can only be *anshik avatar* (partial incarnation) in which only a part of the deity incarnates. See, Prashanta Miranda, *Avatar and Incarnation: A Comparative Study* (New Delhi: Herman Publishing House, 1990).
26. Pande, *Jain Political Thought,* op. cit., p. 110.
27. That the Jainas believe in the existence of the soul is beyond doubt. But this is not so in the case of the Buddhism. It is argued by many that Buddhism denies not only the self but also the Self. This denial is, to say the least, simple-minded. Note, for example, that one cannot be selfless without having a self. As Edward Conze admits, "the doctrine of *anatta* is very deep. One assumes that it will need more than one life-time to get to the bottom of it" (see *Buddhism: The Essence and Development*, New York: Harper Torchbooks, 1959, p. 19). The Buddhist doctrine of *nibbana* (liberation) is akin to Meister Eckhart's saying, "The kingdom of God is for none but the thoroughly dead." And, as Ananda Coomaraswamy notes, "*Nirvana* is death, a being finished (both in the meaning of ended and of perfected)." *Buddhism: Its Essence and Development* (Bombay: Jaico Publishing House, 1958), p. 28. The means employed to get *nibbana* are not themselves *nibbana*, they aim at removing all that obscures the visions of *nibbana*. The means are directed towards taming conquering, curbing, and rejecting the self (*atta*) and making it quiet. Thus, for Buddhism, the Arhant is "one whose self has been cast off (*atta-jaha*); his burden has been laid down (*atta-bharo)*, what there was to be done has been done (*katham-karaniyam*) (ibid.). What needs to be stressed here is the fact that Buddhism does talk of the distinction between the Great Self (*mahatman*) and the little self (*alpatman*). As *Dhammapada, 160* points out, *atta hi attano natho* (The Self alone is the lord of the self) and, again, at 380: *atta hi attano gati* (The Self alone is the destiny of the self). Thus, Buddhism recognizes many selves and only one Self. That is why it insists that it is

One that many are to find. Cf. "He who conquers One, conquers many; and he who conquers many, conquers One." *Jaina Sutras,* tr. Herman Jacobi (New Delhi: Motilal Banarsidass, 1964), Part I, *The Akaranaga Sutra, The Kalpa Sutra,* Vol. XXII of *The Sacred Books of the East.*

28. G.C. Pande, *Studies in the Origin of Buddhism* (Allahabad: University of Allahabad, 1957), p. 356. Buddhaghosa notes that the Nirgranthas regarded the soul as *arupi. Sumangalavilasini I*: 119. Cf. "It does not have a body, is not born again, has no attachment and is without sexual gender. While having knowledge and sentience, there is nonetheless nothing with which it can be compared. Its being is without form, there is no condition of unconditioned." *Jaina Sutras,* op. cit., p. 52.
29. Akalanka, *Tattvarthavarttika*, quoted in Paul Dundas, *The Jains* (London: Routledge, 1992), p. 83.
30. Paul Dundas, op. cit., p. 86.
31. *Jaina Sutras,* tr. Herman Jacobi, op. cit., p. 37.
32. Ibid., p. 24.
33. Ibid., p. 28.
34. Ibid., p. 53.
35. A person who is sunk in the whirlpool of the senses "destroys this (earth body) by bad and injurious doings, and many other beings besides, which he hurts by means of earth, through his doing acts relating to earth". Ibid., p. 4.
36. G.C. Pande, *Jain Political Thought* , op. cit., p. 35.
37. Loc. cit.
38. G.C. Shrivarya, *Bhagavati Aradhana,* p. 1616, quoted in Paul Dundas, op. cit., p. 83.
39. G.C. Pande, *Studies in the Origin of Buddhism,* op. cit., p. 357.
40. *Jaina Sutras,* tr. Herman Jacobi, op. cit., p. 33.
41. Ibid., p. 40. Self-mortification, it must be stressed, is aimed primarily at suppressing wrath. As *Jaina Sutra* (p. 34) puts it:

    He who knows wrath, knows pride; he who knows pride, knows deceit; he who knows deceit, knows greed; he who knows greed, knows love; he who knows love, knows hate; he who knows hate, knows delusion; he who knows delusion, knows conception; he who knows conception, knows birth; he who knows birth, knows death; he who knows death, knows hell; he who knows hell, knows animal existence; he who knows existence, knows pain.

    Since wrath is symptomatic of self-adulation, freedom from it lies in self-abnegation which is not possible without, Jainism emphasizes, self-mortification to the extent that the individual becomes dead to the world and what it signifies.

42. G.C. Pande, op. cit., p. 367.
43. *Jaina Sutras,* tr. Herman Jacobi, op. cit., p. 28.
44. Ibid., p. 29.
45. For the list of *gunasthana*, see Padmabh S. Jaini, *The Jaina Path of Purification* (Berkeley: University of California Press, 1979), pp. 272–73.
46. *Jaina Sutras,* tr. Herman Jacobi, op. cit., p. 28.
47. Ibid., p. 29.
48. *Sutrakritangasutram* in Muni Jambuvijaya, ed. *Acharangasutram and Sutrkritangam* (Delhi: Agamodaya Samiti, 1978), 2.11.9–10.
49. G.C. Pande, *Jain Political Thought*, op. cit., p. 23.
50. *Digha-Nikaya,* I:202; *Samyutta-Nikaya* I:14–15.
51. *Anguttara-Nikay, IV:* 137.
52. Vinaya-Pitaka, I:13; *Samyutta-Nikaya,* III: 66ff.
53. *Samyutta-Nikaya,* III:44–45; *Majjhima-Nikkaya,* III:1190.
54. *Dhammapada,* 165, 161.
55. *"Sermon on Fire".*
56. Ananda Coomaraswamy, *The Living Thoughts of Gotama the Buddha* (Delhi: Munshiram Manoharlal, 1982), p. 29.
57. *Anguttara-Nikaya,* IV:445; *Dhammapada,* 5,223.
58. Ibid., I: 261.
59. *Dhammapada,* 160.
60. Ibid., 379, 380.
61. Ibid., 218.
62. *Anguttara-Nikaya,* III:444.
63. *Dhammapada,* 276
64. *Samyutta-Nikaya,* IV:298.
65. Cf. Plato, *Republic,* 515c7–9.
66. Darrell Dobbs, "The Piety of Thought in Plato's *Republic,* Book I", *American Political Science Review,* 88, 3 (September 1994), p. 670.
67. *Jaina Sutras,* tr. Herman Jacobi, op. cit., I.I.5.1–3.
68. *Sutrakritangasutram,* I.14.
69. It is interesting to note that Haribhadra is very critical of the laity insofar as even a religiously minded lay person continually experiences the pull of familial and social ties; he is like a turtle which rises up from the depths of the ocean to a glimpse of the sky, only to sink down again. See *Commentary on Bhadrabahu's Avashyakaniryukti* (Bombay: Agamodaya Samiti, 1981), p. 97.
70. Paul Dundas, op. cit., p. 38.

71. That the householders are indispensable for the life of the community of Jaina ascetics is reflected in the concept of *chaturvidhasangha* (fourfold assembly) incorporating almsgiving supporters, laymen and laywomen, monks and nuns.
72. Conze raises this and other such questions about Buddhism regarding its approach to the question of temporal power, op. cit., pp. 72–77.
73. See Paul Dundas, op. cit., pp. 161–62. Etymologically, *shravaka* is the one who attains (*shri*) faith in the Jaina doctrines, sows (*va*) wealth unceasingly upon appropriate objects and makes (*ka*) merit by serving good monks.
74. Ibid., p. 165.
75. George Grimm, *Buddhist Wisdom: Mystery of the Self* (Delhi: Motilal Banarsidass, 1978), p. 23.

7

Man, Cosmos and Political Order

The quest for liberation must, it is true, be pursued in the world of here and now, in the world characterized largely by the concerns of everyday life. This fact is important not only because the world is necessary for the sustenance of the *sadhaka* or the individual *shramana;* it is also necessary for the community of *shramanas.* This quest is also important insofar as it points to the attitude one has towards the world and the network of social relations it incorporates. Liberation does not only mean liberation from one's base appetites, desires and passions; it also means complete withdrawal from or the cessation of all activities one has to engage into in the world of everydayness. Complete detachment from the world may be the end-result of the quest of liberation. But it is not inconceivable that the quest for liberation may be triggered off by an attitude that considers the world as corrupt and corrupting, diverting and waylaying the journeying self from its true vocation, that is, the care of the divine in man. This attitude, it must be added, reflects a particular view of the role of man in the world of everydayness, a view that gives primacy to the Self and its welfare as against the environment – physical, social, etc., in which the individual is located.

Thus, the quest for liberation may be grounded in two mutually contradictory perspectives. These perspectives present cosmic (*saprapancha*) and acosmic (*nisparapancha*) views of reality. The cosmic (*saprapancha)* view of reality, as does the acosmic (*nisprapancha)* view, underlines the need to realize the supreme end of life, that is, release from *samsara* (cycle of birth and death). However, there is a fundamental difference between the two. The cosmic view treats the *samsara* as the emanation of the Absolute. It is the Absolute that is real; it is the one and the only substance out of which the many modes of constituting the world have come forth. It is because of this that the world, too, is considered to be sacred and, therefore, real. And, since the world is sacred and real, it as well as human existence in it must be taken seriously. In contradistinction to this, the acosmic view of reality "regards the Absolute as the distinctionless substrate wherefrom the illusory world-show appears ..."[1] And, since the world is simply a shadow, it is unreal and, therefore, something that constitutes obstacles in the path of liberation, if it is not downright profane; its concerns, too, are polluting; they divert man from his true vocation, that is, liberation.

Needless to say that whether one gives allegiance to the cosmic or the acosmic view of reality, it makes a lot of difference insofar as the world and the management of worldly affairs, including political life and relations, are concerned. Since the acosmic view of reality considers the world as unreal, corrupt and corrupting, the world and all that it signifies are to be shunned, if one is to get release from *samsara*. And, since one cannot escape from the world, its concerns and affairs are to be tolerated without entangling oneself in them or being intimate with them. Thus, the world is recognized to be out there; it cannot be wished away. One can only try to protect oneself from its bewitching allurements, its not-easy-to-identify traps and its deceptive concerns, so that the real vocation of man, that is, liberation, can receive proper attention.

But, while the world has the tendency to take one's mind away from one's real vocation, it is completely worthless and useless. Its usefulness can be justified on two important grounds. In the first place, the world needs to be won over to the ways of saintly life. In order for the way to prevail and influence profoundly the ways of the world, the world needs to be converted to the way. In the second place, as long as the way does not prevail fully and totally, it needs those who take upon themselves to spread the word and to inspire people to embrace the way. And, these people need the support of the world to meet their existential needs of food, shelter, etc. As such, the world is necessary because it supports the community of the mendicants. But for all that, it is the lowest on the scale of valuation. It is already dead to those who have attained liberation. But even for those who are forced to live in it or cannot leave it, it is expected that they too would get away from it as soon as possible. And, as long as they have to live in it, they would tolerate it.

It is this perspective that informs the attitude of both Jainism and Buddhism as it concerns the world and its affairs. As we have already seen, both of them recognize that man's nature is bivalent; that is, implanted in man's breast are two divergent tendencies, one of which impels him to seek the pleasures of the body and, as a consequence, get immersed in materiality and suffer *dukkha* as well as cause *dukkha* to others. The other tendency prompts him to turn inward and explore the divine in him and yoke the ship of his life to the firm and spiritually elevating anchor of the divine ground of being. But man has the choice to seek either the pleasures of the body or to work for the enrichment of his soul. The acosmic view of reality, as reflected in Jainism and Buddhism, does not see the possibility of pursuing both at one and the same time. Each of them considers these two ends of life to be polar opposites, each of them going its own different way. Both Jainism and Buddhism treat these two as oriented to mutually contradictory ends of life with their respective impulse located in different parts of man, that is, body and soul.

The opposition between the pleasures of the body and the good of the soul is the result of the perceived difference between the role the two play. The body is supposed to be the locus of base desires, while the soul, as the sensorium of the divine, is the proper instrument of cultivating the divine in man. Jainism does not accept the existence of God and Buddhism is prudently silent about it. However, both of them recognize that it is only the soul, or the Self, that, when liberated from the rule of the senses and allowed to regain its purity, can earn for man his release from the world. This, in itself, is enough to indicate the downgrading of the cosmos to merely a physical world.[2] And since man's primary responsibility is the care of the soul, and since he cannot discharge this responsibility without withdrawing fully from the world of the senses, it follows that the phenomenal world is a place which not only lacks divine values but is also possessed of certain qualities of its own, qualities that not only reflect the autonomy of the world but are also antagonistic to the ways of the God. It is in this sense that the world becomes auto-telic and traps man in the net of worldly pleasures. As Jonas puts it:

> The withdrawal of the divine from the cosmos leaves the latter not as a neutral value-indifferent, merely physical fact but as a separatistic power whose very self-positing outside God betrays a direction of will. Thus the darkness of the world denotes not only its being alien to God

> and devoid of his light, but also its being a *force* alienating from God, so God is that which alienates and liberates from the world.[3]

Since the world is alienating, it also follows that man must, in his endeavour to realize the divine in him, cross all barriers that intervene between him as a psycho-physical entity and his divinity. It is only then that he can establish a direct relationship between himself and his coveted divinity. He must, therefore, jump over these barriers, i.e., personal, familial, social ties that bind him to this world. Thus, the necessary concomitant of the spiritual journey is the denial of the intervening social realities associated with a variety of social connections, ties and obligations. As such, the regaining of the purity of the soul means "jumping across all intervening realities, which, for direct relationship, are nothing but fetters and obstacles, or disturbing temptations, or at best, irrelevant."[4]

This means that when liberation becomes the primary aim of life, that is, the exclusive concern for regaining the divinity of the soul, the intervening realities are, so to say, "denatured"; as a result, the surpassing interest in liberation takes the heart out of worldly concerns even when they become unavoidable. When the worldly concerns are looked at from the distance of the beyond, the psycho-physical individuality, too, is viewed with suspicion and distrust insofar as it is this component in man's being that is supposed to be dragging him into the mire of materiality. It is so for the simple reason that the forces alienating man is thought to be located in his own interior; it is these forces that weave snares around him and drag him into these snares. That is why, a man who has fixed his gaze on liberation must look at these forces with suspicion, attribute to them all the demonic trickery in the world and fear them as something that betrays him into bondage of his appetites. It is, therefore, not surprising that the psycho-physical individuality is supposed to be incapable of being elevated to the condition of purity and, therefore, made worthy of becoming the true vessel of divinity. It must, therefore, either be left to the free play of its own interior forces and appetites, or be reduced to zero by mortification. But since to leave it to the free play of its own interior forces is alienation from and rebellion against the God, only the second alternative can be pursued. This is true especially of Jainism.

In short, the psychological consequences of a perspective that gives exclusive importance to liberation are highly upsetting and pessimistic. Liberation is the highest value; it must be pursued with determination; to pursue it and seek to realize it in one's life is extremely difficult; and to slacken in it is to suffer the pangs of guilt. But the pursuit of this highest value is not possible for all. This is so not only because of the lack of proper inclination, not also because of the difficulty involved in it, but also because a large number of persons are so deeply enmeshed in the world and its affairs that they cannot even think of turning their back on the world, because of their inability to do so as well as their commitment to it. But to remain in the world and be greatly interested and enmeshed in its concerns while all the time being painfully aware of the need to seek one's own liberation is to suffer the pangs of guilt and become indifferent to the worldly concerns. The upshot is that the world must be left if one is to earn liberation; but since liberation eludes a large number of persons, those, who are unable to work for it, must play their role in the world of here and now. But this situation requires that everyone must go on playing his role without either even thinking why he must play the role he has been saddled with by fate or society or trying to find out whether his role playing has any genuine relevance to the outcome which is not of his making alone.

It is against this background that we can understand and appreciate why the ontological premises underlying the Jaina and Buddhist thinking cannot provide a reliable basis for political order for it to perform its expected role. For the journeying selves, the world has no real significance except for the fact that it constitutes an arena where the individual can try to wipe up the consequences of accumulated *karma* so that the path of his *nirvana* gets unblocked. Thus, the world of here and now has only an instrumental value for the journeying self in the sense that, without it the exhaustion of the accumulated karmic fruits cannot be guaranteed; nor can any effort towards this is possible without receiving support and succour from it. This is symptomatic of the fact that the world is not valued for its own sake, for its significance as what it is and what it implies. The divine is not an integral part of the world. Devoid as it is of the divine essence, it is prone to corruption as well as to corrupting all that it contains. It is because of this that it becomes necessary to snap all worldly relations that involve man in *kamma* and become the cause of his corruption. Liberation can, therefore, be achieved only through renunciation. As such, renunciation is a primary value for both Jainism and Buddhism.

The de-divinization of the world in itself is indicative of the disruption of its organic unity with the divine source of beings.

Drained of its divine quality, the world exists by itself and stands on its own; it has its own inherent order, an order that does not help in working for liberation; it only binds. It is true that the world may be conceived of as a link in a chain of *lokas*. But these *lokas* do not represent any ensemble of possibilities waiting to fructify; they are usually conceived simply as locations where *jivas,* differentiated on the basis of virtuous attainments, take abode after their earthly sojourn. It is true that it is the only world as we know it that is the arena of *karma* but it is not by any means the source of value or the protector of morality. Cultivation of virtue in the world becomes possible only after a person has been convinced of the utter futility of earthly existence, an existence that effectively blocks the way to liberation. This conviction is possible either through experience or *upadesha* (instruction). However, *upadesha* is not a reliable source of *upashrama* (ceasure from action that binds). But experience means that one must live the life of a householder and, therefore, engage in action, and, perhaps, get lost in the world. The householders are, of course, expected to practice detachment. However, again, the weakness of the word against experience becomes obvious. As such, something mightier than the word, something that enleavens the word and makes it potent and, therefore, efficacious, is necessary.

It is against this background that we can appreciate the need to restore to the world its organic unity with the divine and treat it as a cosmos. It is, again, in this context that the world needs to be redivinized, on the one hand, by treating it as a link, albeit an important link, in the great chain of being and, on the other, by considering it as something that partakes of the divine essence. To meet these two conditions as prerequisites for a political order to remain benign and play its role effectively means that one has no alternative but to think of the world as fully ordered. It is by virtue of its being fully ordered that it becomes theoretically and pragmatically possible to order individual conduct and social relations. But, the idea of an ordered world is not necessarily ruled out, even if the world is thought to be an entity that lacks divine essence. "A world emptied of divine content (has) its own order: an order empty of divinity."[5] But, the order inherent or imagined to be existent in a dedivinized world has only a cognitive significance. The principles underlying or constitutive of this order are only descriptive of the nature of the order underlying the world. They are by no means evocative of a condition that must be fully realized by men located in different life situations to sustain the order of the world. And, as a result, they have no ethical significance, in the sense that their realization in life does not make a man moral. They are, in short, value neutral.

Thus, the order articulated or discovered in a world emptied of the divine content is not in a position to provide the ground for order in the social world by inspiring individuals to put their soul in order. It is in this context that the conception of the cosmos as an ordered entity, as something that is not only the perfect exemplar of order but also as the cause of all order in particular beings can be appreciated. By the same token, the order evident in the cosmos is evocative of the need to not only contemplate the cosmic order but also to imitate it in one's life. This is what, in fact, is indicated by the term *praxis* or *shastra.* Such an order, it needs to be emphasized, has a religious or, to be precise, a spiritual significance in that it regulates and guides man's motivation and behaviour in channels that sustain the social order. And this religious or spiritual significance of order is not possible if the cosmos were empty of divine content. As such, the real import of the cosmos as an ordered entity is that the God who, as the creator God, endows it with divine qualities, governs it.

It can, however, be asked: Why should one give credence to a conception of the cosmos that is based on conjecture as against that which has the support and is backed by the authority of science? There is no doubt that scientific enterprise uses "hard" facts in apprehending the nature of what Aristotle calls *tode ti* or, to use the phrase used by *Ishopanishada* – *idam sarvam* – the world spread out before our eyes. But the *idam sarvam*, the phenomenal world is characterized by diversity and multiplicity of *nama (*names) and *rupa* (forms). It is this world that we encounter in our everyday experience and know it as the world of *nama* and *rupa.* But our everyday experience can yield only a commonsensical view of the world that usually proves treacherous and unreliable. This is so for the simple reason that whatever we see around ourselves is subject to growth, decay and death, that is, a process of constant change. And, whatever changes may not yield a reliable knowledge about the world to the common man who lacks the ability, or even the inclination, to delve deeper and discover or know the laws of nature that govern the process of the genesis, growth, decay and death of beings is not at all useful. If the commonsensical view of the world is inadequate as a guide to action and establishing a proper relationship with the world, can we rely on the scientific knowledge of the world? It needs to be emphasized that science deals with the world of becoming and, in dealing with it, it has to rely on a methodology that proves deficient in several ways. In the first place, science does not recognize anything beyond the world of becoming; it does not take cognizance of something that not only supports the process of becoming but also constitutes the point of origination for the process of becoming to proceed. This means that the world as we know it is simply made of stones and water, a view that Plato attributes to the Sophists, and, therefore, has no intelligence whatsoever or has been designed by an intelligent being even though most of the natural objects have life. In the second place, treating the phenomenal world as devoid of intelligence as well as something that is not available for direct apprehension, science must rely for its understanding of the phenomenal world on a method that allows it to apprehend the nature and structure of this world. This method is nothing else than the projection of a conceptual framework on reality as we see it in order to disconceal its essential characteristics. Through repeated projections, it is hoped that the ultimate knowledge of the world will finally be available to mankind. It is with the help of this process that the knowledge of the world constructed by science is supposed to acquire fullness, adequacy and reliability.

It is true that scientific findings are subjected to repeated checking before they are produced before the world as definitive. However, these findings suffer from certain limitations. First, science takes only a partial view of the world insofar as it treats the world only as a concourse of cause-and-effect, a world of becoming. However, beyond the flux caused by the process of becoming, there are also fixity, durability, regularity and order. Also, the process of becoming cannot be said to be self-subsistent; this process assumes that there is something that becomes and supports the process of becoming. Thus, diversity itself needs to be explained with reference to something else, something that constitutes its ground. Obviously, such a ground cannot be anything else but a unitary principle or entity because a non-unitary principle or entity would itself need to be explained with reference to something unitary. This inexorably gives rise to an infinite regression till the one source from which diversity has naturally grown is finally reached. Second, the method that science employs for acquiring knowledge of the world yields only its description. However, this knowledge acquires a normative dimension ruling out any other description/explanation than the one established by science. And, lastly, the world devoid of intelligence has simply an instrumental significance. It is, therefore, there to be used and exploited by man for realizing his purposes. This is symptomatic of the subject-object divide which reduces the world to something that is drained of all those qualities that shape not only man's external existence but also influences, in many important ways, his inner being.

It is because of these limitations that the world must be seen differently. And, when looked at differently, the world is experienced to be a cosmos, signifying an entity that is completely ordered and, as such, there is some entity that does the ordering. And, what does the ordering is something that is the substratum of reality. It is true that this "something" cannot be directly experienced or apprehended because it is beyond the realm of discursive logic and sense perception. But as seers and mystics insist and as their experience underlines, there is a power beyond the sensible world who creates the cosmos, regulates it and supervises over its functioning. In contradistinction to the world of the scientist, which only yields a tentative knowledge of the world, the knowledge of the cosmos and the mode of its functioning is definitive and conclusive. Scientific knowledge of the world has no bearing on man's interior except for the fact that such knowledge proves helpful in transforming/manipulating the external world. The knowledge of the cosmos is, in contrast, definitive, conclusive and transformative; it inspires men to mould their life according to the principles underlying the cosmos.

Thus, the real purport of the cosmos is not only that it is an exemplar of order but is also the source and cause of order in particular beings that constitute it. It is true that the source of order in the universe is always referred to as beyond the ken of the senses; it is supposed to be something that cannot be known by man's ordinary sensory faculties. It is suggested that it can only be experienced, even though this experience is ineffable. Yet this ineffable experience demands articulation, expression and communication principally through the medium of language. But the use of language or logical categories tends to reduce the truth in reality to truth in language. Obviously, then, the truth in language is quite incapable of explicating, elucidating and elaborating the truth in reality. Thus, the truth acquired by experience, an ineffable truth that makes all truths real and significant, remains unavailable to language.

Insofar as the cosmos is embedded in the divine and is, therefore, imbued with divinity, it holds the key to the understanding of the phenomenon of order, its origin and its preservation in a world resisting order. But the universe is not all disorder or resistant to order.[6] The celestial world, for example, displays a remarkable degree of regularity and order.[7] Regularity and order in the cosmos do ravish Hume[8] and Edgeworth into admiration, to be sure. But they are not willing to admit that the universe has anything divine in it or is governed by mind; for them, nature does not reveal or represent divine design or presence. It is simply a "great machine" for Hume or "mecanique celeste" for Edgeworth.[9] But, for Plato, the heavenly bodies like the sun, moon, stars, and earth are the proof that God exists; these bodies are not earth and stones only; they are divine beings partaking of divine essence.[10] Thus, in contrast to the scientific view of the universe, there exists another view that treats the universe not as a machine but as a cosmos, a living organism which is designed by an intelligent being.

It is true that the heavenly bodies display regularity and order. However, can the same be said of the human world that resists order? In contrast to the celestial world, the human world presents entirely a different picture. That order has to be installed and safeguarded in the human world, both in individual psyche and the social universe, to ward off chaos induced by *matsya nyaya*, indicates that the human world is not completely in tune with the celestial world. It may and does have all the characteristic features, principles of functioning, and modes of exemplary behaviour. However, it frequently deviates from and contravenes them. Individuals may, for example, have attributes that, if fully developed, make them perfect men. However, as Coomaraswamy observes, "man's distinctive endowment is not equally developed in all men, however it may be latent in all ..."[11] It is indicative as well as confirmatory of the fact that human nature is bivalent. Human beings evidently partake of both the pure, divine essence of the unknown as well as the impure, shadowy character of the beast.[12]

In view of this combination in man of the pure and the impure, the noble and the vile, and the light and the shadow, the question of curbing or suppressing the vile and helping realize the noble assumes a critical significance. It is in this context that the conception of the cosmos as a *psyche,* as Plato calls it, becomes very relevant for man who must reflect in his own psyche the divine reality that pervades the cosmos. But since the presence of this reality is buried deep in man's psyche under the heavy layers of materiality, the reminder that the life of man is the part of what Plato calls "animated nature" (*empsychos physis*), makes man constantly aware that he must, in living his life, be animated by the divine reality. To be animated by this reality is to arrange and put in proper order all those forces that constitute or inhere in his psyche.

The need to be animated by the divine reality in ordering the forces existing and working in man's interior is all the more pressing in view of the fact that it is this ordering that maintains order in society by curbing and controlling *pleonexia* (the tendency towards self-aggrandizement) in individual beings. To restrain the inferior forces in man's interior by subordinating them to the rule of higher forces is necessary not only for the well-being of the individual but also for social concord, harmony and peace. However, since only a few persons are capable of or willing to work for the establishment of the rule of the higher elements in their interior, the installation of political order and ensuring its proper functioning constitute an essential prerequisite of maintaining social harmony and concord. Needless to say that the state and its commands signify only an external source from which issue forth impulses aimed at controlling and curbing unlawful behaviour of individuals. However, we must ask whether the commands of the state represent something that transcends private goods.

As has already been pointed out, if the political order is meant to prescribe the conditions governing the competition among individuals for goods and services that yield the pleasures of the body, to act as an umpire in this competition, and to take care of the adverse consequences of this competition, the commands of the state assume entirely a different character. This character is determined by the fact that when the pleasures of the body become the pivot of man's life activities, the conception of good necessarily assumes a private character. Private goods come to edge out the notion of collective good and tend to become the dominant, even exclusive source, of providing the guiding principle of individual and collective action. As a result, power, not any concern for safeguarding and promoting the common good, dominates political life and relations. The reason for this is not far to seek. When the pleasures of the body take precedence over non-bodily concerns and become the centre of all other activities of life, effectiveness in acquiring and retaining the resources that yield these pleasures become strategically very important. This is dependent on the extent to which the individual succeeds in generating and/or mobilizing power in concert with others. Thus, power holds the key to who gets what, when and how.

Two consequences flow from this state of affairs that are of very vital importance to political life and relations. In the first place, when the pleasures of the body acquire precedence, the soul is relegated to the limbo of forgetfulness. It means the life of passion buries the soul deep down under the frenzy of the body from where it is very difficult to excavate it. Even if it is excavated, it is likely to be buried again under the heavy demands of everydayness. When the rule of the soul is overthrown, the sense of what Heraclitus calls *xynon* (shareable commonality) that inhabits the interior of every individual is also deadened. While *xynon* remains active or is consciously and actively acknowledged, man remains awake, awake to his essential relatedness with the divine ground of being and to his destiny in the phenomenal world. As Heraclitus puts it, "Only one cosmos ... exists for the 'waking' alone, while the sleepers each have their own private world, a world of dreams."[13] When the world of private dreams takes hold of men, consensus as the foundation of community is weakened and finally destroyed. Value subjectivity produces a situation of eristic or, alternatively, every difference of opinion becomes the cause of eristic in which every person, moved by his own conception of what is good for him, sticks to his own gun. This is symptomatic of the break down of the bridge of a common humanity, as Voegelin puts it.[14]

In the second place, with the break down of consensus, political arguments lack persuasiveness and often lead to quarrels and politics, instead of paving the way for fair and efficient management of public affairs, generates and exacerbates dissension. But the pre-eminence of the private good does not, and cannot, rule collective life out of existence. It does, however, eclipse collective good and, as a consequence, increase the possibility of the curtailment of private welfare. In order, therefore, to safeguard the sanctity of collective life and save the individuals from the dangers of their own cupidity, some effective means of making collective decisions have to be evolved. But no matter which means is chosen, it always gets involved in the struggle for power for controlling decision-making offices and institutions. It is true that those who succeed in controlling the power apparatus of society become responsible for making collective decisions according to certain established rules and procedures. However, all these decisions are reached by some decision mechanism "designed to make one view, one interest, one order of preference prevail over others most of the time by the application of established rules peacefully, without recourse to violence."[15]

It must, however, be emphasized that, as Jassay puts it, "the morality of requiring all to abide by the decision of some as a matter of duty or, less ambitiously, as a matter of inclining before the threat of force, has always seemed problematical."[16] As such, it is necessary to take the help of some myth, whether religious or secular, to induce the people to think that collective decisions and the law(s) under which they are made are in the interest of not just a particular socio-economic interest but for all.

> Thus, most of the people in a political system obey the law because they are deceived into thinking it represents some common good greater than many tempting private goods. In fact, the regime and its laws almost always exist for the sake of some private goods – of some class alliance or of some individuals. Those who are privately benefited may or may not be aware of the deceptiveness of the claim of the regime to exist for the sake of the common good.[17]

But when this deception is exposed or proves too debilitating for the good of a large section of the people, the political regime loses its credibility and, as a consequence, its legitimacy. Then, the regime faces the possibility of either rebellion or a large-scale violation of its commands. It may be able to put the rebellion down by the use of force. However, it is ill prepared to prevent violations of its commands and laws. As Plato frequently notes in Book Nine of *Laws*, penal law is effective only if the criminal is caught. But magistrates cannot look into the hearts of men and, therefore, cannot detect all crimes. Moreover, there always exists the possibility that the machinery of law enforcement may not only apprehend innocent persons for a particular crime but also that they may be actually punished for the crime they have not committed.

We need to look at yet another aspect of this matter. As Plato points out, "no man's nature is able to know what is best for human society; or knowing always able and willing to do what is best."[18] This is so for the simple reason that only a few people can or will make a distinction between what is good for the individual and what is good for the collectivity. Failing to make this distinction, most of the people have difficulty in apprehending that the "true art of politics is concerned not with private but with public good (for public good binds together states, but private good only distracts them); and that both the public and the private good as well of individuals as of states is greater when the state and not the individual is first considered."[19] Even if a person is able to make this distinction in the abstract, he is not able to do so for long because he soon falls a prey to his cupidity. This is due to the fact that "human nature will be always drawing him into avarice and selfishness, avoiding pain and pursuing pleasure without reason, and will bring these to the front, obscuring the just and better; and so working darkness in his soul will at last fill with evils both him and the whole city."[20]

Given this strong tendency, man chooses to live in the shadowy world of appearances forsaking the world of truth and reality. As a result, the individual, whose soul is afflicted by the ill effects of appearance, cannot see the whole for the parts and is, therefore, prone to give preference to his own good. As Dobbs observes:

> Once freed of any mooring in reality, appearance no longer offers even an oblique clue to what truly is. Appearance then exists as nothing more than a temptation to willful manipulation. As a result of the soul's turn wholly towards appearance, reason becomes cramped and deformed. Reason ceases to search for the true and the good in considering the merits of justice and injustice; instead, it is wholly subsumed in "calculation" (*logizomenos*), specifically in that calculation which concludes that injustice is mightier than justice always and everywhere as long as one has the capacity to manipulate appearances.[21]

In a situation where reason degenerates into calculation, the law loses its importance as an educative character. Reason as calculation does not recognize any authority beyond itself. As a consequence of the law losing its educative value, reason as calculation transforms into what Dobbs calls "rational commensuration".[22] This means that a person, who makes the pleasures of the body the quest of his life, may gain the whole world but he certainly forfeits his soul. And since he forfeits his soul, he is prone to failure in discerning the fundamental difference between the sacred and the profane. Rejecting the claim of anything higher than his own good and, convinced of the central importance of calculation in realizing his purposes, he simply brushes aside all those objections and obstructions put in his path by the consideration of the sacred that are not expressible in terms common with the principal objects of (his) interest. This is accomplished most easily in the case of the law by disregarding the educational significance of penalties and interpreting them simply as prices. As such, Dobbs notes, laws do not educate, they merely regulate. Nothing is sacred everything has its price.[23]

It is enough to suggest that when the existence of the sacred is denied, political life and relations degenerate into *matsya nyaya*. The law, which is relied upon to lift society from the mire of *matsya nyaya* and lend it a semblance of order, harmony and peace, also loses its significance. This also suggests, as Plato recognizes,[24] that unless people recognize that the sacred exists and that it must influence different life activities, the law, too, loses its significance as something that educates and trains men in good behaviour. Along with it, it also loses its sanctity. It is, therefore, necessary to make the law impregnated with divine sanctity so that it can play its proper role effectively. But what does, it must be asked, mean to impregnate the law with divine sanctity? It must be emphasized that a political order, responsible for the regulation of the process of acquiring the wherewithal of securing the pleasures of the body, must depend for its effectiveness on laws that have their origin in human will rather than any divinely impregnated wisdom. And the laws that have their origin in human will, can be changed by will. As such, these laws do not represent a pre-existent consensus grounded in what Heraclitus calls *xynon* (shareable commonality); they are the outcome of the contest of power and are, therefore, symptomatic of the dominance of one particular section or, alternatively, an alliance of different socio-economic interests in a particular society. And, the laws that claim to regulate political life and relations lack divine sanctity insofar as the contestations for power take their inspiration from the experience of the natural man who does not recognize or deliberately ignores the existence of the divine.

We should note yet another side of the question related to this. It is quite likely that the laws meant to regulate the quest of the pleasures of the body may not prove effective. They may not, for example, succeed either in curbing the excesses involved in the pursuit of pleasures or fail to create a situation in which it is possible for all to succeed in their search for pleasure. Alternatively, they may not succeed in even making it possible for all to effectively engage in this pursuit. As a result, inequality of conditions governing the acquisition and utilization of the resources that conduce to the enjoyment of the pleasures of the body proves to be deleterious to public order. This is so for the reason that inequality of possessions, in a situation where augmentation of fortune holds the key to individual good and public well-being, proves to be the mother of jealousy and envy. And, a society where jealousy and envy become regnant, the search for glory meets its untimely death. As Plato puts it,

> ... the envious, who thinks that he ought to get better by defaming others, is less energetic himself in the pursuit of true virtue, and reduces his rivals to despair by his unjust slanders of them. And so he makes the whole city to enter the arena untrained in the practice of virtue, and diminishes her glory as far as in him lies.[25]

Lacking virtue, the city does not only lose glory; it also faces ruination. It does not need to be pointed out that it is greed that makes persons jealous and envious. People, under the sway of greed, see and work for only their own good jeopardizing the good of others. This disrupts civic wholeness and, in the lack of civic wholeness, the city languishes because of increasing dissension.

In addition, the atrophy of virtue can first be discovered in the individual. When the soul of the individual gets diseased, the disease of the soul, then, spreads out in the society at large and pervades it as a dense cloud of putrid matter resisting even the strong gust of the wind of good will and pious intentions. When this happens, it becomes very, very difficult for the individuals to shun vice and cultivate virtue. One of the obstacles in the cultivation of virtue, as Plato underlines, is the insistence on making a sharp contrast between "nature" and "convention". What this contrast points to is the understanding of nature as a blind, irrational force. As Guthrie puts it:

> The universe and all that it contains ... are products of nature. They are prior to reason, which only came to birth with man, and are therefore the result of purely fortuitous circumstances. Later came art or design, a more insignificant force of purely human origin, and created some shadows with little reality about them. Now law and its assumptions are products of art and reason, not nature, and justice is only a creation of law. Hence, the 'life according to nature' ... consists in satisfying one's personal desires uninhibited by any subservience to law or convention.[26]

This understanding of "nature" and "convention" drains the cosmos of its divine quality and reduces conventions, laws, customs, etc., to the status of instruments that can be used in realizing personal or sectional purposes. It is against this perspective that one can appreciate why a political system continually changes its laws, even its fundamental laws, and its regimes. These changes are indicative of the fact that there is no common good apart from sectional good and that the aggregation of private good does not add up to public good. More important in this regard is the fact that each version of what is common good is, in reality, the proxy for sectional interests. Everyone of the opinions about what is good for all and the various notions of justice grounded in and reflecting these opinions that the political system legislates into law is given with the same authority.[27] This is a clear indication of the arbitrary character of the laws insofar as their origin does not lie in any impersonal, universal standard of what is good for all. On the contrary, it lies in personal and sectional interest which is projected as common interest. As such, the laws do not represent anything more than the interest of those who happen to be in power at a particular time. In Pangle's words:

> Each decision about what is just or noble can be traced to essentially chance circumstances which precluded the consideration of other notions of what is just, and the circumstances which made one individual or group the strongest and hence able to impose its interest and opinions.[28]

Implicit in this perspective is the denial of the possibility that there could be any non-arbitrary, reasoned legislation based on the consideration of what is good by nature for all men in a particular society or, for that matter, in all societies. But to insist that such a common standard of what constitutes good for all is not at all possible is tantamount to denying that nothing else than the pleasures of the body can be the ground of law-making. However, it is precisely the problems created by the projection of a sectional good as the good of all that makes it necessary to look for a ground for law-making that is above and beyond sectional interests. But what is this ground? Such a ground cannot be found in the external world, whether society or nature. It is true that society does represent an institution that symbolizes collective identity of its members. It may for this reason become very powerful and its norms may prove restrictive and, therefore, oppressive curtailing even the legitimate freedom of individuals. Moreover, it is not something that is separable from the lives of its members. Its significance is derived, in a very important sense, from the fact that it is there to help its members to fulfil their destiny. As such, the standard of what is good for all cannot be derived from anything in the society. Similarly, nature, particularly nature that is supposed to be made of stones and water, cannot yield any such standard. It is true that there are certain laws that underline it and regulate its functioning. However, these "laws" have no moral significance; they are simply descriptive. It is in view of this that the search for a universally applicable standard of what is good for all must return to the individual.

But, as we have already seen, pleasures of the body cannot be the basis of this standard. Does it not, then, mean that we have to focus on the superior element in man's interior as Freud hints? And is not this element the soul? But, then, it has to be shown that the soul has a particular interest and this interest is common to all men and that, when the interest of the soul is promoted, it conduces to the good of all. In other words, it is to be shown that the good of the soul can become the basis of the good of all. Needless to say it is the soul that, as the sensorium of the divine, has the responsibility of keeping man's interior in order. And it is by installing order in man's interior that the soul is able to discriminate between good and bad and, thus, inspires the individual to resolve within him, the tension between the private and the public dimensions of his existence. But the soul, as Plato reminds us, becomes good when it "takes as its helper Mind (*nous*), god in the true sense of the word for the gods."[29] It is only when man looks to the divine and the divine looks to their leader, mind (*nous*) that the soul is able to perform its responsibility of keeping man's interior in order. But to admit the existence of the soul is also to admit something that orders and regulates everything as well as the fact that man is neither self-complete nor autonomous.

Thus, for Plato, there lies a conscious and designing mind behind everything in the world; this conscious and designing entity is nothing else than Mind. This suggests that the cosmos is a divinely created world. In addition, not only is the cosmos created by God; also it is itself a living creature. As Plato observes, the creator God

> was good; and in the good no jealousy in any matter can ever arise. So being without jealousy, he desired that all things should be good and, so far as near as possible to being like himself ... Desiring, then, that all things should be good and, so far as might be, nothing imperfect, the god took over all that is visible – not at rest, but in discordant and unordered motion – and brought it from disorder into order, since he judged that order was in every way the better. Taking thought ... he found that, among things that are by nature visible, no work that is without intelligence will ever be better than one that has intelligence, when each is taken as a whole, and moreover that intelligence cannot be present in anything apart from soul. In virtue of this reasoning, when he formed the universe, he fashioned reason within soul and soul within body, to the end that the work he accomplished might be by nature as excellent and perfect as possible.[30]

Thus, for Plato, the universe is not a lifeless body of stone and water; it is something that has come to be by the providence of the god, in very truth, a living creature with soul and reason.[31] It is this fully ordered cosmos that man is an integral part of. This cosmos, as Jonas points out, "is considered to be the perfect exemplar of order, and at the same time, the cause of all order in particulars, which only in degrees can approximate the whole."[32] It is true that the particular components of this universe approximate the whole only in degrees. However, it is also true that "the totality has no 'being' except through the expression of these components, and the individual particulars have no 'being' except by reason of their mutual relation both with the totality and with other parts"[33] that constitute the whole. Needless to say that it is this "fitting together" of different parts of the cosmos with each other as well as with the whole and of the cosmos with its creator that is the basis of *harmonia* in the world. This *harmonia* is symptomatic of the manifestation of the One through its manifold characters that make the *idam sarvam*.[34] In this harmony, "the responsible dignity of men's minds and will was felt to consist not specifically in their differences from one another but in the variety of their characteristic individuality, thrown into relief, precisely, by their mutual relation and their unity as component differentiated parts of one whole."[35]

In this living, ordered cosmos, man, as an integral part of it, is related to God by virtue of his being the abode of the divine; he, too, is able to actively relate himself to the divine in him because he can use the reasoning capacity he has been endowed by nature. However, he is also associated with a material body. As such, he is also subject to the "necessity" of physical forces and has, as a result, to face many difficulties in realizing completely the possibilities pertaining to the cultivation and actualization of the divine in him that is encoded and immanent in his nature. It is in view of this fact that man's nature is considered to be bivalent. It is true that man is a composite being, that is, his nature is such that it incorporates the possibility both of becoming completely engrossed in materiality and of overcoming his tendency towards particularism as a precondition of cultivating the divine in him. It is also true that the tendency in him towards materiality tends to conceal, suppress or even rule out the divine in him. However, despite his being a contingent creature, he nonetheless possesses the ability to share somehow the *prajnana* (the knowledge that illuminates), the distinctive characteristic of the creator of the cosmos. But this ability remains dormant because of the ignorance induced by what the traditional Indian thinking identifies as *maya*. It is *maya* that engulfs and effectively shrouds the divine light, the light that is the source of man's self-understanding and the beacon of self-development. This, however, does not, in any case, rule out the possibility that man can turn his back to the source of the darkness of ignorance, overcome this ignorance, and seek the divine light. As Tucci puts it:

> While it (*maya*) may disperse more and more into the negation of that light until it entirely obscures it, it may also, as though impelled by the glimmer that is not entirely extinguished in it, disengage itself from the night, discover once more our essential divinity, and induce us to bend our way back along the path that leads to the plane beyond night.[36]

To go beyond the night of ignorance brought on by our attachment to the world of everydayness is to discover within oneself the divine spark that has been enveloped by the overwhelming hold on our being of the *samsara* itself. To discover this inner light is to reintegrate oneself with the God, to return to the original unity that has been enfeebled and, but not, perhaps, completely disabled, by the process of living itself. The process of living that enfeebles and, in many cases obliterates, this unity is nothing else than the understanding that reduces the cosmos to a lifeless entity made of merely water and stones. But this understanding is by no means ineradicable; it can be eradicated provided we accept the fact that this universe is not lifeless body of stones and water nor a concourse of cause-and-effect. It is rather a well-ordered and well-regulated cosmos. The universe as a cosmos is distinguished from the lifeless world by the fact that it manifests order and regularity; it is this characteristic of the universe that testifies to its divine origin, an origin that human beings also share.

It is this understanding of the universe that is capable of restoring the original unity between human beings and their creator. It is this understanding, again, that reminds man that he is neither self-complete nor autonomous; he is part of a larger order symbolized by the concept of cosmos and by virtue of this, he is an integral part of the divine. It must, however, be emphasized that this original unity can be recovered, if lost, or activated if dormant or passive, only when, as Cicero puts it, man "contemplates the cosmos and imitates it."[37] The need to contemplate the cosmos lies in the fact that, even while man shares the divine origin along with the cosmos, "he is far from being perfect, but he is a little part of the perfect."[38] Thus, for Cicero, the purpose of human existence is, first, to discern and understand the order and regularity that characterize the universe. It is only this understanding of the universe that, given the right orientation and impetus, prompts, encourages, and sustains man in his endeavour to realize order and regularity in his own life. Thus, the message that the universe as a cosmos has for man is quite clear, even though it is seldom heeded: man as a part of the universe must conform to the pattern it displays. That is, man must mould his existence in accordance with the principles that undergird order and regularity in the universe. Thus, the order in the universe constitutes the paradigm of human existence and establishes the necessary "connection between the apotheosis of the universe and the ideal of human perfection . . . ."[39]

Man as the part of the cosmos shares in the highest cosmic attributes of the soul and mind, but he is not the most perfect of beings. He is, however, endowed with the potentiality of transforming himself in a way that allows him to share in these attributes. This potentiality can become a reality, if man exploits fully his capacity to perfect himself. This is possible, if he assimilates his being to that of the whole through its contemplation in order to re-orient his understanding based on ratiocination. But simple understanding is not enough; going beyond the mere understanding, he should also seek to imitate in his own life the principles of order inherent in the cosmos. But the full exploitation of this capacity depends, to a great extent, on the veneration of the cosmos of which man is only a small part. To recognize this is to act in accordance with the given characteristics of his real, substantive status, that is, as only a part of the cosmos. To do so is to establish a proper relationship with the universe by moulding his conduct in accordance with the principles undergirding order in the cosmos. In Jonas' words:

> It is based in the interpretation of his existence in terms of the larger whole, whose very perfection consists in the integration of all its parts. In this sense, man's cosmic piety submits his being to the requirements of what is better than him and the source of all that is good.[40]

This submission to the requirements of the whole does not, however, mean denial of freedom to man or the imposition on him of a preconceived and pre-arranged freedom. The fact that man is related with others in the cosmos and with the whole does not signify that man cannot will what he can or know what he is capable of; it simply means that the creative power of each individual resides ultimately in his natural relation with others, and with the whole of which every person is a reflecting facet. This mutual relationship can become salubrious and benign only when man realizes that he is

> not just a part like other parts making up the universe, but through the possession of a mind, a part that enjoys *identity* with the ruling principle of the whole. Thus, the other aspect of man's proper relation with the universe is that he makes his own existence, confined as it is as a mere part, of *adequating* the essence of the whole, of reproducing the latter in his own being through understanding and action.[41]

Thus, the real significance of the cosmos, the universe reflecting order and regularity, is not only that it is a structure incorporating different parts of the universe, and the universe itself as well as its creator. It also signifies that there are certain intelligible principles which, when realized in the life of the individuals, become the instrument of not only the installation of order in man's interior but also of safeguarding and preserving harmony in the world. It is in this sense that the cosmos and what Plato calls "a likely story" detailing the way the cosmos came into being and the principles of order that underlies it become relevant. It is this "likely story" or cosmogony or what *Brihaddevata* calls *bhavavrittam* that helps man to understand the world he is a part of and how to shape his own life as well as his environing socio-cultural order so that he can contribute his own share in safeguarding and preserving the order he is a part of. It is this "likely story" that constitutes a paradigm of human existence; by the same token, it is also the source of inspiration for all to accept this paradigm for moulding their motivation and conduct in accordance with the principles of order inherent in the cosmos. Thus, the "likely story" is an exemplar of human existence and suggests the ways and means of determining the proper course of man's life in the phenomenal world. But not all are in a position to understand "the likely story" of the cosmos or what lies behind it. If they do understand this story, they are not prepared or able to act according to the cosmic paradigm of human existence. It is, therefore, necessary that the environing socio-political order must be grounded in and reflects the cosmic paradigm so that it can prevent individual motivation and conduct from deviating from the principles of order underlying the cosmos.

It is this perspective on man, cosmos and man's relationship with the cosmos, as delineated above, that is the theme of the Vedic "likely story". This "likely story" has, as its main objective, the presentation of the account of how One becomes many. In doing so, it also delineates the relationship between One and many, that is the creator and the world he creates; it also highlights those aspects of this relationship that help in installing and/or maintaining order both in the cosmos and in the interior of man. Needless to say that the process of the One becoming many is the process of creation, of the One taking manifold *nama* (name) and *rupa* (form). The One that assumes manifold names and forms does not remain outside the world he creates as does the *demiurgos* of the Platonic "likely story". As a matter of fact, he enters the world he creates and becomes an integral part of it. In the words of *Yajurveda* 31.19, Prajapati, even though unborn, enters and remains in the womb of everything; the wise know the womb from which he issues forth. However, every being abides in him. It is because of this that he is said to be all-pervasive, abiding in everything that he creates. However, he is *avyaya* (inexhaustible), *anirukta* (inexplicable or undefined), *aparimita* (immeasurable, *apeiron in gk.*), etc.

The process of creation begins when the *aparimita* begins to be *parimita,* that is, bounded. This One, the Veda makes it very clear, is *Swayambhu*, that is, self-born, who, in becoming manifest in the form of the cosmos, the *idam sarvam,* that is, all this, as *Ishopanishada* calls it, does not fully exhaust itself. As a matter of fact, the One, the creator of the universe, is, in the Vedic cosmogony, claimed to be *chatushpada,* that is, he is supposed to have four feet only one of which manifests as this universe, the *idam sarvam* or *tode ti,* as Aristotle calls it. Thus, the *idam sarvam* does not fully reveal what is beyond the universe or what is its source of origination. It is the Vedic "likely story" which articulates what this beyond is and how it is related with the world that he creates. Thus, there are necessarily two parts of the universe, one visible and the other invisible. It is the sensible and the visible universe that the Vedic seers call *praketa*, the sign of the *apraketa*[42] of what is beyond our senses, that is, the unmanifest aspect of the creator. Thus, the *idam sarvam* is only a visible symbol or *eikon*, to use a Platonic term, of the invisible creator.

In order to create, *Swayambhu* has to undergo the process of what is called *dwedhapat,* that is, the splitting of the One into two. This *dwedhapat* is symptomatic of the coming into being of two distinct but complementary principles, that is the father-essence (*para prakriti)* and the mother-nature (*apara prakriti).* Needless to say that these are the two aspects of the One who is also called *ardhanarishwar,* that is, half male and half female, in his undivided form. It is the *sahavasa* (copulation) between these two aspects that splits the One into its two different natures. It is this *dwedhapat* that symbolizes the beginning of the process of creation. While the father-essence is identified with Brahma who, as the creator God, is known as Prajapati, Purusha,[43] etc., as the process of creation gets underway, the mother nature is variously described as Vak, Aditi, Viraj, etc. It is the syzygy between the father-essence and the mother-nature that initiates the process of creation. This process of creation is completed in two distinct but continuous stages, *purvarddha* (the first stage) and *uttararddha* (the second stage); the former denotes the realm of what is, in the Vedic cosmogony, known as *asat,* that is, non-material elements or something that has neither a centre nor a form. In contradistinction to this, the latter signifies embodied beings or *sat,* that is, *enhylon eidos,* as Plato calls it.

These two stages of creation signify the embodiment of the Idea, that is, the God or the luminous entity. The transformation of the Idea into embodied beings is made possible through the performance of what, in the *Rigveda* (X. 90), is known as the *Sarvahuta Yajna.* The significance of this *Yajna* lies in the fact that Purusha performs the *Yajna* in which he sacrifices himself fully and totally for creating the world. It is through this *Sarvahuta Yajna* that the *tadekam* (that One) becomes the *sarva,* the all, the *idam sarvam.* The world and everything contained in the phenomenal world becomes the *medhya* (food) of Purusha. That is to say, the *idam sarvam* itself becomes the *avasa* (residence) of the *Isha* (the God) and the world and every being in it must, therefore, become worthy and proper residence of the divine substratum of reality by offering themselves as the *medhya* (food) of Purusha. Thus, the *Sarvahuta Yajna,* known alternatively, as *Purushamedha Sukta* underlines not only that the God created the world but also that he made it divine by himself residing in it.[44]

His *Yajna* is not a one-time affair; as a matter of fact, it goes on for ever.[45] In this *Yajna,* it is the generation of gods that takes place first; this is indicative of the progressive descent of the Absolute into materiality leading finally to the appearance of the *idam sarvam.* In this process, the Absolute, as already indicated, is split into its two (*dwedhapat*)[46] essential aspects or natures, *para (natura naturans)* and *apara (natura naturata).* The former represents the *amartya* or immortal aspect of the godhead while the latter stands for the *martya* or perishable aspect of the Absolute, also known alternatively as *Vak.* It is interesting to note that *Vak,* that is the female principle or matter, when not in *sakavasa* with the male principle, that is *natura naturans*, is characterized as *anaksha duhita* (a blind daughter, unmanifest *prakriti*); it becomes *janitri*, that is capable of reproducing, but only when it unites in syzygy with Prajapati.[47] As a result of its coupling with Prajapati, *Vak* gives birth to Agni who, along with Soma, engenders gods and other beings in this world. This process of generation occurs gradually at different levels and dimensions. One aspect of the process of creation is the transformation of Brahma into five *vivartas* or stages of development. These *vivartas* are: Swayambhu, Parameshthi, Indra, Chandra and Prithiwi. These *vivartas* symbolize the procession of Brahma through these stages till it finally becomes the *vishwa* or the cosmos. It is interesting to note that these five *vivartas* represent, in an alternating sequence, three different aspects of Agni, that is, Swayambhu, Indra and Prithiwi and two different aspects of Soma, that is, Parameshthi and Chandra.

These *vivartas* are alternatively known as five *mandalas* that symbolize the stages through which the Absolute as pure non-matter descends gradually into materiality and takes concrete forms. Each of these *mandalas* represents a particular ensemble of energy; each of these sets of energy has its own distinctive characteristics, mode of functioning, and ways of interacting with other sets of energy. Each of these *mandalas* has its own presiding deity; it is this deity who is responsible for activating different ensembles of energy forces associated with different *mandalas.* These *mandalas* are the expanded form of *triloka*, or three worlds, which, when triplicated,[48] transform into *saptaloka* (seven worlds) in each of which a *Rishi prana* (life-breath)[49] abides. These *lokas* represent different ways of looking at the procession of the Absolute in which the *anirukta* (undefined) Prajapati becomes increasingly *nirukta* or defined. Each of these *lokas* represents different aspects of Prajapati in procession.

This necessarily very abbreviated account of Vedic cosmogony underlines the fact that, according to the Vedic "likely story", the universe is comprised of both visible and invisible parts. Plato may be right when he insists that only one and no other world was created. But this does not, however, mean that this solitary world is not a hierarchical cosmos with layers and layers of graded worlds one within the other. All these graded layers form only one and unique cosmos. As Needleman puts it,

> ... (Man) stands before a universe which exceeds him in quality as well as quantity. The spheres which encompass the earth ... "surround" the earth much as the physiological function of an organ such as the heart "surrounds" or permeates each of the separate tissues which comprise

it, or as the Captain's distinction "encompasses or "pervades" the life and activity of every crewman on his ship.[50]

All these "pervading", "encompassing" energies, purposes, functions, entities form a compact, cohesive and organic system in Vedic thinking. The earth, to use Needleman's words again, "is inextricably mixed in a network of purposes, a ladder or hierarchy of intentions. A cosmos – and, of course *the* cosmos – is an organism, not in the sense of an unusually complicated industrial machine, but in the sense of a hierarchy of purposeful energies.[51]

The network of purposes or purposeful energies constitutes, in the Vedic perspective, a concentric circle, each circle being the repository of energies or possibilities which are compatibly interrelated and which, taken together, constitute a state pregnant with the potentiality of transiting to another different but organically linked state. Each of these centres of possibilities is the locus of a particular state or outcome of certain forces that, in turn, are the outcomes of certain antecedent forces occupying another circle. Even while antecedent forces have engendered the forces occupying a particular circle, they are uniquely constituted and have a different role to play. Despite this, the forces occupying different circles are organically interconnected and functionally interrelated. These circles or spheres or *lokas* do not refer to actual spatial units descriptive of the cosmos; they are meant to be understood symbolically.[52]

The Vedic notion of the universe is, thus, indicative of an organism. This organism can be described as cell in the service of tissue; tissue in the service of organ; organ in the service of the whole governed by a supreme consciousness or intelligence. At each level of being, there are "gods" or "angels" representing particular bundles of energy which progressively get entrapped in material covering as we come to the last of these spheres. The *lokas,* as the loci of purposeful energies, are fields where creative action or effects of creative action take on concrete forms. These forms need to be put into a shape proper and relevant for the process of creation by the interaction of four constitutive principles: Veda (knowledge or *prama*), *chhandas* (limits or boundaries for keeping the movement of pranic energy within certain well defined space), *dik* (space, direction), and *yajna*. But it is *yajna* that is a factor of prime importance in integrating these and transforming them into the *vishwa*.[53]

The Vedic cosmogony or "the likely story" of creation posits an organic world that is created by the Supreme Intelligence. In this world, all beings are related in a network of interdependence, harmony and cooperation. Also, there operates a continuous process of exchange between these beings and it is the fairness or justness of this exchange that preserves order in the cosmos. In the cosmic metabolism gods give rain; a good rain enables a good crop; good crop enables man to make offerings to the gods; and the gods, pleased by these offerings, give good rain; and so on. If this exchange process is obstructed under the influence of greed leading inevitably to hoarding, the cosmic order is disrupted. As such, it is incumbent upon men to safeguard the process of exchange operation in the cosmos by internalizing and acting upon the principles that sustain and preserve cosmic order.

Thus, at the root of the Vedic perspective on man and his relationship with the world at large, lies the idea of a well-ordered, organic cosmos. It is this organic cosmos that provides the paradigm of human existence. Political order, as an important part of human existence, is, as we shall see later, patterned after this cosmos and is responsible for maintaining order in this world in a situation of changing socio-political circumstances marked by the decline of *dharma*.

Notes

1. T.M.P. Mahadevan, "The Religio-Philosophic Culture of India," in Suniti Kumar Chatterji et al. (eds.), *The Cultural Heritage of India* (Calcutta: The Ramakrishna Mission of Culture, 1937), 3 vols., Vol. 1, p. 169.
2. On this point, see Hans Jonas, *The Gnostic Religion: The Message of the Alien God and the Beginning of Christianity* (Boston: Beacon Press, 1963), p. 250.
3. Ibid., p. 252.
4. Ibid., p. 267.
5. Ibid., p. 250.
6. As Anaxagoras argues, it is mind or intelligence which is the source of all order, all arrangement in everything. Mind is present in nature, just as in animal and is the cause of order and all arrangement therein. See Aristotle, *Metaphysics,* edited and translated by John Warrington (New York: Everyman's Library, 1978), p. 62.
7. In his *Timaeus,* Plato makes use of the regularities of the heavenly bodies and their effects in the cosmos as a whole, in order to demonstrate that the whole universe works in accordance with a rational and moral law.

8. David Hume, *Dialogues Concerning Natural Religion,* quoted in Carl L. Becker, *The Heavenly City of the Eighteenth Century Philosophers* (New Haven: Yale University Press, 1960), p. 56.
9. Francis Edgeworth, *Mathematical Physics,* p. 12, quoted in George J. Stigler, "Economics or Ethics," in Sterling McMurrin (ed.), *The Tanner Lectures in Human Values,* II (Salt Lake City: The University of Utah Press, 1981), p. 168.
10. Plato, *Laws,* 886c-d.
11. Ananda K. Coomaraswamy, *What is Civilization?* (Delhi: Oxford University Press, 1989), p. 77.
12. cf. Plato, *Republic,* 501b7.
13. Heraclitus, quoted in Werner Jaeger, *Paideia* (Oxford: Oxford University Press, 1957), 3 vols.,Vol. I, p. 180.
14. Eric Voegelin, *Order and History: Plato and Aristotle,* III, p. 29.
15. Anthony de Jassay, *Against Politics: On Government, Anarchy, and Order* (London: Routledge, 1997), p.1.
16. Ibid.
17. Thomas L. Pangle, "The Political Psychology of Religion in Plato's *Laws,*" *American Political Science Review,* 70, 3 (September 1976), p. 1068.
18. Plato, *Laws,* 875a (Jowett translation).
19. Ibid.
20. Ibid., 875b-c.
21. Darrell Dobbs, "Choosing Justice: Socrates' Model City and the Practice of Dialectics," *American Political Science Review,* 88, 2 (June 1994), p. 264; see Plato, *Republic,* 366a6–7.
22. Darrell Dobbs, "Reckless Rationalism and Heroic Reverence in Homer's *Odyssey,*" *American Political Science Review,* 681, 2 (June 1987), pp. 491–508.
23. Ibid., p. 500.
24. Plato, *Laws,* 880b-c.
25. Ibid., 731b.
26. W.K.C. Guthrie, *In the Beginning: Some Greek Views on the Origins of Life and the Early State of Man* (London: Methuen & Co., Ltd., 1957), pp. 106–07.
27. Plato, *Laws,* 889e7–8.
28. Pangle, op. cit.
29. Plato, *Laws,* 631d5.
30. Plato, *Timaeus,* in F.M. Cornford, tr. *Plato's Cosmology* (London: Routledge and Kegan Paul, 1971), pp. 33–34.
31. Ibid.

32. Jonas, op. cit., p. 242.
33. Collum, *Manifold Unity: The Ancient World's Perception of the Divine Pattern of Harmony* (Calcutta: Rupa & Co., 1995), pp. 59–60.
34. It must be emphasized that the cosmos Plato talks about is not, in any sense of the term, the manifestation of the One. The Platonic form does not enter anything nor does it allow anything else to enter itself. As such, there exists a duality in the world and its supposed creator. This has profound consequences for man and his world. Needless to say that this duality does not exist in Vedic cosmogony.
35. Collum, op. cit., p. 60.
36. Guiseppe Tucci, *The Theory and Practice of Mandala with Special Reference to the Modern Psychology of the Subconscious* (London: Rider & Co., 1974), p. 12.
37. Cicero, *De Natura Deorum II.II.II.* quoted in Jonas, op. cit., p. 245.
38. Jonas, op. cit.
39. Ibid., p. 246.
40. Ibid., pp. 246–47.
41. Ibid.
42. *Rigveda* X. 129.2.
43. Purusha has, strangely enough, been frequently identified with the primordial giant or a "hermaphrodite god-man".See R.N. Dandekar, *Insights into Hinduism* (Delhi: Ajanta Publications, 1979), p. 156; or a Titan, etc. As a matter of fact, the real significance of the term "purush" points to the entity that is resident in *pura* where *pura* stands for any body, i.e., a material cover, in a three-dimensional space, that is, *adhyatmika, adhibhautika and adhidaivika.* But before the creation of the *pura*, the resident is only a potential resident in search of *pura*; that is, it is only *svadhaya tadekam*, RV X.29.2. It is only Brahma who sacrifices himself to become the *vishwa,* the *idam sarvam.*
44. As *Shatapatha Brahman* 13.6.2.1 puts it:

    And as to why it is called *purushamedha,* the stronghold (*pura*) doubtless is he that blows here (the *prana,* the wind), he bides (*si*) in this stronghold (*pura)* hence he is the Purusha. And, whatever food there is in these worlds that is its '*medha',* its food, therefore (it is called) *purushamedha.* And inasmuch as at this sacrifice he seizes men (purusha) meet for sacrifice (*medhya),* therefore also it is called *purushamedha* (Julius Eggeling translation).
45. cf. RV X.130.1–3.
46. *Brihadaranyaka Upanishad* (Br. Up.), 1.iv. 1.
47. Prajapati begot a daughter (*vak*) and in syzygy with this daughter he created the world. This is known as Brahma *kilvisha,* the sin of Prajapati.

48. Triplication refers to the differentiation of Brahma into *manas (*intelligence, *prana (*energy), and *vak* (matter) as a consequence of the action of *vak* upon consciousness.
49. See Ramashray Roy, *Beyond Ego's Domain: Being and Order in the Veda* (Delhi: Shipra Publications, 1999). For the concept of *lokas,* see Jacob Needleman, *A Sense of the Cosmos: The Frontier of Modern Science and Ancient Truth* (Garden City, New York: Doubleday & Co., Inc., 1975), p. 17.
50. Needleman, op. cit.
51. On this point, see Madhusudan Ojha, *Vijnana Vidyuta* (Jaipur: Rajasthan Patrika Pvt. Ltd., 1990), p. 24.
52. It is against this background that Dandekar's characterization of the system of *lokas* or worlds or cosmographical regions as being marked by a "considerable vagueness, inconsistency and confusion" is unwarranted. See R.N. Dandekar, *Insights into Hinduism* (Delhi: Ajanta Publications, 1979), p. 162.
53. On this point, see Madhusudan Ojha, *Rajovada* (Jaipur: Manav Ashram, n.d.), Shloka 26.

8

State as Surrogate of Order

The central importance of creation myth, whether Vedic or any other, lies in the fact that it forges a link between the finite existence of man and the larger order, the cosmos, and the absolute whose creation this larger order is. This linkage is symbolized by the idea of God and since creation myth deals with a realm which is beyond the range of experience of most human beings and beyond the scope of discursive reasoning, its usefulness does not lie in its descriptive account of what this cosmos looks like or how it came into being; it lies rather in its evocative power. To put it differently, the world beyond this world is not perceptible; it is knowable only through the eyes of the heart. But, the language of the eyes of the heart is beyond communication. It can be communicated only through myths and symbols. It is in myths and symbols that the world beyond this world takes a concrete shape and becomes knowable. It is in this sense that myth cannot be considered as an instrument of description of the cosmos; it is an instrument *par excellence* of its creation. Creation myth is only to a very limited extent descriptive of reality; its primary function is not a cognitive but a formative one. To take the creation myth seriously is to endow it with the power to form not only the idea of who man is but also what relation does he stand in with the world around him.

Given the creative power of creation myth, its significance for man's existence in the cosmos is manifold. In the first place, creation myth constitutes a constant reminder that man is not an autonomous being. As a part of an order that is larger than what it is made out to be even by very imaginative persons, man must overcome his *hubris*, that is, defying god's law and seeking to assert his independence, and thus to redefine and change reality to suit his convenience.

In the second place, to check his *hubris*, he must be aware of the order that controls, regulates and sustains the functioning of the cosmos and consciously endeavour to imitate this order in his own being so that he does not upset the very delicate balance between order and disorder by self-regarding action. Creation myth constitutes a very important source of apprehending what this order is and what it signifies for man enmeshed in the manifold ties of this world. It is true that, as Plato underlines, creation myth is only a "likely story" of the cosmos. And, as a "likely story," it is only an intuitive and imaginative account of what the cosmos looks like. As such, this "likely story" of how this cosmos looks like may not match with how the cosmos in reality is structured. But this does not mean that this "likely story" is, therefore, a mere fabrication without any real worth or significance. What needs to be emphasized is that it is a story that has its basis in the ineffable experience of the unknowable on the part of saints, seers and philosophers. It is based on what Gonda calls "the heart's eye" which penetrates to the depth of the mystery of the unknown, unravels its structure and disconceals the order inherent in it or that flows from it like a river from its source in the unreachable higher reaches of a tall mountain. And, lastly, the order inherent in the structure of the cosmos and regulating its functioning has a deeper meaning for human existence. It is this meaning that helps man to give a semblance of order to his existence. It is with the help of this order and its reflection in his psyche, again, that man can rise above the contingencies of his limited experiences by relating himself to an entity larger than human existence and, as a result, endow his life with truth and meaning.

Given these ramifications of creation myth, it is not difficult to see that, even while the story of the creation of the cosmos is not "factual" in the phenomenal sense, it is over-pregnant with significance for human existence in the substantive sense. Substantively, it provides the basis for linking the finiteness of human existence with the absolute; it helps man discover the meaning of his life by outliving the fragmentary personal life by a projection onto the realm of infinity. It is this projection that provides man to apprehend the principles and precepts for organizing and regulating the pattern of his life that he thinks is proper for his own existential needs. It enables him to order pragmatic affairs of his life relating to the fulfilment of ordinary life needs involved with the process of production and reproduction and, beyond it, cater to the emotional and spiritual needs of his existence. Thus, the real significance of creation myth lies not only in the fact that it enables man to put his pragmatic affairs in order but also in and additionally in the fact that it helps him create a world of meaning out of desires, appetites and aspirations of his worldly existence. It is in view of this that even while creation myth is simply a "likely story", its principle virtue lies not in its factuality, but in its evocative power. That is, by evoking man's relatedness with the external world as a part of the cosmos and its creator, it inspires him to initiate a dialogue between his psyche and the divine ground of reality and participate, through this dialogue, in the process of community formation and/or maintenance, on the one hand, and world transcending experience of the divine, on the other.

It does not need to be emphasized that creation myth, when it succeeds in evoking appropriate response in man's psyche, becomes the substratum of the experience of transcendence. This experience of transcendence is undoubtedly intensely personal; however, it has trans-individual ramifications. Creation myth is fundamentally a projection of human psychic process[1] forging a connection – a spiritual connection – between the *martya* (mortal) and the *amartya* (immortal) inhabiting the man's interior; it provides us with the glimpse, even if only a dim one, of spiritual connections which elude us on a rationally differentiated level. It provides an insight into the structure of order that constitutes the source of spiritual connections. It is these connections that prove instrumental in not only keeping man's soul in order but also of evoking and sustaining what Voegelin calls "community substance". It is this substance that defines what Heraclitus calls *xynon* (shareable commonality) without which the existence of a community – whether religious, political or any other – is unthinkable. As such, it is this spiritual connection that provides the basis for the formation and continuity of a community.

It must, however, be stressed that the claims of the finite existence of man and the call of the absolute cannot be easily reconciled insofar as claims of finite existence have the ingrained tendency to resist restriction and externally imposed limitations. This tendency becomes very strong; it takes hold of man and pushes him in the direction of disobedience of "God's laws". As a result, the organization of man's pragmatic affairs into different spheres as social, economic, political, etc., becomes vulnerable to the encroachment and erosion by man's natural inclination to shape his life by the strong tendency towards what Nagarjuna calls "particularism". When seized by this tendency, man tends to seek privileged access to and control over strategic societal resources. As a result of this, individuals and groups afflict all these spheres with disorder induced by self-interested actions. In order, therefore, to (re-) instal order in these spheres, it is necessary to treat these different spheres as different parts of the larger reality of human existence. Needless to say that all the spheres constitute arenas where the conflict between the finite character of human existence and the absoluteness with the help of which man seeks to order his own life and his pragmatic affairs goes on unabated. In order to put an end to this conflict or, at least, minimize its occurrence, it is necessary to somehow overcome this conflict. This he can do only by going beyond the givens of nature (including his own) and society and linking his finite existence with the absolute as the source of truth, meaning and value.

It is in this sense that principles of order, which are meant to regulate and control the working of different spheres of human activities, are said to be derived from the primordial insight of seers, saints and philosophers into the structure of reality. It is this insight that is embodied and elaborated in creation myth. We can, therefore, appreciate why creation myth is constitutive of reality insofar as it stands as the surrogate of "the penultimate truth, of which all experience is the temporal reflection".[2] As the constitutive principle of reality, the "truth" contained in the creation myth must get its expression not only in man's life and his social relations but also in the organization of different spheres of man's pragmatic affairs. This means not only that man, as an individual person, must contemplate and imitate in his own personal life the order inherent in the cosmos. It also means that the internal urge to conform to and model one's dispositions and actions on the structure of cosmic order must get sufficient sustenance from his social environment in order for it to assume a practical shape. Thus, compatibility between the ordering principle of man's inner world and the environing social institutional arrangement is a necessary condition of keeping intact and alive the spiritual connection between the finite and the absolute. Without ensuring this compatibility, efforts by scattered individuals to order their interior in the light of this spiritual connection can bear no fruit.

In order to ensure this compatibility, two things are vitally necessary. In the first place, as has been pointed out earlier, simple contemplation of the order inherent in the cosmos is not enough either to initiate the quest for the unknown or to sustain one in this quest.

What is also necessary is the imitation of this order in one's life. Imitation does not mean doing mechanically what the gods did;[3] it means inner transformation in the light of the meaning of what the gods did. And, doing what the gods did in a way that forms the soul spiritually is to participate, actively and wholeheartedly, in the dialogue between man's psyche and the unknown beyond. And "participation is impossible without growth in stature within the personal limitations toward the rank of the best; and that growth is impossible unless one recognizes authority and surrenders to it".[4] This best is nothing else than the divine ground of reality, the entity beyond perception but not beyond experience even if it is ineffable. It is to surrender to this authority that paves the ground for man's journey towards perfection.

In the second place, it is true that the recognition of this best authority and surrender to its benign rule is a personal responsibility. But this responsibility can be discharged only in a society that reflects "right-mindedness" (*eunomia*). But how is this "right-mindedness" possible when individuals are immersed in their own self-assertive egoism? The establishment of a society marked by right-mindedness and its continued existence in history is possible if social institutional arrangement reflects the cosmic principles of order. But the problem of the conflict between the claims of man's pragmatic life and affairs and the pull of the need to keep the spiritual connection intact, alive and effective may get accentuated slowly and gradually eat into the vitals of social institutions if the former proves unresovable. As a consequence, man's thought-ways and work-ways may deviate from God's way and, as a result, introduce elements of disorder. To prevent order from sliding into disorder, and create and sustain order when elements of disorder disturb order, is the special responsibility of political order or the state headed traditionally by the king symbolizing the function of *regnum*.

Regnum represents an organized system of power. But its functioning has a double reference. If, on the one hand, the *regnum* is a system of coercive power, it is, on the other, also a system of moral authority. Its commands are not only backed by force but also by right. It is in this sense that *regnum* spans and joins two distinct orders of being, the order of positive reality and that of moral necessity. In order to be able to successfully join these two distinct realities, *regnum* needs to be grounded in and ruled by an eternally subsistent body of knowledge that lies beyond the ken of humanity immersed in materiality. It is only by being so grounded that the political order becomes capable of creating and sustaining a commonly shared world of meaning that groundedness in the knowledge of the beyond creates out of diverse human emotions, aspirations, appetites and desires This world of meaning will lack force and effectiveness as long as it does not evoke an appropriate response on the part of man whose emotions, aspirations, affections and desires it aims at ordering through the transformative act of self-transcendence. This evocative act can be facilitated if the *regnum* represents a unit sufficiently ordered to transform the amorphous field of human force into a well-integrated unity. And, the most essential and convenient object to be transformed into a symbol of unity is always man himself. One of the important functions of the *regnum* is to create a political order, which prevents the unity from being broken, or which restores it, when the aberrations of the movement of human desires break it.

But, the role of the *regnum* is dependent on the extent to which man himself takes care of his unity which, in the Vedic perspective, signifies *sarvata* (wholeness). But how is *sarvata* realized? It is true that *sarvata* is beclouded by man's immersion in everydayness. However, as the Vedic worldview underlines, man is well-endowed with spiritual, psychological and physical properties by virtue of which he is fully capable of discovering/recovering his *sarvata* if he so chooses. Structurally, he is homologically linked with the cosmos; spiritually, he is the son of light, although he might not be aware of it; and psychologically, he is in possession of faculties with the help of which he can know his true destiny by discovering, noetically or erotically, his true relationship with the Beyond. The Vedic perspective also underlines the fact that, in knowing himself and his relationship with the world at large and the divine forces, his different faculties function cooperatively, not discretely. Given this, attainment of *sarvata* is consequent upon man's regaining his oneness with the cosmos at large which, in turn, calls for imitating the order inherent in the cosmos. But this imitation is possible only through the realization that, as *Yajurveda* (XVII. 29) underlines, there is something "that is earlier than this earth and heaven, before the *Asuras* and Gods had being" (*parodiva para ena prithivya paro devebhirsurairyadasti*) and this something is the Father, who made us (*yo nah pita janita,* YV, XVII. 27) and it is the friendship of this Father of ours that helps in gaining or regaining *sarvata*. That is why, *Yajurveda* (IV. 8) prays that "may every mortal man elect the friendship of the guiding God (*divyo devasya neturmarto vurit sakhyam*). And, the clue to the identity of this Father of ours is contained in the Vedic creation myth.

The Father who begot us is not like the Platonic idea or form that is unchanging (*avyaya*). To quote Plato:

> ... (we) must agree that there is, first, the unchanging form, ungenerated and indestructible which neither receives anything else into itself from elsewhere nor itself enters into anything else anywhere, invisible and otherwise imperceptible; that, in fact, which thinking has for its subject.[5]

Positing the idea of unchanging form as the substratum of reality, Plato makes a distinction between being and becoming. While being exists in the state of permanent sameness,[6] becoming is something that comes to be and passes away, but never has real being. Everything that becomes must come to be by the agency of some cause; for without a cause, nothing can come to be.[7] For Plato, being is always real and has no becoming.[8] In contrast, there is something which is always becoming and is never real. But since Form or Idea is unchanging and does not enter anything, Plato must solve the problems of what sets the process of becoming in motion, on the one hand, and what it is that constitutes the model or pattern of the process of becoming, on the other. Plato rejects out of hand the idea that the world of becoming represents a good model;[9] for it to be good, it has to be modelled upon something eternal, the idea itself, which is the best of the causes. The world of becoming is, then, a changing image or likeness (*eikon*) of an eternal model "fashioned on the model of that which is comprehensible by rational discourse and understanding and is always in the same state".[10]

Since the world of becoming and all the objects in it are only moving images of form, it means that Plato must bifurcate reality into two distinct segments, one representing half-fashioned and discordant materials, and the other referring to an ordering entity which must refashion the aberrant objects with a view to bringing them closer to their model. This latter is Demiurge who uses half-fashioned and discordant materials created by *Ananke* (Necessity). Thus, every object in this world is a combination of reason symbolized by Demiurge and Necessity or *Ananke*. It is the process of compounding and mingling of the two order of things, the intelligible but unchanging and the sensible but changing, that has produced the cosmos and everything it contains. Given the fact that the cosmos and all that it contains are the combination of intelligence and necessity, a mixture of being and becoming, what is the relation, it must be asked, between the one (the being) whose *eikon* the world is and the many that the process of becoming engenders. As is quite clear from Plato's "likely story" of creation, he juxtaposes idea and necessity as two autonomously given and conditionally viable entities. This is evidenced by the fact that matter is shapeless and erratic and the Form itself is disembodied. Each of them alone or even in combination "would never coalesce into a 'world' without the cosmically creative force of psyche".[11] However, the creative force does not fully erase the separateness of the two orders of things. The creator of the cosmos remains aloof from its creation by not being a part of it. Moreover, even if the Demiurge puts objects in an ordered form they cannot be fully ordered since to manifest completeness is to transcend their own nature which is beyond the range of possibility.

Unlike the Platonic "likely story" of creation, the Vedic *Bhavavrittam* does not keep the God out of its creation; the creator is an integral part of its creation. Eliade is quite out of his depth when he argues that "the world that surrounds us, the world in which the presence and the work of man are felt – the mountains that he climbs – all these have an extra-terrestrial archetype, be it conceived as a plan, as a form, or purely and simply as 'double' existing on a higher cosmic level."[12] This is true of the Platonic form which constitutes the model or archetype of all the *nama* (name) and *rupa* (form) in the cosmos, but not of the Vedic God who is the arche of everything that we subsume under the rubric of *idam sarvam.* According to the Vedic *anupravesh* theory of creation, the God made this world and then entered it. As *Katha Upanishad* (II. II. 9) points out:

> *Agniryathaiko bhuvanam pravisto rupam rupam pratirupo babhuva:*
> *Ekastatha sarvabhutantaratma rupam rupam pratirupo bashisca.*

Just as fire, though one, having entered the world, assumes separate forms in respect of different shapes, similarly, the self inside all beings, though one assumes a form in respect of each shape; and (yet) it is outside.

It is clear that the Absolute is the creator of the world but it does not remain outside its own creation; it becomes an integral part of it. It is true that the one or *Tad ekam*, That One as the Veda calls it,[13] is not only the source of the world, but also the *paradigm* (*pratimana*), the substance and the knowledge which goes into the creation of the world. But before it transforms itself into the world *Tad ekam* is modeless in his omnipresence, not yet selfed (*atmanvi*),[14] as

Coomaraswamy puts it, is undifferentiated, yet unmanifest. Before the process of creation begins, before *Tad ekam* begins to grow, transmute and take different shapes, it is neither the creator nor the God the world comes to know about.[15] It is only with the help of the primordial self-sacrifice, known as the *Sarvahuta Yajna,* that He not only becomes aware of Himself but also becomes the world that is, He becomes the creator of the world (*Purusha Sukta,* RV, X. 90). Unlike the Platonic Demiurge who must act on materials already fabricated by *Ananke,* the Vedic God acts upon himself and fashions a world out of his different organs and limbs. The process through which One becomes many is described in the Veda as *Yajna*. Purusa, the universal spirit animating all creation, envelops everything but does not as, *Rigveda* (RV, X. 90.1) underlines, exceed ten fingers in measurement. This Purusa, the cosmic man, is so vast that he covers, even overlaps, the earth, not only in space but also in time, for he covers the three ages of the past, the present and the future. *Purusa evedam sarva yadbhutam yacca bhavyam (*RV, X. 90.2). And yet only a fourth portion (or leg) of this cosmic man represents the whole universe while his three portions (or legs) are beyond this universe, in the realm of immortality.

From this cosmic man was born Viraj, that is to say, the mother principle,[16] which gave birth to man. It was this man that was sacrificed in the *Sarvahuta Yajna*. *Rigveda* (X. 90. 4–15) describes the sacrifice of the Purusa in which he performs the act of his dismemberment and the scattering of his different portions for the completion of the work of creation was carried out. The Purusa performs an act of self-immolation so that the universe may come into being. Everything in this world has come out from this act of self-immolation involving the creation of seven *paridhis*[17] and three *samidhas.*[18] Insofar as the phenomenal world, *idam sarvam,* is the result of the sacrifice of the Purusa, there is no doubt that it is the God who transforms himself into the world. As *Shatpatha Brahmana* (SB, 3.5.3.1) points out, "Purusa is sacrifice ... it is for the reason that it is Purusa who spreads or stretches *yajna*. That is why, Purusa is *yajna*. In being stretched, *yajna* becomes as large as Purusa (*Pursuso vai yajna. Purustena yajno yadenam Purusastanuta esa vai tayamano ya vaneva Purusasta-vanvidhiyate tasmat puruso yajna*)."[19]

It should be noted here that the cosmic *yajna* which created the world did not proceed smoothly; there was an obstruction in the form of Vritra. Unless this obstruction was removed, the process of creation would have to be given up. Indra is, therefore, of central importance in the process of creation because it was he who slew Vritra and removed the obstruction that was impeding the free flow of *sapta sindhus*, or rivers. But who was Vritra? Is he really what he is made out by numerous Vedic scholars, that is, as an evil Asura who had captured cows of gods and obstructed the course of rivers, etc.? To answer this question, it is necessary to look at the act of creation from a slightly different but not incompatible perspective. As *Nasadiya Sukta* of *Rigveda* (X.129) makes it clear, there was neither *asat* nor *sat* nor anything else before the world came into being. In this state of "thinglessness", commonly interpreted as void (*sunya*), there arose a desire as the first occurrence of something before the process of creation began. It is this desire that, as *Rigveda* (X.129.4) underlines, links together the existing with the non-existing. The advent of desire splits the one into two opposite but complementary entities or principles, that is, Agni and Soma whose syzygy becomes instrumental in creating the world. Underlying the Vedic perspective is the idea that when the creator is disturbed by the desire to create *praja*, he becomes two and the two together beget the many. Thus, desire represents an act of diremption in that One is split into two (*dvedha*) *Brihadaranyaka Upanishad* (BU, 1.4.3). This diremption would not have been possible if the One were not the living conjoint, the unity of cohabitant parents (RV, I.140.3; III. 7.1). This diremption coincides with the birth of the son (*Indragni*), of light (*jyotis*), of the sun, "Savitur the creator who wears the visible forms of all things" *(viswa rupani prati muncate kavih,* RV, V. 81.2). Thus, the diremption of the conjoint principle is also the beginning of the process of remotion or becoming. "By the separation of the prior, the latter come forth (RV, X. 27.23). And, the coming forth of the latter is symptomatic of "the act of fecundation inherent in eternity".

It is because of this fecundation that *asat* is transformed into *sat*.[20] The transformation of *asat*, something without a centre or form into *sat*, that is, something with a centre and form, is the crux of the Vedic *bhavavrittam*, that is, the coming out of *sat* from *asat* (RV, X. 72.1.3). This, in fact, signifies the transformation of primal energy into mass (*pinda*) or, as Plato suggests, *enhylon eidos.* The Vedic *bhavavrittam* assigns a crucial role to *prana* in this transformation. For example, Parameshthin Prajapatya is *apah*, the ocean of possibilities of *nama* and *rupa*, which, in turn, symbolizes Rishis; *Shatpatha Brahmana* (6.1.1.1) identifies Rishis with *asat* and *prana*. But *asat* exists only as a potentiality, that of assuming *nama* and *rupa* (RV, X. 125.7). Parameshthi is the inexhaustible source of Soma or *apah* or *Ritasadan*, the abode of *Rita* (RV, VII. 36. 1). It is in the ocean of *apah*, the source of all possible *nama* and *rupa* that Atharva, the *Purishya*, the Lord of Parameshthi, brought Agni to life by "rubbing from the Pushkar" (YV, II. 32). With the birth of Agni from the womb of Paramesthi or *karan salil*, the sea of causes, the transformation of *asat* into *sat* or the transformation of energy into matter, takes place. By the same token, this transformation signifies the materialization of possibilities of *nama* and *rupa* inherent in the *karan salil*.

This materialization is facilitated by the right admixture and configuration of *vak* and *pranic* energy. Before the birth of *Agni*, Parameshthi simply represents a stage in the procession of Brahma where it has differentiated, to be sure; however, it has not yet manifested into *pinda* (mass) form; it is not enhylon *eidos*. It is not, therefore, accidental that Atharvan is described in *Atharvaveda* (AV, VII. 2.1) as father Atharvan who is like a brother to the gods (*deva bandhu*), mother of foetus (*maturgarbha*), the *prana* (*asa*) of the father and ever young. Parameshthi, under the charge of Atharvan, signifies the *Janat Loka*, the world where the process of creation but not of procreation begins. However, at this stage Parameshthi is a reservoir of different kinds of pranic energy. It is this stage in which, as *Rigveda* (IX. 74.2) underlines, the (*soma*) juice "has held two worlds (the Earth and the Heaven) together" (*une mahi rodasi yaksa davrita samichine*);[21] the three worlds of *rodasi* have not yet been separated by Indra (RV, V. 31. 6 and X. 113.5) and propped up by Varuna (RV, VI. 70.1). Parameshthi is, at this stage, simply a womb, not sterile but also not yet capable of creation.

In this state, *apah* is referred to as the abhorrent heavenly *apah* (*bi-bhatsunam apam divyanam)* (RV, X. 124.9; I. 164.8), in the state of menstruation, so to say, meaning that *apam divyanam* is obstructed in its onward march in the process of creation. Unless this obstruction is removed, it remains incapable of becoming as it were, "pregnant" and, therefore, unable to engender anything. To use another metaphor, the reservoir of *apah*, that is Parmeshthi, is characterized by *Atharvaveda* (X. 4.8 cd) as harbouring two snakes, one male and the other female, but both of them sapless. Once this state of saplessness is terminated, the process of creation moves forward. This state of saplessness is terminated once Agni, who lies in the womb of *apah*, becomes manifest. But its manifestation is obstructed by what in the

Vedic cosmological account is called Vritra,[22] an Asur. It is also interesting to note that even the gods are called asur and, like numerous Vedic words, the word "asur" too, is over-pregnant with meanings.[23] In one of the senses, Vritra, as Asur is a kind of pranic energy which has the effect of obscuring, obstructing or concealing something. This *prana* is called Atreya *prana* which is characterized as *adhamacchad*, i.e., the *prana* that intercepts and blocks light.[24] Another sense of the term 'Vritra' refers to the material covering, of the non-material Brahma. As has already been indicated, without this covering the transformation of primal energy into mass is inconceivable. However, this covering can be of two types, one subtle inclining to spirituality, or spiritually benign and symbolized by *Chandra* or *Soma* (moon), and the other gross or inclining to particularity or spiritually malign as symbolized by Vritra.[25] Vritra is Soma is confirmed by *Shatpatha Brahmana* (III. 4.3.13) when it says that "Soma (the moon) is god, since soma is in the sky. Soma, forsooth was viritra ..." *Shatpatha Brahmana* (11.1.5.7) also confirms that "... *papma vai vritro*", that is Vritra is sin, which ever keeps him from well-being, from virtue, and the good work." And, since Vritra is *papma*, he obstructs the good work of creation at its source.

It is because of the intervention of the Atreya *prana* that, even while Soma, as *Rigveda* (IX. 74.5) underlines, puts the embryo into the womb of the Infinite and *apah* receives the primordial germ (*tamidgarbha prathamam dadhra apo*, YV, 17. 30a), the birth of Agni did not take place. When Indra killed Vritra, fertile waters were released. *Rigveda* (X. 89.7) puts it:

> *Jaghana vrtram svadhitirvaneva ruroja puro ardanna sindhun;*
> *Vibheda giri navaminna kumbhama ga Indro akrnuta svayugbhih.*

(Indra) slew Vritra as an axe (cuts down) a tree; he demolished the cities (of the foes), he dug out the rivers. He shattered the cloud like a new pitcher; with his allies he recovered the cattle (cf. RV, I. 32.1; I. 32.7; IV. 19.3 and VI. 17.9).

The slaying of Vritra is so only in a metaphorical sense. As we know from *Shatpatha Brahmana* (1.1.3.4), "Vritra in truth lay covering all the (space) which here extends between heaven and earth. And because he lay covering (*vri*) all this, therefore, his name is Vritra. We also know from *Shatpatha Brahmana* (1.6.3. 13), when Indra was moving on in pursuit of Vritra, Agni and Soma and then Dyawa and Prithivi deserted Vritra on Indra's request. This made Vritra very weak and, when struck by Indra's vajra, "he lay contracted like a leather bottle drained of its contents, like a skin bag with the barley meal shaken out". But when Indra wanted to kill the weakened Vritra, he requested Indra not to kill him saying "thou art now what I (was before)[26] Only cut me in twain" (SB, 1.6.3.17). Indra accepted Vritra's request and cut him into two parts, one part which was benign (*yatsaumyam nyaktamas*) became the moon and the other which was malign or demonical (*yadasyasuryamasa*) entered different creatures as their belly. The cutting down of Vritra did release the fertile waters for the work of creation to proceed and restore strength to Indra; however, it also filled the creatures with hunger so that when they crave for food they pay tribute to Vritra (ibid.).

With the release of the fertile waters, procession of Brahma into *vishwa* (cosmos) began and the One, which alone was the self-subsistent entity that existed in the beginning, began to differentiate. In the beginning he was *aja* (a = not +Ja = born, unborn) and is called *aja ekapada* (one legged unborn).[27] He then becomes *chatushpada* when he fully transforms himself into *vishwa* through *Sarvahuta Yajna.* As *Rigveda* (X. 117–18) underlines:

> the sun with one foot outruns man with two!
> The man with two overtakes the hoary with three!
> Four-footed creatures come when the two-footed summon,
> And stand (as watchdogs) near the herd, observing.[28]

What this *mantra* symbolically refers to is the differentiation of *Tad Ekam* into two (*dwaidhapata)*; from the two – *para* and *apara prakrti* – the birth of the third, the sun, followed by the birth of everything in this world. And as the originator and supporter of the universe, the *Aja Ekapada* is identified in *Rigveda* (X. 65.13) as the upholder of the heaven, oceans, the water of the firmament, *vishwedevas* and Saraswati (cf. RV, X. 66.11). In confirmation of the procession of *Tad Ekam* into the universe, *Atharvaveda* (IX. 5.20–21) observes that when it strode out here in the beginning, the earth became its breast, the sky its back, its middle, the quarters its sides, the oceans its paunches; truth and right its eyes, all truth (and) faith its breath, *Viraj* its head.[29] It is this *Aja Ekapada* that, as *Atharvaveda* (X. 8.13) underlines, moves in every womb; although he is not seen, he is born and assumes manifold forms (*prajapatiscarti garbhe antardrsyamano bahudha vi jayate*; cf. YV, 31.19 and *Katha,* V. II. ii.9). It must be added here that the *Aja Ekapada* manifests itself into *vishwa*[30] and in doing that he becomes *catuspada,* the being with four feet. However, only one of its feet becomes the phenomenal world. The universe is the expression of the greatness of Purusa, but he is greater than all this (or *tode ti as* Aristotle calls it); all beings are one fourth of him; his other three-fourths (being) immortal (abide) in Heaven (*Etavanasya mahimato gyauansca purusah; pado'sya viswa bhutani tripadasya mrtam*, RV, X. 90.3).

Aja Ekapada, as *Atharvaveda* (X. 8.1) underlines, is that "who is set over both what is and what is to be and everything and whose alone is the heaven ..." (*yo bhutam ca bhavyam ca sarva yascadhitisthati, svaryasya ca kevalam tasmai jyesthaya brahmane namah).* It is because of its rootedness in this *Aja Ekapada* that the universe cannot be called something apart and separate from its creator. The swan (*hamsa*) ascending does not extract one foot from the sea; verily, if he should extract that, there would not be today nor tomorrow; there would not be night nor day; at no time whatsoever would it dawn (AV, X.4.21). It is this *Aja Ekapada* who, when fully transformed into *catuspada,* is called *Aswa* (horse). This horse is equated to *aswatha*, the cosmic tree, because it supports itself like a horse on three legs (*tripada*) while the fourth leg is held loose which stands for *idam sarvam.* This *Aswa* is, as *Taittiriya Brahmana* (TB, 2.8.9.6) points out, the Brahma whose procession into *vishwa* is the substantive theme of the *Sarvahuta Yajna.* To put it differently, it is this *Aswa* that is scarified (*aswamedha*) in order for the process of creation to be completed and the universe to take a concrete shape. The appearance of the *Aswa* on the world scene is the indicator of the completion of the first half, the *purvardha,* of creation ending with the birth of Agni from the womb of *apah*, that is, the ocean of Soma. It is this Agni that shines in the firmament as the sun. As *Rigveda* (I.163.1) indicates:

> *Yadkrandah prathamam jayamana udyantsamudra duta va purisat;*
> *Syenasya paksa harinasya bahu upastutyam mahi jatam te arvan.*

The great birth, O Horse, is to be glorified; whether first springing from the firmament or from the water, inasmuch as thou hast the wings of the falcon and the limbs of the deer.

It should be pointed out that the process of creation proceeds in two distinct stages, *purvardha,* the first half, and *uttararddha*, the second half. The whole process comprising these two stages is identified as *samvatsar.*[31] The *samvatsar* Prajapati, when identified with the first half (*purvardha*) of the transformation of Brahma, is called *anirukta* (undefined, unmanifest) Prajapati; he becomes *nirukta* when he becomes manifest in the second stage of the procession of Brahma.

As has already been pointed out, the universe is, in Vedic perspective, *agnishomatmaka,* that is, it is composed by Agni and Soma, two opposite but complementary principles. Soma, as *Samaveda* (SV, 124) underlines, *pavaswa Soma mahan samudrah* (the great ocean of Soma) that dwells in the high sky. It is described in *Rigveda* (VII. 47.2) as lightenings moving in the sky and in *Rigveda* (X. 124.9) it is called divine waters (*apam divyanam*) in which cows drink (*yatra gavah pibanti,* RV, I.23.18). It is also interesting to note that *Rigveda* (VII. 47.2) calls Soma "the waves of sweet waters" (*tamurnimapo madhumattama*). It is enough to suggest that Soma is *rasa* (fluid, ocean of energy); it was put in the vessel of Aditi by the Rishis (or *pranas* as SB, 6.1.1.1 put it), as *Rigveda* (IX. 68.7) notes. Parameshthi is the abode of *apah* who was engendered by Swayambhu. These two, Swayambhu and Parameshthi, are two universal parents. The former is equated with *Brishabha,* the Bull, and the latter with Dhenu, the cow (*brisabhasca dhenu,* RV, X. 6.7). They are like two bowls with one of them inverted; they constitute *yoni,* omphalos, in which, as *Rigveda* (X.121.7) indicates, the *brihatah apah* (vast waters) over-spreading the universe contained the germ which gave birth to Agni.

It is thus clear that *apah* represents the mother principle (cf. SB, 6.1.1.9, 11; 10.1.1.14). That is why, *Rigveda* (VII. 96.1) declares *apah* to be Indra's mother and *Rigveda* (X. 91.6) takes note of the fact that *apo agnim janyanta matarah* (Mother Apah gave birth to Agni). But, the relationship between Soma and Agni is not fully explained by mother-son relationship, it is, in fact, multifaceted; it is what *Satpatha Brahmana* (2.1.1.4) describes as *Yosha-Vrisha* (female-male) relationship underlining the mating (syzygy, *mithuna*) between the two as a precondition of creation. As *Rigveda* (VI. 58.8–9 and IX. 2.3) underline, Soma, bedecked with jewels and well decorated, goes to meet her husband, Agni. Agni-Soma relationship is also characterized as that between brothers or friends (RV IV. 44.15), on the one hand, and that between *Annada* (eater) and *Anna* (food) (BU, I.4.6), on the other (cf. CU, 5.10.4; BU, 6.2.16; SB, 10.6.3.1). *Satpatha Brahmana* (10.6.6.3) identifies the eater with the sun (Aditya) and the food with the moon (Soma). Without the support of Soma, Agni as pranic energy would ever lack a body; it will fail to live and be embodied. As such, Soma is Agni's body (*Agnistanurasi*, YV, 5.1). In addition, it is Soma that sustains Agni (*somenadityabalam,* RV, 1.92.22). Without the constant intake of Soma, Agni will become weaker and ultimately die. And, conversely, the dying fire gains strength when the fuel, that is *stoma*, is added to it.[32] It is with reference to this that the myth stated in *Satpatha Brahmana* (8.7.3.1517) is understandable. When Prajapati became unwell because he exhausted himself in creating the world, he rested his head in the lap of Parameshthi and recovered. It is, thus, clear that Parmeshthi is the birth place of Agni who ascends to the heaven and becomes Surya (the sun). It is as Surya that Agni or Prajapati represents the source of *bhutasrsti* (procreation) and the impeller of *samvatsar.*

It is against this background that we can appreciate the fact that the sun represents a dynamic element symbolizing both *Kala* (time) and energy that is the source of creation. It is because of this Surya that the phenomenal world has not only come into being but is also sustained and preserved. As *Atharvaveda* (XIX. 53.1) puts it;

> *Kalo aswo vahati saptarasmih sahasrakso ajaro bhuriretah;*
> *Tama rohanti kavayo vipascitastasya cakra bhuvanani viswa.*

Time drives the horse with seven reins, thousand eyes, unagaing, possessing much seed; him the inspired poets mount; his wheels are all beings (*bhuvana*).

The word *saptarasmih* refers to seven *pranas* (*sapta prana)* with the help of which beings in the world receive their lives and are able to sustain it. It also refers to *sapta bhuwan or lokas* insofar as the process of creation is spread over what *Rigveda* calls *sadas* because, as *Shatpatha Brahmana* (3.5.3.5) notes, *udar amevasya sadah* (sadah is their house); it is called *sadas* because all gods sat in it (*yadasminvishwe deva asidamtasmatsado nama*). The process of creation is divided into these seven *sadas*, also known as *lokas* and *dhamas,* each of which is presided over by a divine being called Prajapati (or *prana*). It is the task of this presiding deity to oversee that the elements located in each of these *sadas* play their role well. The aggregation of seven Prajapatis is the Prajapati who, as the Supreme Being, engenders other Prajapatis. That is why he is described as *prathamaja ritasya* (the first born of Rta, AV, IV. 35.1) and is the father of gods, such as, Indra, Soma (AV, 10.13) as well as the support of all the *lokas (prajapatir lokantsarva adharayat,* AV, X. 7.7).

The appearance of the sun in the firmament is, then, indicative simultaneously of the operation of three-interlinked processes. In the first place, it is indicative of the ongoing process of the transformation of Brahma which comes to completion when Prithivi is finally created. It is the process of becoming or *abhavan* which, as Coomaraswamy notes, "... is employed in the Rgveda to denote ... the passing over from one name and function to another."[33] But this passing over from one name and function, i.e., from one form to another, is neither accidental nor arbitrary. It is consequent upon the preparation of the ground, maturing of entities, qualities, processes, etc., appropriate for the transition from one state to another, from one stage to the next. Thus, the *idam sarvam* or what Gonda calls the visible parts of the universe is not the whole of the universe. As Needleman puts it, " ... it exceeds (man) in quality as well as quality" and is composed of spheres "which encompass the earth" and "represents" levels of conscious energy and purpose which surround the earth much as the physiological function of an organ such as the heart "surrounds" or permeates each of the separate tissues which comprise it ... .[34]

In the second place, all these "pervading" encompassing energies, purposes, functions and entities form a compact and cohesive organic system and the earth is inextricably enmeshed in a network of purposes, a ladder or hierarchy of purposes.[35] The network of purposes or purposeful energies constitute, as it were, a concentric circle each of which is the repository of energies or possibilities that are inter-related and that, taken together, constitute a state pregnant with the possibility of transiting to another different but organically linked state. Each of these circles is the locus of a particular state or outcome of creative forces which, in turn, are the outcome of certain antecedent forces occupying another circle. Even while the forces occupying a particular circle have been engendered by antecedent forces, they are uniquely constituted and have a different role to play.[36] These circles, or spheres or *lokas*, do not represent any spatial units; they are meant to be understood symbolically in the sense of "ensembles of possibilities" which, when conditions are ripe, transit into another more advanced stage of creation.

Thus, the *lokas* as the loci of purposeful energies, are fields where concrete action or effects of creative action take on concrete forms. Thus, these forces assume proper shape with the help of four constitutive principles: *Veda* (knowledge or *prana*), *chhandas* (limitation of the movement of pranic energy within certain field), *dik* (space, direction), and *yajna*. The *Ashwamedha Yajna* denotes the process through which the process of creation is brought to completion symbolized by the appearance of Prithivi and along with it of *praja* (beings) and *vitta* (resources necessary for the support of beings). Although the *Aswa* is constantly sacrificed, it neither can be cut nor does it die (RV, I.162.21). In the third place, the universe that is created as a result of *Aswamedha* has, as already indicated, multi-level, each level of which is linked with others in a great chain of being spread over seven *lokas.* This chain is called in the Vedic literature variously as *aswatha, cosmic tree, yupa, skambha, etc.* Everyone of these terms refers to the same entity, that is, tree of the universe whose roots lie in *parame vyoman*, the highest empyrean. As *Katha Upanishad* (II. II) puts it:

> *Urdhwanuto'vaksakha eso'swattha sanatanah;*
> *Tadeva sukram tadbrahma tadevamrtamucyate;*
> *Tasminlokah sritah sarve tadu natyeti kas'can.*

This is the beginningless Aswatha tree that has its roots above and branches down. That (i.e., its roots) is pure, is Brahman and is called immortal. On that are fixed all the worlds; none transcends that (cf. AV, X. 8. 7,13).

It is this tree that *Taittiriya Brahmana* (2.8.96) declares to be Brahma:

> *Brahma tadvanam brahma u sa vrksa asa yato dyawaprthiwi nistatataksuh;*
> *Manisino manasa pra brabinu tad brahdmadhyatisthad bhuvanani dharayan.*

What is underlined here is the equation of the cosmos with a forest called in *Rigveda* (VII. 33.9) as *Sahasravalasa* tree, each of the branches of which stands for a particular world and leaves represent different beings. The branches, the trees and the forest, all of them represent an integrated Being. Each leaf, and the smallest blade of green grass, is the embodiment of Prajapati. The leaves of this *Sahasravalasa* tree are, as *Yajurveda* (1.1) underlines, the source of food and energy (*ise tworje twa*). What is important to note here is that the nourishment and support of every being is derived from the branch of the cosmic tree. This is enough to suggest that man, too, is an integral part of the cosmos and, through it, linked to its creator. The fact that the roots of the cosmic tree lie in the *parame vyoman* indicates that the whole world and all beings in it are rooted in the absolute just as all the spokes of a wheel are fixed in the mane and the felloe of a chariot wheel. As *Brihadaranyaka Upanishad* (II. 4.15) puts it, all individual selves are rooted in the self (*sarva eta atmanah samparpita*). Since man stands in a homologous relationship with the cosmos, there is not only a structural similarity but also they are bound by the threads of integral relatedness.

These threads are, as *Aitereya Aranyak* (AA, III. 2.1) points out, breath, and the breath is a beam on which other beams rest. We also know from *Atharvaveda* (X. 8.9) that seven *pranas* are implantated in the body and from *Rigveda* (X. 82.2) that Viswakarman, who is beyond seven *pranas*, holds them together with *vatarajju* (wind-cord, cf. *Mundak Upanishad*, MU, II. 1.8; AV, VIII. 8.9). It is from this One beyond the seven *pranas* that, as MU (II. 1.8) underlines, all the senses have emerged. These seven *pranas* or Rishis are, as the creation of the One beyond them, its keepers (*risayah sapta sakam ye asya gopa mahati babhuvah,* AV, VIII. 8.9). It is this One who is the *sutram sutrasya* (thread of threads). The Vedic seers do not tire in reminding us that Brahma entered the body and Prajapati is its ruler (*Sariram brahma praviscchariredhi prajapati*, AV, X. 1.8.30). And, as *Yajurveda* (17.14) underlines, no abode can ever become sacred without gods (*Yebhyo na rte pavate dhama kincan*). In view of all this, it is clear, as *Samaveda* (1515) underlines, man is a combination of both *martya and amartya (adurita yo bhadamrta martyesu)*. And, since there is present in man the divine element that is why man's body is called by *Chhandogya Upanishad*(CU, VIII. 101) as *Brahmapura*, the abode of the Purusa.[37]

It is in this context that we can understand the implication of *Rigveda* (I. 164. 20) when it refers to two birds sitting on a tree, where one is eating the sweet fruit while the other looks on. It is a clear reference to the presence of two souls (*atmas*), *jivatma* or *bhoktr suparna and paramatma or the saksi suparna,* that is why *Rigveda* (VII. 86.6) notes that the elder (*paramatma*) lives with the younger (*atma*) brother (*ati jyayana kaniyasi upare*). However, the younger brother does not usually acknowledge the presence of and refuses to be guided by the elder brother. It is true that the chariot of the body has the *amartya* in it as its master, intellect as the charioteer and mind as briddle (KU, I. III. 3). In the chariot, senses are like horses which have their own mind and objects as their way. It is only when the inner dweller is actively associated with the body, senses and mind, that the chariot moves well and ensures its own as well as others well-being. But, the difficulty is that the senses, though created by Swayambhu, were damaged in the process of creation. As a result, they can see only the outer things, not the divine being within (*Paranci khani vyatrnat. Swayambhu stasmatparangpasyah nantaram,* KU, II. 1.1). And, this tendency of the senses to look only outward came to be reinforced when Vritra was cut asunder into two parts, one divine and the other demonic associated with *ashanaya* (hunger) for what Gandhi characterizes as "bodily comforts". And a person who gives preference to the appeasement of hunger, that is, his desires and appetites, worshirs Vritra (SB, I. 6.3.17).

As long as the demonic part of the slain Vritra, which has become an integral part of every being, rules or inspires the life activities of a person, he takes no note of the divine presence in his interior. He tends to become an individual in Jacques Martain's sense; that is, if the individual follows the direction of material individuality, "he will be carried in the direction of the 'hateful ego', whose law is to snatch, to absorb for oneself".[38] And, the individual dominated by material individuality becomes self-engrossed, acquisitive and possessive or what Sennet calls "narcissistic man",[39] who treats the external world – both society and nature – as potential means for the realization of his self-defined purposes. Such an individual, as *Chhandogya Upanishad* (CU, 8.12.1) puts it, becomes *kamacara* (one who is moved to act under the pressure of his desires) and, as a result, becomes *arthasamgrahi* (one who goes an acquiring wealth). In a social order dominated by *arthasamgrahis* the process of exchange[40] between man and others in the cosmos including gods comes to be disrupted and bonds of inter-dependence between man and God and society and world come to be snapped. And, when this exchange process is disrupted, order, too, is disrupted. Those who become acquisitive and possessive do not succeed in gaining the friendship of the god (*naki revantam sakhyaya vindase*) because "those who are puffed up with wine" offend him (*piyanti te suraswah*, RV, VIII. 21.14).

The God entered into man and made the mortal his house (TS, V. 5.21). However, since he divided himself into many parts as beings, he was unable to emerge out of them whole and well-integrated. He could become whole only if he is re-assembled and integrated when gods and men make sacrifices. The gods did the sacrifice and Prajapati began to regain his wholeness. Moreover, by doing sacrifice, the gods went up to heaven. But then they were afraid that, doing *yajna*, men and Rishis too would become like gods. They, therefore, joined the heaven with a *yupa* (pole) in order to confuse and, therefore, prevent them from going to heaven. They buried the front end of the *yupa* in the earth. When men and Rishis wanted to do the *yajna*, they found the *yupa* only with the wrong end pointing towards the heaven. They, therefore, uprooted the *yupa* and buried it again with its head pointing towards the heaven. And, then, they could know the *yajna* and go to heaven (or become god-like) by performing it (AB, II. 1). It does not need to be pointed out that the *yupa* is no other than the *Aswatha*, the Cosmic Tree with its head turned towards the highest empyrean so that men can know it and become godlike by performing it (*tadadyupa urdhwo nimiyate yajnasya prajnatmai lokasya nukhyatyai,* AB, II. 1).

But, for many, the God does not exist; nor do many people believe that there exists a cosmos which is well-ordered and regulated and its different parts are interlinked and sustain each other. Such a cosmos has no meaning for them. As a result of this, the God buried in the cave of man's interior and concealed by the Vritra and his scaly reptilian skin, cannot be released and made whole. "'You' and 'I' are the psychological prison and Constrictor in whom the First has been swallowed up that 'we' might be at all."[41] Unless this Vritra within us is slain, "neither can the God be made whole nor can man overcome his *ashnaya* (hunger for possession and power)". As *Aitareya Aranyaka* (II. 1.8) puts it, the self or the sense of "I" is "the hiding place (*giri*) eye, ear, mind, speech, and breath. They call it the hiding place of Brahman, who knows this throws down the enemy, the evil one, who hates him." This hateful enemy, this adversary, is none but the self, the *bhoktr suparna* who as the Outer Man submerges the Inner Man; unless this Vritra is killed by vajra, that is, the shaft of light (cf. RV, II. 11.5 and X. 95.4), the *jyotir abhayam*, the light that makes one fearless, neither we nor the God can become whole and acquire *sarvata* (wholeness). And, this *sarvata* can be gained only when man commits himself to exploring truth.

Without this commitment, man can never succeed in controlling his passions and will ever remain what Plato calls "the slave of many mad masters" or as *Chhandogya Upanishad* puts it, *anyarata.* It is in this sense that we can appreciate what *Aitereya Brahmana* (AB, I. 1.6) has to say about gods and men: *Satyam Samhita vai daiva anrtasamhita manusya* (it is only the gods who are imbued with truth, not men, cf. SB, I. 1.1.4). To turn away from *anṛta* and begin the search for truth is to look inward to the eternal light that is located in the cave of man's interior. This is possible only when man performs *yajna*. But what kind of *yajna*? There is in Vedic literature a clear distinction between the mere performance of *yajna* and *yajna* as a means of inner spiritual transformation. For example, *Rigveda* (VII. 76.3) underlines the fact that none attains Him (Indra) by works of sacrifice.[42] As such, what is important in the Vedic perspective is not what is enacted outwardly, but what is accomplished inwardly by the understanding sacrificer. The emphasis in the Veda is on *adhyatmika antaram agnihotra*. In it no external *havya* (offering) is used insofar as *vihavya* (without any external oblation) is superior (*asti nu tasmadojiyo, yad vihavyenejire,* RV, VII. 5.4). In this *antaram agnihotra* the sacrificer, *Rigveda* (4.6.1) declares, yokes himself like an understanding horse (*swayam ayuji hayo na vidwana*, cf. *Geeta*, V. 27). And, when the sacrificer engages in *antaram agnihotra*, he becomes a ladle for the gods (*ayam yascamaso devapanah*) who, drinking from it, revel (*tasmin madayantam*, AV, X. VIII 3, 53).

It is in this context that the distinction the *Shatapatha Brahman* makes between *satisada* and *satrasada* assumes importance. While *satisada* signifies a sacrificer who is seated in the *yajna* in reality, that is, he performs the *yajna* by supporting it with his mind (*manasa adhavayati*, SB, II. 2.4.8) and he is, in essence, seated amongst the gods (*satisu devatasa sidantah*), the *satrasada* refers to a sacrificer who just sits at the session of the *yajna* to offer oblation to the gods. The *satisada* does not offer any external *havya* but, instead himself becomes the oblation (cf. RV, X. 124.6, SB, XII, 5.2. 13; AB, II. 4; BU, VI. II. 14). In contradistinction to *satisada*, *satrasada* goes on performing *yajna* offering not himself as oblation, as the sacrificial beast, but only external oblation to please gods in order to acquire sons, riches, prowess, etc. This brings into play another Vedic distinction, that is, between *atmayaji* and *devayaji*, the former referring to a sacrificer who offers himself as oblation and the latter signifying tributes paid to the gods (SB, XI. 2.6.13–14).[43] This distinction, Coomaraswamy suggests, "is of active and passive viae, of 'salvation' from liberation."[44] The *atmayaji* is the one who sacrifices in himself (*atmanneva yajati*).

It is clear, then, that for men to do as gods did in order to become god like, that is to say, they have to imitate what *Aitareya Brahmana* (30.1) calls "*devasilpa*" which sublimates man's base desire and appetites. However, the natural man is spiritually blind.[45] That is why, he cannot make a distinction between the sun whom everyone sees and the sun which not all know with the mind (*pasyanti sarve caksusa na sarve manasa vida*, AV, X. 8.14). As a result, his interior is marked by disorder which spreads outward and disrupts order in society. It, therefore, becomes necessary to create and instal the state as the guardian, defender and promoter of order.

Notes

1. On this point see, Eric Voegelin, *History of Political Ideas: Hellenism, Rome, and Early Christianity* (Columbia: University of Missouri Press, 1977), Vol. I, esp. 'General Introduction' to the series by Thoman A. Hollweck and Ellis Sandoz, pp. 26–27.
2. Ananda K. Comaraswamy, *Hinduism and Buddhism* (Delhi: Munshiram Manoharlal Publishers Pvt. Ltd., 1986), p. 6.
3. *Shatpatha Brahmana* (SB), VII. 2.1.4.
4. Eric Voegelin, op. cit., p. 29.
5. *Timeaus* 51 E52. All references to *Timeaus* are to Francis M. Cornford, *Plato's Cosmology: The Timeaus of Plato,* translated with a running commentary (London: Routledge & Kegan Paul, 1971), if not otherwise mentioned.
6. Ibid., 29A.
7. Ibid., 28A.
8. Ibid., 27D.
9. Ibid., 28D.
10. Ibid., 29A.
11. Eric Voegelin, *Order and History: Plato and Aristotle* (Baton Rouge: Louisiana State University, 1957), III, p. 197.
12. Mircea Eliade, *The Myth of the Eternal Return,* trans. Willard R. Trask (New York: Pantheon Books Inc., 1954), Bollingen Series XLVI, p. 9.
13. *Rigveda* (RV) X. 129.1; *Taittiriya Samhita (TS)* VI. 4.8. 3; SB X. 5.3.1–2, etc.
14. Ananda K. Coomaraswamy, *A New Approach to the Vedas* (Delhi: Aparna Publications, 1985), p. 58; cf. RV.1.164.4.
15. On this point, see R. Panikkar, *The Vedic Experience: Mantra Manjari* (Pondicherry: All India Books, 1983), p. 50.
16. Viraj has been variously translated as "the cosmic water" (Edgerton), "the cosmic egg" (Raghavan), "Mother principle" "*mahat*", "*yoni*" (V.S. Agrawal). It can be understood as the primal *Shakti*, a cosmic source, a womb fecunded by the Purusa. As a result of this fecundation, a Purusa came into being, whose total sacrifice initiated the chain of Aditi-Daksha-Aditi (RV X. 72.4–5) meaning the beginning and continuance of the process of creation. See also AV VIII. 10; IX. 2. 5; IX. 8.30; BV IV. 2.3. See also Ramashray Roy, *Beyond Ego's Domain: Being and Order in the Veda* (Delhi: Shipra Publications, 1999), pp. 121–26.
17. Wilson refers to Sayan's interpretation of the term "*paridhi*" (or enclosures) as seven metres, Gayatri, Tristubha, Jagati, etc., also as meaning shallow trenches, three of which are dug round the *Ahvaniya* fireplace,

three round the northern altar, and the seventh ideally dug round the sun to keep off evil spirits. Mahidhar, however, takes this term to mean "the seven oceans". But according to V.S. Agrawal, the term signifies seven directions of space (RV, IV. 13.3) as well as *sapta dhama,* the seven *lokas* (RV, I. 22.16) in addition to boundaries. *Vedic Lectures*, p. 184.

18. The term '*Tri Sapta*' refers, according to Agrawal, to the seven-fold *suparna-chitti* and "tri" to three fold *Purusha.* "The life in the person is conceived of as *Gayatra* chant and it is said to complete its course in its three fuel-sticks (*Gayatrasya samidhas tisra ahut,* RV, I.164.25). The number refers to manifestation on the plane of matter and three to that on the plane of *Prana*, or the lower and the higher Prakritis respectively. Both are integrated, so that the Purusa Yajna may be possible. The human body or the living organism is the object of the symbolical enunciation. See *Vedic Lectures,* p. 189.

19. It is, thus, clear that it is the Purusa who becomes the *yajamana* (the sacrificer) of the *Sarvahuta Yajna* in which he immolates himself so that the world may become a real possibility. Thus, we must reject Eliade's observation that everything in the world that surrounds us does not have a prototype of this kind. For example, desert regions, inhabited by monsters, uncultivated lands, unknown seas on which no navigator has dared to venture, do not share with the city of Babylon, ... the privilege of a differentiated prototype. They correspond to a mythical model, but of another nature: all these wild, uncultivated regions and the like are assimilated to chaos, they still participate in the undifferentiated, formless modality of pre-Creation. That is why, when possession is taken of a territory – that is, when its exploitation begins – rites that are performed symbolically to repeat the act of Creation. See *Myth of the Eternal Return,* p. 9.

    Citing the example of the possession by Scandinavain colonists, of Iceland Landnama, Eliade further observes that "they regarded this act neither as an original undertaking nor as human and profane work. Their enterprise was for them only the repetition of a primordial act; the transformation of chaos into cosmos by the divine act of Creation. Ibid., p.10.

    Thus, for Eliade, Creation is nothing but the transformation of chaos into order. It must, however, be pointed out that, true to his commitment to the Platonic "likely story" of creation, Eliade does not recognize any other perspective on creation. That is why he has completely missed the essential point of the Vedic *bhavavrittam.*

20. There is a lot of confusion in translating the term "*asat*". It is variably translated as chaos, non-being, non-existence, etc. Even perceptible commentators like V.S. Agrawal and Nicholas seem to be working under the erroneous idea that chaos prevailed before the process of creation began. See V.S. Agrawal, *Sparks from the Vedic Fire* (Benaras: Benaras

Hindu University), p. 89, where he refers to the sun coming out of incoherent watery chaos. As a matter of fact, *asat* in the Vedic perspective is defined as something which has neither a centre nor a form. See Motilal Shastri, *Vedic Concept of Man and Universe* (Jaipur: Rajasthan Vedic Tattwa Shodha Samasthan, 1950), p. 48; *Veda ka Swaroop Vichar* (Jaipur: Rajasthan Patrika), p. 30 and *Bharatiya Drshti se "Vijnana" Shabda ka Samanwaya* (Jaipur; Rajasthan Patrika), pp. 27–28.

21. Dyava and Prithivi are, according to RV, I.159.4, born of the same womb (*sayoni*); however, they are in close embrace, that is, undivided, unseparated.

22. In explaining the Vritra phenomenon, most Vedic scholars have taken the easy way out. They have treated him as a real historical presence who belonged to a moiety called Asur at enmity with Indra, the leader of another moiety, Sura. Vritra, it is suggested, had stolen the cows *(gavah)* of the Suras and hidden them in the deep caves of a mountain. The battle that took place between Suras and Asuras saw Vritra killed by Indra's vajra; this facilitated the release of the cows. Or, alternatively, if one wants to pitch one's interpretation at the symbolic level, then, *gavah* are equated with light and Vritra with cloud which dispersed when Indra hurled his vajra at it and, as a result, light-rays were released. The first interpretation pits the scholar's opinion against the authority of the Vedic literature itself. What is to be noted in this connection is that RV, X 27.3 ab states that "I know not that man who says he (Indra) is the slayer in battle those who do not reverence the gods (cf. RV,X. 54.3; SB, 11.1.6.10). The second interpretation is slightly better but stays still at the phenomenal level. It is, however, forced into a spiritual significance by treating it as a symbol of the victory of good over evil and of light over darkness. This ethical and spiritual interpretation, however, denudes the richness of Vedic symbols and dirempts them from their luxuriant and nurturing Vedic cosmological and metaphysical ground. In view of this, it is necessary to relocate the Vritra phenomenon in the ground it has sprung from and is nourished by. For another explanation. See V.S. Agrawal, *Asya Vamasya Sukta*, pp. 50–57.

23. We can identify two principal senses in which the term "asur" has been employed in the *Rigveda.* First, it means to be endowed with *prana* (life-breath). For example, in RV, 1.164.4 "asur" refers to *prana* and, therefore, even gods are called in Rigveda "asur". Later, asuras came to be differentiated from *suras* (*Tandya Brahmana,* 18.1.2) with the latter meaning asur, that is, the elder sons of Prajapati. See also Banarasi Tripathi, *Rigvediya Subantapadon ka Vyutpatti-Chintan* (Varanasi: Sampurnanada Sanskrita Vishwavidyalaya, 1990), pp. 69–70.

24. In the Vedic literature two types of *prana* – *dhamacchada* (or Agni, cf. Monier-Williams, *Sanskrit-English Dictionary*, p. 514) and *adhamacchada*

have been identified. As AB (III.1.7) points out, one of the three *vasatkaras* is *dhamacchda* which signifies a place to which a demon cannot have access; it helps in the creation of *praja* and *pasu.* By contrast, *adhamacchada prana* is vulnerable to the entry of *asuras* (demons). According to SB (1.4.5.13), Atri was born as a result of the miscarriage of *vak.* The miscarriage occurred because she was given an unfavourable verdict by Prajapati who declared *manas* as superior against vak's claim to be declared superior. Since Atreya was born of miscarriage, *atreya prana* is incapable of producing anything because it is *adhamacchada.* Another explanation of why a category of *pranas* becomes *adhamacchada* is given in RV (X. 124.8) which talks of *bibhatsuvoapa vrtradalishtan* (the water made impure by the presence of Vritra). *Bibhatsu* is a state of being in menstruation and, therefore, prohibitive of copulation and procreation. And, as RV (X. 124.9) makes it clear, the abhorrent *apah* has a friend or companion in a golden bird, a Hamsa, called Indra, who rushes to her help when called by *Anushtubha.* See V.S. Agrawal, *Asya Vamasya Sukta*, p. 43.

25. See Harishankar Joshi, *Vaidik Vishwa Darshan* (Banaras: Banaras Hindu University, VS 2025), II, pp. 543 and 573–74.
26. *Taittiriya Samhita* (TS), I.4.12; II. 501.
27. *Aja Ekapada* is so called because it transforms from the stage of one-leggedness to four-leggedness (*anjati ekena padeneti aja ekapat*).
28. R. Panikkar's translation in *Mantra Manjari,* op. cit., p. 851.
29. Cf. AV XIII.1.42 and IV. 14.1.
30. *Ekam vartata ekanimi sahasraksaram pra puro ni pasca;*

    Viswam bhuwanam jajan yadasyardha kva tad babhuva.

    One-wheeled it rolls, one-rimmed thousand-syllabled, forth in front, behind, with a half it has generated all existence; what its (other) half – what has became of that (AV, X. 8.7.)?
31. *Samvatsar=sam* (the state of equilibrium)+*vas* (*sthiti*, existence)+*sar* (motion). See Motilal Shastri, *Iswar Krishna Rahasya* (Jaipur: Rajasthan Patrika), p. 80. *Samvatsar,* thus, refers to that which moves but does not abandon its place (cf. AV, XI 4.21). It refers to one underlying reality, Brahma, who creates all gods (*sarva atsarat*) and symbolizes the movement of the One who has no leg (*apada*). Brahma is also identified with *samvrit* which, again, stands for *samvatsar* (see YV, 15.9). As such, Prajapati (*samvrit*) becomes *samvatsar* because he moves (*saratiti*). For further details, see *Jaiminiya Brahmana,* 260.
32. The term, '*stoma*' is one of those terms that have been so interpreted as to distort their real significance. Take, for example, Suryakant who (in his *Vaidik Kosha*, p. 589) equates *stoma* with a song of praise or prayer. However, *Tandya Brahmana* (2.5.4) equates it with *viryam* (virility,

vigour). As RV III. 5.2 notes, "*pridvagnirvavrdhe stome* ..." Wilson translates it to mean that the adorable Agni is magnified by the hymns. This may be true but not significant. However, if, as Agrawal suggests, *stoma* means piling, then the real significance of *stoma* is the increase in the virility and vigour of Agni which is possible only when it feeds as *annada* on more *anna,* that is Soma. See V.S. Agrawal, *Vision in Long Darkness,* p. 59. Thus, *stoma* means, in numerous contexts, the growing strength of Agni, that is, the rise in temperature in heat generated by the input of more and more fuel. In RV (III. 58.1), there is a reference to the fact that *usasah stomo Aswinavaigah* (*Stoma* wakes up Aswina at dawn). In SB (8.4.3.2) Prajapati is said to have asked the cooperation of *Prana* for producing *praja.* On being asked who *prana* would pray with, Prajapati replied that they two together should pray. Thus both began to pray (*stosya*). The conclusion is that *yajno vai stoma* (*yajna is stoma*). In both these cases, the symbolical significance is clear: If Aswins need vigour to scale the height of the sky, so does Prajapati in creating the world. In both cases, there is a frightful consumption of energy which must be "stock-piled", as it were, to be able to do the assigned task effectively. It is interesting to note that in YV (14.28.31) are offered praises to all those who were either overlords of the process of creation or beings created. The last verse refers to the thirty-third *stoma* being offered to Prajapati, the overlord of all. For the ritual significance of *stoma,* see especially SB (9.5.2).

It is against this background that we can appreciate the fact that *stoma* signifies energy. *Pranagni* that is emitted form the centre of any *pinda* (mass) is called *gau* which is said to have one thousand parts; when divided by 30 (15 days and 15 nights) *gau* yields 33 *stomas* which describe the spread of Agni and Soma, the rest 10 *stomas* constitute Prajapati.

33. Ananda K. Coomaraswamy, "Vedic Monotheism" in *Selected Papers* II, p. 172.

34. Jacob Needleman, *A Sense of the Cosmos: The Encounter of Modern Science and Ancient Truth* (Garden City, New York: Doubleday & Co. Inc. 1975), p. 17.

35. Ibid. This organism or hierarchy is conceived, in the Vedic perspective, as forming a circle at the centre of which stands *Nabhya* Prajapati as the effulgent Aditya. The rays of Aditya describe the procession of the *sthanu* that is, *Nabhya* Prajapati; the end of the these rays, forming a circle, symbolizes Prajapati's *mahima* which is discernible in the manifested world. Needless to say that it is only the *mahima* of *Nahbya* Prajapati that is or can be perceived.

36. On this point, see Madhusudan Ojha, *Vijnaan Vidyut* (Jaipur: Rajasthan Patrika, 1990), p. 24.

37. As AV (X. 2.30) notes, *puram yo brahmano veda yasyah purusa ucyate* (purusa is called because he resides in a *pura*).
38. Jacques Martain, *Challenges and Renewals: Selected Readings. Eds,* Joseph W. Evans and Leo R. Ward (Notre Dame: University of Notre Dame Press, 1966), p. 290.
39. Richard Sennet, "Destructive Gemeinschaft," in Norman Birnbaum, ed., *Beyond the Crisis* (London: Oxford University Press, 1977), p. 176.
40. The process of exchange between man and god is underlined in *Taittiriya Samhita* (8.4.1) *as follows:*

    Give thou to me, I shall give to thee;

    Bestow upon me; I shall bestow upon thee;

    Accept my offering, I shall accept thy offering.
41. Ananda K. Coomaraswamy, *Hinduism and Buddhism* (Delhi: Munshiram Manohar Lal Publishers Pvt. Ltd., 1986), p. 8.
42. For a very useful discussion, see Ananda K. Coomaraswamy, "*Atma-Yajna:* Self-sacrifice," in *Selected Papers,* p. 108.
43. Cf. *Jaiminiya Upanishad Brahmana* (1.14.1): "He should not be one whose gods are far away. Verily, it is insofar as he approaches the gods with himself *(atmanadeva upasate)* that becomes god for him;" and BU (1.1V. 10), " so whoever approaches a deity as being other, thinking he is one, and I another,' does not comprehend; he is a mere victim of them".
44. Ananda K. Coomaraswamy, *Selected Papers,* p. 132.
45. Ananda K. Coomaraswamy, "Windows of the Soul" in *What is Civilization?* (Delhi: Oxford University Press, 1989), p. 53.

9

The Philosopher and the King

The need for political order arises not because man is by nature bad; its need arises because man is easily persuaded to seek the pleasures of the body. Once he is swayed by his appetites, he turns his back on Purusa who is the real citizen residing in the city of man's being. This is, as has already been suggested, symptomatic of Vritra. It is Vritra who entices man away from the path of virtue. Deserting the path of virtue, man loses the power of discrimination, that is to say, the power of judging what is right and what is wrong. Loss of discriminatory power also signifies the loss of judgement of discriminating among needs for ascertaining which needs to fulfil, which to defer and which to discard forever. What, then, assumes central importance in man's life is the desirability of fulfilling whatever needs appear to be necessary and pressing for realization.

When the fulfilment of needs, as and when they arise and press for realization, assumes central importance in man's life, it signifies that needs can no longer be judged at the bar of reason.[1] When released from the limitations imposed on them by reason, needs become the ground of their own justification; they no longer have to look for their legitimacy in any rationale or principle outside themselves. The claim of auto-legitimacy by needs signifies further the fact that only two *purusharthas*, *kama* (desire) and *artha* (means of satisfying desires) assume a pivotal role in man's life. The result is that the question of what man substantively is pushed to the margin of existence. As a result of this, individual life loses its balance and, therefore, harmony and social life its concord. This further means that appetites and desires (*kama*) assume the direction of the course of human action and claim the rulership of the soul that properly belongs to *prajnana* or *sophia*. But appetites and desires are numerous and their demands are not only too many but also usually conflicting. Even if they are not conflicting, it is impossible, for various reasons, to meet all of them; in addition, the attempt to meet them all produces only deleterious consequences for the individual himself as well as for his relationship with the external world, both nature and society.

One very far-reaching deleterious consequence has, of course, to do with the erosion of auto-control signifying the failure to make a distinction between right and wrong. With the erosion of auto-control, man's interior becomes a veritable playground of riotous appetites. Since it is believed that it is for the good of the individual himself that he does the bidding of his desires, the attempt to satisfy these desires must be made. However, while doing the bidding of his desires, the individual treats the external world as a potential means for the realization of his purposes.[2] When the individual goes on doing the bidding of his desires, it must be said that he lives lustfully and when a person lives lustfully, he becomes dead, entombed in the passion and frenzy of his body, dead to the call of his own "inner" voice warning him against the malign consequences of his willing surrender to his passions. What needs to be emphasized is that when the individual becomes dead to his own "inner" voice, he also becomes dead to the real significance of the external world, both society and nature. And, above all, he does not know which good to pursue. In the absence of the knowledge of what is the greatest good and, lacking the basis for choosing reliably among a multiplicity of apparent goods, it is very difficult to achieve completeness of existence or integration of being. Man is, therefore, forced to welcome them all and try to determine in what manner and to what extent all the goods that he seeks might fit together.

Fitting together is difficult in want of what Plato calls "synoptic vision", that is, the capacity of establishing a principled relationship among various goods as well as among various elements of the external world. Without the synoptic vision, the soul loses its discriminating, regulatory and disciplining power, appetites and desires fill the gap created, by the withdrawal from the centre stage of man's existence of the ordering element. Integration of different capacities of the individual as well as that of the individual and the cosmos he is an integral part of gets disrupted; the consequent disorder of the soul leads to what Plato calls *polypragmosyne*, the readiness to engage in multifarious activities which are not the individual's own concern and *allotriopragmosyne* (meddlesomeness, officious interference).[3]

This leads to the merger of ego and *id* in Freudian parlance that exemplifies the well-known saying of Freud "where *id* was, there ego shall be". It does not mean that the ego should replace the *id*, but that the *id* should come to exist in the realm of the ego, it (i.e., the ego) should shed the illusion of integrated selfhood and dissolve into those associative chains normally repressed into the unconscious.[4] This also means that the self emerges, as Rieff suggests,

> as a subject of a struggle between two objective forces – unregenerate instincts and overbearing culture. Between these two forces there may be compromises but no resolution. Since the individual can neither extirpate his instincts nor wholly reject the demands of society, his character expresses the way in which he organizes and appeases the conflict between the two.[5]

This struggle is real and escape from it is either surrender of the self to the *id* or to the super-ego. If it is the former, the self is ruled by the mob of appetites and desires, and in the case of the latter, it is governed by oppressive traditions, conventions, customs or regnant fashion of ideas and opinions. The individual has, in this situation, no other choice than what euphemistically is called adaptation. In any case, the individual is ruled not by his better self, i.e., his soul which is the sensorium of divine. He is, to put it differently, not his own master; he is ruled either by his passions or impersonal social norms in whose making he has had no hand.

It is this situation that is identified in the Vedic perspective as leading to the loss of essential selfhood and therefore freedom. It is this situation that reduces man to what *Chhandogya Upanishad* (CU, VII. 25.2) calls "*anyarata*".[6] This suggests that integrated, controlled and well-disciplined selfhood cannot be attained if the individual surrenders either to his *id* or to the super-ego. It should, however, be noted that the prime cause that impels the individual to surrender his freedom is, as the Vedic perspective makes it clear, nothing else but the demonic part of Vritra that becomes an integral part of every being as *ashnaya* (hunger).

It is this *ashnaya* that impels man to engage in the quest of bodily comfort. In the process, the *bhoktr soparna* becomes the dominant element in deciding what man must do and be. What man does and becomes is, as John Dewey points out, defined by the dictum, "I possess, therefore I am."[7] Those who come under the complete sway of the demonic aspect of Vritra, become acquisitive, possessive and get puffed up with wine; as a result, they do not succeed in gaining the friendship of gods (RV, VIII. 21.14). The result is that the outer man pushes out the inner man, the Purusa, and becomes the arbiter of what man must do and become. It is in this sense that the natural man becomes spiritually blind. As a result, man's interior is marked by disorder that spreads outward and disrupts order in society. When order in society is disrupted, a vicious circle is created in which it becomes difficult for any individual to cure the sickness of his soul; this inability further adds to the prevailing disorder in society increasing disorder in the psyche of individuals. It is this situation that makes it necessary to form and instal the state as the guardian, defender and promoter of order. It is in this sense that the state becomes the surrogate of order.

But, it must be asked: what kind of political order can quell the rebellion of passions and succeed in creating or restoring order both in the individual psyche and social cosmos? It is quite clear that when persons become *anyarata*, their internal and external controls break down to such an extent that "an appreciable number of persons in a society can live, in various degrees of realization, as it were in the dream of their desires".[8] With the dream world becoming a prominent feature of the life of passion, *xynon* (shareable commonality), as Heraclitus calls it, is lost and consensus as the foundation of community is destroyed. As long as individuals remain conscious of a shareable commonality, the people remain attuned to a larger reality which undergirds the cosmos. But, the loss of this commonality breaks the unity of the cosmos and brings into being a diversity of dream worlds in its place.[9]

The destruction of the foundation of community life is symptomatic of the predominance of value subjectivity which produces only a situation of critics in which people assume the role of a critic because they seek to live by the rules of their own making, rules that they derive from their own private dream world and tend to downgrade the way other people live and act. As Voegelin observes:

> The doxa now comes more clearly into view as the type of rational construction ... that will appear when order is interpreted from the position of dream existence. The experience of participation in a universal order (in the *xynon* in the Heraclitian sense) is lost; reality is reduced to the life of passions in the individual human being; hence the universality of order must be reconstructed out of the only elements that

> are experienced as real. If passion is the only reality, as the order – which after a fashion exists in a corrupt society – must be construed as the result of an agreement between the passionate individuals.[10]

But, the creation of the political order inspired by the life of passion is, as argued earlier, does not prove benign since passion itself has to be disciplined, regulated and, if need be, repressed. The order has, therefore, to be constructed on the solid rock of a perspective that draws its inspiration from and is modelled upon the divine order. As Voegelin puts it:

> To establish a government is an essay in world creation. When man creates the cosmion of political order, he analogically repeats the divine creation of the cosmos. The analogical repetition is not an act of futile imitation, for repeating the cosmos man participates, in the measure allowed to his existential limitations, in the cosmic order itself. Moreover, when participating in the creation of order, man experiences his consubstantiality with the being of which he is a creaturely part. Hence, in his creative endeavor man is a partner in the double sense of a creature and rival of God.[11]

One such paradigm of analogically repeating the creation of the cosmos is, of course, available in Plato's *Republic*. The point of departure for Plato is the search for the principle that ensures *eunomia* (right-mindedness) which alone can prove effective in overcoming the disorder of the soul and thereby pave the way for installing order as a precondition of true order in society.[12] Such a principle must "bear a definite and intelligible relation to the cosmic principle which lies deeper than mere conventions of behaviour, whether of individual or communal life".[13] This principle is the transcendental cosmic mind or intelligence (*nous*), which, as the arche, the beginning of motion, underlines the structure of the universe and all that it contains. This principle does not, however, operate in *vacuo*; it presupposes a substrate of matter that is not yet ordered; it is ordered as a result of the intervention by Demiurge who shapes it in accordance with form or intelligence.

The interaction between intelligence and matter engenders a Trinitarian principle in nature as it does in the case of human beings. Intelligence, energy and matter constituting the world of matter become respectively the soul, spirit and appetite. The homology between the natural and the human world also extends to the polis. This homology makes it possible to identify one single principle of order that is applicable to all the three spheres. This principle involves basically the recognition that (a) the superior element must rule over those elements that are inferior; and (b) each of these elements must do what each of them is best suited for. Of these elements, the soul, as Plato notes, is deathless (*psyche pasa athanatos*)[14] because it sees and, through the vision it is endowed with, participates in the idea.[15] In respect of the second criterion, Plato insists on acting on the principle of "one man, one art".[16]

Plato believes that once different elements are graded and ranked and the superior element rules over all other elements, their self-aggrandizing tendency will be extirpated and, as a result, moderation and harmony will prevail. This equally applies to polis because "the psyche is a society of forces, and society is the differentiated manifold of psychic elements".[17] The same principle must apply to both of them. Thus, justice belongs to the polis as it does to the psyche, "for justice, which is the determination of what is just, is an ordering of the political association"[18] as it of the psyche. And, the ordering of psyche for ensuring justice in man's interior calls for a wisdom or what Plato calls synoptic vision or sharp sightedness that enables one to establish a principled relationship or *politeia* among the city's diverse parts. And, since the city is the replica of the psyche, this *politeia* must first be applied to the internal economy of man himself. And, what is important in this case is the regulation of appetites without which the city is forced to admit the myriad of consumer goods. And, since the city is in no position to exclude any goods or service as long as it is technically possible to provide them, the city, like the inflamed appetites is obliged to admit, itself becomes limitless. As such, it lacks the principle according to which its order or its completion can be determined.[19] The result is that in responding to demands for goods and services that inflamed appetites of the residents of the city generate, the city becomes a "promiscuous heap, stuffed and multitudinous".[20]

This "multitudinous heap" can be transformed into an ordered polity if someone who is endowed with the knowledge that can perceive the basis of order and wholeness. To put it differently, a person can develop the capacity of synoptic vision if he is capable of rising above the temptation of his base desires and cultivate wisdom. This is possible if one adopts the strategy of what Plato calls *periagoge* (turn around of the whole soul),[21] from ignorance to the truth of God, from opinion about uncertainly wavering things to knowledge of being, and from multifarious activity to the justice of tending to one's proper sphere of action. This means openness of soul to the divine ground of being and *periagoge* becomes instrumental in the opening of the soul. The opening of the soul is the right step towards establishing true relation to God. And, the person who has found his true nature through finding his true relations to God is none else than the philosopher. He does not only seek salvation for himself and others insofar as he apprehends the nature of right order. Also, the reconstitution of this relationship in his soul then becomes the substantive centre (*xynon* in Heraclitian sense) which, by its existence, relieves the pressure of the surrounding corrupt society. In addition, since the order of the soul is recaptured through resistance of the surrounding disorder, the principles derived from the order of the soul representing its resistance to disorder become the ground of political order.

It is for this reason that Plato thinks it desirable to instal the philosopher-king as the ruler who can successfully steer the ship of the state to safety in the troubled waters of this troubling phenomenal world. But, for various reasons,[22] this becomes very difficult to achieve. For one thing, the substrate of matter resists order and cannot be fully reshaped because to do so is to destroy the nature of matter as posited by Plato. Since different types of men that constitute society have their nature fixed, it precludes self-transformation for all but the philosopher. And, since matter resists order, knowledge has to be transmuted into power. This transmutation reduces the analogically created divine order into a human political machine – a machine which becomes a thing in itself and for itself, machinery "independent of the rest of the mind and life of the people".[23] This possibility of the mimetically created earthly paradigm of divine order slipping into the mould of artificially created political order signifying a contract among passionate persons has to be warded off. The key to the real appreciation of the Vedic perspective or political order is the separation of *Brahma* (intelligence or *sacerdotium)* and *Kshatra* (executive power, *regnum)* but not their divorce. It, however, underlines the need to treat them not as antagonistic power. They are considered to be complementary to each other, to be sure; but the *regnum* has to be subordinated and must act according to the guidance of Brahma.

It must be made clear at the outset that *Brahma* and *Kshatra* are not concrete objects like persons, things, etc., they are rather psycho-mental powers or qualities that are differentially distributed and manifest in different degrees in different objects.[24] And, since *Brahma* and *Kshatra* are the qualities or properties that represent the manifestations of the absolute in the process of creation and since they represent different aspects, properties or qualities of the some reality or the arche of creation, each of these properties, that is *Brahma* and *Kshatra,* is not complete in itself. It is their combination or union that can produce benign results. Each by itself is not only incomplete but also capable of arrogating to itself more power than what is necessary for the good of itself and for the good of others. It is to check this self-aggrandizing tendency inherent in each of these properties that their combination or *mithuna* (syzygy), as it is called in the Vedic literature, becomes necessary. It is this combination that is also deemed necessary insofar as the question of political order is concerned. To apprehend the need and character of this combination, it is necessary to backtrack a bit and see how it is grounded in Vedic *Bhavavrittam*.

The arche of the world is, of course, *Tad Ekam* (That One) who is, as it were, the omphalos of every beings in this universe. In this form, that is, in the *anirukta* (undefined) form, the *Tad Ekam* is known as *Ardhanarishwar* (half male and half female). The conjoint parents must be split in two opposite but complementary principles and produce the third before the appearance of the many. This is accomplished by what is, in the Vedic literature, called "*Brahma kilvisha*" (Brahma's sin). That is to say, Brahma begets a daughter, vak[25] and cohabits with her. The father, that is, Brahma, working his will, and the daughter coming together, did the "incestuous" deed,[26] the seed was scattered all over as a precondition of the creation of *praja* (beings). This exemplifies what in *Rigveda* (RV, I. 105.2) is referred to as a wife enjoying her young husband and the union of husband and wife engendering progeny. It is this coming together of and interacting by two contrary but complementary principles that is termed in the Vedic parlance as *yajna*.

It is from *yajna* that *praja* (beings) are produced, and being produced from *yajna*, they are produced from *yajna,* they are produced, as if, from *mithuna* (union).[27] Or, again, *Shatpatha Brahmana* (SB, IV, 5.6.1) puts it, the *yajna* is Prajapati; it is from it (*yajna*) that *praja* (being) have been produced and in the manner they are produced therefrom even today. It is because of this *mithuna* between the Mother and the Father in the primeval ages in the *Ritusadan* that the whole universe, this *idam sarvam*, or *tode ti*, as

Aristotle calls it, came into being. As *Pancavimsa Brahmana* (PB, XX. 14.2) puts it:

> Prajapati was alone; the Word was his only possession; Word was the second. He thought, "Let me emit this, Word, it will pervade this whole (universe). He emitted the Word and it pervaded this whole (universe). It rose upwards as a continuous stream of water. Speaking (the syllable) "a", he cut off a third part of it: this became the earth. He thought: "This has come into existence (*abhut*) hence the name *bhumi.*" With (the syllable) "*Ra*", he cut off a second part of it, this became *antariksha*. He thought: "This is between, therefore, *antariksha*." With (the syllable) "*pho*" he threw a (third) part upwards; that became dyau."[28]

But, the process did not end here. He also created certain qualities (*guna*) and endowed beings differentially with these *gunas*. As *Brihadaranyaka Upanishad* (BU, I. IV.10) puts it, in the beginning, there was only Brahma and he knew that he was the only entity. Knowing this, he became all (*sarvam*). But his loneliness did not come to an end. "Being one he did not flourish. He specially projected an excellent form, the *Kshatra.* Indra, Varuna, the Moon, Rudra, Parjanya, Yama, Death and Ishana are *Kshatra* among gods" (BU, I. IV. 11). Next, he created *Visha* and Shudra. As *Shatpatha Brahmana* (IV. 1.4.1–6) underlines *Brahma* and *Kshatra* are psychic or *adhyatmika* forces that are well differentiated because of their separate and distinct properties. Given their separate and distinct properties, they are not equal; they need to be graded according to their nature defined by the degree to which each of them reflects in its own nature the divine nature of Brahma, the source of all beings. That these qualities are so graded is indicated by *Pancavimsa Brahmana* (PB, II. 8.2). Referring to the hierarchical grading of *Brahma*, *Kshatra* and *Visha*, it notes: "The first (verse) is the place of *Brahma*, the middle one that of *Kshatra* and the last one that of *Visha*; the largest share is given to the first (*Brahma*), thereby strength and might accrue to *Brahma* making the *Kshatra* and *Visha* subject to *Brahma.*"

Gradation of these psychic or *adhyatmika* qualities does confirm their inequality and, therefore, the need for putting them in a hierarchical order. However, this does not mean that they are unrelated. They do represent different qualities; however, they are complementary. They are interdependent and their cooperation is, therefore, *sine qua non* for the success for any venture in which different entities, faculties and qualities must collaborate without causing any distortion or conflict. This means that they function compatibly in order that the whole they are parts of does not suffer dissonance or disorder. It is against this background that we can appreciate the real import of *Rigveda* (X. 90. 12) when it underscores the organic relationship among the four faculties, *Brahma, Kshatra, Visha* and *Shudra*. As we shall see later, it is the combination into a reciprocally supportive and cooperative relationship that proves beneficial and fruitful not only for the political order but also for society as a whole.

The gradation of these faculties is also symptomatic of the recognition of the existence of different functions associated with different faculties. But their collaboration and cooperation is not conceived, in the Vedic perspective, to be auto-telic; in this collaborative endeavour the lower principle is, it is thought, governed by a higher principle. This is as true of the art of governance as that of the functioning of social order. The primacy of the higher principle in disciplining, regulating and curbing the self-aggrandizing tendency of the lower principle is symbolized, in the Vedic perspective, as *mithuna* or syzygy representing the process of *yajna* as the means of creating *praja* or, more specifically, some beneficent result.[29] The Veda offers numerous pairs which exemplify the coming together of two contrary but complementary principles, such as, Agni-Soma, Agni-Indra, Indra-Soma, Mitra-Varuna, Prithivi-Dyau, etc. Each of these paired entities represents combination of different qualities, properties, faculties, etc., and comes together for different purposes, performing different functions, and symbolizes the operation of a particular process. The pair of Agni-Soma represents the coming together of two principles whose syzygy is necessary for creation (RV, I. 93.5). In a similar fashion, the pair of Indra and Soma is necessary for sustaining and supporting the process of creation. Indra, as the several roots from which the term "Indra" is derived suggest, is one who kindles or heats and augments strength through the generation of heat.[30] As *Shatpatha Brahmana* (VI. 1.1.2) notes, *asat* as *prana* (life-force) in the middle is called *nabhya* Prajapati, that is, Indra. He, by his power "kindled those Rishis and, therefore, he is called Indra".[31] If Indra invigorates the exhausted Rishis in the process of creation, Indra himself gets his strength restored and augmented by Soma after he exhausts himself in killing Vritra.

Another example of paired gods underscoring its crucial role in the process of creation is that of Prithivi and Dyau. *Atharvaveda* (AV, II. 15.1) refers to them as a pair.[32] But, as *Pancavimsa Brahmana* (VII.

10.1–3) points out, Prithivi and Dyau were at one time together. But then they separated; they again came together and contracted marriage on equal terms. This marriage represents God-marriage (*deva-vivaha*). *Aitereya Brahmana* (AB, VI. 27) also refers to the marriage between Prithivi and Dyau as *deva-vivaha* but adds that when they were separated, it did not rain. But their marriage yielded a beneficient result in that it rained again. In addition, their marriage, as *Shatpatha Brahmana* (IV. 3.2.12) notes, was instrumental in producing *praja*. In contradistinction to these pairs, there are pairs that concern the combination of *Brahma* and *Kshatra* (sacerdotium and regnum), Manas and *Vak* (intelligence and action), or *Kratu* and *Daksha* (authorizing intelligence and executive efficiency). It is these pairs that have a direct hearing on the Vedic perspective on political order as well as of direct concern for us.

To begin with, the combinations of the faculties symbolized by these pairs or syzygies represent the divine paradigm of order and there is inherent in the Vedic perspective insistence on the adoption and implementation of this paradigm at the human level. The Veda underscores the need for human beings to do as the gods did. And, what the gods did was not only to attain divinity for themselves by doing *yajna*, that is, by making themselves sacred through *yajna* but also by making it possible for all to attain divinity or, at least, be governed by God's laws by emulating the ways of the gods. *Yajna* provides the means through which human beings, too, can attain divinity. But, as we have already seen, only rare human beings can become God-like by doing what the gods did.[33] And, it is these rare beings that Plato identified as philosophers who are endowed with "an extraordinary visual faculty" and are in "possession of a divine vision or supersensuous eye".[34] It is these philosophers who Plato would like to be installed as kings to overcome the chaos wrecked by the rebellion of passions and instal/restore order.

In the Platonic perspective, then, intelligence as represented by the philosopher does not only know and can see the true relationship among different elements of the psyche as well as of polity. Also, it is endowed with the capacity to act efficiently and effectively. For various reasons alluded to earlier, however, the Vedic perspective on political order considers this convergence of intelligence and action not only undesirable but also harmful. The *regnum* is the system of power and has, therefore, to be seen in a double light. On the one hand, it is a system of coercive power and, on the other hand, it is a system of moral authority. Its commands are or should be not only backed by force but also by right. It is in this sense that the *regnum* spans and joins two distinct orders of being, the order of positive reality and that of morality. In order to successfully join these two distinct realities, *regnum* needs to be grounded in and ruled by an eternally subsistent body of knowledge which lies beyond the ken of humanity immersed in materiality. Insofar as *regnum* represents energy and power and inclines towards aberration, it needs to be disciplined by a higher principle, that is, intelligence and reason symbolized by Agni or Brihaspati, Manas and Kratu. When *regnum* is disciplined and controlled by these, the political order is said to be controlled by some transcendental principle and, therefore, to be adhering to the divine paradigm of syzygy between *Brahma* and *Kshatra*.

In this syzygy different pairs, such as, Agni-Indra, Manas-Vak, Kratu-Daksha, etc., represent the divine paradigm. Take, for example, the Agni-Indra pair. It is interesting to mention that, as *Rigveda* (VI. 25.5) also notes, both Agni and Indra are mighty ones. Also, if Agni is considered as the ruler,[35] Indra, too, is addressed with the epithet of *samrat* (sovereign).[36] However, *Shatpatha Brahmana* (10.4.1.5) points out, "Now, Indra and Agni were created as *Kshatra* and *Brahma* respectively; the *Brahma* was Agni and *Kshatra* Indra; when created, the two were separate". They spoke: "while being thus, we shall be unable to produce *praja*: let us become one form! The two became one form".

In this syzygy, however, it is Agni who occupies the first rank. This is so for the reason that all those entities who happen to manifest in their being a large proportion of *Brahma* faculty are able to have the synoptic vision. This makes them capable of deeper knowledge of the structure of reality and the true relationship between different constituents of the psyche as well as of what should be the constitutive principle (*politeia*) that should govern the interaction among these constituents. This deeper insight into the structure of order and its proper role in the human world can be obtained only if someone is able to attain what in the Vedic parlance, is called *sarvata*, wholeness – wholeness of senses, mind, the world, and the God. It is this wholeness that helps one to attain the sight with the help of which one can cleave through the mental darkness or limitation that prevents man from seeing further, from seeing the light and penetrating into the beyond ... .[37]

It is this light that makes man what the Veda calls *sura chakshuh*, that is, sun-eyed; this alone makes one capable of seeing by the light of heaven (*svardrishah*). This, in turn, depends upon *dhi* or *dhiti*, a visionary thought which sharpens a far-reaching insight, *suchetas*[38] and yields a flawless understanding, *medham arishtam*.[39] Needless to say that *medham arishtam* involves more than the capability of rational thought,[40] more than mere modification of principle. Rational thought is not to be suspended, it is a thought-provoking and thought-channelling vision that enables man to reach out beyond the senses and the mind.[41] But to go beyond the senses and the mind requires trust and faith in the unseen entity, one seeks to realize in one's own being. This unseen entity is nothing else than the substratum of reality, the Purusa, the indwelling *sat* (truth) in every being. To realize this unseen entity, the Purusa, requires *shraddha* inadequately translated as faith.[42] *Shraddha* is something that, as Panikkar points out,

> is previous to thinking and anterior to willing and deciding. It is precisely faith that makes thinking possible, for faith offers the unthought ground out of which thinking can emerge. It is faith that makes moral and other decisions possible, opening to us the horizon against which our actions become meaningful. Any action performed without faith is only instinctive or automatic movement, without any truly human content; it can hardly be called a truly human action.[43]

It is true that *shraddha* is not only the ground of right thinking; it is also the means of structuring and channeling the process of thinking. It does not posit an opposition between reason and faith.[44] But *shraddha* does not arise automatically; it requires the leavening of *yajna* (*satyam cha me sharddha cha me ... yajnena kalpantam*, YV, X. VIII. 5). But what kind of *yajna*? There is in the Vedic literature a clear distinction between a mere performance of yajna[45] and *yajna* as a means of inner spiritual transformation. For example, *Rigveda* (VII. 70.3) underlines the fact that none attains Him (Indra) by works or sacrifice.[46] What is important in the Vedic perspective is not what is enacted outwardly, but what is accomplished inwardly by the understanding sacrificer. As such, the emphasis is on *adhyatmika antaram agnihotra* through which one can achieve a radical reorientation in his attitude towards one's self and the external world. It is, again, this inner transformation that provides a primordial insight into the structure of reality and the apprehension of the true *politeia*.

A person who is gifted with the insight that can see things in their differences and their interrelationship is called in the Vedic literature as *kavirmaneeshi* (the seer-poet). And, Agni is called *kavirmaneeshi* who has the wisdom, knowledge, discernment and discrimination to know the truth and articulate it. Agni is described as *viproagne* (Brahman Agni);[47] he is *kavimagni satyadharmanam* (one who follows the path of truth),[48] *vishwani kavyani vidwan* (one who is deep-seeing),[49] Kavikratu (endowed with synoptic vision),[50] *ritam chikitwan* (one who knows *ritam*), etc., to suggest the profound intelligence and wisdom with which Agni is endowed. It is because of this that he is considered to be Brahma and that is why he is given the first rank; as *Rigveda* (I. 31.1) puts it, *twamagne prathamo* (you, Agni, are the first).[51] This is confirmed by *Aitereya Brahmana* (VIII. 4) when it says: "*Brahma vai stomanam trivrtt, kshatra panchadasho, Brahma khalu vai kshatratpurva*" (*Brahma* is *trivrtta* stoma while the *Kshatra* fifteen, as such, *Brahma is prior to Kshatra*).[52]

It is also interesting to note that Brihaspati, too, is identified with Brahma and, therefore, said to be the first-born.[53] The priority of Brahma is confirmed in other ways too. Note, for example, that *Aitereya Brahmana* (AB, VII. 19) observes the following:

> Prajapati created *yajna*, then Brahma and Kshatra and then *praja* of two kinds. Those who eat oblation (*hutad*) and those who do not (*ahutad*). Brahma is *hutad* and Kshatra, Visha and Shudra are *ahutad*. The *yajna* departed and Brahma and Kshatra pursued it with their respective weapons (that is, weapons used in *yajna* and those used in war) respectively. Kshatra could not catch hold of *yajna*; it went to Brahma.

Insofar as *yajna* is the means of self-transformation as a step towards becoming *suchetas*, it is a necessary attribute for men to move towards the destination of becoming a *sur chakshus*. Lacking this, however, Kshatra could not catch up with *yajna*. And, since Brahma can have *suchetas*, it is Brahma that can claim precedence over Kshatra. This is also confirmed by *Shatpatha Brahmana* (I. 2.4.1–2), which note that when Indra struck Vritra with his thunderbolt, Vritra was cut into four pieces, that is, *sphya*, *yupa*, chariot and arrow. The first two are used by the Brahman and the latter two by the Kshatriya. Needless to say that Brahmans use the first two in the performance of *yajna* while the latter two by Kshatriya who use them as weapons. And, to add one more evidence, *Aitereya Brahmana* (II. 33) puts it, "Brahma is *Ahava*[54] and Kshatra *Nivid*[55] and *sukta* Visha; the first to be called is Brahma, then Kshatra and then Visha." As A.B. Keith translates it,[56] this makes the lordly power (i.e., Kshatra) dependent on the holy power (i.e., Brahma) ... (and) the people (Visha) dependent on the lordly power. It is no wonder, then, that *Aitereya Brahmana* (VII. 26) declares Brahma as the *Purohita*[57] of Kshatriya and the *Purohita* to be half the self of the Kshatriya. The *Aitereya Brahmana* (VIII. 26) also confirms that Brihaspati is the *Purohita* of gods; this is true of Agni too.

It is against this background that we can appreciate what Agni intimates to Indra in *Rigveda* (VIII. 100.1):

> *Ayam to emi tanva purastadvishwe abhi ma yanti pashchat; yada mahyam didharo bhagamindradimanya krinavo viryani*

I in person go before thee and if thou grant me my share (or due), then shalt thou become worthy through the performance of heroic deeds.

What is the share (or due) that Agni asks of Indra? Undoubtedly, it is the foremost rank that Agni claims to be his by virtue of being Brahma. It is by virtue of his being Brahma and Purohita that Agni places the thunderbolt in Indra's hand so that he may (Indra) overcome the enemies (RV, X. 52.5). As Coomaraswamy notes, *vajra* is the most essential symbol of *regnum* and its placing in Indra's hand by Agni is indicative of the fact that *regnum* is not only subordinate to *sacerdotium* but also that it is nothing more than a delegated power.[58] It is enough to suggest that Agni and Indra constitute a conjoint principle; as a conjoint principle, they form two halves of the whole that is, they are two forms of Brahma (BR, II. 3; MU, VPI. 11.8). But, as is also evident, they represent two aspects of the primordial entity and, as a consequence, neither of them is complete without the other. As *Shatpatha Brahmana* (8.6.1.12), referring to Naksatpanchachuda, points out:

> And, again, as to why he lays down the Naksad Panchachudas – it is for the sake of completeness; for the Naksads are the self, and the Panchachudas the mate, and this, the mate, doubtless, is one half of the self; for when one is with his mate, then, he is whole and complete.[59]

It is also evident from the preceding discussion that it is Indra as the symbol of Kshatra that is assigned the feminine status and Agni that of the male in this syzygy. This is evident from *Shatpatha Brahmana* (X. 4.1.5.8–9) where it is specifically stated that Agni and Indra were made in the form of Brahma and Kshatra. They were separate but they decided to come together for engendering *praja*.

Again, Agni is likened to bricks which are laid down for preparing a *vedi* (the place for sacrificial fire) and Indra to that of *purisha* (anything to fill up interstices in a wall).[60] The use of these epithets is in itself indicative of their complementarity and therefore the need of their alliance. It is further indicated by *Shatpatha Brahmana* (X. 4.1.8) that it is only on the *vedi* that the two forms of Brahma, that is, Agni and Indra, become one. And, when they become one through syzygy, they become effective in whatever they plan to do or actually do.

The significance of the syzygy between Brahma and Kshatra is not by any means exhausted by the intimation that power must be disciplined, controlled and curbed by a higher principle. In this syzygy, Brahma symbolizes *prajnana* or *manas*, that is, intelligence touched by the flash of eternity and is, therefore, in a position to see the true structure of order, articulate what it signifies, and give proper counsel as to how this order can be maintained and safeguarded. It is the combination of all these faculties, qualities and functions that Brahma combines in itself. However, Brahma is not an entity that is *kartr* (executive); it is *abhigantr* (the knower) only. It, therefore, must act through Kshatra who is, in fact, the *kartr*. As such, Brahma is the counselling, authorizing power while Kshatra is the acting, executive power. It is this relationship – the intimate relationship as underlined by the use of the term "*mithuna*" – in which Brahma is prior and first in rank; it is symbolized in different ways, such as Manas-Vak, Kratu-Daksha, Mitra-Varuna, etc., some of which are discussed below.

It does not need to be indicated that *manas* is the first and foremost aspect that was manifested first and *vak* the last. But, as has already been indicated it was through the emission of *vak* that Prajapati created this universe. And, since *manas* which provides the *pratimana* (paradigm) of the universe, it is prior to *vak*. However, *vak* disputed the superiority of *manas* and they began quarreling. They went to Prajapati for a decision who gave his verdict in favour of *manas*, saying, "Mind (*manas*) is indeed better than thou, for thou art an imitator of its deeds and a follower in its wake; and inferior, surely, is he who imitates his better's deeds and follows in his wake."[61] And, this verdict of Prajapati is correct insofar as *Yajurveda* (YV, 4.17) underlines the fact that *vak* is *dhritamanasa*, that is, it is conceived and upheld by *manas*. It is in view of this that *Shatpatha Brahmana* (III. 2.4.11) notes that "*manohidam purastad vakaskurati*" that is *manas* goes before *vak* (and prompts her), speak thus! Say not this! For, were it not for the *manas*, *vak* would talk incoherently. It is thus clear that *manas* is not only the source of *vak* but also its controller; without the disciplining act of *manas*, *vak* only simply be a babble without any rhyme and reason.

It is true that, as *Shatpatha Brahmana* (XI. 2.3.6) underlines, it is only through *nama* (name) and *rupa* (form) that Brahma becomes the *idam sarvam,* the *vishwa. Manas* is the means through which one knows the form; thus, knowing by *manas,* Brahma assumes different forms. And, it is the combination of *nama* and *rupa* that forms this universe. That is why, *nama* and *rupa* constitute two great powers of Brahma. *Aitereya Brahmana* (V. 23) further confirms this when it says that: "*manasa prastauti, manasodgayati, manasa pratiharati* ..." (with mind he alters the prelude, with mind he sings, with mind he responds). All this underlines the fact that *manas* alone as the locus of intelligence can conceive *rupa*; it is, therefore, prior and superior to *vak*. However, it is also apparent that without *vak*, *manas* can only remain silent; it is only through *vak* that *manas* can make articulate and give expression to what is only a thought. As such, even while *manas* proposes, sings (silently) and responds (again silently) to whatever is sung silently, it is *vak* that utters what is proposed silently and recites (*vasha shamsati*). That is why, *Shatpatha Brahmana* (IV. 6.7.5) observes:

> Both the Riks and Saman are speech (*vak*), and the *yajus* are the Mind (*manas*);[62] Now wherever this speech was, there everything was done, everything was known; but wherever mind was there, nothing whatever was done, nothing was known, for no one knows (understands) those who think in their mind.

It is in this sense that "speech and mind are a pairing of the gods (*devanam mithunam*), verily thus with a pairing of gods they win a pairing, by the pairing of gods they are propagated in pairings ..." (AB, V. 23). What it refers to is the fact that the syzygy between *manas* and *vak* constitutes primarily a divine paradigm, which must be adopted and emulated by human beings to ensure their own welfare. It is what is emphatically underlined in *Shatpatha Brahmana* (X. 5.1.1):

> The mystic import of this fire altar, doubtless, is speech; for it is with speech that it is built: with the *Rik*, the *Yajus* and the Saman as the divine (speech; and when he (the Adhvaryu) speaks with human speech, 'do ye this! Do ye that, then also it (the alter) is built therewith'.

It is, thus, clear that *manas* and *vak* are complementary to each other. One is ineffective and, therefore, helpless without the other. As such, syzygy between them is *sine qua non* for successfully bringing about some positive outcome. In this syzygy, Brahma or *manas* represents Kratu, that is, mental or intellectual process, the authorizing counsel, while Kshatra or *vak* symbolizes efficient power. As such, syzygy between Kratu and Daksha is as necessary as that between Brahma and Kshatra or *manas* and *vak*. It is interesting to note that Kratu and Daksha are also identified with Mitra and Varuna respectively. As *Shatpatha Brahmana* (IV. 1.4.1) puts it:

> Mitra and Varuna, forsooth, are his intelligence (*kratu*) and will (Daksha); and as such belonging to him is his self (*adhyatma*), whenever he desires anything in his mind, as "would that this were mine", I might do this! that is intelligence; and whatever that is accomplished, that is will. Now intelligence indeed is Mitra and will is Varuna; and Mitra is priesthood (*Brahma*) and Varuna the nobility (*Kshatra*), and the priesthood is the conceiver, and the noble (*Kshatra*) is the doer.

It is true that as *Rigveda* (VX. 129.4) emphasizes, *kamas ... manaso retas* (one wills or desire with manas) or, as *Atharvaveda* (X. IX.52) and *Aitereya Aranyak* (I.3.2) put it, "*manasa hi sarvakamandhyati ...*". That is,

> All desires rest on the mind, for with the mind man conceives all desires ... speech yields all desires, for by speech man expresses all desires.[63]

But desiring also includes the act of authorizing. It is in this sense that Kratu or Mitra is this authorizing power; without it nothing can be done. That is why, Kratu is equated with *yajna-mukha*, that is, the beginning of *yajna*. Kratu is so important for the *regnum* which should be wedded to Kratu. The divine archetype for the marriage between *sacerdotium* and *regnum* is, of course, the syzygy of Mitra-Varuna (RV, V. 63.3). But, as is clear from *Shatpatha Brahmana* (IV.1.4.2–3), they were separate in the beginning. However, Mitra, the *Brahma*, could stand without Varuna, the *Kshatra*. However Varuna did not succeed in whatever he did because he was not inspired by Mitra, the Brahma. In order, therefore, to avoid failure,

> Varuna, the *Kshatra*, then, called upon Mitra, the *Brahma*, saying, turn thou unto me that we may unite: I will place thee foremost, sped by thee (*tatprasutah*), I will do deeds! – so the two united; and therefrom resulted that *graha* to Mitra and Varuna.[64]

Since *graha* signifies an extraordinary power that takes hold of and supports and sustains the syzygy between Mitra and Varuna (or *Brahma* and *Kshatra*) is a precondition of good governance. In this syzygy, as already pointed out, *Brahma* or *sacerdotium* occupies the foremost position; this foremost position he holds by virtue of his deep insight, synoptic vision, penetrating wisdom, and good counselling. To the extent that the *regnum* conforms to the counsel of the *sacerdotium,* the *regnum* succeeds in the performance of his kingly duties. As *Rigveda* (IV. 50.7) notes:

> *Sa idraja pratijanyagni vishwa sushmena tathavamiviryena;*
> *Brhaspati yah subhrtambibharto balguyati vandate purvabhajan.*

That prince overcomes by his strength and processes all hostile people, who cherishes literally Brhaspati and glorifies and honours him as the first sharer (of the offering).[65]

It is not necessary to point out that Brhaspati is the *purohita* of the gods and he constitutes the divine archetype of *Purohita* in the phenomenal world. As *Aitereya Brahmana* (VII. 26) puts it, "Brhaspati is the *Purohita* of the gods; analogous to him are the other *purohitas* of human king." As such, in the words of *Aitereya Brahmana* (VII. 26), "the Brahma represents Kshatriya's *purohita* who forms one half of the whole while the other half is the king." Thus, *Purohita* is a necessary aspect of *regnum* insofar as he represents *manas* or intelligence. But there are other components without which *regnum* remains ever incomplete. The first such component is the king himself who must undergo a process of rebirth or regeneration or *abhisheka* symbolized by the Rajasuya Yajna (ascension ceremony) before he can step on to his throne. The second component is what, in the Vedic literature, is called *ratnins* (literally, jewels) without which his reign will lack the instruments through which the king makes his overlordship effective and efficient. And, lastly, he must have a *rashtra,* a nation in true sense of the term.

What is important in this regard is the fact that the Vedic perspective on political order considers kingship as a *yajna* and, as a consequence, a symbol of effective action that can be sustained, on the one hand, by interdependence and cooperation among various elements and, on the other, the realization of *Brahmatva* (the qualities of Brahma) by the king through the process of inner transformation. It is interesting to note that *Shatpatha Brahmana* (I. 3.5.5) treats the syzygy between Brahma and Kshatra as *sine qua non* for the performance of *yajna*. Note, for example, that it equates Gayatri with *Brahma* power and Trishtubha with that of Kshatra and underlines the fact that it is only these two powers that can kindle the sacrificial fire. Further, *Shatpatha Brahmana* (I.3.5.6) refers to the need of repeating the *mantra* in these metres because they reproduce mimetically the *Trivritta*, that is, the split of Brahma into three constituent elements, that is, *manas, prana* and *vak*. This means that *yajna*, specially the Rajasuya Yajna, becomes the means of recreation in which not only the person who is to become the king is reformed and regenerated but also of transforming the *rashtra* if it has fallen on bad days and safeguarding it against possible threats to its integrity and well-being.

It is against this background that we can appreciate not only the significance of Rajasuya Yajna, but also that of *ratnins* as well as of the need for the king to live a style of life that safeguards and sustains compatibility between his interior and exterior life. As *Shatpatha Brahmana* (I. 3.5.15) prescribes, the king-to-be should offer 15 samadhenis.[66] But, why the number 15? As it points out, the number 15 is the symbol of Vajra and Vajra is identical with *virya*, that is virility, powers. But what kind of *virya*? And, as is evident from various Vedic texts,[67] Brahma is *virya* to Kshatra. But Kshatra needs to be transformed first into Brahma and it is precisely for this purpose that a king-to-be has to first perform Rajasuya Yajna. It is also obvious that without a Purohita, the *yajna* cannot be performed. (AB, VIII. 24). It is through the Rajasuya Yajna[68] that Kshatra is transformed into Brahma and, therefore, the king-to-be prays, *Brahma prapadye* (I ask for the holy power; AB, VII. 22). But the transformation of *Kshatra* into *Brahma* is not possible as long as the former, un-regenerated self of the king-to-be is not annihilated. That is why, Rajasuya Yajna has been termed as the "death" as well as the rebirth of the king-to-be, *tasya mrtyuschcharati Rajasuyam* (death attends the royal consecration of him; AV, IV. 8.1.).

The death of the former self of the king-to-be is, at one and the same time, the rebirth through which he attains *dwijata*. It is through the attainment of *dwijata* that he can arise above the emotions, above attachments, love and hate, and perform his kingly duties in a spirit of detachment. As *Shatpatha Brahmana* (V.5.1.2) observes:

> As to why the performer of the Rajasuya should perform this offering: because he (the priest) makes him ascend the regions, the seasons, the hymns and metres, he now redeems him therefrom by this (offering). But were the performer of the Rajasuya not to perform this offering, then verily he would become intoxicated (with pride) and would fall down headlong.[69]

Thus, *yajna* is the means of self-transformation and it is as a result of self-transformation that the king-to-be overcomes his self-aggrandizing tendency and makes himself worthy of the responsibilities of his new position. The new position he is to assume soon imposes on him certain responsibilities that can be discharged only when the king sheds off his personal likes and dislikes, his personal concerns and becomes attuned to the good and well-being of the people he rules over. The first step towards this is, of course, overcoming arrogance and acquiring humility. But more than this, he needs to be what *Shatpatha Brahmana* (V.3.3.9) calls *dharmapati* (lord of *dharma*). That is why he makes offerings to Varuna because Varuna is *dharmapati* so that the king-to-be may also become *dharmapati*. And, "that truly is the supreme state, when one is lord of *dharma*". And, it is as *dharmapati* that he ascends to the throne to shoulder the heavy burden of the ruler; as *dharmapati* the king becomes the overlord of beings (*bhutanamadhipatirbabhuva*; AV, VI. 8.1). It is *dharmapati*, again, that he is exhorted to approve his royalty. And it is as *dharmapati*, again, that, as *Shatpatha Brahmana* (V.1.5.14) puts it, *eshavai prajapateh pratyakshatamam yahajanyastadekah sanbahunamishte* (he, the Rajanya, is most manifestly of Prajapati: hence, while being one he rules over many).

It is as *dharmapati* that the king assumes the charge of his kingdom and is, as *Aitereya Brahmana* (III. 4.1) notes, exhorted to rise with splendour as the lord of the people (*visha*) because to you has come the kingdom and bear the responsibility of ruling. In bearing this responsibility, the king should place *shri*[70] at the pinnacle of his kingdom (AV, III. 4.2) and share out good things. Furthermore, Ashwins and Mitra-Varuna are exhorted to put the mind of the king to giving out of good things (AV, III. 4.4). When properly consecrated, the king becomes, as already pointed out, like Prajapati and, as Prajapati, he claims his kingdom and becomes a guiding controller for friends (*iyam te ranmitray yantasi yaman urje*; YU, XVIII. 28). It is as Prajapati that he is expected to give succour to his subject. They address the king: "This is thy kingdom; thou art consecrated (anointed)! Thou art thy friend's supporter and sustainer: for our sustenance art thou, for rain unto us art thou, for our lordship of beings art thou" (SB, IX.3.3.11). Again, as *Yajurveda* (9.22) declares, "... *iyam te rad yantasi yamano dhruvoasi dharunah. Krishyai tva kshemayatva rayyai tva poshaya tva*" (This is your sovereignty. You are the ruler, you are controller, you are firm and steadfast. You are for [better] agriculture, you are for peace and quiet, and you are substance).

It should, however, be noted that the king by himself is not complete. Along with his own self-transformation through consecration at Rajasuya Yajna, he also requires certain functionaries and assistance not only to help him in the execution of his kingly duties but also for support. All those who afford him service or support are called *ratnins* (jewels) who the king-to-be visits and makes his offerings to different gods.[71] But most important of these *ratnins* is the *Purohita* who, as indicated earlier, because he represents Brahma, is the chief counseller; it is by following his advice that he is inspirited and inspired and succeeds in whatever he undertakes to do. The king and his *Purohita* represent Indra and Agni respectively. However, it is a combination of Agni and Indra that proves effective insofar as the art of governance is concerned.[72] But, as long as the *regnum* does not carry the *Visha* (the people) along with him by insuring their well-being, the king does not prove worthy of the trust placed in him by his consecration. As *Rigveda* (II. 12) underlines, the king proves his mettle when he pleases his subjects. *Nrimnasya mahana sa janas Indra* (the worth of Indra is capability to be the dear to his subjects; cf. AB V.1.2).

It should be apparent by now that Brahma is the priest of Kshatra with the former constituting the half portion of the Kshatra. Without the syzygy between Brahma and Kshatra, two distinct but complementary principles, governance may turn into tyranny. It is the syzygy between *Purohita* and Rajnam that "quickens" the *regnum;* that is, it is through this "quickening" that Rajnam is set in motion and kept on the proper path. This quickening is symbolized by the consecration ceremony in which the king is "fathered" by the *Purohita.* Quickening thus refers to the fact that "coronation" of the king is both initiatory and sacrificial; the king is brought forth, new born from the initiatory death by the officiating priests who are, in this regard, his symbolic "fathers". Thus "fathered", the king emerges in his new birth as a divine persona (AB, 8.5.1). He is divine not because he becomes divine; he becomes godlike by virtue of being quickened, "fathered" by the higher principle of Brahma.

The king, when "fathered" by the priests, becomes the "father" of his subjects.[73] This does not, however, imply that he is an absolute ruler. The fact that neither man-made constitution nor the wishes of the majority of the people have selected or elected the ruler or a group of rulers, which in fact is erroneously supposed to make the ruler(s) responsive and responsible, does not mean that the ruler does whatever he wants to do. Four important checks must operate to prevent the king from becoming an arbitrary or authoritarian ruler. First, he must submit himself to the wise advice of his Purohita. Second, the king, in the Vedic perspective, is not the law-maker; he is influenced in his decisions by Dharmashastric treatises, opinions of learned Brahmans, usages and customs, as was the case in Greece. Third, *regnum* has been considered, in the Vedic perspective, only a dependent principle (AV, III. 4.1–2). The syzygy between Brahma and Kshatra underlines the king's subservience to the *sacerdotium*. But, apart from this, this syzygy is symptomatic of the fact that the ruler himself is the subject of another king, that is, *dharma*. *Dharma*, the highest principle, other than which there is no other superior principle, is *adhirajo rajnam* (king of kings).[74] While the constitutional monarch may be controlled by his peers or even by his inferiors, the ruler is supposed, in the Vedic perspective, to be controlled by a superior ruler, that is, *dharma*.

To be ruled by *dharma* is to submit to the eternal law, the truth (*satyam*, *dharma*), and the *kshatrasya kshatram*. Even after Prajapati created Brahma, Kshatra, Visha and Shudra, he was not satisfied. He therefore created as *kshatrasya kshatram*, the controller of Kshatra.

> There is no higher than that (so) even a weak man hopes (to defeat) a stronger man through *dharma*, as (one contending with the king). That righteousness is verily truth. Therefore they say about a person speaking of truth, He speaks of righteousness' or about a person speaking of righteousness', He speaks of truth, for both these are righteousness.[75]

It is thus clear that, in the Vedic perspective, the essence of being a Kshatriya, especially a king, is to make *dharma* the sovereign. When the ruler cooperates with and is assimilated to the higher principle that is Brahma, he justifies the dictum that the king is the father of his subject. But when he pursues his own objectives defined by his own whims and caprices and asserts his independence, the way for autocracy is paved and might presumes to rule without any respect for right, and then *anrita* (untruth, disorder) prevails. The syzygy between *Brahma* and *Kshatra* is, therefore, a pointer to the need of the king to submit himself to *adhirajo rajnam*. This constitutes an insurance against *abhwa* (privation), the fear as well as the actual occurrence of disintegration. When this syzygy holds true, even a weak person can perform the responsibilities of kingship quite well. One does not need a philosopher-king to guide the destiny of the *rashtra* (nation).[76] It is in this context that we can appreciate why, when selecting his Purohita, the ruler recites this *mantra*: "I am that, you are this, I am sky, you are earth ... May we two together support and nourish villages and cities."[77] Similarly, the *Purohita*, on the occasion of his selection makes the king agree that if he is antagonized or earns the enmity of the *Purohita*, he would lose everything.[78] If the king respects Brahma, pays him handsomely and listens to his counsel, he becomes prosperous and the earth bears fruits at all seasons.[79]

And, lastly, despite everything, the respect for and the acceptance of the over-lordship of *dharma* is not possible without what Coomaraswamy calls the installation of a proper internal economy. Man is by nature *dvyatman*, that is, he is endowed with two natures, one spiritual and the other the psycho-physical ego inclined to enjoy the pleasures of the body. (RX, 32.2; RV, I. 164.20, etc.). Unless two selves of man are made compatible, the *bhoktri suparna* becomes dominant and leads man astray, away from the path of *dharma.* Given his two selves, man himself becomes a city of God (AV, X. 2.30; BU, II. 5.18) where, too, must exist a government in which his soul must be the ruler over his reasoning faculty and be able to control, curb and regulate man's passions. It is only on this basis that the outer man, who is active and subject to passions and the inner man, who is contemplative and serene are reconciled and well integrated. It is this reconciliation that makes it possible for the outer king to submit himself to the inner priest (AV, X. 2.29–31). This is possible only through *atma-yajna* (self sacrifice).[80]

As we have already indicated, Brahma speaks or becomes articulate through the speech when he does speak with the voice of the divine? In a fully *dharma*-governed society, neither the king nor *danda* is needed. But when the constitutive principle of society gets eroded and when cumulation of deviations from the proper path of *dharma* hampers the normal, orderly functioning of social life, the king needs to use *danda*, first, to correct the imbalance that results from these deviations and, second, to see that the constitutive principle of order itself is not corroded and eroded. Three important questions arise in this connection. First, the installation of the *regnum* itself is the indicator of the erosion of *dharma* as a regulative principle. As such, the king has, in his effort to uphold *dharma* as the organizing principle of social organization, to depend on man-made laws. However, the question is: Can the dependence on man-made laws really sustain or/and safeguard the *dharma* based social order? If the answer is in the negative, how can order based on *dharma* be and is maintained? And, lastly, the *dharma*-governed society cannot depend solely on *regnum* for defending and safeguarding *dharma*. The social order, too, must be so organized that it is informed by and upholds dharmic principles. This means that its institutional structure, practices and social life and relations are based on *dharmic* principles and can, therefore, safeguard and defend *dharma*-based social order. What are the form and substance of such a society? And, what is the relationship between the social order and political order in a *dharma*-ruled society? It is these questions that are explored in the following chapter.

Notes

1. The substantive meaning of reason in this context is not the calculative, prudential reasoning that calculates what means can be appropriate, in terms of lesser costs and larger benefits, for a given end. The reference there is to that reason that helps in discriminating between different ends not in terms of what is good but in terms of what is right. It is this sense of reason that is called *Sophia* by Plato and is known as *prajnana* in Indian classical thinking.
2. Charles Taylor, *Hegel and Modern Society* (Cambridge: Cambridge University Press, 1976).
3. Plato, *The Republic,* 434b-c; 444 b.
4. Sigmund Freud, quoted in Philip Rieff, *Freud: The Mind of the Moralist* (New York: Anchor Books, 1961), p. 29.
5. Ibid.
6. When the cosmos is de-divinized, as it has been in the modern times, it is drained of purpose and is reduced to a cosmic machine, an infinite universe of perfect symmetry and absolute precision, in short, a Great Machine. See Floyd W. Matson, *The Broken Image: Man, Science and Society* (New York: Doubleday Anchor Books, 1966), p. 3. As Hume noted long ago, the world is, for him, nothing else but "one great machine, subdivided into an infinite number of lesser machines, which again admit of subdivisions, to a degree beyond human senses and faculties can trace and explain". As Hume further notes, all these various machines with their minutest subdivisions "are adjusted to each other with an accuracy, which ravishes into admiration all men, who have ever contemplated them". See David Hume, *Dialogues Concerning Natural Religion*, quoted in Carl L. Becker, *The Heavenly City of the Eighteenth Century Philosophers* (New Haven: Yale University Press, 1960), p. 56. See also Niels Bohr, *Atomic Physics and Human Knowledge* (New York: Wiley & Sons, 1958), p. 95.

In the Cosmic Machine even human beings and their action must be treated as governed by extension and motions. It is, therefore, not surprising, then, that John Herman Randall, Jr. declares: "Give me extension and motion and I will construct the universe." *The Making of the Modern Mind* (New York: Houghton Mifflin & Co., 1940), pp. 241–42. Or, Spinoza: "I shall consider human actions and desires in exactly the same manner as though I were concerned with lines, places and solids." Quoted in ibid., p. 247.

If human action can be studied in terms of extension and motion, man himself turns out to be nothing more than a machine and mechanomarphism constitutes the only mode of understanding human behaviour. Since Bacon and Descartes, a serious attempt has been on to rid behavioural science of its contamination by such metaphysical speculations as purpose, freedom, etc. Talking of freedom, the hypothesis that man is not free become unavoidable for worthwhile effort to free behavioural science of all metaphysical speculations and make it a perfect science. See B.F. Skinner, *Walden-II* (New York: Macmillan, 1984), p. 214. It is against this background that we can appreciate the true intent of Spinoza when he says that "true liberty is nothing else than rational submission to the preponderance of the laws of nature in release from all arbitrary personal dictation". And, of course, by "laws of nature" he does not mean God's laws but laws of nature that science discovers.

Man, in this perspective, is supposed to be an irrational being who needs rational control from outside. It is claimed that man acquires a degree of rationality only through submission to the rational processes of society. Thus, central to the modern perspective is the idea that the individual must be divested of his freedom; the individual must become *anyarata* in order to ensure the good of his own as well as that of the collectively he belongs to. This is quite in contrast to the central belief of Enlightenment in the unchallenged and untrammeled primacy of freedom as the basis of individual felicity and collective good.

7. John Dewey, *Individualism: Old and New* (New York: Capricorn Books, 1962), p. 116. cf. Lavater, "Say what you please of your humanity, no wise man will ever believe a syllable while I and Mine are the two only gates at which you sally forth and enter, and through which alone all must pass who seek admittance." Lavater's Aphorism of Man in William Blake, *Complete Works*' ed. Geoffrey Keynes (London: Oxford University Press, 1976), p. 78.
8. Eric Voegelin, *Order and History: Plato and Aristotle,* III (Baton Rouge: Louisiana State University Press, 1957), pp. 76–77.
9. Cf. Heraclitus, "Only one cosmos ... exists for the 'waking' alone, while the 'sleepers' each have their own private world of dreams," Quoted on Jaeger, *Paideia* I, p. 180. The term, waking refers to a person who is spiri-

tually awake while the term 'sleeper' signifies those who are spiritually blind.

10. Eric Voegelin, op. cit.
11. Eric Voegelin, *Order and History*: *Israel and Revelation,* I (Baton Rouge: Louisiana State University Press, 1957) p. 16. To say that man becomes a rival of God in creating a political cosmion does not mean that he undertakes the arrogant task of replacing God. It only means that he proposes, as *Ishavasyopanishad* makes it clear, to make this world worthy as the residence of the divine. It is true that this world is already permeated with the divine. However, it has been polluted with profanity of different kinds. It therefore needs to be cleansed and the creation of political order is considered to be the one means which can not only check the tendency towards further pollution but also restore to the world its original divinity. And political order can, therefore, be effective in it if it is modelled upon the divine act of creation.

    It is true that political order imitates analogically the divine act of creation, but Drekemeier grossly misconceives the import of this imitation. In describing the Vedic perspective on political order, Drekemeier argues that "in effect, the political order is understood cosmologically, and the cosmic is apprehended in terms that are essentially political." See Charles Drekemeier, *Kingship and Community in Early India* (Stanford, California: Stanford University Press, 1962), p. 15. It should be noted, first, that the act of governance is essentially political but not in the modern sense of the term. It is political in the traditional sense in that it joins together the world of man and that of the gods and attempts to inform, influence and transform the givens of both society and nature in the light of certain transcendental values derived as a result of linking the finite existence of man with the absolute. In this point, see John H. Schaar, *Escape from Authority* (New York: Basic Books, 1961), p. 292.

    The second error of interpretation that he commits pertains to his characterizing the Vedic perspective on political order as cosmological. He does quote Eric Voegelin but he misses the essential point related with Voegelin's definition of the term "cosmological". According to Voegelin, the cosmological perspective refers to a particular self-understanding of a society as the representative order and the ruler claims to be the enforcer of the "truth" as reflected in this particular self-understanding, and undertakes expeditions to punish those who deviate from this "truth". See Voegelin, *The New Science of Politics: An Introduction* (Chicago: The University of Chicago Press, 1987), pp. 54–59.
12. For a detailed discussion, see Ramashray Roy, *Beyond Ego's Domain: Being and Order in the Veda* (New Delhi: Shipra Publications, 1999), pp. 276–84.

13. Charles N. Cochrane, *Christianity and Classical Culture: A Study of Thought and Action from Augustus to Augustine* (Oxford: The Clarendon Press, 1940), 78.
14. Plato, *Phaedrus*, 245e.
15. Ibid., 247.
16. Plato, *Republic*, 37b 4–6.
17. Eric Voegelin, *Order and History: Plato and Aristotle,* III, op. cit., p. 125.
18. Aristotle, *Politics*, 1253a 38.
19. Plato, *Republic*, 371e 9–11.
20. Ibid., 373b 3–4.
21. Ibid., 518d-e.
22. For a detailed discussion, see Charles N. Cocharne, op. cit.; my "Freedom and Order: A Fresh Look" in my *Gandhi: Soundings in Political Philosophy* (Delhi: Chanakya Publications, 1984), pp. 47–92, and Ramashray Roy, *Beyond Ego's Domain: Being and Order in the Veda*, op. cit.
23. See Sri Aurobindo's, *The Spirit and Form of Indian Polity* (Calcutta: Arya Publishing House, 1947), p. 19.
24. The Vedic perspective recognizes types of persons reflecting the preeminence of a particular *guna* (attribute). Three basic *gunas, sattwa, rajas,* and *tamas,* are said to produce a diversity of human nature as a result of combination and permutation of these *gunas.* These *gunas* are also identified with three movements such as, *utkranti* (centrifugal), *adana* (centripetal) and *pratishtha* (rest or equilibrium) in which Brahma as the primal energy gets trifurcated in his procession during creation. These movements represent essential qualities, properties or tendencies that inhere in all things and are present in all the dimensions of the universe. When applied to psyche or *adhyatma*, they are called *gunas* each of which represents a particular psychic power or tendency. *Sattwa*, for example, creates cohesion, is surrogate of concentration of energy, a coming together, a power of concentration. Its presiding god is Vishnu. *Tamas*, on the contrary, represents darkness, the power that prevents concentration signifying diffusion of energy. Its presiding deity is Indra or Rudra. There is also *rajas* which symbolizes equilibrium or the base from which different movements spring and get equilibrated. It is represented by Prajapati or Brahma. For a brief but succinct discussion, see Allain Danielou, *Hindu* Polytheism (New York: Pantheon Books, 1964), pp. 22–28.
25. As RV X. 71.2 points out, *vak* is created by mind or, as SB VI. 1.2.9 notes, *vacam mithuna sambhavat* (by his mind he entered into union with *vak*).
26. RV X. 61.6–7. It is this deed that is referred to in AB III. 33 as *Brahma Kilvisha.* Incensed by Brahma's sin, the gods sought for some one who could put him to death; but each feeling his own inability, the gods created

Rudra for this purpose. Rudra cuts off one of the five heads of Brahma. This symbolically confirms the diremption of Vak from Brahma. Cf. RV I. 164.8: "In the region of the universal Rita, the mother separated from the Father and in the primeval ages wedded him in spirit and mind ..."

27. SB VI. 4.2.9 *yajnadvai prajah prajayante yajnatprajayamana mithunatprajayante.* It is interesting to note that in the *Havirdhan*, where the cart carrying Soma was taken, was enclosed on all sides to let it represent a secret place where (Agni and Soma) could co-habit. See SB IV. 6.7.12. Also, as SB IV. 6.7.12 points out, it is there in the Havirdhana that the male, Soma, longs after the female, the *apah* (water). From that *mithuna*, moon was produced. This is symbolic of what Meister Eckhaut calls "the act of fecundity inherent in eternity".
28. Translated by W. Calland. Cf. *Jaiminya Brahman* (Gb). II. 244.
29. The process through which one becomes many is characterized in the Veda as *yajna*. The term "*yajna*" is derived from the root "yaj"; it does not only mean to worship, to pray or to sacrifice but also to bring different things together. On this point, see Motilal Shastri, *Bharatiya Drishti se Vijnana Shabda ka Samanwaya* (Jaipur: Rajasthan Patrika Pvt. Ltd.), p. 46. When several things come together, intermingle and become something else by giving up their former separate form, it is called *yajna*, that is, joining two or more things together, because elements in yoga preserve their attributes. It is, therefore, not surprising that RVI. 164.35. characterizes *yajna* as *bhuvanasya nabhih* (cf. YV 23.62 and AVIX. 1.14).
30. See Ramashray Roy, *Beyond Ego's Domain: Being and Order in the Veda*, op. cit., p. 184.
31. In SB (VI. 1.1.4–6) Agni is said to have seven purusas that is represented by human body or a *suparna* (bird). See RV (1.164.15), AV(IX. 1.16), *Tait Aranyaka* (1.3.1) and *Nirukta* (14.19).
32. AV (II. 15) refers to other pairs as well.
33. *Supra*, Ch. 9. Gods performed *yajna* and went to the highest heaven.
34. These are the terms in which A. Ramamurty describes the seer-poets or Vedic Rishis. See his *The Central Philosophy on Rig-Veda* (Delhi: Ajanta Publications, 1991), p. 49.
35. See RV (I. 59.5, 2.2.8, 3.1.18, 3.10.1, VI. 1.13, VI. 7.1, VI. 15.13, 7.6.1, etc.).
36. See RV (I.100.1 2.14.11, III. 57.1, IV. 17.20, VI. 36.4, VII. 27.3, VII. 30.1; VIII. 16.1; VIII. 64.3; VIII. 70.1, X. 44.3, X. 134.1; YV 8.37, AV VI 98.1–2; XX. 44.1 XX. 105.4, etc.).
37. Jeanine Miller, *The Vision of the Cosmic Order in the Vedas* (London: Routledge & Kegan Paul, 1985), p. 132.
38. RV (VIII. 3.10).
39. RV (II. 34.7).

40. To train the mind through rational thought is tantamount to "grasping the reality of life through the setting up of a world of objectified 'meanings', of Platonic entities amenable to logical handling and of clear and distinct ideas' by which raw stuff of life can be reduced to conceptual order". J.L. Mehta, *Philosophy and Religion: Essay in Interpretation* (New Delhi: Indian Council of Philosophical Research, 1990), p. 104.
41. Jan Gonda, *The Vision of the Vedic Poets* (Delhi: Motilal Banarasidass, 1984), chs. 2–4.
42. *Shraddha* denotes not only faith but also respectful trust and fidelity. *Shraddha* (Sat+dha, that is, holding on to truth), as Nirukta (IX. 30) points out, can also be derived from *shraddha* (truth). *Shraddha* can, as Panikkar shows, also mean the longing of a pregnant woman, her confidence that a new life will spring out of her womb. See *The Vedic Experience: Mantra-Manjari*, p. 398, fn. 221. In this sense, *shraddha* signifies a longing and confidence that a new life of light will emerge from the depth of the darkness of *avidya*. It is also interesting to note here that AV (VI. 133.4) addresses *mekhala* (girdle) to grant *mati* (wisdom), *tapas* and Indra's prowess. *Mekhala* has been identified in the same *mantra* as the daughter of *shraddha* born out of *tapas*. It is also called *rishinamasya yudham*, the weapon of Rishis with the help of which they create the *bhutas*, beings. In view of all these, it is clear that one of the elements of *shraddha* has to do with the disciplining, of keeping man within certain limits, limits that derive their meaning from the bonds of existence, and of joining existence with *sat*. As YV(XIX. 77) notes, Prajapati saw *rita (truth)* and *anrita (falsehood)* and assigned *a-shraddha* (*disbelief*), *anrita* and *shraddha* to *rita*. And, again in YV(XIX.30), it is stressed that truth can be had only on the basis of *shraddha*.
43. The Vedic Experience: Mantra Manjari, op. cit., p. 178.
44. As Mehta points out, there exists in the West a philosophical tradition, deriving from Greece, and another tradition, the religious, having other root, with "truth" as the concern of the former and "faith" that of the latter. "Or, as a more illuminating recent proposal has it, two kinds of faith, one in reason, the other is God. The polarity of their relation to each other, and the constant, unresolved tension between the two has led to the formation of a mode of thinking which appears inappropriate when it addresses itself to a tradition like that prevalent in India, has not been subject to that kind of polarity and dialectical tension", op. cit., p. 114.
45. There is a lot of confusion about the real significance of *yajna*. Most Vedic scholars refuse to treat it as anything else than the mere performance of rituals, as a mere ritual. Nothing can be farther from truth than this. For three vital reasons, Veda puts a great deal of emphasis on *yajna*. First, *yajna* is the means of putting together Prajapati when he allowed

himself to be dismembered for the sake of the *praja*, that is, he divided (*vibhakta*) himself into *praja*. Second, the *praja* constitute his distributive essence (*vibhuti*), to be sure; however, they become unaware of this primordial connection with Prajapati. Thus, although man is a *bhakta* (part) of the Supreme Being, he has come to be *vibhakta*, separated, from the primal source of his being. In order, therefore, to regain his *sarvata* (wholeness), he must do as the gods did, that is, perform *yajna* so that he can consciously relate himself with his source. And, lastly, the preservation of the cosmos and the order inherent in it depends on the continuation of the process of exchange between man, on the one hand, and between men and gods, on the other. (See Taittiriya *Brahaman* 2.8.8). Thus, the performance of yajna is to do as the gods did, and are still doing, in creating, supporting and sustaining this world. And to perform *yajna* faithfully and diligently is tantamount to actively trying to become like gods.

46. For a fruitful discussion on this point, see Ananda K. Coomaraswamy. "*Atma-yajna:* Self-sacrifice," in *Selected Papers,* p. 108.
47. RV (III. 14.5, VI. 13.3, VIII. 11.6).
48. RV (I. 12.7).
49. RV (III. 1.18, IV. 5.3., IV. 11.3, VI. 15.10).
50. RV (III. 14.7).
51. RV (V. II. 4).
52. The conventional Vedic scholarship, whether Indian or Western, has handled the term "*stoma*" very casually without caring to explore its deeper significance. Take, for example, Suryakant who equates *stoma* with a song of praise or prayer. See his *Vaidik Kosha* (Varanasi: Banaras Hindu University, 1963), p. 589. However, *Tandya Brahman* 2.5.4 equates *stoma* with *viryam* (virility, vigour). As RV III. 5.2 notes, "*predvagnivavridhe stoma* ...." Wilson translates it to mean that the adorable Agni is magnified by the hymns. This may be true. However, if, as Agrawal suggests, *stoma* means stock-piling, then the real significance of *stoma* is the increase in the virility and vigour of Agni which is possible only when it feeds as *annada* on more *anna*, that is Soma. See Vasudeva Saran Agrawal, *Vision in Long Darkness,* p. 59. It is thus clear that *stoma* signifies units of energy. When Prajapati begins the process of creation requiring a lot of energy. In his procession, he emitted energy which is called gau which is said to have one thousands parts. When divided by 30 (15 days and 15 nights), gau (rays) yields 33 *stomas* which describe the spread of Agni and Soma, the rest of 10 *stomas* constitute Prajapati himself. See Motilal Shastri, *Shatapatha Brahman Vijnan Bhashya* (Jaipur: Rajasthan Patrika, 2047 VS), pp. 41–42, 446. Out of these 10 stomas, the three *stomas* at the centre stand for the *trivrittakaran (three-fold division) into*

manas, *prana* and *vak* of Brahma. That is why Brahma is prior to Indra who occupies only the 15th *stoma*.

53. *Brihaspativai sarva Brahma, Gopath Brahman,* 1.3.4.
54. *Ahava* is a particular invocation addressed by Hotr to Adhwaryu. Cf. RV (X. 10.1; 1.34.8, VI. 7.2, X.100.5, X.112.6).
55. *Nivida* is a smaller invocation addressed to a god to come to a *yajna*. Cf AB. 2.33.34; 3.10.11; 6.33,35; SB 3.9.3.28; 13.5.1.9, etc.
56. *Rigveda Brahmanas: The Aitereya and Kaushitaki Brahmanas*, tr. by A.B. Keith (Delhi: Motilal Banarsidass, 1971), Harvard Oriental Series, Vol. 25, p. 121.
57. The term "*Purohita*" signifies one who goes in front, that is, who precedes in rank. Or, alternatively, it means a family priest.
58. Ananda K. Coomaraswamy, *Spiritual Authority and Temporal Power* (New Delhi: Munshiram, 1978), p.3, fn. 3; RV II. 11.4; SB I. 2.4.1, V. 4.4.15, XIII. 4.4.1.
59. Cf. SB V. 2.1.10: Being about to ascend, he (the sacrificer) addresses his wife, "come, wife, ascend we the sky! – Ascend we, says the wife. Now as to why he addresses his wife; she, the wife, in sooth is one half of his own self; hence, as long as he does not obtain her, so long he is not regenerated, for so long he is incomplete. But as soon as he obtains her, he is regenerated, for then he is complete.
60. It must be pointed out that the term "*Purisha*", as many other Vedic words, has different meanings. However, as SB (8.7.3.7; 10.4.1.7) indicates, it also refers to Indra.
61. SB (I. 4.5.8–11). See also TS II; 5.11.4: "for what is made perfect by *manas*".
62. Yajus, Rik and Sama represent the three aspects of Agni as Prajapati in his *anirukta* (undefined state) is *yajna*; when he begins to process, he becomes Rik and, when completely transformed into a mass (*pinda*), the outer limits of the *pinda*, is called soma. A circle whose centre is yajus, the diameter Rik and the circumference Sama, can symbolically represent this.
63. *Aitereya Aranyak*, I. 3.2, ed. and trans. by A.B. Keith (Oxford: Clarendon Press, 1969).
64. It is interesting to point out that Eggeling, while translating this passage, has failed to disconceal the true import of the term *graha*. As SB (IV. 6.5.1) notes: "*Esha vaigrahah ya esha tapati yenemah sarvah praja grahitastastmadahurgrahangthnim iti charanti grahagrahitah santa itih* (Now the graha, forsooth, is he that burns yonder, since by him all these creatures are held. Hence they say, "we take (*grah*) the grahas", "they walk seized by the *grahas*)". Agni, as SB (X. 1.1.5) points out, "*yadgrhanti tasmadgrah ah*" (that which holds is *graha*). It refers to extraordinary power that can take hold of, support and sustain.

65. See RV (IV. 50.9); also AV (8.5.24, 26).
66. SB (1.3.5.1): *Samindhe Samidhinir bhirhota tasmat samidhenyo nama* (With the firewood *idhma*, lighting material, the Adhvaryu lights (*indha*) the fire: hence it is called firewood, cf. SB (XI. 2.7.6). notes, *etahi va idam sarvam samindhata etabhiridam sarva samindham tasmad samidhenejs nama* (for it is these that kindle all this (universe) and by them all this (universe) is kindled, whence they are called kindling verses).
67. SB (V. 3.2.4; V. 1.1.2); RV (VIII. 13–1). See also Ananda K. Coomarswamy, *Spiritual Authority and Temporal Power* (New Delhi: Munshiram,1978), the editon used here was published by Kraus Reprint Corporation, New York, 1978.
68. For detailed discussion of Rajasuya Yajna see J.C. Heesterman, *The Ancient Indian Royal Consecration* (S-Gravenhage: Mouton & Co., 1957) and A.M. Hocart, *Kingship* (London: Oxford University Press, 1969).
69. Cf. SB (V. 1.1.1): Once upon a time the Gods and asuras, both of them sprang from Prajapati, strove together. And the asuras, even through arrogance, thinking, 'Unto whom, forsooth, should one make offering? went on offering into their own mouths. They came to naught, even through arrogance; wherefore let no one be arrogant, for verily arrogance is the cause of ruin.
70. *Shri* means light, lustre, radiance, splendour, glory, beauty, grace, loveliness, M. Monier-William, *Sanskrit-English Dictionary,* 1995 edn. p. 1008. See also SB (XI.4.3.1–3); cf. RV (VIII. 2.19), AV (VI. 54.1; VI. 73.1, IX. 5.31, X. 6.26, XI. 1.12,21, etc.).
71. The *Ratnins* whose houses the king-to-be visits for making offerings are: 1. chief commander, 2. purohit, 3. the chief queen, 4. chariot-driver, 5. *gramani* (village chief), 6. *kshatta* (chamberlain), 7. *sangrahita* (collector), 8. *bhagndugh* (tax collector), 9 *akshavap* (surveyor of the dicing hall), 10. *govikarta* (slaughterer), and 11. *palagal* (messenger). At these houses, he makes offerings respectively to: 1. Agni, 2. Brhaspati, 3. Aditi, 4. Varuna, 5. Marut, 6. Savita, 7. Ashwin, 8. Pusha, 9. Rudra, and 10. Marga. See SB (V. 3–2) and Heesterman, op. cit., Ch. 6.
72. As AB (II. 37.5) puts it, in the battle between suras and asuras "these two as Indra and Agni did not conquer; being Agni and Indra they did conquer" (*na va etavindragai santau vyayayetamagnendrau va etau santau*).
73. Cf. AV (IV. 8), SB (IX. 3.3.11), SB (V.1.5.4).
74. Ananda K. Coomaraswamy, *Spiritual Authority and Temporal Power,* op. cit., p. 160.
75. Br. Up. (I. IV. 14).
76. Coomaraswamy, op. cit., p. 63.
77. AB (VIII. 27).
78. Ibid.

79. RV (IV. 50.8, also IV. 50.7 and 9).
80. Cf. AB (II.37): The sacrifice is a chariot of the gods; the *Ajya* and *Prauga Shastras* are its inner reins; in that with the *Ajya* he follows in recitation *pavamana*, with the *Prauga* the *Ajya* (*stotra*), verily thus he separates the inner reins of the chariot to prevent confusion; in imitation thereof they separate the inner reins of the chariot of men to prevent confusion. His chariot whether of the gods or men does not become confused who knows thus.

    Cf. *Katha Upanishad* (I. III 3–9) where man's being is compared with a chariot in which the intellect is the charioteer, senses the horses. It is the intellect that holds the reins of these horses and drives them towards the destination, that is, self-control.

10

Dharma, Society and Political Order

Whenever the issue of creating, sustaining and safeguarding order in society is raised, the tradition of Western thinking gives one unequivocal answer. It identifies the political system as not only the creator of order, but also its guardian and protector when the unruly crowd of passions rises in open rebellion against the harsh rule of the soul and when, as a result of this, order in society is threatened with disruption. Plato recommends the creation of a political order that he calls republic as the panacea capable of saving man from the adverse consequences of disorder. In his view, there is no other agency than the state that can work as the surrogate of order and release man from the slavery of his turbulent passions. Social order does not enter into his reckoning. Even Aristotle assigns the responsibility of transforming the individual into a citizen not to society but to the public realm, that is, the realm of politics.

This tradition of thinking continues uninterrupted even in modern times. In contradistinction to the state, society is considered to be the arena where diverse socio-economic interests compete for articulation, ascendance and control. By virtue of this, society comes to be divided into competing, heterogeneous groups and is transformed into a conflict system. If the conflict that ensues as a result of the aggressive pursuit of interest by different socio-economic interests is allowed to rage unabatedly, order is likely to be jeopardized. The pacification of conflict by settlement, through negotiations, bargaining and compromise, of disputes caused by different claims of entitlement, is supposed to be beyond the capacity of society. It cannot, therefore, provide any framework of integration of diverse socio-economic interests; it is only the state that can provide such a framework.

It is not, therefore, surprising that Voegelin, influenced by this perspective, insists that the creation of a political order, "is an essay in world creation", that constitutes "the little world of order". Such an order is carved out of "a shapeless vastness of conflicting human desires" and leads "a precarious life under the pressure of destructive forces from within and without, and maintaining its existence by the ultimate threat and application of violence against the internal breaker of its laws as well as the external aggressor".[1] The use of violence, however, is instrumental only for the preservation of order, what Voegelin calls the cosmion; its real function is "the creation of shelter in which man may give to his life a semblance of meaning".[2] The meaning of what constitutes the essence of being human cannot be derived from the givens of life of a natural man nor that of society and nature. If the life of the natural man is considered to be meaningful in and by itself, then, it proves to be disruptive of order both in human psyche and in the society at large.

To consider the givens of man, that is, the natural man, society and nature as immutable, is to endow the finiteness of human existence with the quality of the absolute. As a result of this, corporate life is likely to face a variety of problems that must be solved if man is to survive the life of a natural man and maintain his continued existence in history against the hazards that the act of living presents. It is to solve these problems that the little world of order, or the cosmion, is created. Once it comes into being, this little world has to live and work in particular historical conditions which may snap the fragile thread of its existence. It is in this sense that, even while the cosmion, the little world of order, aims at creating permanent structure of order backed by necessary rules and force, is itself nothing more than a finite world. Yet this little world of order aims at endowing human existence with absoluteness of meaning. It is in this sense that, as Schaar points out:

> Political life occupies a middle terrain between the sheer givens of nature and society on the one hand, and the transcendental ends towards which men aspire, on the other. Political action is that type of action through which men publicly attempt to transform the givens of nature and society in the light of values which are above or outside the order of the givens.[3]

The state constitutes this middle terrain between the sheer givens of nature and society that give a definite shape to human existence and certain transcendental values above or outside the givens of nature and society. As such, it has necessarily to deal, on the one hand, with the diversity of human nature with its diverse and not necessarily compatible requirements, hopes and expectations. On the other hand, it is assigned the responsibility of holding different kinds of human beings located in a highly differentiated factual order in some framework of unity. Also, it is responsible for preventing them from breaking those norms, rules and laws that are essential for ensuring collective good, both, negatively, by meting out punishment for infringing these norms and, positively, through inculcating respect for these norms and rules. It is in this sense that the state possesses the dual character of combining power with authority, and force with morality. The historical existence of the state is always threatened with the chaos caused, internally, by the rebellion of appetites and, externally, by powerful rulers driven by the ambition of acquiring ever more territory. The state has, therefore, to take recourse to violence in order to ward off the danger of chaos, if gentler methods fail to have any effect. But apart from this, the authority that the state exercises over the people it claims to rule within its given territory must have a moral force and be grounded in something that is over or outside particular wills.

In addition to this duality, there is yet another feature of the state that allows it to be seen in a double light. It is true that the birth of the state is due largely to human cupidity. The state is thus considered to be a providential check upon human cupidity. However, the state is also a power machine that is used exclusively by the state to maintain its existence as well as to preserve the integrity of the created order. Yet, precisely because it signifies a power machine, it tends to be used by powerful socio-economic interests for preserving and protecting their privileged position and, towards this, prevent the weaker sections of the society from using the state power for a similar purpose against superior forces of wealth, power and privilege. It is in this sense that, as Unger points out, "the state is seen in a double light, as the providential alternative to the blindness of human cupidity and as a supreme weapon of some men in their self-interested struggle against others."[4]

It does not need to be pointed out that the perception of the state in this double light is due mainly to the perilous divide in modern times between reason and will creating in its wake yet another divide, that is, between the private and the public. Given the primacy of the satisfaction of desires as a means of ensuring happiness, sustaining the process of self-making of man and supporting civilizational progress, freedom in modern times signifies the lack of heteronomy, the conception of what is right is reduced to the notion of what is good. As a result of this reduction, the good has no existence outside the will. It is true that the will that decides what is good is supposed to function under the suzerainty of reason. However, for various reasons, both will and reason move on parallel tracks with only infrequent interactions. This is so because, as Kant points out, man is a citizen of two kingdoms, a natural realm of causal determination and a moral realm of freedom. As a citizen of the former, he wants to explain and understand the world for effective action; he must reside in the latter so that he can justify his conduct both in his own eyes and in the eyes of his fellowmen. Kant did claim that a moral law rather than the caprice of the will must take the place of natural determination. However, he was unable to forge an effective bridge between the universality of reason and the particularism of the will.

The fact, however, remains that reason plays only a subsidiary role and is treated by the will as its handmaiden. As such, "reason cannot command us to choose a course of action simply because it is worthy of being chosen nor can it prohibit us from settling on some new aim for our activities. Its industry in the service of desire is indispensable, but limited. The limit is the line that divides the elucidation of relations among desires from the decision about what in the end to choose".[5] The distinction, made especially in modern times, between knowledge and will is at the root of the erosion of the morality of reason. In Pande's words:

> The modern distinction, in fact, arises from the distinction between knowledge and will, the latter being free to follow any fiat within the bounds of desire and impulse, which are regarded as non-rational. On this view, the will becomes arbitrary or non-rationally determined and thus the principles it follows cease to have any connection with reason just as the latter remains connected only with directive principle of the will.[6]

In view of the fact that it is the private concerns of individuals that constitute the woof and warp of politics, the state, too, does not remain immune to the influences of politics that receives its inspiration from the interplay of private passions. It is true that the state is viewed as an association which, unlike other associations in society, is considered to be something above the antagonism and strife of private values. It can also be argued that the state is simply a framework within which antagonistic interests are represented and their conflicts resolved. However, it does not alter the fact that the state has the responsibility of providing as well as safeguarding the integrity of the rules of the game which must be followed while private interests are vigorously pursued by individuals and groups. These rules must be above the competition of private interests and must not be determined by particular or a particular combination of private interests. It is also true that the state is distinguished from other associations on the basis of the distinction between laws of the state and rules prescribed and enforced by other associations. However, this distinction is prone to frequent breakdowns. The government, as Unger observes, "takes on the characteristics of a private body because private interests are the only interests that exist in a situation of which it is a part. Thus the state is like the gods in Olympics, who were banished from the earth and endowed with super-human powers, but condemned to undergo the passions of the mortals."[7]

Thus, the state, even while it is supposed to be above the competition and strife of private values, is forced by existential situation to act frequently as a private body. It must be emphasized that the state becomes indispensable because most individuals are incapable of controlling and curbing the erratic movement of their desires, appetites and passions. This is symptomatic of their inability to exercise control over their passions; that is, it is indicative of the fact that these individuals have already undergone the process of the erosion of auto-control. This further indicates the fact that they have lost the power to discriminate between what is right and what is wrong and what is good for the individual and what is good for all individuals. Since there are no conceptions of the good that stand above the conflicts of private values and impose limits on the tendency of the individual towards self-aggrandizement, artificial limits on this tendency have to be imposed by some outside agency. This agency is considered to be none other than the state which must enact laws or, alternatively, apply rules framed on the basis of some transcendental source and see to it that these laws or rules are obeyed.

The fact, however, remains that the heat of the pursuit of self-interest dissolves respect for the law. To the extent that this happens, the legitimacy of the state as the providential alternative to human cupidity faces severe erosion. The state has, therefore, to safeguard and ensure its legitimacy and seek to restore respect for the law by recourse to violence. But the extensive use of violence by the state to ensure conformity to the law creates its own paradox. As the reliance of the state on the use of force increases, the legitimacy of its claim to rule by virtue of the authority granted to it takes a plunge downward. It is not to deny the state's right to exercise violence in order to shore up the crumbling ramparts of the rule of law and reinforce its authority. However, the very fact that the state is forced to use its power resources frequently is indicative of its sagging authority. This, in turn, is symptomatic of the widespread erosion of the respect for the law in the society at large indicating further that the loss of auto-control on the part of individual members of the society has become an established fact.

It is interesting to note that the tradition of Indian thinking attributes the erosion of the auto-control in the individual and the onset of good or bad times to the ruler. The aphorism that *raja kalasya karanam* (the king is responsible for good or bad times) points just to this. This does not, however, mean that the upward or downward swing in the movement of time is due to the slackening of governmental control over the people and the weakening of governmental fiat. When the state is forced to exercise stricter control over the people, it indicates a deeper malaise, that is, the erosion of the commitment to moral conduct on the part of the people, particularly the leaders or great men (*mahajana or spudaios* in Aristotle's word), that is, persons who set the pattern of ideal conduct.[8] It is only when the leaders of society, who are considered to be the exemplars of good conduct, stray away from it that society becomes afflicted with the difficult-to-cure disease of corruption of its ideals and exemplary conduct. Thus, the source of the corruption of society is always to be found at its apex – the apex occupied by its *mahajanas or spudaios.* And, if the ruler, who happens to be the *spudaios* among *spudaios*, strays away from the path of virtue or right conduct, the condition of the people he rules over must degrade and become miserable.

It is against this background that we can appreciate the fact that the act of governance cannot be the basis of the principle that governs its functioning; this act has to be subordinated to some higher principle. This principle, as we have already seen,[9] is what is known as *kshatrasya kshatram*, that is, *dharma.* This being the case, it is quite clear that *dharma* is a higher principle that is above the state and constitutes the source from which the state does or can derive those principles that should guide and regulate its functioning. Thus, the legitimacy of *regnum* depends on the extent to which it conforms to these principles in discharging its responsibilities and using force in securing conformity to law. In being guided by *dharma* while discharging his responsibilities, the ruler performs his duty of upholding *dharma.* The saying that *dharmo rakshite rakshitah* (when *dharma* is upheld, well-being of every being is ensured) points to just this essential aspect of the act of governance. Even violence used by the state to uphold the order of *dharma* can be justified only if the state accepts and conforms to *dharma.*

It is true that upholding the order of *dharma* is the primary responsibility of the state. This responsibility can be discharged well only if the state is guided in its actions by and accepts *dharma* as its *adhiraja.* However, this is only a necessary but by no means a sufficient condition. The state cannot be effective in upholding the order of *dharma* if this order has either eroded in the society at large or has no meaning in managing the pragmatic affairs of the people. It is, therefore, necessary that people are committed to, respect and give allegiance to *dharma* in handling the problems of personal life and social existence. The social world, without the restraining hand of *dharma,* easily becomes the breeding ground of exploitation and oppression leading to the onset of *matsya nyaya.* Social life and relations must, therefore, be informed and regulated by *dharma.* Since social life and relations are, to a large extent, reflections of actions on the part of individual members of society aimed at fulfilling their various needs related both to their worldly existence and transcendental purposes, it is necessary that their conduct, too, reflect their devotion to and obedience of *dharma.*

What kind of social order, we must ask, can prove effective in providing the much needed benign shelter to the people struggling to find a reliable anchor for the ship of their life tossed around in the seething and surging sea of everydayness? To answer this question satisfactorily, we must make a distinction between three kinds of social order based on easily identifiable different principles of organization and modes of operation. The first to be mentioned in this regard is the one, which is, viewed scientifically, not philosophically.[10] Viewed scientifically, the universe is considered to be the concourse of causal relations; these relations can be studied only by using the methods of the natural sciences. The heavy reliance on the methods of the natural sciences came to be placed because of the radical shift in the worldview that occurred in the 17th century in Western Europe. The main thrust of this shift was to reject the idea of man as an integral part of a larger conceptual order; as such, man was not a self-defining subject but a person who derived his norms and values from the larger conceptual order. This order was considered to be the bedrock of his knowledge and understanding of himself and the world around him. Central to this world view was the notion of intelligible essence, that is, the form that, by becoming embodied in matter, lends each being its unique pattern of development and distinctive identity.

The rejection of the notion of intelligible essence had far-reaching consequences for man and his relationship with the external world. This rejection, as Rosen points out, transformed actuality into possibility.[11] If objects lack intelligible essence, that is, if their development is not governed by what is embedded in their own being, then, it is shaped by their environing conditions. Actuality, then, is not manifested or actualized potentiality; it is simply a possibility. In other words, the possibility of a particular object being shaped in a desired fashion opens up. But, the possibility unfolds in history and incorporates a sequence of changes leading from one level of achievement, capacity and refinement to ever higher and higher levels. In this spiralling process man's individual and social life, it is assumed, could undergo almost unlimited change, a radically new order of social relationships could be established, and in this new order there could be fundamental transformation in human nature.[12]

When actuality is transformed into possibility, form is submitted to the agency of two closely related powers: temporality or history and human will. Virtue now consists in the satisfaction of desires, which becomes possible with the help of science and technology. With this change in the worldview, a new perspective on man and his world came to dominate man's thinking. As Becker puts it:

> We necessarily look upon our world from the point of view of history and from the point of view of science. Viewed historically, it appears to be something in the making, something which can at best be only tentatively understood since it is not yet finished. Viewed scientifically, it is something to be manipulated and mastered, something to adjust ourselves to with the least possible stress. So long as we can make efficient use of things, we feel no irresistible need to understand them.[13]

In the world, viewed both historically as well as scientifically, knowledge must produce concrete results. As Descartes explains:

> In the place of speculative philosophy taught in the schools we can have a practical philosophy, by means of which, knowing the forces and the

> actions of fire, water, air, of the stars, of the heavens, and of all the bodies that surrounded us – knowing them as distinctly as we know the various crafts of the artisans – we may in the same fashion employ them in all the uses for which they are suited, thus rendering ourselves the masters and possessors of nature.[14]

And if man wanted to become "the masters and possessors of nature", then, nature has to be read in the language it is written. This language is, of course, mathematics. And since natural sciences have devised methods of reading nature in the language it is written, science has obtained impressive results. The successes of the natural sciences must, therefore, be attributed, at least in part, to mathematical or quasi-mathematical methods they have employed. As such, the acceptance of such methods as paradigmatic and the application of them in social sciences would result in comparable achievements. This assumption has led to another, more dangerous, assumption that a study of reality could qualify as scientific only if it used the methods of the natural sciences. This further means that subject matters studied by "non-scientific" procedures are either illusionary, that is simply non-existent or, then, at least, capable of being transformed or reduced into suitable forms for scientific analysis.

Now, if the methods used by the natural sciences are to be used in studying society, the procedures employed to study social reality must be objective through a methodologically rigorous exclusion of all value judgements. The exclusion of all value judgements is felt to be necessary because they are supposed to express only individual preferences and decisions and are, therefore, subjective. As such, only propositions concerning facts of the phenomenal world could count as being objective and, therefore, scientific. For one respectable perspective on value-free science, a perspective elaborated by Max Weber, it meant an exploration of the causality of actions by means of ideal types. Weber's scientific analysis could not say whether it was better to be Marxist revolutionary or a liberal constitutionalist, to be sure; but it could indicate what the consequences would be if someone tried to translate his value preferences into action. For, Weber, the task of science with respect to "demonic" values was to make men aware of the consequences of their actions and to awaken in them a sense of responsibility. But Weber was unable to resolve the problems that this perspective gave rise to. The most difficult problem concerned the fact that if the values were truly demonic, there was 'no reason, why anyone should wake up to responsibility, particularly when they fall back upon what Weber himself identified as an "ethics of intention" that dismissed the problem of consequences altogether'.[15]

Needless to say that the fact-value divide, that is, the hallmark of modern social analysis is, of course, the product of the modern idea of what man is. As a bundle of desires, man can expect to be happy and realize the potentialities implanted in his breast only if he fulfills his needs as a natural being by obeying the dictates of his desires. It is true that as a rational man, he can control and regulate the erratic movement of his desires. However, while reason is universal and its endowment also universal, it is reduced in modern times to the status of only instrumental, calculative reasoning concerned primarily with the calculation of means for ends determined by the will. As Unger points out:

> Understanding contributes to the organization of our goals by clarifying their interrelation, but it never ultimately determines their substance. Reason is as formal in the performance of its moral responsibilities as it is in the development of scientific truth. The substance of our goals is the object of arbitrary will just as the substance of material phenomena is left by science to the realm of our everyday sense impressions.[16]

The dichotomy of universal reason and arbitrary desires creates another dichotomy, that between means and ends. Given the primacy of the need to satisfy desires, the determination of what these desires are, which desires to satisfy and how to go about it – all these considerations are subjective and subject to the preferences of the will. It is true that the means to an end is the activity of understanding and, as such, it is supposed to be an objective act. It is also true that the choice of the ends themselves is the work of desire and, therefore, arbitrary. However, the role of reason is limited only to "reckoning"; it is reduced to the status of practical, prudential reason responsible for intelligent calculation of how to encompass ends and means which are themselves beyond the arbitration of reason. It is in this sense that reason serves as the hand-maiden of the will.[17] As a consequences of the downgrading of reason, everything in the world is considered to be potentially an object of appetite or aversion. But whatever the individual does not seek or treat as an end is important to him only as a possible means. In this perspective, the external world, both society and nature, is treated as potential means for realizing individual purposes.

To treat the external world simply as potential means for realizing individual purposes has several important consequences for man's relationship with his environing social and natural world. First, if the individual is to prove effective in realizing his self-determined purposes, he must be able to represent things clearly taking into account comparative costs and benefits of various alternative means of attaining a given end.[18] The power to plan and execute is thus the hallmark of man in modern times. This presupposes and attitude of disengagement towards the external world. To look for significance in the external world is to circumscribe one's ability and willingness to use and manipulate the outer world for realizing one's purposes. To be disengaged is a necessary condition not only for implementing projects but also for safeguarding freedom. As Taylor points out, "To be able to look on everything, world and society in this perspective would be to neutralize its significance and this would be a kind of freedom – the freedom of the self-defining subject who determines his own purpose, or finds them in his natural desires."[19]

Second, the primacy of the satisfaction of desires as the stepping stone to the good life of modern conception has thrown the pursuit of higher life purposes to the dustbin of history. As a result, the fulfilment of ordinary life needs involved with the process of acquiring wealth, power and prestige has assumed a central importance in man's life. But even the satisfaction of ordinary life needs requires a rational control even while rationality is considered to mean only prudence and subjugated to the over-lordship of the will. However, as a reaction to Enlightenment, ordinary life needs have themselves been endowed with higher significance and their realization is considered essential for the full flowering of man's potentialities. As Taylor puts it:

> To fulfil the true impulse of nature in us is not just to meet biological needs but also to satisfy a higher aspiration. It is, at the same time, a moral fulfilment. From Rousseau on, the true "voice of nature" is at one and the same time both the impulse of biological needs and an aspiration to what is experienced as moral self-realization.[20]

From this perspective, the notion of life according to nature involves a fusion of the biological and the moral obliterating the hierarchical ordering as was the case with traditional moralities, or their setting in a relation of rational control that is implied in Enlightenment perspective. What is interesting to note is that the fulfilment of ordinary life needs is not only instrumental in securing happiness and promoting personality development as well as facilitating civilizational progress. It has also helped create and sustain an industrial consumer society supposedly endowed with the capacity to deliver all the goods necessary for sustaining life, safeguarding liberty, and facilitating the pursuit of happiness. All this does not only mean the meeting of certain quantitative targets but also the realization of the individual's status as autonomous, rational agent. For the sustenance of this status, continued accumulation is necessary but destructive, as we shall see shortly, of morality, social harmony and ecological balance. However, it bespeaks of a consistent, disciplined maintenance of instrumental stance to things, as well as the realization of what is erroneously called man's spiritual dimension.

It is true that this perspective on man and his world denies the existence of any transcendental reality other than the phenomenal world and the life and relations of natural man in it. However, it does not mean that this world lacks any order. The order that this de-divinized world is supposed to display is that one discovers in a machine, such as, a clock.[21] This mechanical order is not accounted for in terms of ideas but in terms of a set of interlocking elements whose relations can be explained in terms of efficient causation. As Taylor points out:

> The order (as against disorder) in things does not consist in their embodying Ideas, but rather in their meshing without conflict and distortion. Applied to the human realm, this means that man comes to realize natural order when the company of desiring subjects comes to achieve full satisfaction (happiness), each compatibly with all the others. Perfect harmony is the goal which nature and reason prescribe to men.[22]

And, lastly, the perspective delineated above represents what Iris Murdoch calls the "broken totality"; it manifests itself in splits within man himself, between man and society, and between man and nature. Reason, as we have already seen, is unable to mend this "broken totality". It can, however, be argued that even a society reflecting the mechanical conception of order still retains some measure of culture which can exert some sobering influence on the wayward movement of desires. But here, again, we encounter a great difficulty. Culture, in modern times, has, for all practical purposes, lost its intellectual, chiefly educational, vaguely prescriptive and, above all, the evaluative significance.[23]

The transmutation of culture is due to the rise into prominence of *homo economicus* who must use his power to force nature to yield her hidden treasures to man who can use these treasures to satisfy his needs. It is by satisfying his needs that man launches the process of his self-making.[24] In this process, man develops his capacities, creates institutions and culture, and makes history. While the material artifacts that man creates in this process signifies civilization, non-material artifacts, such as, "knowledge, belief, art, morals, law, customs, and any other capabilities and habits acquired by man as a member of society" is characterized as culture.[25] On this view, culture is not a matter of personal cultivation, but that of the productive system that injects, through changes in the economic realm, ever larger doses of change in society. It is clear, then, that culture itself has no intrinsic core of its own which retains its singularity, as Herder argues, but is only an artifact of changes, especially economic changes, going on in any social system. As such, culture evolves in history, its particular stages signifying different levels of civilizational progress. Each of these stages denotes, perhaps, a structurally inter-related whole unified by some inner principle. If this principle, which is by no means autonomous, changes, so does culture.

When culture enjoys no autonomous status, loses its educative, evaluative and prescriptive value, and is reduced simply to the status of entertainment, society, too, loses its disciplining role and emerges simply as an arena where different persons and groups pursue their private concerns. With all the disciplining, controlling and regulating elements in society losing their salience, the tendency inherent in individuals and groups towards self-aggrandizement gains an upper hand. It is claimed that the political order is capable of coping with the threats of the disruption of the fragile bonds of order. However, what must be emphasized is the fact that order, as already pointed out, signifies, in such a social order, only equilibrium that antagonistic socio-economic forces come to achieve in the process of reciprocal resistance. However, order as equilibrium always tends to be disturbed by the activities of individual and groups aimed at safeguarding and promoting their interest. When order is threatened with disruption, the process of negotiation, bargaining and compromise is initiated and contenders are induced to cease their hostilities after partial satisfaction of their claims. However, this does not prove effective. The contenders bide for time and renew their hostilities when the time appears propitious to them. Also, other socio-economic interests, too, are prompted to channel their demands into the political system and take political action to press for their satisfaction.

It is obvious, then, that order in its mechanical sense does not reflect any *a priori* idea of order against which the state of order can be evaluated and judged. Neither does it incorporate any idea of justice. In this perspective, order is simply a possibility, ever evolving; its character is determined by the comparative power positions of the contending socio-economic interests. As such, power displaces the substantive notion of justice and becomes the determinant of who gets what, when and how. It does not need to be pointed out that order and its maintenance or disruption, depend essentially on the extent to which rebellion of desires is or can be pacified. The state cannot pacify it because it is capable only of taking care of the consequences of the rebellion of desires; it cannot limit or abolish altogether man's desires. The rebellion of desires takes place in man's interior. When it does take place and disorder ensues, mind, as Freud notes, ceases to be a peacefully self-contained unity. A prudent superior class is, then, needed to restore the unity of mind.[26] If the disorder in man's interior persists, it pervades society and makes it diseased. A diseased society can destroy a man's soul because "the disorder of society is a disease in the psyche of its members".[27] And, a diseased society can become healthy if it is capable of curbing and curing the disorder of the soul, *nosos*. A society can succeed in doing so if it recaptures its full significance as an entity as the guardian of man's psyche. How can it be done? What kind of society is or can prove capable of it?

It should be quite clear by now that what is distinctive about the perspective on society we have been discussing is its treatment of society as something external to man. But the very assumption that society is external to man, that is, its ontological status as an external world, is questionable. Relegating society to the status of an external world, it is further assumed that it exhibits a uniform and homogeneous structure, which can be fruitfully studied by using a single method of analysis. It must be emphasized that society is neither homogeneous nor external to man. But when it is supposed to be both, it, then, becomes possible to study it by using the methods of the natural sciences. In order to lend precision to analysis and acquire predictive quality for the result of the analysis, the complexity of society engendered by the varieties of human nature it contains within its ambit and the variation in its structure in time and space is totally ruled out of court. As a result, the crucial question of the relevance of the image of society disconcealed by the methods of the natural sciences remains unanswered.

It must be emphasized that when society is assumed to be an external world, it is attributed with being and existence apart from the being and existence of individuals it is composed of. But, as Pande argues, it is only the individual that has being and distinct existence; society cannot be imagined to have its own being. It signifies the totality of all the individuals that compose it; its character is formed and determined by the nature of its members.[28] Human nature is varied and diverse; it is as a result of the diversity of human nature that congeals into different types of society in time and space. Given the variety of human nature, the most important question that needs to be answered concerns the coherence and significance of the social order in weaving the resistant diversity into a benign unity. As we have already seen, if the essential nature of man is conceived in terms only of a natural man, society loses its significance as well as its coherence. As a result, society emerges simply as an arena of the interplay of conflicting interests and not a framework of thought-ways, and work-ways that shapes man's orientation and guides and channels his energies in a proper direction for realizing his purposes.

In order, therefore, to apprehend the proper relationship between the individual and society, it is necessary to take into account the totality of human nature composed of diverse elements. But, what is this totality? Without specifying this totality endowed with a multifacetedness that allows man to participate in the creation and sustenance of social order, the apprehension of the proper relationship between the individual and the society he is a part of, will remain elusive. "Without an idea of man," Voegelin notes, "we have no frame of reference for the designation of human phenomenon as relevant or irrelevant. Man is engaged in the creation of social order physically, biologically, psychologically, intellectually and spiritually."[29] And, it must be added, only some of these engagements admit of "general laws".

Add to the multifacetedness of man's participation in the creation and maintenance of society three kinds of hierarchy that impinge heavily on man's existence in history. The first hierarchy refers to the *sapta loka* (seven worlds) at the apex of which is *satyam* or the absolute, pure consciousness, whose transformation through different layers of graded worlds one within the other forms a compact, cohesive and organic system. In this organic whole, the earth and all the beings inhabiting it are inextricably enmeshed in a network of purposes, a ladder or hierarchy of intentions, purposes, functions, and possibilities.

There is yet another hierarchy of beings that refers to the tripartite division of all beings based on differential combinations of body, sense organs, and minds.[30] There are beings with only body and are called *asanjna* (inanimate without consciousness); those who have both body and mind are *antah-sanjna* (sentient but without intelligence), such as, birds, animals, etc., and, then there are beings, such as, men, who have all the three qualities, that is, body, mind and intelligence, or *sasanjna*. The last hierarchy pertains to the constitution of man as *sasanjna* being. Here, two factors, one related with the structure of man's interior and the other pertaining to the psycho-physical constitution of man influence what man is and becomes in this world. First, there is the hierarchy of the soul, life force and appetites and, second, there are three *gunas* (qualities) – *sattwa*, *raja*s, and *tamas* – whose differential combination determines the nature of man in terms of his natural inclinations, or *pravrtti*. It is these three hierarchies that are intimately related with man's existence in history.

We must, then ask: How are these hierarchies integrated in man's being and what ramification does this integration have for society? What is obvious is the fact that man has not only a dual character; he has also to live simultaneously on different planes of existence. Insofar as man's dual character is concerned, this cannot be explored and ascertained by focusing on his existence and activities in the phenomenal world alone. It is true that man has to engage in the handling of the pragmatic affairs of his life; but his whole nature is not fully defined by them. Underlying the external, pragmatic existence of man is his subtle existence defined by the spiritual dimension of his being.[31] Once this spiritual dimension of man's being is recognized, it leads to the awareness that, while man, in his external, existential dimension, is immersed in the objective, material world, he also transcends this world. It is in this sense that while man is biologically, psychologically and sociologically determined, his ultimate destiny, as Nagarjuna emphasizes, is that of an unconditioned being;[32] he is, in short, an ethico-religious entity. It is because of this that man does not just live his life, he leads it.

Having discovered himself to be an ethico-religious entity, man can no longer pretend to be simply a part of the phenomenal world, precisely because spiritual experience is accompanied by the insight and awareness that one's person transcends the forms of worldly being, namely, space and time. This insight and the awareness engendered by it are kept alive by a conscious effort to maintain a strict hierarchical order in his interior, a vertical hierarchical order in which the soul provides the "superior element" Freud talks about; it is this "superior element" that controls and regulates his energies or life force and appetites. This superior element is, of course, the soul as the sensorium of divine. When the soul is attuned to the divine ground of being, man transcends his determination by biological, psychological and sociological factors and proceeds to explore the extent of his unconditioned being. It is against this background that we can appreciate why Indian thought ascribes greater value to rising above the conditioned and relating the self to the unconditioned and identifying with it. Everything in the realm of the conditioned is always becoming. "Now whatever becomes, is transformed, dies, and disappears, is not the part of the sphere of being."[33] Indian thought has, therefore, emphasized dissociation with, but not rejection of, the realm of becoming and concentrating on and informing the everydayness by the cultivation of the inner self as the centre of experience. This inner self is

> an independent, imperishable entity, underlying the conscious personality and bodily frame. Everything that we normally know and express about ourselves belongs to the sphere of change, the sphere of time and space and the veiling net of causality, beyond measure, beyond the dominion of the eye.[34]

It is this imperishable entity that constitutes the vital centre of every person. In the discovery of this vital centre, deeply embedded in the unconscious behind the waking consciousness, the knowledge of things that are changeable is of no help. The primary concern therefore of Indian thought – in striking contrast to the interest of modern philosophers of the West – has always been, not information, but transformation; a radical changing of man's nature and, therewith a renovation of his understanding both of the outer world and his own existence, a transformation as complete as possible, such as will amount when successful to a total conversion or rebirth.[35]

It is this rebirth that provides the basis for acquiring a passing glimpse of the structure of order, which, then, becomes the paradigm of ordering both man's interior and his social world, including the political. It is this rebirth that, for Plato, makes a man a philosopher and provides him with a synoptic vision that can discern the true *politeia* for creating a just political order. Plato, however, gives priority to political order, not to social order, as the entity capable of integrating the individual with the larger order as the basis of his commitment to the requirements of justice. However, when the social world is left untouched by the transforming alchemy of spiritual experience, political order slips into the mire of ineffectiveness. That is why, in contrast with the Platonic paradigm, the Vedic perspective gives equal, if not greater weight, to society as the keeper of the morals of its members. As the keeper of morals, society must derive its organizational structure from the self-knowledge of man, especially the self-knowledge of seer-poets or *kavirmaneeshis* that constitutes the norm for the formation of individual psyche and the structuring of collective life and relations.

The real significance of self-knowledge is that it consciously forges a link between the finiteness of human existence and the absoluteness of *satyam*, the *arche* which transforms itself into the cosmos. It is true that the cosmos is one organic whole. It is, as Giordano Bruno observes, one in substance, but many in form. One of these forms, the spirit, is the self-consciousness of that substance. It is this self-consciousness which, when pervasive in society, becomes the ground of what Heraclitus calls *xynon* or what Pande calls *samanchittata* (shareable commonality). Social consciousness is not, therefore, the aggregation of different varieties of individual consciousness in modern psychological sense but the socialized form of consciousness of the cosmos as spirit transcending but moulding individual consciousness. This social consciousness plays the essential role of keeping the individual "awake" to his relatedness with the ground of being, the prime source of spiritual consciousness. When the world of dreams takes hold of men, consensus as the foundation of community is destroyed. Value subjectivity produces only a situation of eristic in which people stick to their own guns. This is symptomatic of the breaking down of the bridge of common humanity, as Voegelin puts it.[36] If this bridge is allowed to collapse or is considered to be not worthy of rebuilding if it collapsed, the problem of communication and intelligibility in a decadent society becomes very acute. Argument fails or leads to quarrels,[37] politics exacerbates dissensions. It is because of this that prior consensus grounded in the conscious experience of the shareable commonality by the members of society becomes the *sine qua non* of building and sustaining the sense of community as the basis of harmonious and salubrious collective life and relations.

Harmony in man's interior is necessary but is not automatic; each individual cultivates it by his self-effort. However, two things need to be noted in this regard. First, it is not possible for every person to engage in the onerous task of self-development through self-knowledge. Second, it is, therefore, necessary that a social order capable of keeping the individual on the path of virtue must exist. Even self-effort must be matched by a social system that supports and sustains it or, at least, does not create hefty roadblocks that discourage or kill self-effort. The urge to harmonize one's interior and thus cultivate certain virtue necessary for a harmoniously functioning social order may germinate in man's interior. However, it needs proper environmental condition to allow it a healthy and vigorous growth. In many cases, the values necessary for harmonious social existence, if not the urge for properly ordering man's interior, have to be inculcated and prevented from erosion through processes which, for their effectiveness, depend on a suitable institutional environment.

To provide such an institutional structure undergirded by a value system and expressed through and reinforced by certain practices is the responsibility of society. It is in this sense that society cannot be considered as a mechanical aggregate of self-defining subjects; it is something larger than all the individuals that comprise it and its structure and function are not changed by individual in the short haul of lime. In Pande's words:

> Social consciousness can be distinguished by the fact that it regulates as a partially manifest order of things, understanding, the *samskaras* (acquired traits that help in the refinement of character), memories and faith of its individual members in a relatively longer temporal framework. In this sense, society can be understood as the deeply embedded soul, as the sub-stratum of individuals; it is in this form that it makes its members aware of and sustains their identity, ideals, rights and duties and provides them with the opportunity to live their life and engage in action in accord with the way it sanctions. All individuals find themselves related with a tradition of knowledge and understanding and a network of relationships that are larger than their own finite existence. If this tradition of knowledge and understanding can be characterized as culture, then, the network of relationships can be called society. Man as a being endowed with consciousness is, in this sense, a resident of a socio-cultural cosmos, which has an external form and internal consciousness.[38]

Thus, society and its substance cannot be fully grasped by exploring its external form alone. It is necessary to relate the manifest, visible, external form to its internal substratum. Externally, social life and relations assume a particular form because of the concatenation and cumulation of the effects of action men engage into for realizing their different purposes. But these purposes themselves draw their inspiration and derive their legitimacy from the underlying ideals that are beyond the dominion of the eye and principles that give a particular form to distinctive character and significance.[39]

What must also be emphasized here is that the dynamic and intimate relationship between the external and internal aspects of social consciousness and its widespread acceptance in society are due to its groundedness in spiritual consciousness and the awareness of the cosmos as the abode of the Supreme Being. It is this interrelation among (a) the transcendental truth as experienced by seers, sages and philosophers, (b) the internal springs of values derived from the interpretation of the transcendental truth as the society's self-interpretation of truth, and (c) the external aspect of society constituting the realm of action that is symbolized as society. It is this inter-relationship, again, that articulates, in terms of institutional arrangement, thought-ways, and work-ways, the experience of order. This articulation, it does not need to be pointed out, is made possible with the symbols that give concrete expression to the ineffable experience of order. It is as the result of the "interpretation of institutions and experiences of order that a society's form is a unique and authoritative articulation of the truth of being".[40]

It is by virtue of all this that society possesses not only an external but also an internal dimension of meaningfulness through which its members interpret existence to themselves. This internal structure of social reality is not experienced merely as an accident or a convenience by the members of the society, but is expressive of their human essence. And, inversely, the symbols express the experience that man is fully man by virtue of his participation in a whole which transcends his particular existence.[41] The articulation through a constellation of symbols, myths, rites, etc., the society's self-interpretation of truth and order, constitutes a society and orders it in a distinctive way. As such, it is the symbolic form of existence that creates a society. In the course of being preserved and reaffirmed through ritual observance, the symbolic form sustains the society by harmoniously securing the attunement of its members to the truth of being. This is the means by which a society attains and retains its identity in history. A society's civilizational form is, therefore, "its mode and allotted measure of participation in the world-historic process of experience and symbolization of order that extends indefinitely into the future".[42] It is in this sense that society's civilizational form has historical singularity that can never be absorbed by phenomenal regularities, because the form itself is an act in the drama of human beings striving towards truth of being.

It is against this perspective that we can see why the form and substance of a society can be fully misapprehended and misunderstood if we focus our attention on its externalities alone. It is true that the form of a society is the most visible and, therefore, easily apprehensible aspect of its existence in history. However, the form itself arises from the society's self-interpretation of the substratum of reality and its concrete expression in a particular mode of order concretely articulated and expressed in the society's institutional arrangement. It is true that the experience of the truth of reality or the Unknown is gained by seers and philosophers. It is this experience of transcendence that, when widely accepted and communicated through different methods, forms the substance of society and gives meaning to its form. It is this experience that constitutes and sustains the fundamental consensus based on shareable commonality. Also, it is this experience that finds expression in elaborate symbols

> communicating the fundamental consensus of the society and shaping the fabric of its institutional life and the public and personal lives of the people. It forms the belief structure which is the distinctive foundation of association in society, and it also shapes the essential humanity of the individual members of the society by supplying meaning in their existence as participants in a reality which they experience as transcending merely private existence.[43]

Needless to say that the Vedic idea of social order exemplifies the perspective delineated above and it does it rather well. The substance, which shapes its existence in history and animates its members for engaging in the realization of life purposes, both pragmatic and transcendental, is derived from the Vedic "likely story" of creation or *shrishti vidya*. The creation of the cosmos, as we have already seen, becomes possible through *yajna* in which Brahma is gradually transformed into *vishwa* or the cosmos. It is this *yajna* that constitutes the fundamental paradigm of Vedic society. The pursuit of different life purposes, subsumed under the generic term, *purushartha,* must be subjugated to transcendental values that are derived from the effort to promote self-development through self-knowledge. It is this subjugation that constitutes in the social world yajna, that is, the act of making everything sacred. It is for this reason that society is treated in the Vedic perspective as *yajna* in which different classes of people cooperate to fulfil its fundamental requirements. As Coomaraswamy observes, the "form of order (*yatharthata*) and impartiality (*samadrsti*) will mean that every man shall be enabled to become and by no misdirection prevented from becoming, what he has in him to become."[44]

The social order reflecting the way of sacrifice must encompass a hierarchy of sacerdotial, royal, and administrative powers, and of physical organs of sense and action.

> In the sacramental order there is need and place for all men's work; and there is no more significant consequence of the principle than, work is sacrifice, the fact that under these conditions ... every function from that of the priest and the king down to that of the potter and scavenger, is literally a priesthood and every operation a rite.[45]

The sacramental order of society takes on, in the Vedic perspective, the form of *varnashrama vyavastha* the fundamental institutional arrangement that constitutes the reliable instrument of realizing common well-being. If *varna* arrangement of society fixes functions, duties and rights of persons according to their native attributes,[46] the *ashrama* prescribes the duties of each person according to four life stages, that is, *brahmacharya* (education), *garhasthya* (householder), *vanaprastha* (preparatory stage for renunciation), and *samnyas* (renunciation). The real significance of *varnashrama vyavastha* lies in the unique Vedic perspective on human existence that combines, as Pande points out, the realization of different life-purposes based on end-means relationship with the order of ideals and duties grounded in certain transcendental values. In this combination, the fulfilment of ordinary life-needs is incorporated in the framework of *artha-tantra* or the joining of means with end and the mobilization of necessary resources for this, while the ideals and duties that must govern the fulfilment of different life-needs are included in *dharma-tantra* (just order).[47]

Recognizing as it does the need to combine this "worldly and the other-worldly" ends in a benign and personally and socially beneficial pattern of, combination and integration, the Vedic perspective, as already pointed out, accepts as given the diversity of the human and natural worlds. It posits a tripartite division of all beings in the world, such as, *asanjna, antah-sanjna* and *sasanjna*. In this varied and variegated world, man, although endowed with consciousness, is a highly differentiated species. The Vedic perspective recognizes types of persons reflecting the pre-eminence of a particular *guna.*[48] It is their differential combinations that produce a variety of human nature. As a result of all these, the social world itself comes to be characterized by a diversity which is not in any sense less bewildering and difficult to manage.

Apart from the diversity of human nature that characterizes society, there is also a plethora of human purposes that must be recognized and opportunities for realizing these purposes must be made available so that men of different types can give full scope to their potentialities to develop, attain maturity and be fully realized. But diversity must not be allowed to become antagonistic and make the social world an arena of conflict. As such, the prime responsibility of social order is to link and coordinate diverse human nature, purposes and efforts directed to realize these purposes in a way that safeguards the viability, integrity, and distinctness of the social order without blocking the opportunities for individuals to grow in the direction their nature prescribes and society sanctions. It is against this perspective that we can truly appreciate the substance and the form of the society of Vedic conception has assumed.

If the diversity of human nature and plurality of purposes growing out of it are reflected, on the individual level, in four *purusharthas*, combining both pragmatic and transcendental concerns, they find their concrete expression, on the social level, in *varnavyavastha*. Based as it is on a division of functions, functions that, in turn, are grounded in the natural inclination (*pravritti*) of the individuals, *varnavyavastha* permits individuals to pursue vocations in keeping with their capacities. Each *varna* has, therefore, its own *dharma* both in the sense of naturally ingrained inclination and of the ideal principles (*dharma* in the moral sense) that should guide and govern the functions performed by a person belonging to a particular *varna*. It is in this latter sense that *varnadharma* is distinguished from *sadharanadharma*, that is, moral principles applicable to all.

What is the relationship, we must ask, between *varna dharma and sadharna dharma*. One school of thought underlines the fact that there are occasions when *varna dharma and sadharana dharma* come into conflict; in such cases, the former must take precedence over the latter.[49] However, to treat *varna dharma* as prior to and superior than *sadharana dharma* is, according to another school of thinking, to make the former above the consideration of all virtue, such as, forgiveness, self-control, non-stealing, etc., implied in the latter. This is likely to open the way to the aggressive pursuit of *varnadharma* as a means of advancing self-interest masquerading as collective good. That is why the Vedic perspective insists on the need to inform *varna dharma* with *sadharana dharma*. As Mitra points out:

> The end in these common and universal duties is not the common well-being, which is being correctly realized in specific communities; but the common good as the precondition and the foundation of the latter; it is not the good which is common-in-the-individual but common-as-the-prius-of-the-individual.[50]

It is thus clear that even while *varna vyavastha* divides the society into numerous functional segments, these segments are integrated into an organic whole because of the existence and operation of several factors. In the first place, none of the *varnas* is sufficient in itself; it has to depend on other *varnas* not only for survival but also for sustenance and support. This in itself makes interdependence and cooperation necessary among different *varnas*. But it is symptomatic only of functional interdependence which in the lack of proper normative underpinning, may degenerate into business, and, therefore, exploitative relationship. In the second place, therefore, functional interdependence is undergirded by two important factors. First, there is the need to link the conduct of pragmatic affairs of everyday life with the pursuit of higher life purpose. This, means that the pursuit of *kama* and *artha* must be subjugated to the discipline of *dharma*. In addition, it is also necessary to seek release from bondage from the world of attachments after one has performed his duties in the phenomenal world. This, again, requires a person to live a virtuous life by regulating his life according to moral principles. The second factor to be taken into account is the need to subjugate the observance of *varna dharma* to *sadharana dharma*.

It should be obvious by now that the Vedic view of man and his world does not deny the claim of everydayness and the need of fulfilling ordinary life needs. While giving due importance to ordinary life-needs, it also gives due place in man's life to the pursuit of a higher life purpose. This requires that the *artha-tantra* must be subordinated to *dharma-tantra*. To pursue all life-activities in accordance with *dharma* is the Vedic way of linking the finite existence of man with the absolute which is the source of truth, value and meaning. This linkage is possible because of the Vedic insistence on following *dharma* in realizing different life purposes. *Dharma*[51] here signifies the eternal laws which maintain the world and is the later version of the Vedic *rta*. According to the Vedic way of thinking, the world "is not the product of a fortuitous concourse of elements, but is ruled by certain norms and sustained by an order necessary to its preservation. The order is an objective one, inherent in things; and the gods are only its guardians".[52]

When extended to the moral realm, *dharma* refers to "the totality of duties which bears upon the individual according to his status (*varna*) and the stage of life (*ashrama*) at which he stands, the totality of rules to which he must confirm (sic)"[53] if he is to manage his pragmatic affairs well while enriching his spiritual existence. It must, however, be emphasized that *dharma* is disembodied; it takes a concrete form in concrete social situations characterized by diversity of human nature creating a multiplicity of climate of opinion and interest. Diversity of opinion and interest creates diversity of contexts in which action takes place.

It is through action in varying contexts of interests and opinions that *dharma* takes on a concrete shape. The embodiment of *dharma* into practice is *vyavahar*, which differs from place to place because of the fact that the practices of the people located in a highly differentiated factual order vary greatly. Insofar as the application of a particular principle of *dharma* is mediated through the diversity of the lived world, a world differentiated on the basis of *desha* (space), *kala* (time) and *patra* (agency), different customs, conventions, interpretative systems, and different patterns of *lokachara* (practice of the people) come into being. It is this diversity (*vividhata*) that marks a social system irrespective of its size. It is this diversity, again, that makes it difficult for the shareable commonality (*samanchittata, xynon*) to become a dynamic force in social life and relations. However, without a sense of shareable commonality, diversity poses a serious threat to order. But order is not worth a penny if diversity is destroyed. To do so would be tantamount to abolishing freedom and tampering with natural gifts men are endowed with. Diversity has, therefore, to be preserved and the integrity and autonomy of each of the elements defining diversity must be respected. This raises the question of combining freedom and order in such a way that it does not unnecessarily curb individual freedom, nor does it put the order of *dharma* in jeopardy. It is such a social system that the Vedic vision of man and his world envisages. It is the sovereignty of *dharma* that, in the Vedic perspective, forges a benign bridge between freedom and order ensuring that neither freedom is excessively restricted nor order is infringed.

The reason why *dharma* can successfully forge the link between everydayness and eternity is that it expresses at once a three-dimensional principle relating to the natural, metaphysical and ethical aspects of the cosmos; it enjoins man to shape his life in accord with it. *Dharma,* thus, refers to the structure of reality as well as the need to follow its precepts in life for harmony at personal and collective levels. In this sense, *dharma,* as an ethical principle means the cosmic law which constitutes the source for deriving principles of right conduct in highly differing contexts. As such, *dharma* can, for the sake of convenience, be termed as "laws in actuality" as the symbol of the cosmic law. When applied to the human world, the cosmic law can be said to be "the law in action" as the embodiment through the actual conduct of the people in differing contexts of interest and opinion.

Dharma, as the product of the primordial insight into the structure of reality, does not render a fully developed and finished body of material rules of conduct. It only shapes human experience by revolutionizing it through the soul's attunement to the divine ground of being or, alternatively, through adherence to established social norms, practices, customs, conventions, etc., that symbolize the embodiment of "the law in actuality" and that have been sanctified by and conforms to tradition. The conformity to established social norms and practices, it does not need to be emphasized, is a means of linking the two realms of the material and the non-material and everydayness and eternity. As such, it impregnates every act, whether pragmatic or religious, with symbolic meaning. It also shapes man's orientation, which is transformed into *samskaras* (acquired attributes that refine and shape human character) and becomes instrumental in nurturing, sustaining and supporting the sense of shareable commonality. The dharmic order is, it is true, perceived by some seer, sage or philosopher. But then it is articulated in doctrines which influence institutional arrangement, shapes practices, moulds men's minds and sustains the dharmic order in history through memory, tradition, rites, customs, etc.[54]

It is only when *dharma* assumes a live presence in the minds of men reinforced by social norms and practices that "the rule of *dharma*" becomes "rule of law" by a process going beyond the expression of it, a process which enables it to enter society armed with the power of constraint which is not inherent in it, something that assumes coercive character once it is declared and sanctioned by the act of the ruler. But the ruler cannot, in a definitive and general way, substitute his will for the principles of *dharma, or* custom or *vyavahar.*[55] It is *dharma*, not law made by the king or some body whether representative or appointed, that rules not only the people but also the ruler who accepts *dharma* as his *adhiraja*. And as the *adhiraja* of the ruler, *dharma* makes the *danda* its ally in enforcing and sustaining the order of *dharma.*

The order of *dharma* not only joins the sphere of everydayness with eternity as the source of value and meaning. As manifestation of the One, it forms the basis of unity but allows this unity to assume diverse forms in time and space without, however, allowing this diversity to break the bond of unity. As a framework of unity, *dharma*-ruled society provides ample opportunities to its members to use their freedom in creating and innovating new patterns of thought-ways and work-ways provided they adhere to the basic tenets of *dharma*. In such a society, the institutionalized public order, if it is to be operationally satisfactory as a habitat for men, must truly represent the *dharmic* order and be reflected in every individual's orientation and behaviour. Only when *dharma* gets sustenance in society from its members' thinking and action, does it instill respect for and obedience of law as declared by the ruler. The Vedic idea of an appropriate social order, based as it is on the firm foundation of *dharma,* provides, perhaps, the most effective basis for the reconciliation of the good of one individual and the good of all individuals. As Pande observes:

> Affection and hospitality, tolerance and acceptance, charity and philanthropy, non-violence and compassion, have been widely accepted values in Indian tradition. Virtual autonomy of groups in regulating their accustomed mode of social life and harmony between them have been a marked feature of that tradition. The modern notion of the struggle of the individual against the group or groups against groups, whether classes, races or nations, were largely strangers in the context of the ancient ethos. The freedom which the individual sought was ideal freedom, not the freedom to maximize his competitive gains by any means. Instead of the notion of right, that of duty was pre-eminent. It was accepted that justice means non-discrimination but this did not lead to any notion of social or economic equality. Inequalities in these respects were accepted as inevitable on account of the diversity of human capacities, effects and virtue.[56]

It is from such a society that the principle of *regnum* gets proper support and sustenance. That is why the Vedic perspective on order makes the political order only an adjunct of the social order and assigns to it the responsibility of protecting the fundamental elements of the dharmic order from the depredation of human cupidity.

Notes

1. Eric Voegelin, 'Introduction' in *History of Political Ideas: Hellenism, Rome, and Early Christianity* (Columbia: University of Missouri Press, 1997), Vol. I. Appendix A, p. 225.
2. Ibid.
3. John H. Schaar, *Escape from Authority: Perspectives on Eric Fromm* (New York: Basic Books, 1961), p. 296.
4. Roberto M. Unger, *Knowledge and Politics* (New York: The Free Press, 1975), p. 75.
5. Ibid., p. 49.
6. G.C. Pande, *Spiritual Vision and Symbolic Forms in Ancient India* (New Delhi: Books and Books, 1984), p. 24.
7. Roberto M. Unger, op. cit., p. 73.
8. See G.C. Pande, *Bharatiya Parampara ke Mula Svara* (New Delhi: National Publishing House, 1981), p. 61.
9. Supra, Ch. 9.
10. G. C. Pande, *Bhartiya Samaj: Tattwika aur Aitihasika Vivechan* (New Delhi: National Publishing House, 1994), Ch.1.
11. Stanley Rosen, "Man's Hope," *Social Research,* 48, 3 (Autumn, 1980), p. 619.
12. Maurice Mandelbaum, *History, Man and Reason: A Study in Nineteenth Century Thought* (Baltimore: The John Hopkins University Press, 1971), p. 146.
13. Carl L. Becker, *The Heavenly City of the Eighteenth Century Philosophers* (New Haven: Yale University Press, 1952), pp. 27–28.
14. Rene Descartes, *Philosophical Writings, ed. and trans.* Norman Kemp Smith (New York: Modern Library, 1958), pp. 130–31.
15. See, Barry Cooper, *Eric Voegelin and the Foundations of Modern Political Science* (Colombia: University of Missouri Press, 1999), Ch. 3.
16. Roberto M. Unger, op. cit., p. 45.
17. The relegation of reason to an instrumental role raises the question of the regulating principle for keeping passions, some of which are turbulent and destructive, on a leash. Recognizing passions to be the dominant trait of human personality and recognizing, too, the inadequacy of moralizing philosophy and religious precepts, the search for a regulating principle came to centre around, first, entrusting the state with the responsibility of keeping passions under control and, later, subordinating them to one master passion. This passion was identified as self-interest, in the sense of the grand passion for augmenting fortunes and the desire for bettering one's material condition, in a word, avarice.

See Albert O. Hirschman, *The Passions and the Interests: Political Arguments for Capitalism before its Triumph* (Princeton: Princeton University Press, 1987). With avarice becoming the propelling force, man comes to be considered nothing more than "an externalized creature", an object, self-interest crowding out man's inner being. See Ellen M. Wood, *Mind and Politics: An Approach to the Meaning of Liberal and Socialist Individualism* (Berkeley: University of California Press, 1972), esp. 111. It is in self-interest, then, that the fleeting, fluid self gains a firm anchor, which lends it a particular character and prompts it to action. It is in this sense that John Dewey's dictum, " I own, therefore I am", expresses a better characterization of man in modern times than the Cartesian "I think, therefore I am."

18. On this see Charles Taylor, "The Concept of a Person," B.N. Ganguly Memorial Lectures, Centre for the Study of Developing Societies, Delhi, March 1981, 3rd Lecture, p.11.
19. Ibid.
20. Charles Taylor, "Growth, Legitimacy and the Modern Identity", *Praxis International*, 1, 2, (only 1981), p. 113.
21. See, for example, David Hume, *Dialogues Concerning Natural Religion,* where Hume identifies the world with "one great machine, subdivided into an infinite number of lesser machines, which again admit of subdivisions, to a degree beyond human senses and faculties can trace and explain." Quoted in Becker, op. cit., p. 56.
22. Charles Taylor, *Hegel and Modern Society* (Cambridge: Cambridge University Press, 1979), p. 75.
23. See A. Merquior, *The Veil and the Mask: Essays on Culture and Ideology* (London: Routledge & Kegan Paul, 1979), p. 39.
24. From Vico through Hegel to Marx, the process of the self-making of man has been the organizing perspective on man and his world.
25. E.N.B. Tyler, *Primitive Culture* (London: Murray, 1871), pp. 2–3.
26. Sigmund Freud in Phillip Rieff, *Freud: The Mind of the Moralist* (New York: Anchor Books, 1961), p. 31.
27. Eric Voegelin, *Order and History: Plato and Aristotle* (Baton Rouge: Louisiana State University Press, 1957), III, p. 69.
28. G.C. Pande, *Bharatiya Samaj,* op. cit., p. 16.
29. Quoted in Barry Cooper, op. cit., p. 78.
30. Based on Max Schelar's version of philosophical anthropology, Voegelin categories all beings into four classes: Human, Animal, Vegetative, and Inorganic. See Cooper, op. cit., p. 169.
31. See G.C. Pande, *Bharatiya Samaj,* p. 23. This is indicative of *dual nature* of man; it is this symbol dual nature that has a genuine ontological status

that can be explored only with the help of proper philosophical deliberation. This deliberation will fail to yield a proper understanding of man and his world if this ontological reality, expressed in the symbol dual nature, is reduced to one or another of its constituent elements.

32. See Venkata K. Ramanan, *Nagarjuna's Philosophy* (Delhi: Motilal Banarsidass, 1978), pp. 100–02.
33. Mircea Eliade, *Patanjali and Yoga,* Trans. Lam Markham (New York: Schocken Books, 1976), p. 6.
34. Heinrich Zimmer, *Philosophies of India,* ed. Joseph Campbell (London: Routledge & Kegan Paul. Ltd., 1952), p. 3.
35. Ibid., p. 4.
36. Eric Voegelin, *Order and History: Plato and Aristotle*, III, op. cit., p. 29.
37. Jurgen Habermas recommends "communicative competence" based an discursive logic as the instrument of building consensus is society. However, he also argues that, for this competence to be effective, prior consensus is necessary. But he fails to indicate how this "prior consensus" can be achieved. He also fails to realize that in a social situation marked by the breakdown of consensus, discursive logic cannot be effective in building consensus. See his *Legitimation Crisis,* Introduction by Macarthy.
38. G.C. Pande, *Bharatiya Samaj,* p. 12.
39. See Ibid., p. 13.
40. Eric Voegelin, *Order and History: Israel and Revelation,* I, op. cit., p. 60
41. Eric Voegelin, *The New Science of Politics,* p. 27.
42. Eric Voegelin, *Order and History: Israel and Revelation,* I, op. cit., p. 61.
43. Ellis Sandoz, *The Voegelinian Revolution: A Biographical Introduction* (Baton Rouge: Louisiana State University Press, 1981), p. 98.
44. Ananda K. Coomaraswamy, *Hinduism and Buddhism* (Delhi: Munshiram Manoharlal Publishers Pvt. Ltd., 1986), p. 26.
45. Ibid., p. 27.
46. The origin of the caste system in India is traced by many back to Purusha-sukta, a creation hymn, which depicts the characteristics of an organic cosmos. When it refers to *varnas,* it describes qualities that are necessary in forming a social world whose harmonious blending in the social whole is *sine qua non.* It identifies different categories of people distinguished by qualities unique to each of them. Described in these terms, the *varnas* referred to in the Sukta do not constitute hierarchically graded caste groups in sociological sense, but refer to attributes that are not hierarchically organized but horizontally woven into a network of interdependence, cooperation and harmony.
47. G.C. Pande, *Bharatiya Samaj,* p. 23.

48. We have already discussed these three basic *gunas*. For a brief but succinct discussion, see Alain Danielou, *Hindu Polytheism* (New York: Pantheon Books, 1964), Bollingen Series LXXII, pp. 22–28.
49. S. Dasgupta, *A History of Indian Philosophy* (London: Cambridge University Press, 1965), vol. 2, pp. 507–8.
50. S.K. Mitra, *Ethics of the Hindus* (New Delhi: Asia Rule Service, 1978), pp. 3–4.
51. The word *dharma* is used in several widely different senses. The most general sense is provided by what is strong, firm, durable and reliable.
52. Robert Lingat, *The Classical Law of India,* by J. Duncan M. Derrett (Berkeley: University of California Press, 1973), p. 3. Lingat further observes "during the Vedic period the fundamental laws of the universe were identified with laws of the sacrifice. Consequently, *dharma* was *par excellence* the sacrificial act which maintains and even conditions the cosmic order" (ibid). Two grievous errors can be detected in this statement. In the first place, even while Lingat ascribes this view to the Mimamsa School, he projects it back on the Vedic world view which is, to say the least, anachronistic because he identifies *rta* with the laws of the sacrifice. It does not need to be pointed out that the meaning of sacrifice, insofar as the Vedic sense of its meaning is concerned, is the process through which Brahma becomes the *vishwa.* See Ramashray Roy, *Beyond Ego's Domain: Being and Order in the Veda* (Delhi: Shipra Publications, 1999), ch. 4. Sacrifice (*yajna)* in this context means self-transformation of the Idea into *nama* and *rupa.* By the time we come to Mimamsa, the process of self-transformation is turned into an externalized system of rituals (*karmakanda*). In the second place, it is a misnomer to say that the sacrificial act "maintains or even conditions the cosmic order". As a matter of fact, it is the cosmic order as symbolized by *rta* that constitutes and paradigm as well as the source of sacrifice. The performance of *yajna* by a person is for self-transformation, which helps the preservation of the cosmic order by safeguarding the process of exchange between man, gods and other beings. It is the process of exchange that, as *Taittiriya Brahman* points out, maintains the cosmic metabolism.
53. Robert Lingat, op. cit., p. 4.
54. See G.C. Pande, *Bharatiya Samaj,* pp. 14–15.
55. Lingat, op. cit., p. 224.
56. G.C. Pande, *Foundations of Indian Culture: Dimensions of Ancient Indian History* (New Delhi: Books and Books, 1984), pp. 169–70.

11

Overview

The discussion in the preceding chapters has ranged over a wide variety of themes related with the question of political order. Our point of departure in this respect has been determined by several questions. These questions, for instance, are: what does political order substantively signify? Where does it draw its inspiration from for assuming the form and substance it actually does? And, what precise role does it play in man's life and relations? It has ever been man's endeavour to give to his finite existence a deep sense of durability. This refers not only to his resolve to ensure the continuity of his type organized territorially in different ways and manners. It also refers to his concern for and efforts to elevate his existence above the level of mere animal existence. It is true that man has to respond to the claims of his lower nature. However, to remain tied to his animal nature is to live merely an animal existence. That is why, it is necessary for man to consciously try to rise above his base nature and cultivate his superior manhood. To put it differently, man does not intend simply to live; he also intends to live well and meaningfully.

To live well and meaningfully means different things to different people. Minimally, it may mean only a life of subsistence with the full assurance of whatever provisioning is felt to be necessary for such a life. Even a life of subsistence, that is, a life devoted primarily to the fulfilment of ordinary life needs at the barest minimum level, requires a minimum degree of security without which provisioning may prove to be a difficult task. This is so for the simple reason that one may perhaps fail in holding on to what one has acquired by working hard. Security here means the prevalence of a condition which indicates that people are well imbued with the idea that they should respect the right of others to hold on to what they have come to possess after toiling hard and that they should, in turn, be also secure in their own possession.

Such an existence may prove to a Glaucon that it is fit only for pigs. He might therefore prefer to have some relish so that he and people like him may enjoy a life of ease, comfort and elegance. This means that the people must have access to a full array of goods and services as supplement to the indispensable staples of human life that are commonly accepted and expected as pertaining to an elegant lifestyle. To make the elegant lifestyle the preferred value in life is to create and sustain a social system that can cater to the needs of elegant lifestyle. It is needless also to say that this system must differ, both quantitatively and qualitatively, from the one that has nothing else as its goal than the assuring of security of subsistence. For one thing, a system concerned only with the provisioning of goods and service necessary to support and sustain a simple lifestyle that usually is the case with subsistence economy does not have to deal with a multiplicity of goods and services that must be provided to the people who wish to live an elegant lifestyle. As such, such a system will not require a large number of specialists who must be trained and recruited to service limitless appetites.

When the need of the people is quite limited and goods and services required to fulfil these needs are quite simple, the territory needed for habitation by simple and, perhaps, small communities would not be large. As such, these communities need not be swollen up with a multitude of callings insofar as there are only a few, simple needs to be supplied. In addition, given the smallness and localized nature of communities, it is also quite likely that social relationships in these communities would be based on blood and kinship ties allowing for the fusion rather than differentiation of functional and normative integration. It is this fusion that allows not only for the development of the structures of social cooperation and interdependence. It also allows for the development and strengthening of those normative considerations that reinforce these structures of social cooperation and sustain social harmony. This is so for the simple reason that provisioning in a subsistence economy is facilitative of the fusion between the functional and normative dimensions of human existence.

The argument that provisioning is neither value-neutral nor incapable of generating normative considerations does not need an elaborate demonstration. If human race were not to last for more than one generation, the question of provisioning will become trivial. However, since this is not the case, there is also the question of making sufficient arrangements for the care and nurturance of the offsprings. This takes mankind beyond the question of provisioning in the present. Thus metabolism and reproduction constitute integral aspects of economic life and relations of the people. To recognize this is also to recognize the sense of responsibility that one generation must evince and bear with respect to the coming generations translated in terms of preserving and protecting the available natural resources. Thus, the process of provisioning may have its origin in self-interest incorporating both self-preservation and a good life. It is in this context that the underlying self-interest that happens to be the hard rock of responsibility not only towards oneself but also towards the generations coming after. The sense of responsibility has, of necessity, two dimensions, temporal and spatial. As Jonas puts it:

> ... through the counterpoise of mortality, with its powerful commitment, a horizon of self-transcendence is added to the reference of need and interest; self-preservation is widened into preservation of progeny; needs beyond one's own become an integral part of concern; and with the unique length of human childhood and dependency, what would otherwise be short-range and surely optional providence in the service of self-interest, becomes long-range providence enjoined by responsibility.[1]

As a result of the need to add a long-range providence enjoined by the sense of responsibility underlying self-interest, the centre of focus in provisioning extends from the sense of "me" to "mine". This in effect signifies a temporal dimension added to the factor of self-preservation. Added also is a spatial dimension as a consequence of the linear spread of kiths and kins. When this spread assumes a larger sized, blood ties envelop a small community in an extended network of interdependence and cooperation. Thus, the sense of responsibility moves beyond the circle of immediate kiths and kins and embraces larger and expanding circles of relatives and friends. It is this sense of responsibility that gets reinforced by blood ties and a network of obligations and the process of exchange of gifts. It is, then, obvious that in a subsistence economy marking a small community, economic relations are undergirded by moral considerations as well as a cooperative social structure.

In contradistinction to this, a lifestyle based on relish gives birth to the need of having a complex society, which contains not only a diversity of human nature but also a complicated mixture of races. The territorial spread of a society given to satisfying a multitude of appetites must be quite large. The geographical base of such a society must be big as a consequence of incorporating a diversity of occupations engaged in producing an array of goods and services necessary for supporting an elegant lifestyle. This further means that functional relationships become far-flung, distant and invisible; they lose the intimacy and warmth of face-to-face relationship and assume autonomy from the nexus of social relations. The gaining of this autonomy is in itself indicative of the separation of functional and normative integration. Add to it the fact that the very socio-cultural diversity becomes the source of social divisiveness and, therefore, a factor of considerable importance in the breakdown of normative integration.

It is for these reasons that a society, that values an elegant lifestyle, has to accommodate a multitude of appetites for maintaining such a lifestyle, build requisite infrastructures and create necessary facilities for satisfying these appetites. It must also depend upon some effective mechanism of disciplining, regulating and controlling individual dispositions in such a way that social harmony is not disturbed even if structures of social harmony get frayed and fragile. To have an effective mechanism of regulation and control is also to create and instal a public order equipped with a full array of rules and regulations meant to regulate and control people's conduct. These rules and regulations may either be prior to or independent of the creation of public order or may be created and enforced by the installed public order itself. No matter what the situation, public order is necessary not only in the case of a complex society grown very big because of its preference for an elegant lifestyle but also in that of a simple, face-to-face society. The only difference between the two types of society is that the form and substance of public order differ rather substantially from one to the other.

The real function of the public order is not merely to enforce certain rules and regulations. The real function is to use these rules and regulations to instill in the minds of individuals the awareness of the wholeness of their collective life and to animate them with the consciousness that, as an integral part of the collectively, it is incumbent on them to preserve and sustain its wholeness. This can be done only when they are able to see the essential relatedness between the good of one and the good of all. But, since the awareness of this essential ingredient of the good health of collective life is not present in everybody in equal degree, the consequent lack of a good fit between the private and the public introduces distortions that may disturb the smooth tenor of public life. It is, first, to prevent these distortions from occurring and, then, to see to it that these distortions either do not occur or, if they do occur, they do not disturb the smooth functioning of public life.

Given the diversity of the phenomenal world as well as the extreme heterogeneity of orientation, altitude and purpose of human beings, and given the tendency of man towards self-aggrandizement, interaction among men, between man and society, and man and nature cannot be left to the wayward movement of individual desires. The consequence of giving a free rein to man for satisfying whatever desires he feels strong enough to successfully resist postponement or outright rejection is likely to give rise to disorder. This is reflected in what is known, in the West, as the state of nature (especially the Hobbesian concept of it) and, in Indian tradition, as *matsyanyaya* (the law of the shark). And, since self-aggrandizement tends to lead to anarchy which, in turn, threatens to extinguish the light of culture and to snap the fragile thread of life, order turns out to be a necessary condition for preserving life and allowing and sustaining constructive employment of human energy.

To order human energy in such a way that its diverse uses by a multitude of individuals do not produce tension and distortion in collective life and relations is to employ a trans-individual principle for ordering and organizing collective existence. The main objective of this principle is to link different components of the community of people with each other in a principled relationship. The need for order arises precisely because the community of the people is characterized by diversity. However, the creation of order is meant not to eliminate or suppress diversity; it must be accepted as given. Only after we recognize this diversity, can we mount efforts to organize different components in such a way that energy of different components finds its own direction and fulfilment without, however, creating roadblock for others. When this principle is applied to and employed in managing political affairs of a particular community with a view to giving a definite shape by actions taken by individuals and groups for realizing their purposes, political order emerges.

Political order is not in any sense apart and different from order that may prevail in any particular community of people. It is true that many scholars treat political order to be different from, say, the social order. What needs to be emphasized here is the fact that man has always looked to nature for deriving his conception of order. But, the meanings we give to nature and the attributes we discover in it have not remained fixed through the ages. Even a cursory reading of Collingwood's *The Idea of Nature*[2] would argue against the notion of fixed "nature". Even if nature may not have changed, man's idea of order including that of political order has differed over time and space.

The reason why man has always turned to nature for deriving the conception of order lies in the fact that the paradigm of order cannot be located either in the individual considered to be a self-sufficient entity or in the mankind as an abstraction or as on aggregation of self-sufficient individuals. To ground the notion of order either in man or Man, whether in the abstract and organic or the atomistic sense, is to subject order to the whims and caprice of man as well as to the changing fashion of opinion in time and space. And, if order is as fragile and fickle as the things in the phenomenal world or as man-made objects, it would fail in performing the role expected of it. The concept of order must, therefore, transcend the varieties and vagaries of time and space; it has, therefore, to be grounded in something larger and more durable than man in particular or universal aspects. This something is undoubtedly nature, which is endowed with order, or undergirded by principles that maintain order.

It is true that nature provides the model of order in the human world. It is also true that the idea of nature has been undergoing periodical changes. But, the nature of these changes need not detain us here since they are not germane to the discussion here. What concerns us here is the fact that nature has been viewed in ways that posit polar conceptions of order. It is this polar conception that has a great bearing on the notion of order both an ideal to be attained and as a category of description of the world as it is. There is, first, the conception of nature which ascribes to nature as something that is not ordered by the interaction of its own forces immanent in it but to something beyond it, something that transcends nature. It is this transcendental entity that is considered to be the source of the multiplicity of names and forms. It is held that the process of becoming characterizing the phenomenal world is inconceivable without the firm ground of being, that is, something eternal and unchanging, as the ultimate source of order in nature.

In contradistinction to this, nature is supposed to be self-sufficient and self-complete. It is not supposed to depend for its working on something distinct from and beyond itself insofar as its working is completely explicable in terms of cause-and-effect. The nature, in this perspective, is seen, as for example, by David Hume, to be self-subsistent; its working is said to be governed by something inherent in itself. By virtue of this, nature is also seen to be self-regulatory. The image of machine comes easily to mind when referring to order one discovers in nature. According to this mechanical model of order, nature is considered to be one great machine, sub-divided into an infinite number of lesser machines with further subdivisions, all these various machines with the one great machine are not only interlinked with each other; they are also adjusted to each other so accurately that they preclude distortion of any kind.[3] Insofar as it pertains to human perspective, there is, at least, the recognition of a creator even if he is nothing more than an engineer of the clock-work universe. Later on, however, the very idea of the creator is replaced by spontaneity and automaticity in the working of nature. Nature is described as composed of such entities as particles, atoms, etc., which, obeying the law of energy, constitute the warp and woof of creation. It is these particles, atoms, etc., that interact in such a way that equilibrium in nature is maintained.

These polar views of nature yield differential conceptions of order. If we consider nature not as a self-subsistent entity but, instead, as something that is governed by an entity transcending it, the significance and implication of the concept of order grounded in this understanding of nature is quite different from the one based on nature conceived as a self-subsistent entity. On the former view, man is supposed to be an integral part of a larger, cosmic order. To the extent that man participates in this order by attuning himself to the divine ground of being, he becomes endowed with a higher range of values and, by ordering his own interior, he contributes meaningfully to the preservation and sustenance of order in society.[4] If, on the other hand, it is the idea of nature as a self subsistent entity that provides the model of order, order that is seen to be operating in nature has to be discerned, imitated, and artificially created in the human world. It is, then, hoped that the artificially created order will become a real force in regulating man's existence in the phenomenal world.

Given the variety of conceptions of order, due not only to the difference in the perspectives projected on to nature but also to differences within a particular perspective, two questions assume importance. First, what precisely is the Vedic conception of order?

And, in what way is this conception meritorious in comparison to other conceptions? As is evident from our discussion in chapter two, the point of departure for the exploration of these two questions has been the modern conception of order, one germane to the world with God and the other pertaining to the world without God. This is by no means arbitrary. As is well known, it is the modern conception that has come to undergird political order first in Western Europe as the regnant paradigm of order. Its dominance has been made possible by the disintegration of the unity of Christian worldview and its predecessor, the classical Greek conception of order. The modern conception of order is supposed to successfully bridge the gap between the private and the public and ensure compatibility between the good of one and that of all without putting any conscious brake on the individual's liberty to engage in entrepreneurial activities. But, since this promise remains, for various reasons, unfulfilled, it is necessary to put it in a right perspective by juxtaposing it with other conceptions of order. It must also be mentioned in this connection that there is the Chinese conception of order, based principally on the Confucian thinking that talks of cosmic order, to be sure. However, it comes to be based primarily on a system of ethics that prescribes the proper conduct of persons according to age, gender and rank.

In modern perspective, order, based on the Newtonian conception of the natural universe is the model of order in the human world. However, the human world has yet to attain completeness that the natural universe displays. But, what kind of order is perceived in nature that is considered to be an appropriate model to be initiated in the human world? As discussed earlier, Francis Edgeworth saw nature comprised of particles, each of which has its own fixed movement. Even, while all these particles move according to the force inherent in them, their separate movement does not in any way obstruct the movements of each other. These particles are, so to say, onto only unconditionally viable but also autonomous of each other. However, despite their autonomy and their movement unrestrained by other particles, the combined effect of all these separate movements is to contribute to the generation of one maximum sum total of accumulated energy. It is to this sum total of accumulated energy that the separate movements of different particles contribute and submit.

Thus, while separate particles go their own way and follow the pattern of movement encoded in their own being, their separation and separate movements do not produce distortion or conflict; their movement is regulated and controlled by the order inherent in nature. It is this conception of order in nature that is projected in modern times on to human realm. In projecting this model, the movement of particles is equated with the movement of individual souls and it is expected that, even while the souls move in different directions, their movements may combine to produce not only the maximum energy of pleasure but also of love and concord. But, what does the movement of the soul mean? This movement does not refer to the yearning of the soul for God or some ultimate entity; it refers to the quest for felicity, which is possible only when man engages in satisfying one's desire after another in a ceaseless manner.

The satisfaction of desires is considered essential not only for ensuring felicity but also for man's self-development and civilizational progress. It is as the over-all result of this that the individual, so it is claimed, acquires a distinctive personality, involving the effective use of man's creative faculties in transforming nature and creating social institutions as well as the development of faculties themselves. Existing as potentialities, these faculties are actualized refined and expanded in the process of self-making of man.[5] It is true that the search for felicity promotes jealousy and swells self-love. Taken together, they breed discord. However, as Kant asserts, discord itself must be valued because without it "all the excellent capacities implanted in mankind would slumber eternally undeveloped".[6]

In the modern perspective, then, it is the movement of desires that constitutes the most dynamic element of what Edgeworth calls, "mecanique social". What is natural to man is his desires since they are derived from his nature. The satisfaction of these desires is *sine qua non* for his felicity. But more than this, their satisfaction is also rational since it is only by satisfying his desires that man can not only secure his felicity but also ensure his development and social progress. On this view what is striking about a person is not his quest for self-realization in the traditional sense but "his ability to conceive different possibilities, to calculate how to get them, to choose between them, and thus plan their lives".[7] Calculation of means-ends relationship does point to the role of rationality in man's life activities. However, this rationality is what Aristotle calls *phronesis*. It does not anymore refer to a vision of true order; it is not an active principle of the soul that allows man to rise above the particularities associated with his contingent experiences. It is concerned simply with the meeting of needs in a sober, disciplined, clairvoyant, and rational way.

On this view reason turns out to be nothing more than the hand-maiden of appetites signifying instrumental, prudential, calculative reasoning. What is distinctive about this perspective is that the pursuit of felicity is supposed to be both natural and rational. As such, every individual seeks to acquire felicity or enhance its stock for himself. Doing so, he fails to confront in his own action "the distinction between what is available as a result of getting ahead of others and what is available from a general advance shared by all".[8] As a result, he single-mindedly pursues his own self-interest unmindful of whether or not it helps or hinders others engaged in a similar pursuit. And, if every soul moves on the course set by its own search for felicity, how does order get established and sustained? The answer that his perspective yields is the tendency in nature to maintain equilibrium or restore or create a new equilibrium when the pre-existing equilibrium is somehow disturbed and upset.

When projected on to the social universe, it displays three distinctive features. First, social universe is the aggregate of self-defining subjects who, propelled by the movement of their own desires, engage into action. The social universe comes to be characterized by a plurality of orientations, intentions and purposes. Pluralism is, therefore, an essential characteristic of the social universe and its violation is tantamount to the extinction or, at least, serious disability, of the social universe itself. Second, apart from the inviolability of the plural character of the social universe, what is also essential is to ensure is that no restraint is put on individual freedom insofar as the determination of individual purpose and the mode of its realization is concerned. This condition must be respected as long as "company of desiring subjects comes to achieve full satisfaction (happiness), each compatibly with all others".[9] And, lastly, it is quite likely that self-interested actions of individuals may introduce distortion in the functioning of the social universe. However, the maintenance of order is not the responsibility of the individual, but it is the charge of an impersonal, "natural" mechanism that adjusts claims of individuals, disburses rewards and punishments and maintains order[10] by correcting imbalances.

It is in this context that we can appreciate Mandeville's dictum of private vices leading to public benefit. What is emphasized in this perspective is the assumption that there is a natural harmony of interest. Even when order is disturbed by self-interested actions of individuals and groups, the Invisible Hand that Adam Smith talks of intervenes and sets things right. As Smith notes:

> The natural effort individual to better his own condition, when suffered to exert itself with freedom and security, is so powerful a principle, that it is alone, and without any assistance, not only capable of carrying on the society to wealth and prosperity but of encountering a hundred impertinent obstructions with which the folly of human laws too often encumbers it operations ... .[11]

In Smith's view, then, concatenation of actions by individuals impelled by the desire to maximize their own satisfaction conduces to perfect order. Even when order is disturbed, the mechanism of self-adjustment inherent in the social universe intervenes to put order on the right track. The social universe is thus a machine, "mecanique social", implying the dual notion of the rationality of self-defined purpose and that of a perfect order. It is this dual notion of rationality that is expected to put both "mecanique celest" and "mecanique social" on a throne "each upon the double sided height of one maximum principle, the supreme pinnacle of moral as of physical science".[12] It is evident, then, that, when nature is de-divinized, cosmic order is no longer available for creating order in the social universe. It is only nature, nature as a self-subsistent and self-regulating system that can now provide any model of order. This now means interaction among autonomously given individuals without conflict or distortion and without any human or non-human intervention.

The assumption of natural harmony of interest proves untenable and order becomes fragile and vulnerable to frequent disruptions. But when "mecanique social" fails to fully conform to "mecanique celest", reliance for preserving order is placed on two factors. First, it is assumed that individuals possess certain qualities, which moderate the excesses of the pursuit of self-interest. Individuals are supposed to act in "calm moments" (Hume and Edgeworth); they follow their duty (Mill and Bentham); or obey their conscience (Butler) or the "impartial spectator" residing in their breast (Smith). And, second, when the invisible hand falters in coping successfully with the responsibilities placed on it, the way for the state to intervene to take care of the adverse consequences of self-interested actions of individuals and groups is cleared. The fact that the social universe has to depend on the state for preserving order is indicative of the erosion of auto-control. In the lack of support to order coming from the individuals and groups, state action in preserving order proves anaemic and ineffective.

It needs to be stressed that the modern conception of order gives prominence to the satisfaction of desires. But, the endeavour by individuals and groups to satisfy their desires and appetites introduces life-corroding competition in the social universe because the propelling force in man's existence today is, as Mahatma Gandhi puts it, "the hunger for wealth and the greedy pursuit of worldly pleasures". When the hunger for wealth and pleasure occupies the centre stage of man's life, "the vision of thing above" loses it relevance rendering the search for spirituality and morality also irrelevant. Since the need to satisfy one desire after another rules contentment out of reckoning, the aggressive expression of possessiveness breeds exploitation, domination, inequality and oppression. As a result, violence becomes endemic and pervades all areas of human existence. Desires and appetites take hold of the soul and direct the course of human action. As a result, disorder sets in the soul and spreads out to society. And, when society becomes diseased, it begins to destroy man's soul.[13] The resultant vicious circle can be broken only when the soul sets on a course of asserting its superiority and resisting society. But this is not possible within the frame of order for the world without the God. Then, what about the Chinese conception of order? It is true that order in China has proved very durable in Chinese society. However, it has to pay a heavy price in the sense that human creativity and innovation have been seriously eclipsed.

Given the necessity of the soul to regain its benign influence on man's passion, it is essential that the soul regains its function of reigning over man's passion. But how does the soul regain its over-lordship and resist the society's attempts to corrupt it? It is needless to say that the soul's corruption is the consequence of its immersion in the world of appearance which forces it to turn its back on reality, that is, the divine ground of being. This immersion is *prima causa* of differentiation of men between "I" and "you" and "We" and "they" giving rise to a multiplicity of antagonistic interests. Swayed by this differentiation, men get to set in the multiplicity of changing forms and allow fickle and changing opinions to influence and shape their orientation and attitude towards the world. As a result, failing to transcend the multiplicity of changing forms, they become forgetful of and or unconcerned with the truth of reality, that is, the oneness in many. True knowledge escapes those who are under the sway of *nomos* (changing opinion or convention) and are, therefore, prone to embrace a distorted and wrong view of what they really are and what kind of relationship they must establish with the external world.

Only contemplating the eternal, unchanging form behind the perishable, changing forms, can have true knowledge. This requires overcoming *philodoxos* (love of opinions) and cultivating *philosophos* (love of wisdom). Wisdom requires a transition from the concern with becoming to being. It is being that is the substratum of reality and to know it is the necessary condition of wisdom; to have wisdom is to end the rule of babble, since the babble of the many induces the abortion of reason.[14] To check the abortion of reason is possible only when one attunes his soul to the divine ground of being, that is, intelligence. For Plato, it is intelligence or the idea that constitutes the model of order with the help of which Demiurgos puts in order the erratic objects that *Ananke* creates. If intelligence is the source of order in the cosmos, intelligence, the locus of idea and the attribute of the soul keeps in check the exuberance and aberrations of spirit and appetites. To accept the rulership of the soul as the sensorium of divine is to establish order in man's interior.

When man's interior is put in order, it becomes the model of order in society or what Plato actually means, *polis*. For Plato, *polis* is nothing else than man writ large. There is a homology between the structure of man's being and that of *polis*. Like man's being, *polis,* too, exhibits tripartite division of faculties and capacities. Unless they are brought under the rulership of intelligence personified by the philosopher-king, these faculties tend to be self-aggrandizing. Endowed as he is with a clear vision of the idea and, therefore, is blessed with a synoptic vision, he becomes holy, just and wise.[15] And, since he is holy, wise and just, he can, therefore, rule wisely. As a wise ruler, he can devise an institutional order in which appetites, working under the rulership of the soul, that is intelligence, do not proliferate and, consequently, specialization, too, does not increase beyond a limit. As a result, men restrict themselves to the specific area of their naturally endowed functional capacity and refrain from meddling into the affairs of others.

Such a political arrangement will conduce to individual well-being and collective good since it is based on the recognized superiority of *sophia* (intelligence or *prajnana*) in ordering, disciplining and controlling different components of both man's being and the polis.

In positing a homology between man and the polis, Plato does recognize that human nature is diverse. As such, the *polis*, too, is made up of diverse elements. But, the elements that make for diversity in the case of both man and the polis are not competitors, as they are supposed to be in the modern conception of man and his world, but collaborators in a collective enterprise in which each component is, at one and the same time, linked with each other as well as to the whole.

As such, these components form a Great Chain of Being, in which the strength and vitality of all the links are ensured. While recognizing the diversity of human nature, Plato also recognizes the need, on the one hand, of interdependence, collaboration and cooperation among these diverse elements and, on the other, that of their subordination to a superior element, that is, the soul in the case of the individual person and the philosopher king in the case of the polis. Incorporation of these two essential elements in the creation of the polis is necessary for promoting justice which alone is capable of eliminating the opposition between the *idion* (private) and the *koinon* (public) and thereby ensure harmony and concord.

Three factors intervene to make Platonopolis a less desirable an object. First, the perfect ordering of the objects created by *Ananke* is not possible since they are part of nature and are, therefore endowed *ab definitio*, with aberrant nature. To transcend it is to cease being nature or the product of nature and become something else than what in reality it is. Thus, there is an inherent opposition and, therefore, the possibility of conflict, between necessity and freedom cannot completely be eliminated. As a consequence, the tension between the two ever poses a threat to order. Second, this tension tends to be all the more heightened insofar as diversity is a frozen diversity in the Platonic scheme of things because different elements constituting diversity, except for a few rare souls, can never hope to undergo the process of self-transformation. As such, the king must rule over them. However, even if he is a philosopher and claims to have the monopoly of wisdom, the political system would eventually grow rigid and, therefore, become oppressive. Thus, the Platonic or, to be exact, Socrates' preference for self-rule, turns out to be the self-rule for a rare person who must rule over others. And, lastly, given the ineradicable tension between matter and form, knowledge does not prove too effective in curbing the aberrations of matter. As such, the ruler has to necessarily take recourse to power as a prop of effective governance. Thus, the purpose of governance by knowledge is likely to be progressively defeated by the ever-present possibility of the depredations of untamed nature of man.

Similar to Platonic perspective on man and his world, the Vedic perspective, too, considers man to be an integral part of a larger order presided over by the Absolute. But, unlike Plato, the Vedic perspective posits the idea that beings in this world are like so many sparks of the Absolute. By virtue of this, they are a part of the divine and are endowed with the capacity to recover their divinity if they have lost it or have become unconscious of it. If the divine part in them were ascendant and dominant, they would not require to be ruled by any agency external to them, nor will they need to be controlled or punished by *danda*. But, since the divine part is not active in all or, if active, not in the same measure, both a ruler and the arrangement of *danda* are required to protect and preserve the rule of *dharma*. But for any system of governance to be an effective instrument of protecting and preserving the rule of *dharma*, the ruler must himself have no personal stake in the act of governance. This means that he himself, first, be fully governed in his thinking and acting by *dharma* and should not use his power or authority to promote his own self-interest as something apart from the good of all.

The requirement that the ruler must accept the sovereignty of *dharma* means that the act of rulership is essentially a conjunction of what, in the Vedic perspective, is recognized as Brahma *(sacerdotium)* and ksharta (*regnum*). It is true that *kshatra* derives its authority to rule from its submission and conformity to *dharma*. However, *regnum* is also the surrogate of power and is susceptible to power drive. It is, therefore, necessary to curb the power drive of the ruler by making the act of ruling as a conjoint of two different but complementary principles, characterized in the Vedic perspective as Mitra-Varuna, Kratu-Daksha, etc. In this conjoint, it is the Brahma part that is the dominant partner whose counsel and advice, the ruler must heed.[16] As a dominant partner, Brahma counsels the ruler about the right course of action and, therefore, it is a necessary counterpart to the waywardness of power. It is also the ruling element since, endowed as it is with a deep-knowing intelligence, it has the necessary knowledge of what is right thing to do in a particular context of action. It is in this context that we can appreciate the fact that rulership is a partnership between wisdom and power.

In addition, what the Vedic perspective underlines is that the ruler is not the source or maker of law; he is only the enforcer of law as interpreted by those who know dharmic tradition and reflected in *vyavahar* that is, tradition custom, conventions, etc. In this sense, what is important in this regard is that law is not made; it is already given through various authoritative interpretations of *dharma* that is supposed to be an impersonal or transpersonal (*apaurusheya*) source of origin. *Dharma* is thus something that is formulated in principles of right conduct on the basis of the primordial insight into the structure of cosmic order. Thus, law in this context does not mean something that is the product of human will, it is eternal and abstract and assumes a concrete shape through interpretation and embodiment in personal and social practices. And, since the ruler has to submit himself to the over-lordship of *dharma*, his main functions are limited to security of the people and of the territory ensuring the well-being of the people, preventing the basic characteristics of the social system from being eroded and the resolution of conflicts according to the dharmic principles. That is why, the Vedic perspective makes it utterly clear that the real over-lord of the ruler is not his whim, nor his caprice, nor even his discretion but *dharma,* that is, *Kshatrasya kshatram*.

What also needs to be emphasized in this regard is that the Vedic perspective, unlike the Platonic one, does not assign centrality to the political order either for integrating the diverse components of society into a unified whole or for making the people just or, at least, to keep them on the path of justice. In the Vedic perspective, it is rather the social system that has to bear the major responsibility of making men truly men. The fact that the social order projected by the Vedic perspective is, in the real sense of the term, cosmion, that it is a replica of the cosmic order which, through its foundational ideas, institutional arrangement, practices and processes, enables its members to transform and shape their lives in the light of the experience or, at least, conscious awareness of the divine ground of being. It is by virtue of this that men become virtuous and lead a life of righteousness. It is only the righteous men who can understand what justice is and why it is necessary to act righteously and sustain the dharmic order.

What also is interesting to note in this context is the fact that, unlike the Platonic insistence on the immutability of human nature except for a few rare souls, the Vedic perspective underlines the possibility of acquiring the properties of a higher nature and, therefore, of transcending the baseness and limitations of the natural man. This possibility becomes real not because, as Aristotle insists, *polis* provides the opportunities to men of ruling and being ruled and, through it, of their becoming aware of and responsible for safeguarding public order from the infection of *pleonexia*. If the social realm is, for Aristotle, the realm of necessity and if it only promotes an instrumental perspective on the world, it is then certain that the values it will embrace and propagate will not be supportive of a good public order. To the extent that this happens, the *polis,* even if a philosopher-king rules it, will not serve the cause of justice nor will it be able to keep men on the path of virtue.

It is against this backdrop that we can appreciate the Vedic insistence, on the one hand, on the possibility of every man attaining higher nature and, on the other, the need to treat the social order as the repository of those values, practices and processes that aim at making men good men as a precondition of becoming a good citizen. It is only on this basic that a political order can ever hope of succeeding in the effective discharge of its responsibilities. It is, again, only on this basis that people can exert influence on the conduct of the king and check the excesses of an ambitious ruler. It is clear, then, that what assumes a greater significance for protecting, safeguarding and preserving public order in the Vedic perspective is the social order. But when the social order becomes deficient, for one reason or the other, political order needs to be created for preventing the social order from degeneration into an impersonal, objective arena where different interests vie among themselves for articulation, ascendance and control. It is clear, then, that what is primary in the Vedic perspective is not the political order but the social order of which the former is only a part, a necessary adjunct and an unavoidable supplement. As such, it is the social order, not the political order that is the source of values and meaning.

A political order based on the Vedic perspective is eminently capable of ensuring and preserving compatibility between the private and the public. By virtue of this, it can effectively prevent the public order from sliding into the mire of *matsya nyaya*.

Notes

1. Hans Jonas, "Economic Knowledge and Critique of Goals," in Robert L. Heilbroner, ed., *Economic Means and Social Ends: Essay in Political Economy* (Englewood Cliffs, N.T.: Prentice Hall, Inc. 1969), p.77.
2. R.C. Collingwood, *The Idea of Nature* (London: Oxford University Press, 1976).
3. This is how David Hume describes order in nature in *Dialogues Concerning Natural Religion*.
4. Eric Voegelin, *Order and History: Israel and Revelation* (Baton Rouge: Louisiana State University Press, 1957), I, p. 2.
5. This is what is reflected, in various ways, in the writings of Vico, Hegel and Marx.
6. Immanuel Kant, *Political Writings*, ed. Hans Reiss (Cambridge: Cambridge University Press, 1980), p. 45.

7. Charles Taylor, *Social Theory as Practice* (Delhi: Oxford University Press, 1983), p. 55.
8. Fred Hirsch, *Social Limits to Growth* (London: Routledge and Kegan Paul, 1977), p. 10.
9. Charles Taylor, *Hegel and Modern Society* (Cambridge: Cambridge University Press, 1979), p. 75.
10. For a useful discussion on this point, see Ernest Gellner, *Spectacles and Predicaments: Essay in Social Theory* (Cambridge: Cambridge University Press, 1979), p. 283.
11. Adam Smith, *Wealth of Nations* (Oxford: Clarendon Press, 1979), I, p. 580.
12. Francis Edgeworth, *Mathematical Physics* (1881). Quoted in George J. Stigler, "Economics or Ethiss" in Sterling McMurrin, ed. *The Tanner Lectures in Human Values,* II (Salt Lake City: The University of Utah Press, 1981), p. 181.
13. Eric Voegelin, *Order and History: Plato and Aristotle,* III, op. cit., p. 69.
14. Plato, *Republic in the Works of Plato,* Jowett edition (New York: Tudor Publishing Co., n.d.), I, p. 233.
15. Plato, *Thaetetus,* in Jowe II, IV, p. 357.
16. Heesterman argues that inherent in the Vedic perspective is a fundamental dilemma. The *Purohita,* the symbol of *Brahma* has authority but no power, while the ruler has power but no authority. As such, there is inherent in this perspective the ever-present possibility of conflict and statement insofar as the *Purohita* is helpless in case his counsel is ignored or flouted by the ruler, on the one hand, and the ruler's decisions may lose legitimacy if they are taken despite the *Purohita*'s advice to the contrary. If Heesterman's argument is based only on theoretical possibility alone, then his position is untenable. If, or the other hand, he takes note of historical cases, then, he is guilty of preparing a undesirable connection of theoretical and empirical perspectives.

Bibliography

Original Sources

Rigveda

Yajurveda

Samaveda

Atharvaveda

Maitereya Brahman

Gopath Brahman

Jaiminiya Brahman

Pamchavimsha Brahman

Shatapatha Brahman

Taittiriya Brahman

Tandya Brahman

Aitereya Aranyaka

Taittirya Aranyak

Taittiriya Samhita

Aitereya Upanishad

Brihadaranyaka Upanishad

Chhandogya Upanishad

Isopanishad

Kathopanishad

Maitreyi Upanishad

Mundaka Upanishad

Mandukya Karika

Shwetashwatar Upanishad

Brihaddevata

Shrimadbhagwat Geeta
Valmiki Ramayana
Mahabharata
Commentary on Bhadrababu's Abashyakaniryukti
Jaina Sutras
Acharaya Jinasena, *Adipurana*
Mahavastu
Jataka
Jaina Sutras
Tattvartha Varttika
Sutra Kritangasutram
Digha-Nikaya
Anguttara Nikaya
Samyutta Nikaya
Majjhima-Nikaya
Dhammapada

Secondary Sources

Acharya, Nanda K., *The Cultural Politics of the Hindus* (Prikant: Surya Prakashan Mandir, n.d.).

Agrawal, Vasudeva Sharan, *Sparks from the Vedic Fire* (Banaras: Banaras Hindu University, 1962).

——, Vedic Lectures (Banaras: Banaras Hindu University, 1967).

——, *Vision in Long Darkness* (Varanasi: The Author, 1968).

Altekar, A.S., *State and Government in Ancient India* (Delhi: Motilal Banarsidass, 1992).

Arendt, H., *The Human Condition* (Garden City, New York: Anchor Books, 1959).

Aristotle, *Nichomachean Ethics.*

——, *Politics.*

Aurobindo, Sri, *The Secrets of the Veda* (Pondicherry: Sri Aurobindo Ashram, 1987).

——, *The Spirit and Form of Indian Polity* (Calcutta: Aryan Publishing House, 1947).

Bandopadhyaya, N.C., *Development of Hindu Polity and Political Theories* (Calcutta: R. Camberay & Co., 1927).

Barker, Ernest, *Greek Political Theory: Plato and His Predecessors* (London: Methuen and Co. Ltd., 1952).

——, *Principles of Social and Political Theory* (Oxford: Clarendon Press, 1962).

Basham, A.L., *The Wonder that was India* (London: Sidgwick and Jackson, 1961).

Becker, C.L., *The Heavenly Cities of the Eighteenth Century Philosophers* (New Haven: Yale University Press, 1960).

Berlin, Isaiah, *Four Essays on Liberty* (London: Oxford University Press, 1977).

Bhandarkar, R., *Some Aspects of Ancient Hindu Polity* (Varanasi: Banaras Hindu University, 1963).

Birnbaum, Norman, ed., *Beyond the Crisis* (London: Oxford University Press, 1977).

Bloomfield, Maurice, *The Religion of the Veda: The Ancient Religion of India: From Rigveda to Upanishad* (Delhi: Indological Book House, 1972).

Chardin, Teilhard de, *Toward the Future* (London: William Collins Sons Co. Ltd., 1973).

Cochrane, Charles N., *Christianity and Classical Culture* (Oxford: Clarendon Press, 1940).

Colletti, Lucio, *From Rousseau to Lenin: Studies in Ideology and Society* (New York: Monthly Review Press, 1981).

Collingwood, R.C., *The Idea of Nature* (London: Oxford University Press, 1976).

Conze, E., *Buddhism: Its Essence and Development* (New York: Harper Torchbooks, 1959).

Coomaraswamy, Ananda, *Spiritual Authority and Temporal Power in the Indian Theory of Government* (New York: Kraus Reprint Corporation, 1967).

——, *A New Approach to the Vedas* (Delhi: Aparna Publications, 1985).

——, *Hinduism and Buddhism* (Delhi: Munshiram Manoharlal, 1986).

——, *The Living Thoughts of Gotama the Buddha* (Bombay: Jaico Publishing House, 1958).

——, *What is Civilization?* (Delhi: Oxford University Press, 1989).

Cooper, Barry Eric, *Voegelin and the Foundations of Modern Political Science* (Columbia: University of Missouri Press, 1999).

Cooper, John M., *Reason and Human Good in Aristotle* (Cambridge, Mass.: Harward University Press, 1975).

Danielou, Allain, *Hindu Polytheism* (New York: Pantheon Books, 1964).

Dasgupta, S., *A History of Indian Philosophy* (London: Cambridge University Press, 1965), 5 Vols.

Descartes, Rene, *Philosophical Writings*, ed. and tr. Norman Kemp Smith (New Work: Modern Library, 1958).

Dewey, John, *Individualism: Old and New* (New York: Capricorn Books, 1962).

Drekemieir, Charles, *Kingship and Community in Early India* (Bombay: Oxford University Press, 1962).

Dundas, P., *The Jains* (London: Routledge, 1992).

Eliade, Mircea, *The Myth of the Eternal Returns: Cosmos and History* (London: Arkana, 1989).

Gadamer, Hans G., *Dialogue and Dialectic: Eight Hermeneutical Studies on Plato* (New Haven: Yale University Press, 1980).

Gandhi, M.K., *Selected Works of Mahatma Gandhi*, ed. Shriman Narayan (Ahmedabad: Navjivan Publishing House, 1969).

Gerth, Hans and C. Wright Mills, *From Max Weber* (New York: Oxford University Press, 1946).

Ghoshal, U.K., *A History of Indian Political Ideas* (London: Oxford University Press, 1962).

Gonda, Jan, *Ancient Indian Kinship from the Religious Point of View* (Lieden: E.J. Brill, 1948).

——, *The Vision of the Vedic Poets* (Delhi: Munshiram Manoharlal, 1984).

Greene, David, *Greek Political Theory: The Images of Man in Thucydides and Plato* (Chicago: University of Chicago Press, 1965).

Grimm, G., *Buddhist Wisdom: Mystery of the Self* (Delhi: Motilal Banarsidass, 1978).

Heesterman, J.C., *The Ancient Indian Royal Consecration* (The Hague: Mouton de Gruyter, 1957).

Hegel, G.W.F., *The Philosophy of History* (New York: Dover Publications, 1950).

Heilbroner, Robert L., *Economic Means and Social Ends: Essays in Political Economy* (Englewood Cliffs, N.J.: Prentice-Hall, 1969).

Heschel, A.J., *Who is Man?* (Stanford: Stanford University Press, 1965).

Hirsch, Fred, *Social Limits to Growth* (London: Routledge & Kegan Paul, 1977).

Hirschman, A.O., *The Passions and the Interests: Political Arguments for Capitalism Before its Triumph* (Princeton: Princeton University Press, 1987).

Hobbes, Thomas, *Leviatham* (New York: Dutton, 1950).

Hobhouse, L.T., *Social Evolution and Political Theory* (New York: Kennikat Press, 1968).

Hocart, A.M., *Kingship* (London: Oxford University Press, 1969).

Jaeger, Werner, *Aristotle: Fundamentals of the History of His Development*, tr. Richard Robinson (Oxford: Clarendon Press, 1962).

——, *Paideia* (New York: Oxford University Press, 1959), 3 Vols.

Jassay, Anthony de, *Against Politics: On Government Anarchy and Order* (London: Routledge & Kegan Paul, 1997).

Jayaswal, K.P., *Hindu Polity: Constitutional History of India in Hindu Times* (Calcutta: Butterworth & Co., 1924).

Kant, Immanuel, *Political Writings*, ed. Hans Reiss (Cambridge: Cambridge University Press, 1980).

Keane, John, *Public Life and Late Capitalism: Towards a Socialist Theory of Democracy* (Cambridge: Cambridge University Press, 1984).

Krishna, K.B., *Theories of Kingship in India* (Vijaywada: Vishalandhra Publishing House, 1932).

Law, M.N., *Aspects of Ancient Indian Polity* (Oxford: Oxford University Press, 1921).

Lingat, Robert, *The Classical Law of India* (Berkeley: University of California Press, 1973).

Lowe, Adolph, *On Economic Knowledge: Toward a Science of Political Economy* (New York: Harper & Row, 1965).

Lowi, Theodore J., *The End of Liberatism: The Second Republic of the United States* (New York: W.W. Norton, 1969).

Lowith, Karl, *Meaning in History* (Chicago: The University of Chicago Press, 1950).

MacIntyre, Alasdair, *Whose Justice? Which Rationality?* (London: Gerald Duckworth & Co. Ltd., 1988).

Mandelbaum, Maurice, *History, Man and Reason: A Study in Nineteenth Century Thought* (Baltimore: The John Hopkins University Press, 1971).

Maritain, Jacques, *Challenges and Renewals: Selected Readings* (Notre Dame: University of Notre Dame Press, 1966).

Matson, F.W., *The Broken Image: Man, Science and Society* (New York: Anchor Books, 1966).

McMurrin, Sterling, ed., *The Tanner Lectures in Human Values*, II (Salt Lake City: The University of Utah Press, 1981).

Mehta, J.L., *Philosophy and Religion: Essays in Interpretation* (New Delhi: Indian Council of Philosophical Research, 1990).

Merquior, A., *The Veil and the Mask: Essays on Culture and Ideology* (London: Routledge & Kegan Paul, 1979).

Miller, Jeanine, *The Vision of Cosmic Order in the Vedas* (London: Routledge & Kegan Paul, 1985).

Miranda, P., *Avatara and Incarnation: A Comparative Analysis* (New Delhi: Herman Publishing House, 1990).

Mitra, S.K., *Ethics of the Hindus* (New Delhi: Asian Publishing Service, 1978).

Morgenthau, Hans, *Politics Among Nations: The Struggle for Power and Peace* (New York: Alfred A. Knopf, 1964).

Mukerjee, K.P., *Ancient Indian Political Experience* (Colombo: M.D. Gunasena & Co. Ltd., 1961).

Muller, Max, *Auld Lang Syne* (New York: Charles Scribner's Sons, 1899).

——, *Chips from a German Workshop* (New York: Charles Scribner's Sons, 1895).

Needleman, Jacob, *A Sense of the Cosmos: The Encounter of Modern Science and Ancient Truth* (Garden City, New York: Doubleday & Co., 1975).

Nussbaum, Martha, *The Fragility of Goodness: Luck and Ethics in Greek Tragedy and Philosophy* (Cambridge: Cambridge University Press, 1986).

Ojha, Madhusudan, *Vijnana Vidyuta* (Jaipur: Rajasthan Patrika, 1990).

Pande, G.C., *Bharatiya Parampara ke Mool Swara* (New Delhi: National Publishing House, 1981).

——, *Bharatiya Samaj: Tatwawik Aur Aitihasik Vivechan* (New Delhi: National Publishing House, 1994).

——, *Spiritual Vision and Symbolic Forms in Ancient India* (New Delhi: Books and Books, 1984).

——, *Jain Political Thought* (Jaipur: Prakrit Bharati Samsthan, Centre for Jain Studies, University of Rajasthan, 1984).

Panikkar, K.M., *The Ideas of Sovereignty and State in Indian Political Thought* (Bombay: Bharatiya Vidya Bhawan, 1963).

Panikkar, R., *The Vedic Experience: Mantra Manjari* (Pondicherry: All India Books, 1983).

Plato, *Republic*

——, *The Symbolism*

——, *The Law*

——, *Phaedo*

——, *Gorgias*

——, *The Seventh Letter*

——, *Timeaus*

Prasad, Beni, *Studies in the Origin of Buddhism* (Allahabad: University of Allahabad Press, 1957).

——, *The State in Ancient India* (Allahabad: The Indian Press Ltd., 1928).

Ramanan, K. Venkata, *Nagarjuna's Philosophy* (Delhi: Motilal Banarsidass, 1978).

Randall, H., *The Making of the Modern Mind* (New York: Houghton Mifflin & Co., 1990).

Rieff, Philip, *Freud: The Mind of the Moralist* (New York: Anchor Books, 1961).

Ronen, Duv, *The Quest for Self-determination* (New Haven: Yale University Press, 1979).

Roy, Ramashray, *Beyond Ego's Domain: Being and Order in the Veda* (Delhi: Shipra Publications, 1999).

——, *Captive Vision: Ideas as Weapon* (Delhi: Ajanta Publications, 1993).

——, *Gandhi: Soundings in Political Philosophy* (Delhi: Chanakya Publications, 1984).

——, *Self and Society: A Study in Gandhian Thought* (New Delhi: Sage Publications, 1984).

——, *The World of Development: Theoretical Dead End?* (Delhi: Ajanta Publications, 1994).

Scitovsky, Tibor, *The Joyless Economy* (New York: Oxford University Press, 1976).

Shastri, Motilal, *Bharatiya Drishti Se "Vijnana" Shabda ka Samaniyaya* (Jaipur: Rajasthan Patrika, n.d.).

——, *Vedic Concept of Man and Universe* (Jaipur: Vedic Tattwa Shodh Sansthan, 1950).

Sinha, H.N., *The Development of Indian Polity* (Bombay: Asia Publishing House, 1963).

Skinner, B.F., *Walden II* (New York: Macmillan, 1984).

Soloman, R.C., *The Rise and the Fall of the Self* (New York: Oxford University Press, 1989).

Taylor, Charles, 'Growth, Legitimacy and the Modern Identity', *Praxis International*, Vol. 1, No. 2, 1981.

——, *Hegel and Modern Society* (Cambridge: Cambridge University Press, 1979).

——, *Social Theory as Practice* (Delhi: Oxford University Press, 1983).

Tocqueville, Alexis de, *Democracy in America*, ed. Phillips Bradby (New York: Vintage Books, 1956), 2 Vols.

Tyler, E.N.B., *Primitive Culture* (London: Murray, 1871).

Unger, R.M., *Knowledge and Politics* (New York: The Free Press, 1975).

Varma, V.P., *Studies in Hindu Political Thought and its Metaphysical Foundations* (Delhi: Motilal Banarsidass, 1959).

Vlastos, Gregory, *Studies in Greek Philosophy*, ed. Daniel W. Graham (Princeton: Princeton University Press, 1995).

Voegelin, Eric, *Anamnesis* (Notre Dame: University of Notre Dame Press, 1978).

——, *History of Political Ideas* (Columbia: Missouri University Press, 1997).

——, *New Science of Politics: An Introduction* (Chicago: The University of Chicago Press, 1952).

——, *Order and History: Israel and Revelation* (Baton Rouge: Louisiana State University Press, 1956), 8 Vols.

——, *Plato* (Baton Rouge: Louisiana State University Press, 1966).

Weber, Max, *The Theory of Social and Economic Organisation*, ed. Talcott Parsons (New York: The Free Press, 1966).

Wolin, Sheldon, 'Post-Modern Politics and the Absence of Myths', *Social Research,* Vol. 52, No. 2, 1985.

Wood, Ellen M., *Mind and Politics: An Approach to the Meaning of Liberal and Socialist Individualism* (Berkeley: University of California Press, 1972).

Index

P000655 RW 30Y

Rawat
546
8.7.16